Domino Development

Domino Development with Java

ANTHONY PATTON

MANNING

Greenwich
(74° w. long.)

For online information and ordering of this and other Manning books, go to www.manning.com. The publisher offers discounts on this book when ordered in quantity. For more information, please contact:

Special Sales Department
Manning Publications Co.
32 Lafayette Place   Fax: (203) 661-9018
Greenwich, CT 06830   email: orders@manning.com

Manning Publications Co.   Production Services: *TIPS* Technical Publishing
32 Lafayette Place   Copyeditor: Jeannine Kolbush
Greenwich, CT 06830   Typesetter: Lynanne S. Fowle
                                  Cover Designer: Leslie Haimes

Printed in the United States of America
1 2 3 4 5 6 7 8 9 10 – VHG – 03 02 01 00

Vickie, you've given me hope and a purpose. I am truly blessed.

brief contents

1 ✧ Domino development with Java 1

2 ✧ Domino Designer IDE 5

3 ✧ Java basics 23

4 ✧ NotesFactory/NotesThread/NotesError classes 33

5 ✧ Session class 38

6 ✧ Database class 44

7 ✧ Working with views 57

8 ✧ Document class 77

9 ✧ Item class 94

10 ✧ The RichTextItem class 106

11 ✧ Working with collections 130

12 ✧ Activity logging 144

13 ✧ Working with the ACL 153

14 ✧ Agent class 169

15 ✧ Name class 188

16 ✧ Date-time values 196

17 ✧ Working with outlines 219

18 ✧ Working with your classes 231

19 ✧ Reports 244

20 ✧ Searching 261

21 ✧ Working with the Web 270

22 ✦ Developing outside the Domino IDE 288

23 ✦ Applets 306

24 ✦ Standalone applications 324

25 ✦ Servlets 329

26 ✦ JDBC 346

27 ✦ WebSphere 357

28 ✦ Lotus connectors 362

29 ✦ Third-party tools and code 369

30 ✦ The future 375

31 ✦ Example: shopping cart 381

32 ✦ More examples 406

A ✦ Domino Java class reference 412

B ✦ Error codes 432

contents

preface xxi

about the cover illustration xxiii

acknowledgments xxiv

1 Domino development with Java 1

1.1 Why Java? 1
Java is object-oriented 2 ✧ Java is interpreted 2
Java offers broader support 2 ✧ Java has standard network communications
features 3 ✧ Java is portable 3 ✧ Java has skillset transportability 3

1.2 LotusScript comparison 3

1.3 Learning the Java language 4

1.4 The future 4

2 Domino Designer IDE 5

2.1 Domino Designer environment 5

2.2 Imported Java 6

2.3 Java 10
AgentBase class 18 ✧ Java console window 18 ✧ Help documentation 19
Form events 20 ✧ Agents 20 ✧ Third-party IDEs 20 ✧ Special keys 20

2.4 Chapter review 21

3 Java basics 23

3.1 Building blocks 23
Output 23 ✧ Semicolon 24 ✧ Braces 24 ✧ Escape character 24
Data types 24 ✧ Logic 25 ✧ Concatenation 25 ✧ Increment/decrement 26
Looping 26 ✧ Controlling program flow 27 ✧ Comments 28
Arrays 28 ✧ Vector class 28 ✧ Access 29 ✧ Import 29 ✧ Package 29
Implements 29 ✧ Extends 30

3.2   Classes, methods, and properties 30
       Constructor 30 ⬩ Final 30 ⬩ Static 30 ⬩ Casting 31 ⬩ Overloading 31
       Using your own classes 31 ⬩ Case-sensitivity 31

3.3   Chapter review 32

4   *NotesFactory/NotesThread/NotesError classes*   33

4.1   NotesFactory class 33

4.2   What is a thread? 34

4.3   NotesThread class 35

4.4   What is an exception? 35

4.5   NotesException class 35
       ID property 35 ⬩ Text property 36

4.6   NotesError class 36

4.7   Memory management/recycle method 36
       recycle method 36 ⬩ Syntax 37

4.8   Chapter review 37

5   *Session class*   38

5.1   Using the Session class 38

5.2   Property list 42

5.3   Method list 42

5.4   Chapter review 43

6   *Database class*   44

6.1   Syntax 44

6.2   Properties 46

6.3   Methods 48
       Full-text index 48 ⬩ Access 49 ⬩ Create, remove, and
       duplicate 49 ⬩ get methods 50

6.4   All documents 50

6.5   Replication class 50
       Syntax 50 ⬩ Properties 51 ⬩ Methods 51

6.6   DbDirectory class 53
       createDatabase 53 ⬩ getFirstDatabase 54 ⬩ getNextDatabase 54
       openDatabase 54 ⬩ openDatabaseByReplicaID 54
       openDatabaseIfModified 54 ⬩ openMailDatabase 54

6.7   Chapter review 56

7   Working with views   57

7.1   Syntax 57
getView 57 ❖ getViews 58

7.2   Working with view columns 59
getColumn 59 ❖ getColumns 60

7.3   ViewColumn class 60
Properties 63

7.4   Working with view entries 64

7.5   ViewEntry class 64
Document property 67

7.6   ViewEntryCollection class 68

7.7   ViewNavigator class 69
createViewNav method 70 ❖ createViewNavFrom method 70
createViewNavFromCategory method 70 ❖ createViewNavFromChildren
method 70 ❖ createViewNavFromDescendants method 70
createViewNavMaxLevel method 70 ❖ Methods 71
List of get methods 71 ❖ List of goto methods 72

7.8   Searching a view 74

7.9   Deleting a view 75

7.10   Refreshing a view 75

7.11   Folders 76

7.12   Chapter review 76

8   Document class   77

8.1   What is a document? 77

8.2   Syntax 78

8.3   Accessing individual elements/fields 79
getItemValue 79 ❖ getItemValueDouble 79 ❖ getItemValueInteger 79
getItemValueString 79 ❖ appendItemValue 79 ❖ replaceItemValue 80
hasItem 81 ❖ getFirstItem 81

8.4   Other methods 82
computeWithForm 82 ❖ copyAllItems 82 ❖ copyItem 83
copyToDatabase 83 ❖ createReplyMessage 83 ❖ createRichTextItem 84
encrypt 84 ❖ getAttachment 84 ❖ makeResponse 84 ❖ putInFolder 84
remove 84 ❖ removeFromFolder 84 ❖ removeItem 85
renderToRTItem 85 ❖ sign 85

8.5   Properties 85

8.6   Working with profile Documents 90

8.7   Chapter review 92

9   Item class   94

9.1   What is an Item? 94

9.2   Creating an Item 94

9.3   Getting an existing Item 95

9.4   Removing an Item 96

9.5   is properties 97

9.6   More properties 99

9.7   type and values properties 102
List of type constants 102

9.8   Other methods 104
abstractText 104 ⬧ appendToTextList 105 ⬧ containsValue 105
copyItemToDocument 105

9.9   Chapter review 105

10   The RichTextItem class   106

10.1   What is the RichTextItem class? 106

10.2   Accessing an existing rich text item 106

10.3   Creating a new rich text item 107

10.4   Adding data 109
addNewLine 109 ⬧ addPageBreak 109 ⬧ addTab 109
appendDocLink 109 ⬧ appendRTItem 110 ⬧ appendText 110
getFormattedText 110

10.5   RichTextStyle class 111
Bold 111 ⬧ Color 111 ⬧ Effects 112 ⬧ Font 112 ⬧ FontSize 112
Italic 113 ⬧ Parent 113 ⬧ StrikeThrough 113 ⬧ Underline 113

10.6   RichTextParagraphStyle class 115
Alignment 115 ⬧ FirstLineLeftMargin 115 ⬧ interLineSpacing 115
LeftMargin 116 ⬧ Pagination 116 ⬧ RightMargin 116
SpacingAbove 116 ⬧ SpacingBelow 116 ⬧ Tabs 118 ⬧ clearAllTabs 118
setTab 118 ⬧ setTabs 119

10.7   RichTextTab class 120
Properties 120 ⬧ Position 120 ⬧ Type 120 ⬧ Methods 120 ⬧ clear 120

10.8   EmbeddedObject class 122
Accessing embedded objects 122 ⬧ Creating embedded objects 122
Properties 123 ⬧ Methods 123 ⬧ OLE 123 ⬧ Attachments 124
Creating a link object 126 ⬧ Deleting objects 127

10.9   Chapter review 128

11   *Working with collections*   130

11.1 What is a collection? 130

11.2 DocumentCollection class 130

11.3 Creating a DocumentCollection object 131

11.4 Properties 131
Count 131 ✦ isSorted 131 ✦ Parent 132 ✦ Query 132

11.5 Accessing documents in a collection 132
getDocument 132 ✦ getFirstDocument 132 ✦ getLastDocument 132
getNextDocument 132 ✦ getNthDocument 134 ✦ getPrevDocument 135

11.6 Refining a collection 135

11.7 Adding/removing a document to/from a collection 136
addDocument 136 ✦ deleteDocument 136

11.8 Working with folders 138

11.9 Updating documents in a collection 139

11.10 stampAll 139

11.11 Working with profiled documents 140

11.12 Sorting a collection 140

11.13 Newsletter class 143

11.14 Chapter review 143

12   *Activity logging*   144

12.1 Overview 144

12.2 Creating 144

12.3 Properties 145

12.4 logAction 145

12.5 logError 145

12.6 Using the agent log 146

12.7 Logging to a file 148

12.8 Logging via Email 148

12.9 Logging to a Domino database 151

12.10 Chapter review 152

13   *Working with the ACL*   153

13.1 What is the ACL? 153

13.2 Seven access levels 153
Manager 154 ✦ Designer 154 ✦ Editor 154 ✦ Author 154
Reader 154 ✦ Depositor 154 ✦ No access 155

13.3 ACL class 155

13.4 Properties 156
InternetLevel 157 ✧ IsUniformAccess 157 ✧ Parent 157 ✧ Roles 157

13.5 Save 158

13.6 ACLEntry class 158
Accessing ACL Entries 158 ✧ Removing an Entry 162

13.7 Working with roles 164
ACL Class Methods 165 ✧ ACLEntry Class Methods 166

13.8 Chapter review 168

14 *Agent class* *169*

14.1 Overview 169

14.2 Syntax 169

14.3 Properties 171

14.4 Methods 177
run 178 ✧ runOnServer 178 ✧ remove 178

14.5 Passing parameters 179

14.6 AgentContext class 181
getCurrentDatabase 182 ✧ getCurrentAgent 182

14.7 Processing documents 182
unProcessedFTSearch/unProcessedSearch 182 ✧ SavedData 184
DocumentContext 186 ✧ PrintWriter class 186

14.8 Chapter review 186

15 *Name class* *188*

15.1 Overview 188

15.2 Syntax 189
getUserNameObject method 189 ✧ getUserNameList 189

15.3 Creation 190

15.4 Properties 191

15.5 Putting it to use 193

15.6 Chapter review 195

16 *Date-time values* *196*

16.1 Overview 196

16.2 Creating 196

16.3 Special identifiers 197

16.4 Properties 198
DateOnly 198 ✧ GMTTime 198 ✧ IsDST 198 ✧ LocalTime 198
Parent 198 ✧ TimeOnly 198 ✧ TimeZone 198 ✧ ZoneTime 199

16.5 Adjusting 200

16.6 More methods 201
convertToZone 201 ✧ setAnyDate 201 ✧ setAnyHour 201
setLocalDate 201 ✧ setLocalTime 202 ✧ setNow 202
timeDifference 202 ✧ toJavaDate 202

16.7 Finding the difference between
two Date-Time objects 204

16.8 Searching using date-time values 205

16.9 DateRange class 205

16.10 Free-time search 207

16.11 International class 208
Accessing 209 ✧ Properties 209

16.12 Working with Date-Time fields 213

16.13 GregorianCalendar class 216

16.14 Chapter review 218

17   Working with outlines   219

17.1 Overview 219

17.2 Syntax 220

17.3 Properties 220

17.4 Traversing an outline 221

17.5 Other methods 224
addEntry 224 ✧ removeEntry 225 ✧ moveEntry 225
createEntry 225 ✧ save 225

17.6 OutlineEntry class 225
Properties 225 ✧ Methods 226

17.7 Chapter review 230

18   Working with your classes   231

18.1 Overview 231

18.2 Designing classes 231

18.3 this 232

18.4 Creating a class 232

18.5 Constructors 234

18.6 Multiple objects 237

18.7 Script libraries 239

18.8 Chapter review 243

19 *Reports* *244*

19.1 Overview 244

19.2 Reports as documents 245
Email 247 ✧ Scheduled 248 ✧ Selective/custom reports 248
Form as a front end 248

19.3 Newsletter class 256
Properties 257 ✧ Methods 257

19.4 Chapter review 260

20 *Searching* *261*

20.1 Full-text indexing databases 261

20.2 Logical search operators 263

20.3 Searching a view 264

20.4 Searching a database 266

20.5 Creating a full-text index 267

20.6 Chapter review 268

21 *Working with the Web* *270*

21.1 Overview 270

21.2 PrintWriter class 271

21.3 Browsers 273

21.4 Environment variables 273

21.5 DocumentContext 274

21.6 Events 277
WebQueryOpen 277 ✧ WebQuerySave 278

21.7 Executing agents 278

21.8 Tracking session data 279

21.9   Working with URLs 283

21.10 Chapter review 287

22 *Developing outside the Domino IDE* *288*

22.1 Domino IDE weaknesses 289

22.2 Required files 289
notes.jar 289 ✧ ncso.jar 289 ✧ ncsoc.jar 289 ✧ CLASSPATH 290

22.3 Version 290

22.4 AgentRunner 290
Syntax 290 ✧ Lotus Domino Toolkit for Java 291 ✧ AgentRunner setup 292

22.5 Working with the Sun JDK 293

22.6 VisualAge for Java 296
Developing a Java application in VisualAge 300 ✧ Using AgentRunner with VisualAge 302

22.7 Other environments 304

22.8 Chapter review 305

23 *Applets*   306

23.1 What is an applet? 306

23.2 Issues 306

23.3 Structure of an applet 307

23.4 Security 307

23.5 Referencing applets in HTML 307

23.6 AppletBase class 309
Domino session 309 ✧ Methods 309

23.7 Accessing a Domino server 310

23.8 Standard Domino applets 321

23.9 Installing applets locally 322

23.10 Chapter review 323

24 *Standalone applications*   324

24.1 Overview 324

24.2 Main 325

24.3 Threads 325
Extending the NotesThread class and using the runNotes method 325
Implementing the Runnable interface 325 ✧ Using the sinitThread and
stermThread methods of the NotesThread class 326

24.4 Accessing a Domino server 326

24.5 Chapter review 328

25 *Servlets*   329

25.1 What is a servlet? 329

25.2 Java Servlet Development Kit (JSDK) 330

25.3 Structure of a servlet 330
Servlet request object 332 ✧ Servlet response object 333

25.4 Session tracking 335
HttpSession object 335

25.5 Running servlets on Domino 337
Domino servlet configuration file 338

25.6 The servlet life cycle 339

25.7 Accessing Domino objects via a servlet 340

25.8 Domino forms 343

25.9 Chapter review 344

26 JDBC   346

26.1 What is JDBC? 346

26.2 SQL 346
SELECT 347 ✧ FROM 347 ✧ WHERE 347

26.3 Getting the Domino JDBC driver 348
Setting the CLASSPATH variable 348 ✧ Importing the proper package 348

26.4 JDBC URLs 348

26.5 Connecting to Domino 349

26.6 Statements 349

26.7 Executing 349

26.8 Results 349

26.9 Handling errors 352

26.10 Metadata 352

26.11 Servlets 353

26.12 Chapter review 356

27 WebSphere   357

27.1 Overview 357

27.2 Versions 358

27.3 Getting the product 358

27.4 Installation with Domino 358

27.5 Administrative console 359

27.6 Java Server Pages (JSP) 359

27.7 JSP syntax 360

27.8 Support 360

27.9 Chapter review 361

28   *Lotus connectors*   *362*

28.1 Java classes 363
   LCSession 363 ✦ LCConnection 363 ✦ LCFieldList 364
   LCField 365 ✦ LCException 366

28.2 JavaBeans 368

28.3 Chapter review 368

29   *Third-party tools and code*   *369*

29.1 ArNoNa CADViewer 369

29.2 JClass 372

29.3 Chapter review 374

30   *The future*   *375*

30.1 OverViews 376

30.2 XML 376
   Current support 377 ✦ Future support 378 ✦ LotusXLS 379

30.3 Chapter review 380

31   *Example: shopping cart*   *381*

31.1 Registration 382

31.2 Email agent 385

31.3 Individual store items 388

31.4 Checking out 394

31.5 Putting it all together 404

31.6 Notes 404

31.7 Chapter review 405

32   *More examples*   *406*

32.1 Extracting attachments 407

32.2 Removing a user from ACL 408

32.3 Exporting 409

32.4 XML exporting 410

32.5 Creating a newsletter 411

A   *Domino Java class reference*   *412*

B   *Error codes*   *432*

index 443

preface

Java has developed into a powerful programming language in a very short time, and has helped define the term "Internet time." Initially, the focus for Java was on the development of applets for the World Wide Web. It has, however, grown into a language suitable for many other tasks—including working with the Domino Application Server. Java is a standard language, as opposed to the proprietary LotusScript language, and it allows developers from other environments to immediately feel comfortable in Domino development.

Domino itself is an application development server from Lotus/IBM. It is available for most flavors of Unix, Linux, Windows, OS/2, Apple, S/390, and AS400, with R5 being the current version.

I was very excited at the prospect of Domino development via Java, but was disappointed when I discovered the enormous lack of related, in-depth information available. Numerous books provide the ABCs of the Java language—but where do you go from there?

My learning process involved interactions with experienced Domino developers, Java programmers, the vast resources of the World Wide Web, and Internet Usenet groups—hammering home the axiom: the more you learn, the less you know.

The purpose of this book, therefore, is to provide an overview of development with Domino and Java. A brief introduction to the core Java language is included as well.

About the book

The book begins with a detailed look at the Domino Designer development environment followed with an overview of the core Java language. The first three chapters are devoted to these basics.

Chapters 4 through 17 provide detailed coverage of the Domino Java classes—syntax as well as examples are included.

Chapter 18 offers a glance at developing your own Java classes for use with Domino. Chapter 19 is an overview of reporting techniques. Methods for searching Domino databases and handling the results are outlined in chapter 20.

The Internet is the focus of chapter 21. Domino and Java can be used with web-based clients, and this chapter shows you how.

Other development environments are introduced in chapter 22. As a Java developer, you are not restricted to the Domino IDE. The syntax for developing Java applets for use with Domino is addressed in chapter 23 and chapter 24 includes details on development of standalone Java applications that interact with Domino.

Chapter 25 provides a detailed introduction to Java servlets and how to best take advantage of them in a Domino environment, while chapter 26 is an in-depth look at JDBC and the Domino JDBC driver.

Chapter 27 focuses on the IBM WebSphere Application Server and its use in conjunction with Java, and Lotus Connector technology is covered in chapter 28.

Information on utilizing third-party applets in a Domino application is supplied in chapter 29, and chapter 30 takes a look at the possible future directions of Domino. A detailed example of a Domino application, based on topics covered in this book, is offered in chapter 31. Additional Java code for various tasks is included in chapter 32.

Finally, the two appendices provide other useful information. Appendix A is a quick reference for the Domino Java classes and appendix B provides a listing of Domino Java error codes.

Source code downloads

Source code for all of the examples presented in this book is available from the publisher's web site. Please go to www.manning.com/patton2.

Code conventions used in this book

The following typographical conventions are used throughout the book:

- Code examples and fragments are set in `Courier`, which is a fixed-width font.
- Methods, classes, fields, statements, and other key words in the body text are also set in `Courier`.
- Commands, or lines to be typed by the reader, are set in **`Courier Bold`**.
- Comments in code are set off with a double forward slash (//) at the beginning of each comment line. The comment line or lines precede the line or lines of code being referenced.
- Code annotations accompany certain segments of code. Annotated code is marked with chronologically ordered cue balls, such as ❶. The annotations themselves follow the code in sections entitled "Explanation," and are marked with the corresponding cue balls (❶) for identification purposes.
- Code line continuations are indented 3 spaces.
- Additional code conventions are outlined in chapter 3.

about the cover illustration

The cover illustration of this book is from the 1805 edition of Sylvain Maréchal's four-volume compendium of regional dress customs. This book was first published in Paris in 1788, one year before the French Revolution. Its title alone required no fewer than 30 words.

Costumes Civils actuels de tous les peuples connus dessinés d'après nature gravés et coloriés, accompagnés d'une notice historique sur leurs coutumes, moeurs, religions, etc., etc., redigés par M. Sylvain Maréchal

The four volumes include an annotation on the illustrations: "gravé à manière noire par Mixelle d'après Desrais et colorié." Clearly, the engraver and illustrator deserved no more than to be listed by their last names—after all they were mere technicians. The workers who colored each illustration by hand remain nameless.

The colorful variety of this collection reminds us vividly of how culturally apart the world's towns and regions were just 200 years ago. Dress codes have changed everywhere and the diversity by region, so rich at the time, has faded away. It is now hard to tell the inhabitant of one continent from another. Perhaps we have traded cultural diversity for a more varied personal life—certainly a more varied and exciting technological environment. At a time when it is hard to tell one computer book from another, Manning celebrates the inventiveness and initiative of the computer business with book covers based on the rich diversity of regional life of two centuries ago, brought back to life by Maréchal's pictures. Just think, Maréchal's was a world so different from ours people would take the time to read a book title 30 words long.

acknowledgments

There are numerous people who have influenced this book, including all of my clients (past and present), colleagues, friends, and family. I especially want to thank everyone at TIS Worldwide: Stu, Jennifer, Hank (Mr. C-Span), Mark Waterbury, Mark Elder, Jim, John, Madhu, Prasad, Justin, Anthony, Robert, Anne, Karen, Eric, Manesh, Mohit, Muhammed, Ravi, Rishi, Rob, Ushi, Brooks, Kirsten, and Leslee.

A number of individuals took the time to proofread the manuscript in various stages. Their feedback proved to be invaluable. They included: Ted Thomas, Andrew Watt, Bill Griffith, Don Bunch, Kevin Hakason, and Karl Roberts. Additional gratitude goes to Andrew Watt for checking the validity of the source code.

Special thanks goes to the wonderful staff at Manning Publications: Mary Piergies, Ted Kennedy, Lee Fitzpatrick, and most especially Marjan Bace. Thank you also to Lynanne Fowle, compositor, and Jeannine Kolbush, copyeditor.

Finally, a big hug goes to Branden. Your constant energy and enthusiasm are contagious.

Domino development with Java

1.1   Why Java?   1
1.2   LotusScript comparison   3
1.3   Learning the Java language   4
1.4   The future   4

1.1   WHY JAVA?

You cannot pick up a computer-related publication these days without seeing something concerning Java. Java this, Java that, and so forth. Why the fanfare for a computer language? The languages C, C++, and Pascal have been around for decades. Visual Basic is much newer, but it is no less popular.

Lotus Notes/Domino includes plenty of built-in functions and commands (@Functions and @Commands) as well as the LotusScript programming language. You can use C and C++ as well.

In version 4.6, Lotus jumped on the Java bandwagon by adding limited Java support to the Notes/Domino product. Domino R5 finished the task by adding extensive support for the Java language. You can develop agents, applets, and standalone and servlet Java code that interacts with Domino.

The big question you may ask yourself is, "Why should I care or take the time to learn Java?"

1.1.1 Java is object-oriented

Java is a relatively new technology that has developed at the speed of the Internet (fast!). This is neat because we have had the chance to see it mature and grow. It was developed from the ground up as an object-oriented programming language. This differs from C++, which, while object-oriented, had to be designed to work with procedural C code.

In Java, everything is an object. In Domino you have database objects, agent objects, session objects, and so forth. A Java application consists of a bunch of objects communicating with each other. A Domino session object may tell a database object to create a new document object. The result is a componentized application. The goal is for the individual components of applications to be reused in other programs.

1.1.2 Java is interpreted

Java is known as an interpreted language. Java code is compiled into bytecode, which is interpreted and run by a Java Virtual Machine (JVM). Therefore, a JVM is required to run Java code. Windows 98 comes with its own Java Virtual Machine, the Domino server has a built-in JVM, both browsers from Netscape and Microsoft have JVMs to run Java applets, and so forth. The result is what Sun Microsystems advertises as the "Write Once, Run Anywhere" language. Of course, the *anywhere* portion must have a JVM.

Your Java code does not care whether you are running on an IBM AIX, Windows NT, Windows 98, AS/400, or BeOS. The only thing it needs is the JVM. The result is that the same code will work on multiple platforms. This is in stark contrast to distributing a C, C++, or Visual Basic application. With these applications, you have to know the platform and compile and debug the code for it.

This is a moot point when developing Domino agents. Because they live in a Domino database, they are already platform-independent. When you access Domino objects outside of a Domino database (such as an applet or a servlet), this platform independence becomes a huge plus.

1.1.3 Java offers broader support

How many other platforms or applications support the LotusScript language? Outside of applications from Lotus, the number is zero and will remain zero forever. LotusScript is a proprietary language designed and maintained by Lotus for Lotus. Therefore, no other companies develop LotusScript add-ons or LotusScript development environments.

On the other hand, Java is an open-standards development language. The development of the language is supported by almost everyone in the industry. Due to this fact, JVMs exist for almost every platform. In addition, there are numerous companies developing with and for Java. Third-party class libraries are available to ease your development effort, and the range of development environments is awesome.

VisualAge for Java, JBuilder from Borland, and Symantec's Visual Café are just three of your choices for developing Java code. You can use the Sun command-line environment (free download) as well. These tools give you options such as versioning, debugging, and project management. The native LotusScript development environment (and Java IDE in R5) is very limited by comparison.

1.1.4   Java has standard network communications features

One of the neatest aspects of Java is that it was developed as an Internet language. That is, it has network communications built into the core language. The protocol of the Internet, TCP/IP, is the common communication protocol. With that in mind, you can create network-savvy applications with little or no trouble.

Threading is another aspect of Java that is very appealing. It allows your applications to take advantage of multiple threads of execution. Threading can be painful to learn and comprehend, but the rewards can be great when it is well-used.

1.1.5   Java is portable

We have already touched upon this point—Java is portable—but it deserves to be repeated. Java code developed in Domino can live outside of the Domino environment. Try that with LotusScript. How many LotusScript interpreters for Windows NT are on the market?

1.1.6   Java has skillset transportability

The Java skillset is portable just like Java code. Once you learn the Java language, you can put it to use in other environments. Domino may not survive forever, so it is a good idea to make yourself more marketable by learning a new skill.

1.2   *LotusScript comparison*

The following table is a comparison of LotusScript and Java properties within Domino.

Table 1.1   LotusScript v. Java

LotusScript	Java
Procedural	Object-oriented
Runs in Notes/Domino	Runs in an interpreter (JVM)
Script can exist within events, functions, subs, libraries, and agents	Everything is defined as a class. You can use and reuse classes
Access to both front-end and back-end Domino objects	No front-end support; restricted to back-end access
Restricted to Notes/Domino environment	Can run outside Notes/Domino as a standalone application, applet, or servlet
No third-party support	Direct access to third-party tools and add-ons

1.3　LEARNING THE JAVA LANGUAGE

This book focuses on the Domino Java environment. While this book includes a chapter that covers basic Java syntax, there are several excellent books available for learning the language. Here is a short list:

- *Thinking in Java* by Bruce Eckel (Prentice Hall)
- *Java How to Program* by Deitel & Deitel (Prentice Hall)
- *Distributed Programming with Java* by Qusay H. Mahmoud (Manning Publications)
- *Java in a Nutshell* by David Flanagan (O'Reilly)
- *Exploring Java* by Pat Niemeyer and Josh Peck (O'Reilly)

Thinking in Java has an excellent tutorial CD that you can order separately. I highly recommend it for learning the Java language. In addition to books, numerous Web sites offer a wealth of Java information as well as some tutorials, such as:

- Sun Microsystems (java.sun.com)
- JavaSoft (www.javasoft.com)
- Gamelan (www.gamelan.com)
- Project Cool (www.projectcool.com)
- IBM Java (www.ibm.com/java)
- HP Java (www.hp.com/java)

1.4　THE FUTURE

The future of anything computer-related is hard to predict, but the investment in Java by major corporations such as Sun, IBM, Hewlett-Packard, and Apple (to name a few) is too much to ignore. They are betting the futures of their companies on Java, so why not you?

Domino Designer IDE

2.1   Domino Designer environment   5
2.2   Imported Java   6
2.3   Java   10
2.4   Chapter review   21

2.1   DOMINO DESIGNER ENVIRONMENT

The standalone Domino Designer client was introduced in Domino R5. The former *everything-for-everyone* workspace in previous releases was split into three separate units: Administrator, Designer, and the Lotus Notes user client. The integrated development environment (IDE) included with the Domino Designer client software includes numerous features for working with Java.

Basically, it includes a rudimentary Java editor/compiler. The best part of the environment is syntax checking and error reporting. We will take a closer look at these features later. Figure 2.1 shows the Designer interface when you develop an agent. You can see this screen if you choose Agent from the Create Menu option in Domino Designer, or you can choose New Agent after clicking on Agent in the Design pane. The Run selection drop-down box shows the choices available for development within the IDE. You can use the formula language, built-in processes (Simple action), Lotus-

Script, Imported Java, and Java. The large white space in the IDE is the source code panel this is where you enter all code.

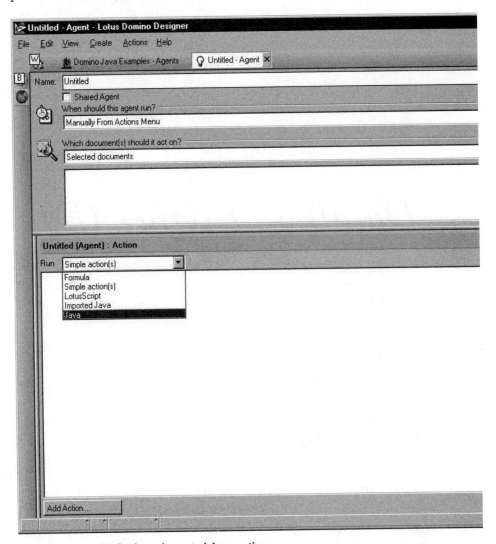

Figure 2.1 Domino Designer Imported Java option

2.2 IMPORTED JAVA

Figure 2.2 shows the environment arrangement when you select Imported Java. This option allows you to import Java class files from your computer file system (network or local drives). The Import Class Files button on the bottom left of the screen allows you to select the class files to import. Figure 2.3 shows the import window.

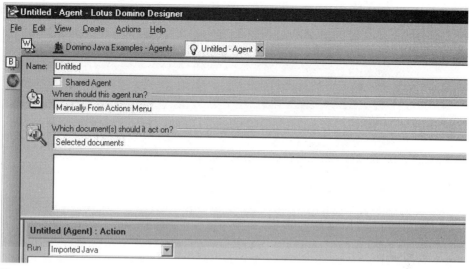

Figure 2.2 Domino Designer Imported Java option

While the button states "Import Class Files," you can import Java classes as well as compressed Jar files. The IDE will compile and get the class files on the fly. Figure 2.4 shows the IDE after you choose to import a Jar file. The system automatically retrieves a base class from the file. You can retype the base class in the text box at the bottom of the IDE window.

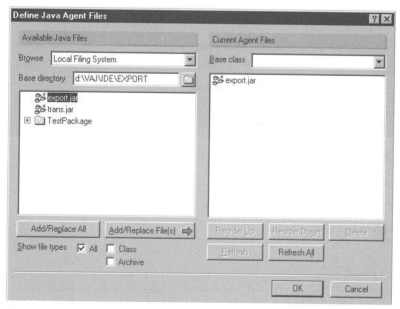

Figure 2.3 Import class files window

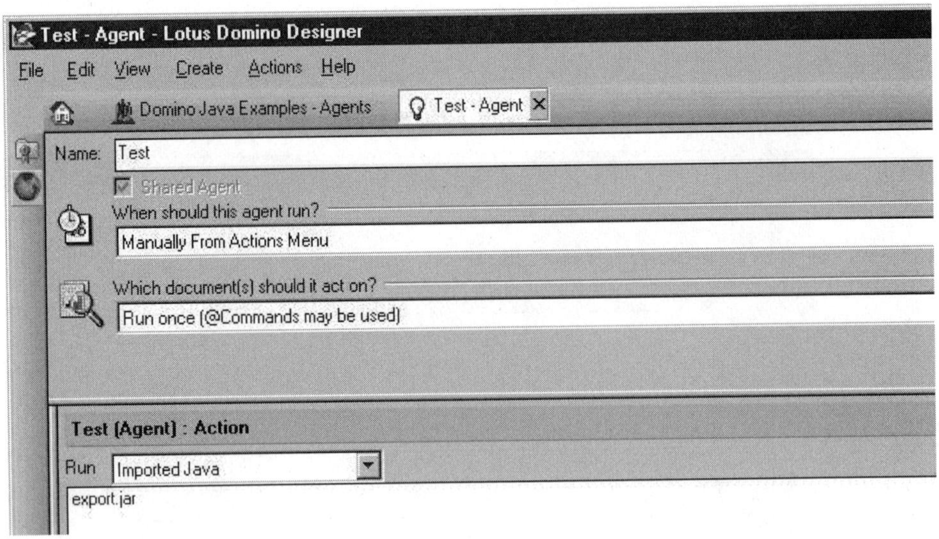

Figure 2.4 IDE after importing a Jar file

Now notice that the Reimport Class Files button appears in the bottom left of the IDE. The Reimport Class Files window shown in figure 2.5 appears when you select this button. This window allows you to refresh (reimport) the imported files if the source files change. Also, it allows you to remove existing files and add newer files.

The base class drop-down list allows you to select the base class. Press OK once you have made your changes, or press Cancel to not save your changes.

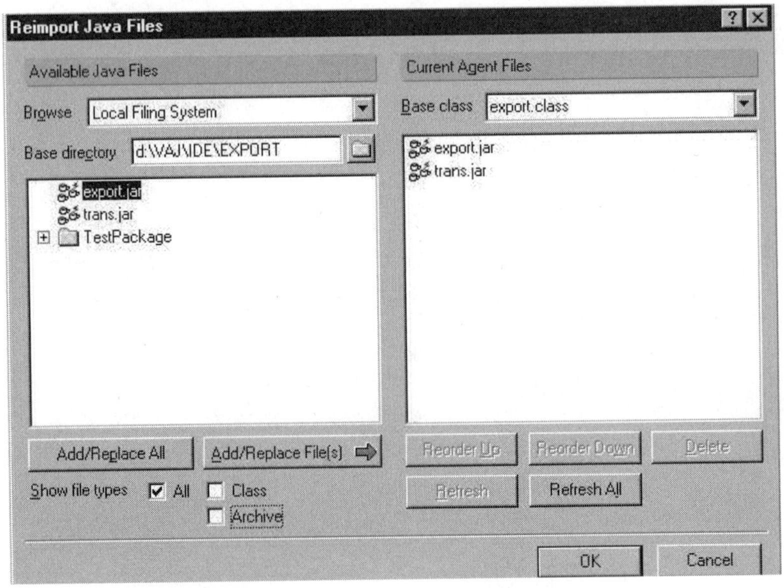

Figure 2.5 Reimport class files window

You cannot edit imported files, so you are restricted to the code imported. If you select the Java option shown in figure 2.1, you can code your own Java. Figure 2.6 shows the window that appears when you select Java.

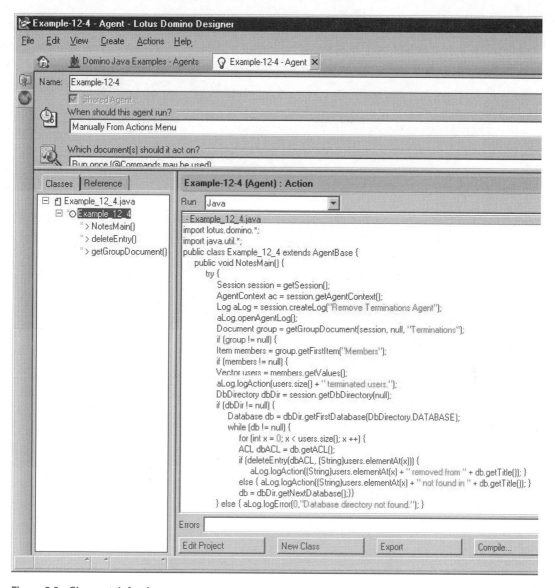

Figure 2.6 Classes tab for Java agent

2.3 JAVA

You will notice that the source code pane shown in figure 2.6 has the skeleton of code required for a Domino agent. To the left of the source code pane is the object browser pane. It has two tabs: Classes and Reference. The Classes tab allows you to browse all objects in your agent. Figure 2.7 shows the Classes tab for an existing agent. You can browse all objects and methods in the code.

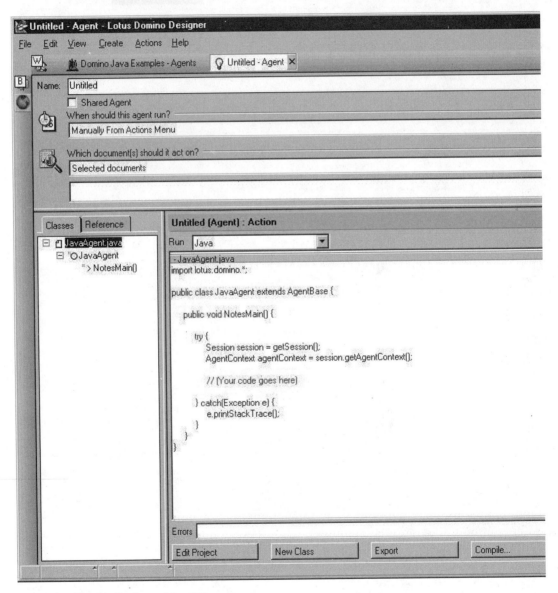

Figure 2.7   Domino Designer Java option

The Reference tab allows you to quickly browse the Sun Java classes and the Domino Java classes. The Sun classes are called "Core Java," and the Domino classes are "Notes Java" in the drop-down menu. The Reference tab displays the class hierarchies with twisties that allow quick navigation. Figure 2.8 shows the Reference tab for the Core Java classes, and figure 2.9 shows the Notes Java classes.

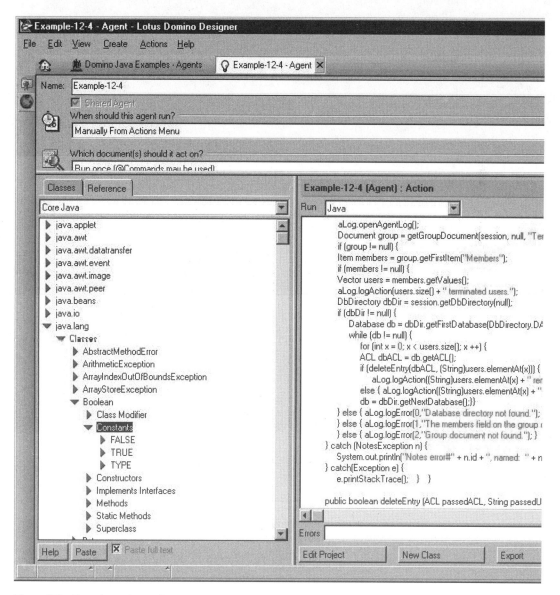

Figure 2.8   Core Java class tab

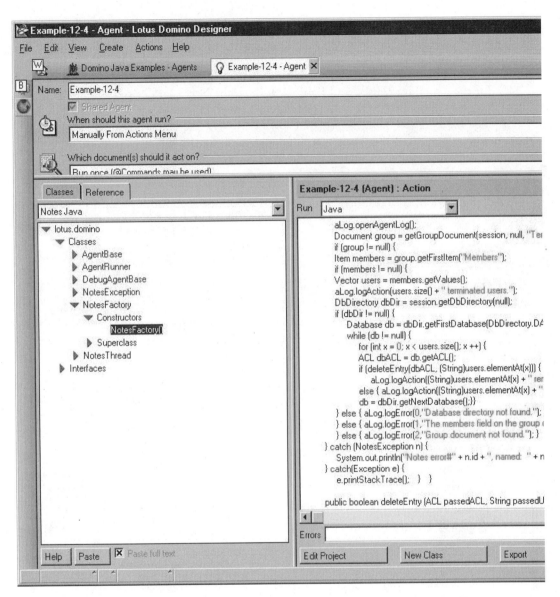

Figure 2.9   Notes Java class tab

Below the object browser pane are two buttons: Help and Paste. The Help button retrieves context-sensitive information from the Domino Designer help database. The Paste button pastes the selected text from the object browser into the source code pane.

Just below the source code pane is the Errors dropdown list, cursor position, and four buttons. The Edit Project button (see figure 2.10) allows you to add Java source, class, or Jar files from the file system. You can also reimport existing files in the project.

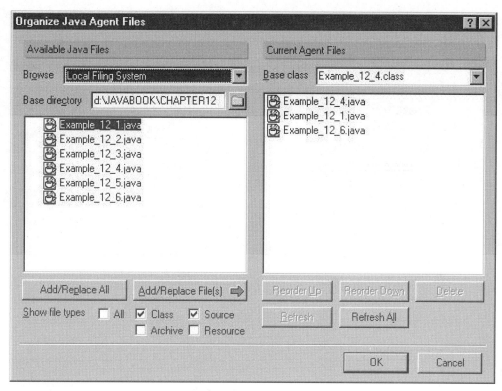

Figure 2.10   Edit project window

Adding a file from the file system via the Edit Project button inserts the class file into the source pane. If there is more than one class file, a plus sign (+) or minus sign (-) will appear to the left of the class declaration in the source pane. This allows you to browse and edit the contents of the class by expanding or collapsing it. Figure 2.11 shows an agent with three classes. The first class is collapsed (-), the middle class is expanded (+), and the last class is collapsed (-).

The New Class button facilitates the creation of a new class within the source pane. Selecting this button inserts an empty class declaration into the bottom of the source pane, as shown in figure 2.12. Notice the new class at the bottom of the source pane.

The Export button exports the Java source from the current source pane to the file directory path designated. Figure 2.13 shows the Export window.

The Compile button compiles the Java source code into Java bytecode (class file). It allows you to compile the selected class (indicated by cursor position) or all classes. Figure 2.14 shows the selections.

The last element to explore is the reporting of errors and cursor position. Just above the four buttons at the bottom of the window is the Errors drop-down list. Syntax errors are reported here. You can choose the drop-down list to view the error and

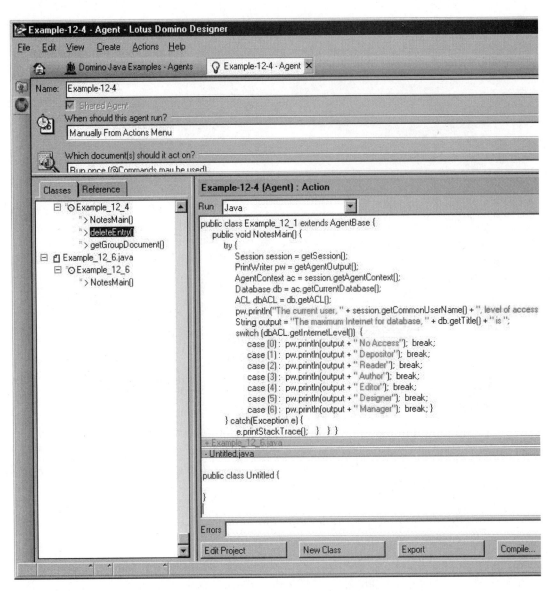

Figure 2.11 Adding a new class

CHAPTER 2   DOMINO DESIGNER IDE

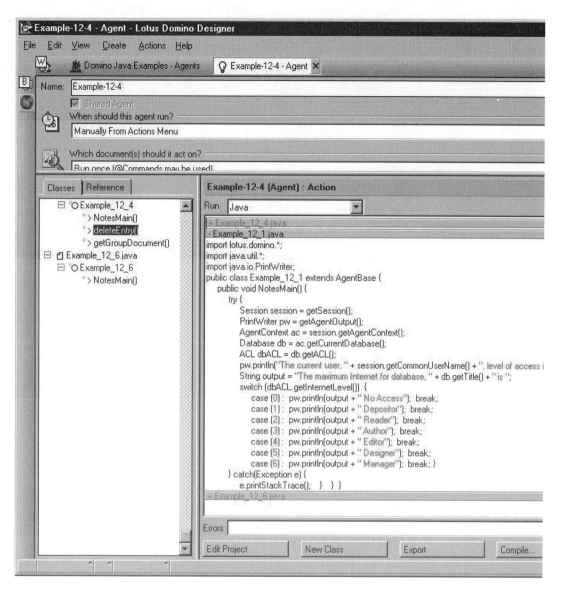

Figure 2.12 Multiple classes in the source pane

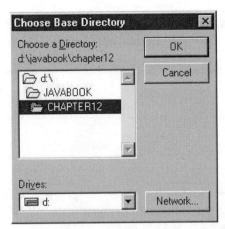

Figure 2.13
Exporting Java source code

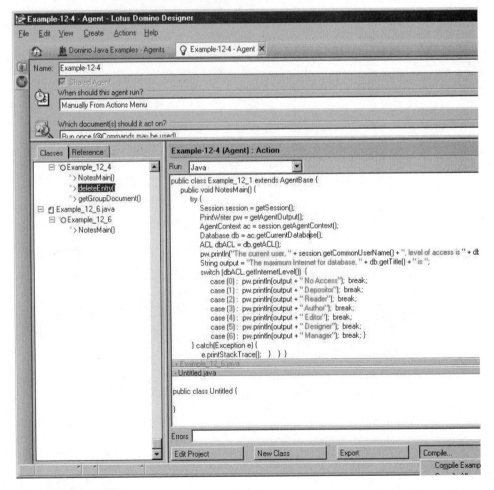

Figure 2.14   Compiling

a pointer (arrow) to the location of the error. Figure 2.15 shows the message box that appears when an error occurs. Figure 2.16 shows the IDE Errors list.

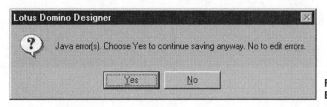

Figure 2.15
Error message

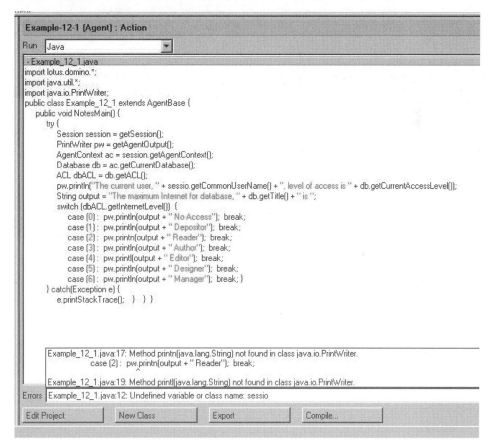

Figure 2.16   Errors drop-down list

You can scroll the errors reported in the Errors drop-down list. The cursor's position in the source code pane is reported to the right of the Errors drop-down list. The cursor position appears in the format (column number, row number). Errors reported in the drop-down list give you the line number, so using the cursor position can help track errors. Runtime errors return the line number as well; you can view these errors in the Java Debug Console Window.

2.3.1   AgentBase class

All Domino agents developed in Java must extend the `AgentBase` class and use the `NotesMain()` method as the entry point (where it starts running) for the agent. These items are automatically placed in the Java code when you select Java as an agent.

2.3.2   Java console window

The Java Debug Console is the standard output area for all Domino Java Agent code. Any code printed will appear in this window, and runtime errors will appear as well. Figure 2.17 shows the Java Console window. It has two buttons: Clear and Close. The Clear button clears the contents of the window, and the Close button closes the window. To view the Java Console window, select File | Tools | Show Java Debug Console, as shown in figure 2.18.

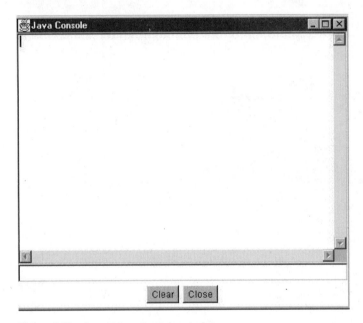

Figure 2.17   Java debug console window

Figure 2.19 shows the Java Console window when runtime errors are encountered. Notice that it gives you the line number in the line containing the "at." The first "at" line is your concern; this is where the error originated.

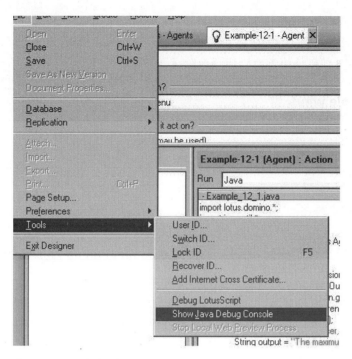

Figure 2.18   Displaying the Java debug console window

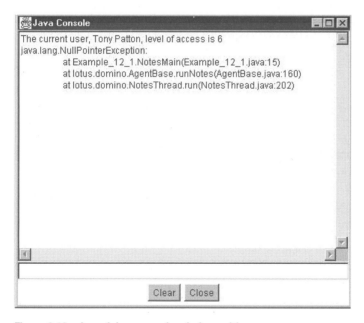

Figure 2.19   Java debug console window with errors

2.3.3 Help documentation

The Domino Java Classes and Domino Designer documentation is available in a few formats. We have seen how you can use the reference tab in the IDE to view Java class hierarchies and syntax. The Domino Designer installation includes optional Domino database files that cover the IDE and Java classes in detail. Both Lotus and IBM offer documentation. Lotus has yellow books and IBM offers Redbooks. You can find both at Lotus' support site (support.lotus.com) through the Technical Library link. Strangely, the very latest IBM Redbooks are not reliably listed on Lotus.com. These can be searched for by going to http://www.redbooks.ibm.com/ and entering "Domino" in the Search option.

2.3.4 Form events

There are a number of Domino Form events that are available to LotusScript, but none are directly accessible to Java. The Lotus Notes client doesn't support Java for programming, but it does allow the use of Java Applets and JavaScript. On the other hand, back-end agents written in Java can be triggered through one of two events: WebQueryOpen and WebQuerySave. These events are fired when a form/document is opened or closed via a browser client such as Microsoft Internet Explorer or Netscape Navigator.

2.3.5 Agents

Java development within the Domino Designer is accomplished in the form of an agent. In addition, Domino objects are accessed by external Java applications via IIOP, Corba, RMI, and more.

2.3.6 Third-party IDEs

While the Domino Designer is nice, it lacks features of a true Java development tool such as IBM's VisualAge for Java, Symantec's Visual Café, and Borland's JBuilder. These tools offer debugging, visual development, and project management features that are out of reach of the Designer client. Lotus offers the AgentRunner to develop Java agents in non-Designer development tools. Standalone applications/applets that access Domino objects can be built in other tools with the importing of the proper Domino Jar files into the environment. Chapter 22 is dedicated to such non-Designer development.

2.3.7 Special keys

There are a number of key combinations that you can use within the Designer code pane to perform much-needed functionality.

CTRL-Z   Undo: Undoes the most recent keystroke or activity; can be pressed multiple times

CTRL-C   Copy: Copies the selected text to the clipboard

CTRL-V	Paste: Pastes the text from the clipboard to the cursor location
CTRL-F	Find/Find Replace: Searches for text instances and replaces one or more instances if desired. Figure 2.20 shows the Search dialog box. It has fields for the text to find and another field for the optional replacement text. The drop-down list at the bottom of the box allows you to specify the scope of the search.

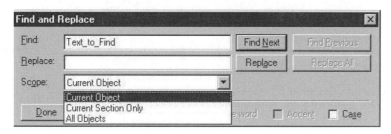

Figure 2.20   Find and Replace window

CTRL-A	Selects all text in the current window. This combination of keys highlights all text; you can use it in conjunction with CTRL-C to copy all text to the clipboard.
CTRL-L	Displays the address box at the top right of the workspace; contains the address (replica ID) for the currently open database
CTRL-N	Creates a new Domino database; displays the New Database window
CTRL-O	Opens an existing Domino database; displays the Open Database window
CTRL-Q	Closes the Domino Designer
CTRL-S	Saves the current work; compiles if used in a Java agent
CTRL-X	Cuts the selected text to the clipboard
CTRL-W	Closes the current window
CTRL-1	Goes to the Core Java classes of the Reference tab of the object browser

2.4   CHAPTER REVIEW

The Domino Designer is a radical departure from pre-R5 environments. For starters, it is a separate client installed alongside the Notes client. Also, it supports functions, Lotus-Script, JavaScript, and Java. You can import and export Java source code from Domino Agents. Standalone Java applications/applets can access Domino objects as well. The Java development environment offers rudimentary debugging and error reporting. You can overcome these drawbacks by using a third-party IDE.

- The Domino Designer is a separate application from the Notes client and the Domino administrator client.
- Domino Designer supports Java in agents only.
- The WebQueryOpen and WebQuerySave form events can refer to back-end Domino Java agents.
- You can direct Domino URLs at Java agents as well.
- The Domino Designer Java development environment offers Java class/reference browsers.
- Rudimentary error and syntax checking is included in the environment.
- You can import, export, and refresh Java files.
- Domino Designer R5 supports SUN JDK 1.1.
- You can use third-party Java development tools to develop Java agents and applications/applets.

CHAPTER 3

Java basics

3.1 Building blocks   23
3.2 Classes, methods, and properties   30
3.3 Chapter review   32

There is practically a ton of Java books on the market, so this chapter does not plan to teach you Java from the ground up. This chapter does, however, cover various aspects of Java development that you will need to understand when building Domino Java. The purpose is to provide a brief introduction that will allow you to get started with the examples in this book.

3.1 BUILDING BLOCKS

This section contains a brief overview of some aspects of the basic syntax of the Java programming language.

3.1.1 Output

You can send output to the standard out (Java Console window in the Domino Designer client) via this command:

```
System.out.println("text");
```

3.1.2   Semicolon

Every Java statement in the source code of a Java application must end with a semicolon. A missing semicolon generates a compile error.

3.1.3   Braces

All groups of code are placed between a pair of curly braces, { }. The body of a class is placed inside braces; the body of an `if` statement or its `else` statement is inside braces; the body of loops, such as `for` and `while`, are inside braces, and so forth. You will see these conventions used in all examples in this book.

3.1.4   Escape character

The escape character in Java is the backslash (\). When used in Java String values, it tells the system that the next character after it is special. The character after the backslash is combined with the backslash to form an escape sequence. The backslash should be used when you need to place such items as quotation marks or a simple backslash in a String variable. The following line of code prints out a string with a backslash and quotes in it:

```
System.out.println("A backslash \\ and double quotes \" \" in my output.");
```

You will also need to use the backslash when you store any directory path/ filename information:

```
String path = "c:\\notes\\data\\";
```

You can combine other characters with the backslash to create special characters. Here is a list of some of them:

    \n   Newline, moves the cursor to the beginning of the next line
    \t   Horizontal tab, moves the cursor to the next tab stop
    \r   Carriage return, moves the cursor to the beginning of the current line
    \'   Single quote
    \"   Double quote
    \\   Backslash

3.1.5   Data types

Java is not a pure object-oriented language, due to the existence of the primitive data types. These are data types built into the Java language; they are not classes. Here is a list of the data types:

- double: double numeric values; the largest primitive type (64 bits)
- float: floating point numeric values (32 bits)
- long: large integer values (64 bits)
- int: integer values (32 bits)
- char: character values, enclosed in apostrophe (16 bits)
- short: small integer values (16 bits)
- byte: 8 bits
- boolean: true/false (1 bit)

Table 3.1 shows a comparison of Java primitive data types and LotusScript data types:

Table 3.1   Java and LotusScript data types

Java	LotusScript	Size (bytes)
short	integer	2
int	long	4
float	single	4
double	double	8
byte	n/a	1
char	n/a	2
boolean	n/a	
n/a	Variant	
n/a	String	

There are a couple of things to remember regarding Java variables:

- You must declare all variables before using them.
- Java is case-sensitive, so a variable named Test is not the same as one named test.

String.   The String class offers a number of methods for working with its contents:

```
String name = "Tony Patton";
System.out.println(name.trim());
System.out.println(name.length());
System.out.println("Tony Patton is " + name.length() + " chars long.");
```

3.1.6   Logic

The following items make logical comparisons:

&&   Logical AND
|| Logical OR
!   NOT operator
==   Equality
<=   Less than or equal to
>=   Greater than or equal to
!=   Not equal to

NOTE   Remember that a single equal sign assigns an integer value, and double equal signs test equality.

3.1.7   Concatenation

The plus sign (+) concatenates two strings or any other value for output or storage in a String variable. All classes in the Java library overload the toString method, so the system automatically converts non-String data types. Therefore, the following code is properly formatted:

```
int x = 1;
double y = 9.1;
System.out.println("x = " + x + ", y = " + y);
```

The result is:

```
x = 1, y = 9.1
```

3.1.8 Increment/decrement

Two plus signs (++) and two minus signs (- -), respectively, increment or decrement a value by one. You can place them before or after a variable. If the plus or minus signs are placed before the variable, the code performs the increment/decrement operation before accessing the variable contents. Otherwise, the value is returned and then the increment/decrement operation is performed. The following bit of code demonstrates this functionality:

```
int x=0;
System.out.println("x = " + ++x);
System.out.println("x = " + x);
int y=0;
System.out.println("y = " + y++);
System.out.println("y = " + y);
```

The output for the code will be:

```
x = 1
x = 1
y = 0
y = 1
```

Also, you can combine the equal sign with the various operators to form a shorthand approach to the operation:

```
x += 2 adds two to the current value stored in the variable x.
y -= 4 subtracts four from the current value stored in the variable y.
```

3.1.9 Looping

Java has a number of looping methods available.

for

```
for (starting index value; condition; increment index value)
{
   // code goes here
}
```

In this example, the loop will repeat twenty times:

```
for (int x=1; x <= 20; x++)
{
   // do something
}
```

do

```
do
{
  // code goes here
} while (boolean condition);
```

while

```
while (condition)
{
  // code goes here
}
```

3.1.10 Controlling program flow

There are a number of Java statements available for controlling the flow of a program.

if/then/else if/else.   The `if` statement checks a condition and executes a block of code. If the condition is false, it can revert to another condition, and finally execute a block of code if all else if conditions are false.

```
if (condition)
{
  // code
}
else if (condition)
{
  // code
}
else
{
  // code
}
```

NOTE   The else if and else blocks are optional.

switch/case.   The switch/case directive checks a value and "switches" it to a block of code with the case value that matches. If there are no matches, the default block is executed. The default block is optional, so execution could be skipped altogether.

```
switch (value)
{
 case(value) :
    // code
    break;
 default:
    // code
    break;
}
```

break.   The break statement can break out of a loop or other control structure. In the previous section, the break statement was used to break out of the switch statement after code for a particular case was executed. The following snippet of code exits the loop after only one iteration, due to the break statement:

```
for (int x=0; x<1000; x++) {
 // some code here
 break;   }
```

continue. The continue statement continues the execution of code. It is the opposite of the break statement.

3.1.11   Comments

You can place comments into your Java programs using two methods. Two forward slashes (//) placed on the line signals the system to recognize everything after them on that line as comments and, thus, nonexecuting code:

```
// Comment
```

Everything between the forward slash and asterisk (/*) and an asterisk and forward slash (*/) is viewed as a comment:

```
/*
   Comments
*/
```

3.1.12   Arrays

Everything in an array must be the same type and is referenced via the same name. Single- and multi-dimensional arrays are legal. Let's take a look at an array declaration:

```
String names[] = new String[20];
```

The index values for the elements in an array start at zero (0) and end with the length of the array minus one. In this case, the last element in our array of Strings is 19.

A two-dimensional array could be declared las follows:

```
String namePairs[][] = new String[5][5]
```

The length property of an array accesses each and every element in an array through the use of a loop:

```
for (x=0; x <=names.length -1; x++)
{
  System.out.println("Name:   " + names[x]);
}
```

3.1.13   Vector class

The Vector class works like an array, but it can hold a variety of disparate objects. It is not restricted to one consistent data type.

```
Vector v = new Vector(5);
for (int x=0; x < v.size(); x++)   {
   System.out.println(v.elementAt(x));   }
```

3.1.14 Access

There are a number of identifiers for assigned access:

Public   The public identifier specifies that the class, property, or method is available to everyone, that is, the public.

Protected   The protected identifier specifies that the class, property, or method is only available to those in or derived from the same package.

Private   The private identifier specifies that the class, property, or method is only available to its own class.

3.1.15 Import

The import keyword brings or imports other Java classes and libraries into your application for use. An item in another class is not available (with the exception of the base java.lang package) to your code. When you work with Domino classes, the next import statement applies:

```
import lotus.domino.*;  // import core Domino R5 classes
```

If you wanted to use the Vector class, which is part of the java.util package, the following two import statements would do the trick:

```
import java.util.*;
import java.util.Vector;
```

Import statements must appear in the first line(s) of your code, before anything else.

3.1.16 Package

Classes that are grouped together are considered a package. The standard syntax for a package name is the directory structure in reverse order. Dots are the separators for directories. Also, the Internet domain name of the company that developed or owns the code is used as the base directory structure (in reverse order). So, a package called utils for the company Baseline, Inc. with the Web address www.BaseLineInc.com would be com.baselineinc.utils. The directory structure for the class files (on a Windows platform) would be <drive letter>:\com\baselineinc\utils\.

3.1.17 Implements

A Java interface can be described as a structure for a class. It is defined to signal what must be included in the class, but you can add your own code. The implements keyword makes a class conform to a particular interface:

```
public void testClass() implements testInterface
```

A class can implement multiple interfaces but can only inherit its design from one parent class. Multiple inheritance is not legal in Java. You can use multiple interfaces to get around this limitation.

3.1.18 Extends

The extends keyword creates a subclass of a class. You can extend a class and add your own functionality to the base class:

```
public void testClass() extends testParentClass
```

3.2 CLASSES, METHODS, AND PROPERTIES

One of the most common ways to explain object-oriented programming is to compare it to the real world. You can think of an object as a noun, that is, a person, place, or thing. This object has certain characteristics called properties, and certain behaviors called methods. You can think of a class as a group of related objects. A mailman is a person object; he or she delivers the mail (method), and is a male or female (property). On the other hand, a person class can define a mailman, programmer, bus driver, or any other type of person. A class is a template for an object. An object is an instance of a class. The terms object and class are often used interchangeably, so it can be confusing.

All development in Java is done with classes. Everything you create, whether a Domino agent, standalone application, or applet, will consist of one or more classes with methods and properties.

3.2.1 Constructor

The constructor method of a class is the method that is called when an object is first instantiated via its class definition. The constructor method has the same name as the class, and it can accept one or more parameters, which can be overloaded.

```
public class1() {
 class1() {
   // Constructor code here
 }
```

3.2.2 Final

The final keyword locks a class or method. Declaring either as final prevents inheritance. Because declaring a class final prevents inheritance, all methods in a final class are implicitly final.

3.2.3 Static

The static declaration defines variables to be statically maintained in storage. Only one copy of the variable is maintained, and it is not deleted between calls to its container. This is like a global variable, but its scope is not really global. Rather, its scope is limited to the class containing it. Static variables are good for items that require a count or anything similar.

3.2.4   Casting

Casting allows you to convert one object to another. You may require casting when you are unsure of the data type, or when you need to have a certain object when you call a method. You will see casting used extensively in the examples throughout this book. A common use of casting is for storing disparate objects in a Vector. When you retrieve the objects from the Vector, you must cast them to the appropriate type. To implement casting, place the new type in parentheses preceding the object to be cast.

3.2.5   Overloading

The overloading of methods allows more than one declaration for a method to be created. You may have different variations of a method depending on the parameters you pass; one may accept an integer, another nothing, and so on. Overloading provides you, the developer, with an enormous amount of flexibility. The next snippet of code has the constructor method overloaded:

```
public class2 {
  class2 (int x) {
    // constructor code for integer parameter
  }
  class2 (String s)  {
    // constructor code for String parameter
  }
  class2 () {
    // constructor code for no parameters
  } }
```

3.2.6   Using your own classes

As with any programming language, you are allowed to create and develop your own classes. In fact, you must create a class to do any type of Java development. The creation of a Domino Java agent creates a class. Your classes can have whatever properties and/or methods you desire. You will see classes in each and every example in this book. Examples in chapter 18 are devoted to creating your own classes. Chapter 19 focuses on reports; it will demonstrate how to add functionality to your own classes.

3.2.7   Case-sensitivity

Java is a case-sensitive programming language, so you must type code in this book as it is listed. You must capitalize the Database class; the IDE will signal a code error if you type database using all lowercase letters.

3.3 CHAPTER REVIEW

Java is a very powerful programming language with or without Domino. The Domino Java classes extend this power to the Domino development environment. Learning Java can prove daunting, so a good book and/or class is a must to get up to speed. The purpose of this chapter is to provide a quick overview of items that will appear throughout the rest of the book. It is meant not to teach you Java, but rather to direct you to aspects of Java on which you may want to concentrate.

C H A P T E R   4

NotesFactory/NotesThread/ NotesError classes

4.1   NotesFactory class   33
4.2   What is a thread?   34
4.3   NotesThread class   35
4.4   What is an exception?   35
4.5   NotesException class   35

4.6   NotesError class   36
4.7   Memory management/recycle
      method   36
4.8   Chapter review   37

For your Java code to work in Domino, it must make itself known to the Domino Server. For Java code (other than Domino agents), this can be done using the `NotesFactory` class.

4.1   NOTESFACTORY CLASS

The `NotesFactory` class is used in non-Domino agent code; that is, code running outside of the Domino environment that accesses Domino objects must use the `NotesFactory` class. Applications that make local calls (on the same machine as the Domino server) should use the `createSession` method with no parameters. Code that makes remote calls to a Domino server must use the `createSession-(serverName)` method. Remote code accesses a Domino server via IIOP (Internet InterOrb Protocol).

The `NotesFactory` class has only one method named `createSession`. The method is overloaded, so there are a number of variations of it. Here are the numerous formats of the `createSession` method:

```
createSession();
createSession("Server IP address");
createSession("Server IP address", "username", "password");
createSession("Server IP address", String args[], "username", "password");
createSessionWithIOR("IOR");
createSessionWithIOR("IOR", "username", "password");
createSessionWithIOR("IOR", String args[], "username", "password");
createSession(Applet, "username", "password");
createSession(Applet, org.omg.CORBA.ORB.ORB orb, "username", "password")
```

The only other method is getIOR:

```
getIOR("Server IP address");
```

Example 4.1 shows a standalone application that uses one variation of create-Session to connect to a remote server.

Example 4.1   (Standalone application)

```
import lotus.domino.*;
public class Example_4_1 implements Runnable  {
 public static void main(java.lang.String[] args)    {
  Example1 t = new Example1();
  Thread nt = new Thread((Runnable)t);
  nt.start();   }
 public void run()    {
  try {
   Session s = NotesFactory.createSession("200.118.34.8","tpatton","password");
   String p = s.getPlatform();
   String cu = s.getCommonUserName();
   String nv = s.getNotesVersion();
   String sn = s.getServerName();
   String un = s.getUserName();
   s.recycle();
  } catch (NotesException n) {
   System.out.println("ID:  " + n.id + " -- Name:  " + n.text);
  } catch (Exception e) {
     e.printStackTrace();  }  }  }
```

Don't worry if you don't yet understand what each part of this Java code does. As we work through further examples of java code, I will explain the significance of the various parts of the code in more detail.

4.2   WHAT IS A THREAD?

The book *JAVA Threads*, by Scott Oaks and Henry Wong, defines a thread as follows:

> "The term thread is shorthand for thread of control, and a thread of control is, at its simplest, a section of code executed independently of other threads of control within a single program."

They continue to explain:

"Thread of control is the path taken by an application during execution…. Having multiple threads of control is like executing items from two lists."

4.3   NOTESTHREAD CLASS

The `NotesThread` class extends the basic `Thread` class in the basic Java language. Threads do not have to be incorporated in Java agents; they are included in the `AgentBase` class that is used as the base class for all Domino Java agents.

You can use threads in Domino in one of three ways:

1   Extend the `NotesThread` class

2   Implement the `Runnable` interface (see Example 4.1)

3   Use static methods to initiate a thread (`sinitThread`) and terminate a thread (`stermThread`)

4.4   WHAT IS AN EXCEPTION?

Java exception handling allows a Java program to catch all types of exceptions. You can use it to catch specific exceptions as well. Java exception handling is designed to smoothly handle errors rather than abruptly crash a program. Exception handling is useful for the following events:

- handling exceptional and unforeseen situations
- processing errors from other components (such as third-party vendors) that don't handle their own very well
- handling exceptions in a clean fashion

4.5   NOTESEXCEPTION CLASS

The `NotesException` class provides the facility of exception handling for Domino Java agents. You should use it in try/catch/finally clauses, such as the following, to catch Domino errors:

```
try {
  // code
} catch (NotesException n) {
  // code
} catch (Exception e) {
  // code }
```

You should include handling for `NotesException` as well as normal Java exceptions. The previous snippet of code provides that functionality.

4.5.1   ID property

The `id` property of the `NotesException` class returns the Domino error code (Appendix B contains Domino error codes). You can access it as follows:

```
NotesException.id
```

4.5.2 Text property

The text property of the NotesException class contains the text description of the error message returned:

```
NotesException.text

try {
    // code
} catch (NotesException n) {
    System.out.println("Exception ID:  " + n.id);
    System.out.prinln("Exception description:  " + n.text);
} catch (Exception e) {
    // code }
```

The exception handling code appears throughout the examples in this book.

4.6 NOTESERROR CLASS

The NotesError class defines error code variables. You can use the defined variables in conjunction with the NotesException class to catch and handle specific Domino errors accordingly. Appendix B lists the possible error codes.

4.7 MEMORY MANAGEMENT/RECYCLE METHOD

One of the most talked about features of the Java language is garbage collection. Languages, such as C and C++, require developers to take care of the objects they use; they must manage the memory themselves. Memory leaks can occur in this scenario if you forget to dispose of an object. This is not a problem in Java, because Java performs automatic "garbage collection" of memory.

Every Java class has a method called finalize. It is often referred to as the finalizer method. Its job is to return resources used by its object to the system. Java guarantees that the finalize method will be called just before garbage collection is performed.

The Java Virtual Machine decides when and if the garbage collector is called. It is out of your hands, so there isn't much to rely on with garbage collection. In fact, the garbage collector may not ever be called.

4.7.1 recycle method

Every Domino Java object has a recycle method. This method handles the cleanup of system resources used by the object. The Java garbage collector runs after the recycle method is called. The Java garbage collector has been disabled in Domino, so it can only run on objects once the recycle method has been called. The garbage collector will not run immediately; it will run when it deems it necessary.

For this reason, you must personally handle the cleanup of your Domino objects. This becomes a real issue in large amounts of code, but it is good practice to always use recycle.

Here are a few tips regarding recycling:

- Always create a new Domino session object for each servlet request, and call its `recycle` method when you are finished with the session object.
- Choose your spots in a Domino agent for recycling.
- Keep the memory footprint small.
- A good spot for recycling is just after exiting a loop.

4.7.2 Syntax

The `recycle` method accepts no parameters, so it is called with empty parentheses. Here is the `recycle` method used for a Domino `Session` object:

```
session.recycle();
```

Avoiding the `recycle` method in your Domino code will cause major memory problems. The Java garbage collector is unpredictable and it cannot "garbage collect" Domino objects until the `recycle` method has been called. For this reason, get into the habit of recycling all Domino-related objects.

4.8 CHAPTER REVIEW

There are a number of special Java classes available for accessing Domino objects via Java. The `NotesFactory` class can create sessions with remote Domino servers. The `NotesException` and `NotesError` classes work with Domino exceptions and errors. Garbage collection of Domino objects requires the use of the `recycle` method.

- The `NotesFactory` class is a special class only used to access Domino objects from outside the Domino agent environment.
- The `NotesFactory` class contains the `createSession` method that is overloaded to provide the capability to create a session for use with local and remote calls and calls via Corba.
- The `NotesException` class provides a means to handle errors specific to the Domino environment.
- The `NotesException` class provides `id` and `text` properties for accessing exception data.
- The `NotesError` class defines error variables for use with Domino.
- The `recycle` method is common to all classes in the Domino Java class library.

C H A P T E R   5

Session class

5.1 Using the Session class   38
5.2 Property list   42
5.3 Method list   42
5.4 Chapter review   43

5.1 USING THE SESSION CLASS

The Session class is the most important class used when you access Domino objects via Java. It is the base class of all other Domino Java classes and represents the environment for the current program. Once a Session object is instantiated, it allows access to databases, which leads to accessing documents and views among other objects. A Session object also allows access to information pertaining to the current environment, such as name of the server, current user name, and platform. The Session class is used extensively throughout this book (in almost every example), so its methods and properties will be discussed when appropriate. Now let's take a quick look at using the Session class in example 5.1.

Example 5.1   (Domino Agent)

```
package Chapter5;
import lotus.domino.*;  ❶
import java.io.PrintWriter;  ❷
public class Example_5_1 extends AgentBase {  ❸
  public void NotesMain() {  ❹
    try {  ❺
      Session session = getSession();  ❻
      String p = session.getPlatform();  ❼
      String cu = session.getCommonUserName();  ❽
      String nv = session.getNotesVersion();  ❾
      String sn = session.getServerName();  ❿
      PrintWriter pw = getAgentOutput();  ⓫
      pw.println("Current platform:  " + p);  ⓬
      pw.println("Current Username:  " + session.getUserName());  ⓭
      pw.println("Current Common Username:  " + cu);
      pw.println("Current Notes Version:  " + nv);
      pw.println("Current Server Name:  " + sn);
      if (sn == "")  {  ⓮
       pw.println("We are working locally.");
      }else {
       pw.println("We are working on the server:  " + sn);  }
      if (session.isOnServer()) {  ⓯
       pw.println("We are working on the server.");
      }else  {
       pw.println("We are working locally.");  }
      session.recycle();  ⓰
    } catch(Exception e) {  ⓱
      e.printStackTrace();  ⓲
} } }
```

Explanation

❶ Import the Domino classes so we can access them in our agent.

❷ Import the `PrintWriter` class from the java.io package. It will be used to print results.

❸ Declare the class name and the fact that it extends the Domino `AgentBase` class. The `AgentBase` class is used for agents.

❹ The required `NotesMain` method for Agents is declared. It accepts and returns no values.

❺ The beginning of our try/catch block. We must gracefully handle all errors.

❻ Create a new `Session` object.

❼ Retrieve the current platform for the agent via the `getPlatform` method.

❽ Retrieve the common user name for the current user via the `getCommonUserName` method.

⑨ Retrieve the version of Domino running the agent via the `getNotesVersion` method.

⑩ Retrieve the current server (blank if local) via the `getServerName` method.

⑪ The `PrintWriter` class is instantiated to the output for the current agent.

⑫ The `println` method of the `PrintWriter` class sends the string variables to standard out. You can view code output via the Java Console (File | Tools | Show Java Debug Console) in the Domino client.

⑬ The `println` method is used like all other lines, but it uses the call to the `getUserName` method in the print statement. This demonstrates that a String variable does not have to be created.

⑭ We use an `if/else` block to determine if the server is local (`getServerName` method returns `""`). Remember that equality is determined with double equal signs (`==`).

⑮ The `isOnServer` method determines if we are working locally or not.

⑯ Reclaim and recycle system resources used by the Domino `Session` object.

⑰ This is the `catch` block of our `try/catch` clause.

⑱ Print the contents of the stack to the standard output if an exception occurs. This will send the results to the Java Console when the code is run from a Domino agent.

Output (via Java Console):

```
Current platform: Windows/32
Current Username: Tony Patton
Current Common Username: Tony Patton
Current Notes Version: Release 5.0 |March 30, 1999
We are working locally.
We are working locally.
```

You can create Domino sessions remotely as well as locally in Domino agents. Example 5.2 creates a session on a Domino server via Corba/IIOP.

Example 5.2 (Standalone application)

```
package Chapter5;
import lotus.domino.*;

public class Example_5_2 implements Runnable  {
  public static void main(java.lang.String[] args)    {
    Example2 t = new Example2();  ❶
    Thread nt = new Thread((Runnable)t);  ❷
    nt.start();  }  ❸
    public void run()    {  ❹
      try {
        Session s = NotesFactory.createSession("200.118.34.8","tpatton","password");  ❺
        String p = s.getPlatform();
        String cu = s.getCommonUserName();
```

```
String nv = s.getNotesVersion();
String sn = s.getServerName();
String un = s.getUserName();
System.out.println("Current platform:  " + p);
System.out.print("Current Username:  ");
System.out.println(s.getCommonUserName());
System.out.println("Current Common Username:  " + cu);
System.out.println("Current Notes Version:  " + nv);
if (sn.trim() == "")  {
  System.out.println("We are working locally.");
} else{
  System.out.println("We are working on the server:  " + sn);
}
if (s.isOnServer()) {
  System.out.println("We are working on the server.");
} else{
  System.out.println("We are working locally.");}
s.recycle();  ❻
} catch (NotesException n) {  ❼
System.out.println("ID:  " + n.id + " -- Name:  " + n.text);  ❽
} catch (Exception e) {
e.printStackTrace();  }  }  }
```

Explanation

❶ Create a new instance of our class.

❷ Create a new thread for our object.

❸ Start the thread.

❹ The run method is required for all classes that implement the Runnable interface.

❺ Create a new session object connecting to a remote server via IIOP. The three parameters passed into the createSession method of the NotesFactory object are Domino server IP address, username, and password.

❻ Recycle the Session object.

❼ Handle any Domino-specific exceptions encountered.

❽ Display the id and text of the exception encountered.

Output

```
Current platform:  Windows/32
Current Username:  Tony Patton
Current Common Username:  Tony Patton
Current Notes Version:  Release 5.0 |March 30, 1999
We are working on the server:  CN=PATTON/O=BASELINE
We are working on the server.
```

Examples 5.1 and 5.2 demonstrate how to access various properties of the Session class on a local server and a remote server. You can also use the Session class in an applet. Chapter 23 covers applets.

5.2 PROPERTY LIST

You access all properties using a getPropertyName method—e.g. getAddressBooks. This is consistent through all of the Domino Java classes. All properties of the Session class are read-only; there is no corresponding setPropertyName for any of the properties. Here is a complete list of the properties of the Session class:

- AddressBooks: Vector containing list of address books
- AgentContext: Agent environment for the session; only used for Domino Java agents
- CommonUserName: Current user's common username
- International: International object for the operating system
- isOnServer: Boolean (true/false) signaling whether or not the current session is on a server (this method is an exception to the getPropertyName style of naming)
- NotesVersion: Current version of Domino being used
- Platform: Platform (operating system) on which Domino is installed
- ServerName: The name of the server being accessed
- UserName: Current user's fully qualified user name
- UserNameList: User name list for current user; includes alternate user name
- UserNameObject: A Name object representing the current user

5.3 METHOD LIST

In addition to the numerous get methods for each and every corresponding property, there are additional methods as well:

- createDateRange: Creates a new DateRange object
- createDateTime: Creates a new DateTime object
- createLog: Creates a new Log object
- createName: Creates a new Name object
- createNewsletter: Creates a new Newsletter object
- createRegistration: Creates a new Registration object
- createRichTextParagraphStyle: Creates a new RichTextParagraph-Style object
- createRichTextStyle: Creates a new RichTextStyle object

- `evaluate`: Evaluates a `Notes` formula (using the formula language)
- `freeTimeSearch`: Searches for free time via Domino Calendaring and Scheduling
- `getDatabase`: Creates a new `Database` object
- `getDBDirectory`: Creates a new `DBDirectory` object
- `getEnvironmentString`: Retrieves the value of an environment variable
- `getEnvironmentValue`: Retrieves the value of an environment variable
- `getURLDatabase`: Locates and opens the Web Navigator database
- `resolve`: Returns the Domino object represented by a Web address (URL)
- `setEnvironmentVar`: Sets the value of an environment variable

These methods will be used extensively throughout the rest of this book, so we will not include any examples at this point.

5.4   CHAPTER REVIEW

The `Session` class is essential to successful Domino Java development. It represents the Domino environment in which code will be working using the `Notes-Factory` class for remote access and the `AgentBase` class for Domino agents. Most examples in this book use the `Session` class, so you will become very familiar with its syntax and uses. The purpose of this chapter has been to construct a base for the rest of the book. We will now move forward to the rest of the classes in the Domino Java library.

- The `Session` class is the base for all Domino Java code.
- A `Session` object can be instantiated for local and remote servers.
- There are numerous properties in the `Session` class; they are accessible via a corresponding `getPropertyName`.
- There are various methods in the `Session` class; they can create various Domino objects.

C H A P T E R   6

Database class

6.1 Syntax 44
6.2 Properties 46
6.3 Methods 48
6.4 All documents 50

6.5 Replication class 50
6.6 DbDirectory class 53
6.7 Chapter review 56

The database is the core element of a Domino application. It is the container for all other elements: views, documents, forms, agents, and so forth. In this chapter we will access Domino databases and take advantage of various methods and/or properties in the Database class.

6.1   SYNTAX

A handle to a database object is established using one of three ways. First, once a Session object is instantiated, a database can be retrieved (if it exists):

```
Session s = getSession();
Database db = s.getDatabase("server", "database filename/path");
```

or

```
Database db = s.getDatabase("server (null for local)", "database filename/
path", boolean);
```

The `boolean` parameter in the second format tells the system to create the database object if the named database cannot be opened.

The second way to access a database object is through the `AgentContext` object. It contains a current database property for accessing the database in which the agent is running:

```
Session s = getSession();
AgentContext ac = s.getAgentContext();
Database db = ac.getCurrentDatabase();
```

The third way to access a Domino database is through the use of the `DbDirectory` class:

```
Session s = getSession();
DBDirectory dbd = s.getDbDirectory("server or null for local");
Database db = dbd.getFirstDatabase(type);
```

NOTE   The type can be one of four types—DbDirectory.TEMPLATE, DbDirectory.DATABASE, DbDirectory.REPLICA_CANDIDATE, or DbDirectory.TEMPLATE_CANDIDATE.

Example 6.1   (Domino Agent)

```
import lotus.domino.*;
public class example_6_1 extends AgentBase  {
 public void NotesMain()   {
  try  {
   Session s = getSession();
   PrintWriter pw = getAgentOuput();
   DbDirectory dbd = s.getDbDirectory(null);    ❶
   Database db = dbd.getFirstDatabase(DbDirectory.DATABASE);    ❷
   pw.println("Title:   " + db.getTitle());    ❸
   db.recycle();
   dbd.recycle();
   s.recycle();}
  catch (Exception e) {
   e.printStackTrace();
 } } }
```

Explanation

❶ Declare/instantiate `DbDirectory` object. The directory for the local Notes installation will be used.

❷ Instantiate a `Database` object to the first database (in the first .nsf file) in the database directory.

❸ Send the title of the database to the standard output.

6.2 PROPERTIES

Example 6.1 demonstrates the use of the title property, but there are numerous other properties of the Database class available. Example 6.2 demonstrates this point.

Example 6.2   (Domino Agent)

```
import lotus.domino.*;
import java.io.PrintWriter;

public class Example_6_2 extends AgentBase {

public void NotesMain() {
 try {
  Session session = getSession();
  AgentContext ac = session.getAgentContext();
  Database db = ac.getDatabase(null,"names.nsf");        ❶
  PrintWriter pw = getAgentOutput();        ❷
  pw.println("Database Title: " + db.getTitle());        ❸
  pw.println("Filename:  " + db.getFileName());        ❹
  pw.println("Path:  " + db.getFilePath());        ❺
  pw.println("Server:  " + db.getServer());        ❻
  pw.println("Maximum Size:  " + db.getMaxSize());        ❼
  pw.println("Size:  " + db.getSize());        ❽
  pw.println("Created:  " + db.getCreated());        ❾
  pw.println("Current Access Level:  " + db.getCurrentAccessLevel());        ❿
  pw.println("Design Template Used:  " + db.getDesignTemplateName());        ⓫
  pw.println("Folder References Enabled: " + db.getFolderReferencesEnabled());        ⓬
  pw.println("Last Full Text Indexed:  " + db.getLastFTIndexed());        ⓭
  pw.println("Last Modified:  " + db.getLastModified());        ⓮
  pw.println("Managers:  " + db.getManagers());        ⓯
  pw.println("Percent Used:  " + db.getPercentUsed());        ⓰
  pw.println("Replica ID:  " + db.getReplicaID());        ⓱
  pw.println("Replication Info:  " + db.getReplicationInfo());        ⓲
  if (db.isOpen())        ⓳
   pw.println("Database is open.");
  else
   pw.println("Database is not open.");
  if (db.isDelayUpdates())        ⓴
   pw.println("Updates are delayed in this database.");
  else
   pw.println("Updates are not delayed in this database.");
  db.setDelayUpdates(false);        ㉑
  if (db.isDelayUpdates())        ㉒
   pw.println("Updates are delayed in this database.");
  else
   pw.println("Updates are not delayed in this database.");
  if (db.isFTIndexed())        ㉓
   pw.println("Database is full-text indexed.");
  else
   pw.println("Database is not full-text indexed");
```

```
if (db.isMultiDbSearch())   ㉔
  pw.println("Database has multi-database search enabled.");
else
  pw.println("Database has multi-database search disabled."); }
db.recycle();
ac.recycle();
session.recycle();
} catch(Exception e) {
e.printStackTrace();}}}
```

Explanation

❶ Create/instantiate a `Database` class to our local Domino Directory (names.nsf). The first parameter is null to signify a local database.

❷ Instantiate our `PrintWriter` object to the agent output via `getAgentOutput`.

❸ Retrieve the title of the database and send it to the standard output, which is the Java Console.

❹ Retrieve the name of the database file.

❺ Retrieve file path information for the database.

❻ Retrieve the server name for the database; ours will be blank because we are working locally.

❼ Retrieve the maximum size settings for the database.

❽ Retrieve the current size in bytes for the database.

❾ Access the date and time the database was created.

❿ Retrieve the current access level.

⓫ Get the design template (NTF file) used to create the database.

⓬ Retrieve the flag that signals whether folder references are enabled or not.

⓭ Retrieve date/time the full-text was last updated; null will be returned if it is not full-text index.

⓮ Retrieve the date/time the database was last modified.

⓯ Retrieve the list of managers from the ACL.

⓰ Get the current percent that is used. One hundred minus this value returns the amount of white space.

⓱ Get the database's replica id.

⓲ Get the replication info for the database.

⓳ Determine whether or not the database is open and send the proper output.

⓴ Determine whether or not delays are updated for the database and send the proper output.

㉑ Set the database to not delay updates; this is the only property that is not read-only.

㉒ Redo the line from item #20.

㉓ Determine whether or not the database is full-text indexed and send the proper output.

㉔ Determine whether or not a multi-database search is enabled for the database.

Output

```
Database Title:  Patton's Address Book
Filename:  names.nsf
Path:  c:\notes5\data\names.nsf
Server:
Maximum Size:  2097152.0
Size:  980992
Created:  06/03/99 11:25:03 AM EDT
Current Access Level:  6
Design Template Used:  StdR4PersonalAddressBook
Folder References Enabled:  false
Last Full Text Indexed:  null
Last Modified:  11/08/99 12:49:19 AM EST
Managers:  [CN=Tony Patton/O=TIS, LocalDomainServers]
Percent Used:  95.5
Replica ID:  852567850054B13C
Replication Info:  lotus.domino.local.Replication@8009cc
Database is open.
Updates are delayed in this database.
Updates are not delayed in this database.
Database is not full-text indexed.
Database has multi-database search disabled.
```

6.3 METHODS

In addition to the property set methods, there are additional methods available for working with `Database` objects.

6.3.1 Full-text index

The following code snippet checks if the database is already full-text indexed. If it is not, then a full-text index is created. If the database is already full-text indexed, it does nothing:

```
Session s = getSession();
AgentContext ac = s.getAgentContext();
Database db = ac.getCurrentDatabase();
if (!db.isFTIndexed())
  db.updateFTIndex(true);
```

6.3.2   Access

There are a few methods for working with a user's access to a database. The following bit of code uses the `queryAccess` method to determine if my access is author. If so, I am granted manager access; otherwise I am removed from the database ACL.

```
Session s = getSession();
AgentContext ac = s.getAgentContext();
Database db = ac.getCurrentDatabase();
String username = "Tony Patton";
if (db.queryAccess(username) = ACL.LEVEL_AUTHOR)
{
   db.grantAccess(username, ACL.LEVEL_MANAGER)
}
else
{
   db.revokeAccess(username);
}
```

6.3.3   Create, remove, and duplicate

The `Database` class also provides a number of methods for working with database files. The following few lines of code demonstrate copying, deleting, compacting, and replicating.

If you want to remove/delete a database, use the `remove` method:

```
Database.remove();
```

The `replicate` method replicates a database with all replicas on a server. The one and only parameter is the server. It returns true or false depending on whether or not replication was successful.

```
boolean = Database.replicate("Server");
```

If you want to create a replica of a database at a new location, use the `createReplica` method. It returns a handle to the newly created `Database` object.

```
Database = Database.createReplica("Server","database filename");
```

To create a new database using the current database as the template (if it is a template), use the `createFromTemplate` method. It returns the newly created `Database` object.

```
Database = Database.createFromTemplate("server","new database filename",boolean);
```

Use the `createCopy` method to create a copy of a Domino database with no documents. It accepts two parameters: the destination server (is empty string if server is local), and the file name for the new copy.

```
Database.createCopy("","new file name");
```

The `compact` method compacts all white space from a database:

```
Database.compact();
```

6.3.4   get methods

There are a number of get methods you can use to access database properties:

- `getAgent`: Retrieves a handle to an agent in a database
- `getDocumentByID`: Gets a handle on a document from a database using its `Notes ID`
- `getDocumentByUNID`: Gets a handle to a document from a database using its `Universal ID`
- `getDocumentByURL`: Retrieves a document given its Web address (URL)
- `getForm`: Gets a form object representing a form in a database
- `getOutline`: Retrieves an outline object from a database
- `getProfileDocCollection`: Gets a collection of profile documents
- `getProfileDocument`: Retrieves a profile document from the database
- `getURLHeaderInfo`: Gets header information from a Web document given its URL
- `getView`: Retrieves a view object from a database

6.4   ALL DOCUMENTS

The `AllDocuments` property of the `Database` class allows you to retrieve all documents from a database in the form of a document collection:

```
Session s = getSession();
AgentContext ac = s.getAgentContext();
Database db = ac.getCurrentDatabase();
DocumentCollection dc = db.getAllDocuments();
System.out.println("There are " + dc.getCount() + " documents in the " +
    db.getTitle() + " database.");
```

Before we close the chapter, let's take a look at the `Replication` class.

6.5   REPLICATION CLASS

The `Replication` class accesses and sets the replication settings for a Domino database.

6.5.1   Syntax

A handle to a `Replication` object is obtained through the `Database` class:

```
Replication = Database.getReplicationInfo();
```

A read-only `Replication` object for the `Database` object is returned; that is, a new `Replication` object cannot be created for a `Database` object. On the other hand, the various attributes of the `Replication` class can be read and set via Java.

6.5.2 Properties

All properties, with the exception of `CutoffDate`, have a corresponding `set` method for changing their value. A partial list of properties for the `Replication` class follows:

- `CutoffDate`: Read-only property that is the sum of today's date plus the cutoff interval
- `CutoffInterval`: Read/write property representing the number of days after which documents are automatically deleted if the `isCutoffDelete` property is in effect
- `IsAbstract`: Read/write boolean property signals if large documents should be truncated and attachments should be removed during the process of replication
- `IsCutoffDelete`: Read/write boolean property signaling whether documents older than the cutoff date should be deleted automatically
- `IsDisabled`: Read/write boolean property signaling whether replication is disabled for the database
- `IsIgnoreDeletes`: Read/write `boolean` property signaling whether deletions are replicated
- `IsIgnoreDestDeletes`: Read/write `boolean` property signaling whether deletions should not be replicated to destination databases
- `Priority`: Read/write property signaling the replication priority for the database. It has the following constants defined in the Replication class:
  - `Replication.CNOTES_REPLCONST_PRIORITYHIGH`
  - `Replication.CNOTES_REPLCONST_PRIORITYLOW`
  - `Replication.CNOTES_REPLCONST_PRIORITYMED`
  - `Replication.CNOTES_REPLCONST_PRIORITYNOTSET`

6.5.3 Methods

In addition to the `get` and `set` methods, the `Replication` class has three other methods that allow you to clear the replication history, reset properties, and save the replication settings:

- `clearHistory`: Clears the replication history
- `reset`: Resets the replication properties to their last saved values
- `save`: Saves the replication properties

Example 6.3 illustrates the use of the various properties of the `Replication` class.

Example 6.3   (Domino Agent)

```
import lotus.domino.*;
import java.io.PrintWriter;
public class Example_6_3 extends AgentBase {
  public void NotesMain() {
    try {
      Session session = getSession();
      Database db = session.getDatabase(null,"names.nsf");   ❶
```

```
            PrintWriter pw = getAgentOutput();
            if (db != null) {   ❷
             pw.println("Database Title:  " + db.getTitle());   ❸
             pw.println("Filename:  " + db.getFileName());   ❹
             Replication rep = db.getReplicationInfo();   ❺
             if (rep != null) {   ❻
              pw.println("Cutoff date: " + rep.getCutoffDate());   ❼
              pw.println("Cutoff interval: " + rep.getCutoffInterval());   ❽
              pw.println("Abstract? " + rep.isAbstract());   ❾
              pw.println("Cutoff delete? " + rep.isCutoffDelete());   ❿
              pw.println("Replication disabled? " + rep.isDisabled());   ⓫
              pw.println("Ignore deletes during replication? " + rep.isIgnoreDeletes());   ⓬
              pw.println("Ignore deletes in destination databases? " + rep.isIgnoreDestDeletes());   ⓭
              pw.print("Replication priority is");   ⓮
              switch (rep.getPriority()) {   ⓯
                case (Replication.CNOTES_REPLCONST_PRIORITYHIGH):   ⓰
                 pw.println("High.");
                 break;
                case (Replication.CNOTES_REPLCONST_PRIORITYLOW):   ⓱
                 pw.println("Low.");
                 break;
                case (Replication.CNOTES_REPLCONST_PRIORITYMED):   ⓲
                 pw.println("Medium.");
                 break;
                case (Replication.CNOTES_REPLCONST_PRIORITYNOTSET):   ⓳
                 pw.println("Not set.");
                 break;
                default :   ⓴
                 pw.println("Not set."); }
             } else {
              pw.println("Replication object not found."); }
              db.recycle();
            } else {
             pw.println("Database object not found."); }
            session.recycle();
           } catch(Exception e) {
           e.printStackTrace();}}}
```

■

Explanation

❶ Create the Database object.

❷ Proceed only if the Database object was found.

❸ Display the title of the Database object.

❹ Display the file name of the Database object.

❺ Get the replication information from the Database object via a   Replication object.

❻ Proceed only if the Replication object was found.

❼ Display the cutoff date.

❽ Display the cutoff interval.

❾ Display whether large documents and attachments are truncated during replication.

❿ Display whether documents older than the cutoff date should be automatically deleted.

⓫ Display whether replication is disabled.

⓬ Display whether deletions are not replicated.

⓭ Display whether deletions are replicated to destination databases.

⓮ Display the beginning of the priority line. The `print` method of the `PrintWriter` class is used; this does not place a new line at the end of the output.

⓯ Retrieve the priority of the `Replication` object; use it in a switch/case block.

⓰ Use the constants to determine if priority is high.

⓱ Use the constants to determine if priority is low.

⓲ Use the constants to determine if priority is medium.

⓳ Use the constants to determine if priority has not been set.

⓴ Access the `default` block of the `switch` block if all `case` statements fail.

Output

```
Database Title:  Patton's Address Book
Filename:  names.nsf
Cutoff date: 08/04/99 01:03:36 AM EDT
Cutoff interval: 90
Abstract? false
Cutoff delete? false
Replication disabled? false
Ignore deletes during replication? false
Ignore deletes in destination databases? false
Replication priority is Medium.
```

6.6   DBDIRECTORY CLASS

You saw the `DbDirectory` class used earlier in this chapter, so let's take a closer look at it. The `DbDirectory` class accesses database and template files on a Domino server. The Domino server's data directory is used as the base (the start of the listing). There are several methods available for use with the `DbDirectory` class.

6.6.1   createDatabase

The `createDatabase` method creates a new `Database` object using the filename specified. The server of the `DbDirectory` class is used. A second optional parameter signals whether the database should be opened after its creation.

```
Database = DbDirectory.createDatabase("filename", boolean);
```

6.6.2 getFirstDatabase

The `getFirstDatabase` method retrieves the first `Database` object of the selected type from the server:

```
Database = DbDirectory.getFirstDatabase(type);
```

Here are the possible values for the type parameter:

- DbDirectory.DATABASE
- DbDirectory.TEMPLATE
- DbDirectory.REPLICA_CANDIDATE
- DbDirectory.TEMPLATE_CANDIDATE

6.6.3 getNextDatabase

The `getNextDatabase` method retrieves the next `Database` object from the server. The reference point and type are determined by the `getFirstDatabase` method that must be called before it.

```
Database = DbDirectory.getNextDatabase();
```

6.6.4 openDatabase

The `openDatabase` method opens an existing database on the server. It accepts the filename of the parameter, and an optional `boolean` parameter signals whether failover is enabled.

```
Database = DbDirectory.openDatabase("filename");
```

6.6.5 openDatabaseByReplicaID

The `openDatabaseByReplicaID` method allows you to open a `Database` object by its replica ID:

```
Database = DbDirectory.openDatabaseByReplicaID("replica ID");
```

6.6.6 openDatabaseIfModified

The `openDatabaseIfModified` method allows you to open a `Database` object if and only if it has been modified since the `DateTime` object passed into it:

```
Database = DbDirectory.openDatabaseIfModified("filename", DateTime object);
```

6.6.7 openMailDatabase

The `openMailDatabase` method opens the current user's mail database:

```
Database = DbDirectory.openMailDatabase();
```

Example 6.4 takes advantage of the `DbDirectory` and `Replication` classes to disable replication for all databases.

Example 6.4 (Domino Agent)

```java
import lotus.domino.*;
import java.io.PrintWriter;
public class Example_6_4 extends AgentBase {
 public void NotesMain() {
   try {
     Session session = getSession();
     PrintWriter pw = getAgentOutput();
     DbDirectory dbdir = session.getDbDirectory(null);      ❶
     Database db = dbdir.getFirstDatabase(DbDirectory.DATABASE);;   ❷
     while (db != null) {   ❸
      pw.print("Database:  (" + db.getTitle());   ❹
      pw.print(db.getFileName() + ") ");   ❺
      Replication rep = db.getReplicationInfo();   ❻
      if (rep != null) {   ❼
       rep.setDisabled(true);   ❽
       rep.save();   ❾
       pw.println(" replication has been disabled.");   ❿
      } else {
       pw.println(" replication has not been disabled."); }
      db = dbdir.getNextDatabase();}   ⓫
     dbdir.recycle();
     db.recycle();
     ac.recycle();
     session.recycle();
   } catch(Exception e) {
     e.printStackTrace();}}}
```

Explanation

❶ Create a new `DbDirectory` object via the `getDbDirectory` method of the `Session` class.

❷ Create a new `Database` object via the `getFirstDatabase` method of the `DbDirectory` class. Return only `Database` objects.

❸ Loop through all `Database` objects in the `DbDirectory` object.

❹ Display the `Database` title.

❺ Display the `Database` filename.

❻ Create a new `Replication` object from the `Database` object.

❼ Proceed only if the `Replication` object was retrieved.

❽ Disable replication for the `Database`.

❾ Save the replication settings.

❿ Display message stating replication has been disabled.

⓫ Retrieve the next `Database` object from the `DbDirectory` object.

6.7   CHAPTER REVIEW

The `Database` class allows access to the most basic element of the design of a Domino application: the database. The database is the container for all design elements: agents, views, documents, forms, collections, and so forth. In addition, it gives you access to various properties and methods for working with Domino databases.

- The `getCurrentDatabase` method of the `AgentContext` class gets a handle on a `Database` object.

- The `getDatabase` method of the `Session` class accesses a `Database` object.

- The `DbDirectory` class has a number of methods for accessing databases.

- There are a number of properties that have `getPropertyName` methods for accessing items based on whether the `Database` is full-text indexed, the file path, the server name, size, and so forth.

- The `queryAccess`, `grantAccess`, and `revokeAccess` methods manipulate a worker's access to a database.

- There are a number of methods available for creating copies, replicas, and new instances of a database. Also, the `remove` method permanently deletes a Domino database.

- Numerous `get` methods exist for retrieving objects from a database, such as `getView`, `getAgent`, and `getOutline`.

- The `AllDocuments` property of the `Database` class returns a collection containing all documents from a database.

C H A P T E R   7

Working with views

7.1 Syntax 57
7.2 Working with view columns 59
7.3 ViewColumn class 60
7.4 Working with view entries 64
7.5 ViewEntry class 64
7.6 ViewEntryCollection class 68

7.7 ViewNavigator class 69
7.8 Searching a view 74
7.9 Deleting a view 75
7.10 Refreshing a view 75
7.11 Folders 75
7.12 Chapter review 76

The Domino view is the most common form for presenting documents. It can be thought of as a type of index that presents documents in a predefined format (according to the design of the view). A view can contain one or more columns, as well as entries. Entries represent individual view elements. The elements can be categories, documents, conflicts, or totals. Folders behave differently than a view, but they are handled the same way in Java. This chapter explores the `View` class and associated classes.

7.1   SYNTAX

While the database object has three ways to get to a `View` object, the `View` class has two. The first way to access a view is to use the `getView` and/or `getViews` methods of the `Database` class. The other method involves the `ViewEntry` class.

7.1.1   getView

The `getView` method returns a specified view (by name) from a database:

```
Session s = getSession();
AgentContext ac = s.getAgentContext();
Database db = ac.getCurrentDatabase();
View vw = db.getView("name of view");
```

7.1.2   getViews

The `getViews` method returns a vector containing all the views from a database:

```
Vector v = db.getViews();
```

Example 7.1   (Domino Agent)

```
import lotus.domino.*;
public class Example_7_1 extends AgentBase {
 public void NotesMain() {
  try {
    Session session = getSession();
    AgentContext ac = session.getAgentContext();
    Database db = ac.getCurrentDatabase();         ❶
    java.util.Vector v = db.getViews();            ❷
    System.out.println("Number of views in " + db.getTitle() + " is " + v.size()); ❸
    for (int x=0; x < v.size(); x ++) {            ❹
    View currentView =(View)v.elementAt(x);        ❺
    System.out.println("View:  " + currentView.getName());  }   ❻
  db.recycle();
  ac.recycle();
  session.recycle();
 } catch(Exception e) {
  e.printStackTrace();   } }   }
```

Explanation

❶ Set the `Database` object to the current database in which the agent is located.

❷ Use a `Vector` object to retrieve a list of all `View` objects in the database. A `Vector` is similar to an array.

❸ Send the title and number of views to the Java console.

❹ Use a `for` loop to access every element in the `Vector`.

❺ Create a new `View` object using the current element (via loop index) in the `Vector`. We have to explicitly cast the `Vector` element to the `View` object type.

❻ Send the name to the Java console.

Output

```
Number of views in Domino Java Examples is 2
View:  Examples \ by Number
View:  Examples \ by Chapter
```

You can use the same approach used in example 7.1 to access views via IIOP. Example 7.2 demonstrates how.

Example 7.2   (Standalone application)

```
import lotus.domino.*;
public class Example_7_2 implements Runnable{
  public static void main(java.lang.String[] args) {
    Example2 t = new Example2();
    Thread nt = new Thread((Runnable)t);
    nt.start();   }
  public void run() {
    try {
      Session s = NotesFactory.createSession("200.118.34.8","tpatton","password"); ❶
      Database db = s.getDatabase(null,"log.nsf"); ❷
      java.util.Vector v = db.getViews();  ❸
      System.out.println("Number of views in " + db.getTitle() + " is " + v.size());
      for (int x=0; x < v.size(); x ++) {  ❹
        View currentView = (View)v.elementAt(x);
        System.out.println("View:  " + currentView.getName()); } }
      db.recycle();
      s.recycle();
    catch (NotesException n) {
      System.out.println("ID:  " + n.id + " -- Name:  " + n.text);  }
    catch (Exception e) {
      e.printStackTrace(); } } }
```

Explanation

❶ Create/instantiate a `Session` object to our remote server.

❷ Create/instantiate a `Database` object to the Notes Log database. The server parameter is set to null to signal the use of our current session.

❸ Populate a `Vector` object with all views from the log database.

❹ Loop through each element in the `Vector`.

7.2   WORKING WITH VIEW COLUMNS

The core element in a view is the column. Columns can categorize, sort, total, calculate, and display data in the view. An abundance of calculated columns can hamper view performance, so discretion is necessary when you design a view. The Domino Java classes provide access to columns in a view via the `ViewColumn` class.

The only way to instantiate a `ViewColumn` object is through the `View` class. There are two methods in the `View` class: `getColumn` and `getColumns`.

7.2.1   getColumn

```
Session s = getSession();
AgentContext ac = s.getAgentContext();
```

```
Database db = ac.getCurrentDatabase();
View vw = db.getView("name of view");
ViewColumn vc = vw.getColumn(column number);
```

7.2.2 getColumns

Working with the getColumns method is similar to working with the getViews method of the Database class. A Vector object is returned with a list of ViewColumn objects representing the columns in the view.

```
Vector vcs = vw.getColumns();
```

Example 7.3 (Domino Agent)

```
import lotus.domino.*;
public class Example_7_3 extends AgentBase {
 public void NotesMain() {
   try {
     Session session = getSession();
     AgentContext ac = session.getAgentContext();
     Database db = ac.getCurrentDatabase();
     View vw = db.getView("Examples \\ by Chapter");  ❶
     ViewColumn vc = vw.getColumn(2);  ❷
     System.out.println("Column 2 Title:  " + vc.getTitle());  ❸
      vc.recycle();
      vw.recycle;
      db.recycle();
      ac.recycle();
      session.recycle();
   } catch(Exception e) {
     e.printStackTrace(); }  }  }
```

Explanation

❶ Set our View object to the specified view from the database. The actual name of the view, not an alias, should be used.

❷ Set our ViewColumn object to the second column.

❸ Display the title of the column in the Java Console window.

Output

```
Column 2 Title:  Example
```

7.3 VIEWCOLUMN CLASS

The ViewColumn class itself lets you access the myriad of attributes associated with a column. Example 7.4 demonstrates the numerous properties of a column.

Example 7.4 (Domino Agent)

```java
import lotus.domino.*;
import java.util.*;

public class Example_7_4 extends AgentBase {

public void NotesMain() {
 try {
     Session session = getSession();
 AgentContext ac = session.getAgentContext();
 Database db = ac.getCurrentDatabase();
 View vw = db.getView("Examples \\ by Chapter");   ❶
 Vector vcs = vw.getColumns();   ❷
 Enumeration en = vcs.elements();   ❸
 while (en.hasMoreElements())  {   ❹
  ViewColumn vc = (ViewColumn)(en.nextElement());   ❺
  System.out.println("Title:  " + vc.getTitle());   ❻
  System.out.println("Alignment:  " + vc.getAlignment());   ❼
  System.out.println("Date Format:  " + vc.getDateFmt());   ❽
  System.out.println("Font Color:  " + vc.getFontColor());   ❾
  System.out.println("Font Face:  " + vc.getFontFace());   ❿
  System.out.println("Font Point Size:  " + vc.getFontPointSize());   ⓫
  System.out.println("Font Style:  " + vc.getFontStyle());   ⓬
  System.out.println("Column Formula:  " + vc.getFormula());   ⓭
  System.out.println("Header Alignment: " + vc.getHeaderAlignment());   ⓮
  System.out.println("Item Name:  " + vc.getItemName());   ⓯
  System.out.println("List Separator:  " + vc.getListSep());   ⓰
  System.out.println("Number Attribute:  " + vc.getNumberAttrib());   ⓱
  System.out.println("Number Digits:  " + vc.getNumberDigits());   ⓲
  System.out.println("Number Format:  " + vc.getNumberFormat());   ⓳
  System.out.println("Column Position:  " + vc.getPosition());   ⓴
  System.out.println("Time Date Format:  " + vc.getTimeDateFmt());   ㉑
  System.out.println("Time Format:  " + vc.getTimeFmt());   ㉒
  System.out.println("Time Zone Format:  " + vc.getTimeZoneFmt());   ㉓
  System.out.println("Column Width:  " + vc.getWidth());   ㉔
  if (vc.isSorted()) {   ㉕
   System.out.println("The column is sorted.");  }
  else {
   System.out.println("The column is not sorted."); }
  if (vc.isIcon()) {   ㉖
   System.out.println("The column is an icon.");  }
  else  {
   System.out.println("The column is not an icon.");  }
 vc.recycle();}
 vw.recycle();
 db.recycle();
 ac.recycle();
 session.recycle();
 } catch(Exception e) {
 e.printStackTrace();}  }  }
```

Explanation

❶ Create `View` object using the specified view name.

❷ Retrieve the list of columns and place them in the `Vector` object.

❸ Create an `Enumeration` object containing all elements (`ViewColumn` objects) in the `Vector`.

❹ Loop through all elements in the `Enumeration` object using a `while` loop.

❺ Create a `ViewColumn` object using the current object from the `Enumeration` object.

❻ Access the `title` property of the column.

❼ Access the `alignment` property of the column.

❽ Access the date format of the column.

❾ Access the font color for the column.

❿ Access the font face for the column.

⓫ Access the font point size for the column.

⓬ Access the font style for the column.

⓭ Retrieve the formula (if it exists) for the column.

⓮ Get the header alignment setting for the column.

⓯ Get the item name for the column.

⓰ Access the list separator for the column.

⓱ Retrieve the number attributes for the column.

⓲ Retrieve the number digits for the column.

⓳ Get the number format for the column.

⓴ Retrieve the column position (starting at 1) in the `View`.

㉑ Retrieve the time/date format for the column.

㉒ Get the time format for the column.

㉓ Get the time zone format for the column.

㉔ Retrieve the width of the column.

㉕ Access the boolean attribute `isSorted` of the column. It signals whether or not a column is sorted.

㉖ Determine whether or not a column is set to display icons via the `isIcon` boolean attribute.

Output for one column

```
Title:  Example
Alignment:  0
Date Format:  0
```

```
Font Color:  2
Font Face:  Gill Sans
Font Point Size:  12
Font Style:  1
Column Formula:
@If(@IsError(@TextToNumber(keyExample));keyExample;@TextToNumber(keyExample))
Header Alignment:  0
Item Name:  $3
List Separator:  0
Number Attribute:  0
Number Digits:  0
Number Format:  0
Column Position:  2
Time Date Format:  2
Time Format:  0
Time Zone Format:  0
Column Width:  9
The column is sorted.
The column is not an icon.
```

7.3.1 Properties

The previous example gave a good demonstration of the numerous properties associated with a ViewColumn object. There are a number of "is"-related properties that return true or false depending on whether or not a property is set for a column.

Here is a more comprehensive list of is properties for a ViewColumn class:

- IsAccessSensitiveSort: Signals whether or not a column is sorted according to accent

- IsCaseSensitiveSort: Signals whether or not a column is sorted according to case

- IsCategory: Signals whether or not a column is a categorized column

- IsField: Signals whether or not a column value is based on a field value

- IsFormula: Signals whether or not a column value is based on a formula

- IsHidden: Signals whether or not a column is hidden

- IsHideDetail: Signals whether or not details for a total column are hidden

- IsIcon: Signals whether or not a column displays an icon

- IsResize: Signals whether or not a column is resizable

- IsResortAscending: Signals whether a resortable column can be resorted in ascending order

- IsResortDescending: Signals whether a resortable column can be resorted in descending order

- IsResortToView:Signals whether or not a column can be resorted by user selection

- `IsResponse`: Signals whether or not a column contains responses only

- `IsSecondaryResort`: Signals whether or not a column is a secondary resortable column

- `IsSecondaryResortDescending`: Signals whether or not a secondary resortable column is in descending order

- `IsShowTwistie`: Signals whether or not a categorized column displays the twistie

- `IsSortDescending`: Signals whether or not a column is sorted in descending order

- `IsSorted`: Signals whether or not a column is sorted

You can access all the column items discussed so far via the column properties window. Figure 7.1 shows a sample property window for a sorted/categorized column via the second tab. It shows whether the column items are sorted in ascending or descending order, case-sensitive sorted, accent-sensitive sorted, or whether or not it is a total column, to name a few. The other tabs give access to countless other column properties.

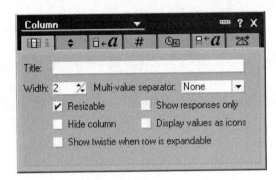

Figure 7.1   Column properties

7.4   WORKING WITH VIEW ENTRIES

The columns in a view run north to south, vertically. Entries run west to east, horizontally. In other words, an entry in a view is a row. Figure 7.2 shows a view in the standard Domino log database. Each row in the view is an entry. Entries can be categories, responses, main documents, totals, and so on. They have many, but not all, of the same qualities as columns.

7.5   VIEWENTRY CLASS

The `ViewEntry` class allows you to access an entry via Java. It can be obtained from the following classes: `View`, `ViewEntryCollection`, and `ViewNavigator`. We will examine the methods for working with a view object now, and cover the other two classes later in this chapter.

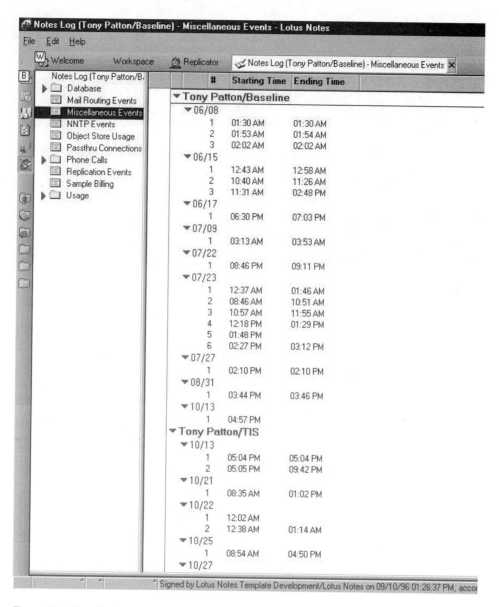

Figure 7.2   Sample view

```
ViewEntry ve;
ve = vw.getEntryByKey("Key Value",boolean)
```

The second parameter uses true/false to signal whether or not an exact match is to
be found.

Example 7.5   (Domino Agent)

```
import lotus.domino.*;
import java.util.*;

public class Example_7_5 extends AgentBase {
public void NotesMain() {
 try {
   Session session = getSession();
   AgentContext ac = session.getAgentContext();
   Database db = ac.getCurrentDatabase();
   View vw = db.getView("Examples \\ by Chapter");
   ViewEntry ve = vw.getEntryByKey("Test",false);        ❶
   System.out.println("Child Count:    " + ve.getChildCount());        ❷
   System.out.println("Indent Level:   " + ve.getColumnIndentLevel());        ❸
   System.out.println("Column Values:   " + ve.getColumnValues());        ❹
   System.out.println("Descendant Count:   " + ve.getDescendantCount());        ❺
   System.out.println("Full-text Search Score:   " + ve.getFTSearchScore());        ❻
   System.out.println("Indent Level:   " + ve.getIndentLevel());        ❼
   System.out.println("Category?   " + ve.isCategory());        ❽
   System.out.println("Conflict?   " + ve.isConflict());        ❾
   System.out.println("Document?   " + ve.isDocument());        ❿
   System.out.println("Total line?   " + ve.isTotal());        ⓫
   System.out.println("Valid?   " + ve.isValid());        ⓬
   System.out.println("Note ID:   " + ve.getNoteID());        ⓭
   System.out.println("Sibling Count:   " + ve.getSiblingCount());        ⓮
   System.out.println("Universal ID:   " + ve.getUniversalID());        ⓯
   System.out.println("Position:   " + ve.getPosition(','));        ⓰
   ve.recycle();
   vw.recycle();
   db.recycle();
   ac.recycle();
   session.recycle();
 } catch(Exception e) {
   e.printStackTrace();}}  }
```

Explanation

❶ Set the ViewEntry object to the ViewEntry returned by searching for the value regardless of case.

❷ Access the ChildCount property of the ViewEntry class. It returns the number of immediate children entries to an entry.

❸ Access the indent level of an entry via the ColumnIndentLevel property.

❹ Get a comma-delimited list of all column values for an entry via the ColumnValues property.

❺ Return the total number of descendents (not limited to immediate children) to the entry via the DescendantCount property.

❻ If an item was returned via a full-text query, the search score for it is returned from the `FTSearchScore` property. A value of zero is returned if the entry was not returned from a search.

❼ The `IndentLevel` property returns the indent level of the entry.

❽ The `isCategory` property signals whether or not an entry is a category.

❾ The `isConflict` property signals whether or not an entry is a save/replication conflict.

❿ The `isDocument` property signals whether or not an entry is a document object.

⓫ The `isTotal` property signals whether or not an item is a total line.

⓬ The `isValid` property signals whether or not an entry is valid.

⓭ The `NoteID` property returns the Notes ID number for an entry.

⓮ The `SiblingCount` property returns the number of siblings, including itself, for an entry.

⓯ The `UniversalID` property returns the Universal ID number for an entry.

⓰ The `getPosition` method returns the current position for an entry. It accepts one character as a parameter; it is used to separate the return values. The return value will be in the form of row, plus separator, plus column.

Output

```
Child Count:  0
Indent Level:  0
Column Values:  [Test, Test]
Descendent Count:  0
Full-text Search Score:  0
Indent Level:  1
Category?  false
Conflict?  false
Document?  true
Total line?  false
Valid?  true
Note ID:  24BA
Sibling Count:  1
Universal ID:  637FF5B87CF09004852568240009970F
Position:  4,1
```

7.5.1   Document property

The `Document` property of the `ViewEntry` class returns a `Document` object for an entry if the entry is a document.

> **Example 7.6   (Domino Agent)**

```
import lotus.domino.*;
import java.util.*;

public class Example_7_6 extends AgentBase {
  public void NotesMain() {
```

```
try {
  Session session = getSession();
  AgentContext ac = session.getAgentContext();
  Database db = ac.getCurrentDatabase();
  View vw = db.getView("Examples \\ by Chapter");
  ViewEntry ve = vw.getEntryByKey("Test",false);
  if (ve.isDocument())  {  ❶
    Document doc = ve.getDocument();  ❷
    // The document would likely be processed further.
    doc.recycle();  }
  ve.recycle();
  vw.recycle();
  db.recycle();
  ac.recycle();
  session.recycle();
} catch(Exception e) {
  e.printStackTrace();} } }
```

Explanation

❶ Determine if the entry is a document or not.

❷ If the entry is a document, create a Document object containing the entry. The
Document object is discussed further in the next chapter.

7.6   *VIEWENTRYCOLLECTION CLASS*

The ViewEntryCollection class works with a group of documents from a view
in the form of a collection. This section briefly discusses this class; chapter 11 covers
collections in more detail. The ViewEntryCollection class is initialized from the
View class, and the ViewEntry class accesses individual entries in it.

Example 7.7   (Domino Agent)

```
import lotus.domino.*;
import java.util.*;

public class Example_7_7 extends AgentBase {
  public void NotesMain() {
    try {
      Session session = getSession();
      AgentContext ac = session.getAgentContext();
      Database db = ac.getCurrentDatabase();
      View vw = db.getView("Examples \\ by Chapter");
      ViewEntryCollection vec = vw.getAllEntries();  ❶
      ViewEntry ve = vec.getFirstEntry();  ❷
      while (ve != null)  {  ❸
        System.out.println("Note ID:  " + ve.getNoteID());  ❹
        ve.recycle();
        ve = vec.getNextEntry();    }  ❺
```

```
    vec.recycle();
    vw.recycle();
    db.recycle();
    ac.recycle();
    session.recycle();
  } catch(Exception e) {
    e.printStackTrace();} } }
```

Explanation

❶ Create a `ViewEntryCollection` object with all entries from the `View` object.

❷ Use the `getFirstEntry` method of the `ViewEntryCollection` class to retrieve the first entry from the collection.

❸ A `while` loop is used to process all entries in the collection.

❹ Print the Note ID of the entry.

❺ Retrieve the next entry from the collection; a pointer to the current entry is used as the placeholder.

Output

```
Note ID:   24AA
Note ID:   24A6
Note ID:   24AE
Note ID:   24B2
Note ID:   24B6
Note ID:   24C2
Note ID:   24BE
Note ID:   24C6
Note ID:   24BA
```

7.7   *VIEWNAVIGATOR CLASS*

Another way to access individual entries in a `View` is through the use of the `ViewNavigator` class. The `ViewNavigator` class can access all entries or a subset of entries in a Domino view. There are six methods of the `View` class that can access and create a `ViewNavigator` object:

- `createViewNav`: Creates a `ViewNavigator` object containing all entries in a view

- `createViewNavFrom`: Creates a `ViewNavigator` object containing all entries starting with the element passed into the method

- `createViewNavFromCategory`: Creates a `ViewNavigator` object containing all entries in a given category

- `createViewNavFromChildren`: Creates a `ViewNavigator` object containing all immediate children of a specific entry

- createViewNavFromDescendants: Creates a ViewNavigator object containing all descendents of a specific entry
- createViewNavMaxLevel: Creates a ViewNavigator object containing all entries in a view down to a specified level passed into the method. The level can be between zero (top level) and 30 (default)

7.7.1 createViewNav method

```
Session session = getSession();
AgentContext ac = session.getAgentContext();
Database db = ac.getCurrentDatabase();
View vw = db.getView("Examples \\ by Chapter");
ViewNavigator vn = vw.createViewNav();
```

7.7.2 createViewNavFrom method

```
Session session = getSession();
AgentContext ac = session.getAgentContext();
Database db = ac.getCurrentDatabase();
View vw = db.getView("Examples \\ by Chapter");
ViewEntry ve = vw.getEntryByKey("Test",false);
ViewNavigator vn = vw.createViewNavFrom(ve);
```

7.7.3 createViewNavFromCategory method

```
ViewNavigator vn = vw.createViewNavFromCategory("Category Name");
```

7.7.4 createViewNavFromChildren method

```
ViewNavigator vn = vw.createViewNavFromChildren(ve);
```

7.7.5 createViewNavFromDescendants method

```
ViewNavigator vn = vw.createViewNavFromDescendants(ve);
```

> **NOTE** The object passed into createViewNavFromChildren, createViewNavFromDescendants, and createViewNavFrom methods can be a Document object as well as a ViewEntry object.

7.7.6 createViewNavMaxLevel method

```
ViewNavigator vn = vw.createViewNavMaxLevel(30);
```

7.7.7 Methods

Once a ViewNavigator object is created, there are a number of methods available for moving around the group of objects in it. The navigation methods can be grouped as get and goto methods. The Domino Java classes documentation suggests that you use the goto method when you navigate, due to the fact that it does not return (create) a ViewEntry object. On the other hand, all get methods return a handle to a ViewEntry object (or Document object).

7.7.8   List of get methods

- `getChild`: Retrieves the first child of an entry
- `getCurrent`: Retrieves the current entry
- `getFirst`: Retrieves the first entry
- `getFirstDocument`: Retrieves the first document entry
- `getLast`: Retrieves the last entry
- `getLastDocument`: Retrieves the last document entry
- `getNext`: Retrieves the next entry using the current entry as the pointer
- `getNextDocument`: Retrieves the next document entry
- `getNextCategory`: Retrieves the next category entry
- `getNextSibling`: Retrieves the next sibling entry to the current entry
- `getNth`: Retrieves the entry at a specified location in the topmost level
- `getParent`: Retrieves the parent of the current entry
- `getPos`: Gets the position of the current entry
- `getPrev`: Retrieves the previous entry
- `getPrevCategory`: Retrieves the previous category entry
- `getPrevDocument`: Retrieves the previous document entry
- `getPrevSibling`: Retrieves the previous sibling to the current entry

Example 7.8   (Standalone application)

```
import lotus.domino.*;

public class Example_7_8 implements Runnable{
 public static void main(java.lang.String[] args) {
   Example_7_8 t = new Example_7_8();
   Thread nt = new Thread((Runnable)t);
   nt.start();  }
 public void run()     {
   try   {
     Session s = NotesFactory.createSession("200.118.34.8","tpatton","password");
     Database db = s.getDatabase(null,"log.nsf");
     View cView = db.getView("Miscellaneous Events");
     ViewNavigator vn = cView.createViewNav();          ❶
     Document doc = (Document)vn.getFirstDocument();     ❷
     while (doc != null)  {  ❸
       String fm = doc.getItemValueString("Form");       ❹
       doc.recycle();
       doc = (Document)vn.getNextDocument();  }          ❺
     vn.recycle();
     cView.recycle();
     db.recycle();
     s.recycle();
```

```
    } catch (NotesException n) {
      System.out.println("ID:   " + n.id + " -- Name:   " + n.text);
    } catch (Exception e)   {
      e.printStackTrace(); } } }
```

Explanation

❶ Create the `ViewNavigator` object. It will contain all entries from the current database because we used the `createViewNav` method of the `View` class.

❷ Create a `Document` object using the `getFirstDocument` method of the `ViewNavigator` object. We explicitly cast the returned item to a `Document` object to avoid any problems.

❸ We will loop through all documents in the `ViewNavigator` object using a `while` loop. We know we have processed all documents when we get a null value.

❹ The `getItemValueString` method of the `Document` class retrieves the contents of the form field. The next chapter will cover this in more detail.

❺ Use the `getNextDocument` method of the `ViewNavigator` class to get the next document from the database.

7.7.9   List of goto methods

- `gotoChild`: Moves the current pointer to the first child of the current or specified entry
- `gotoEntry`: Moves the current pointer to the specified entry
- `gotoFirst`: Moves the current pointer to the first entry
- `gotoFirstDocument`: Moves the current pointer to the first document entry
- `gotoLast`: Moves the current pointer to the last entry
- `gotoLastDocument`: Moves the current pointer to the last document entry
- `gotoNext`: Moves the current pointer to the next entry using the current or specified entry as the reference point
- `gotoNextCategory`: Moves the current pointer to the next category entry
- `gotoNextDocument`: Moves the current pointer to the next document entry
- `gotoNextSibling`: Moves the current pointer to the next sibling of the current or specified entry
- `gotoParent`: Moves the current pointer to the parent of the current or specified entry
- `gotoPos`: Moves the current pointer to the specified position/location
- `gotoPrev`: Moves the current pointer to the previous entry using the current or specified entry as the reference point

- gotoPrevCategory: Moves the current pointer to the previous category entry using the current entry as the reference
- gotoPrevDocument: Moves the current pointer to the previous document entry
- gotoPrevSibling: Moves the current pointer to the previous sibling entry of the current or specified entry

Example 7.9   (Standalone application)

```
import lotus.domino.*;

public class Example_7_9 implements Runnable{
 public static void main(java.lang.String[] args) {
  Example_7_9 t = new Example_7_9();
  Thread nt = new Thread((Runnable)t);
  nt.start();   }
 public void run()      {
  try    {
    Session s = NotesFactory.createSession("200.118.34.8","tpatton","password");
    Database db = s.getDatabase(null,"log.nsf");
    View cView = db.getView("Miscellaneous Events");
    ViewNavigator vn = cView.createViewNav();
    vn.gotoFirstDocument();   ❶
    boolean flag = true;   ❷
    while (flag)      {   ❸
      Document doc = (Document)vn.getCurrent();   ❹
      String fm = doc.getItemValueString("Form");   ❺
      doc.recycle();
      flag = vn.gotoNextDocument();      }   ❻
    vn.recycle();
    cView.recycle();
    db.recycle();
    s.recycle();
  } catch (NotesException n) {
    System.out.println("ID:   " + n.id + " -- Name:   " + n.text);   }
  } catch (Exception e)   {
    e.printStackTrace(); } } }
```

Explanation

❶ The gotoFirstDocument method of the ViewNavigator class moves the pointer to the first document in the database.

❷ A boolean variable is initialized to true. It will be used in the while loop to signal there are no more documents to process.

❸ A while loop loops through all documents in the database.

❹ The `getCurrent` method of the `ViewNavigator` class retrieves the current document. By default the `getCurrent` method returns a `ViewEntry` object, but we cast it to `Document` because we know we are getting only documents.

❺ Retrieve contents of the form field.

❻ The `gotoNextDocument` method retrieves the next document from the database. It returns false if there are no more documents, but true if a document is found.

7.8   SEARCHING A VIEW

You can retrieve entries from a view as the result of a search. A full-text search utilizes a full-text query, which may include logical operators and field names, but not @Functions. It does not require the database to be full-text indexed, but the existence of an index does improve performance.

When conducting a full-text search on a view, you can specify the maximum number of documents to be returned. The return value of the function is the number of matches found. The searched view object contains only matching documents after the search. Thus the view can be processed to view the result set.

```
int x = View.FTSearch("Query",maximum_number_of_matches);
```

Example 7.10   (Domino Agent)

```
import lotus.domino.*;
import java.util.*;
public class Example_7_10 extends AgentBase {
  public void NotesMain() {
    try {
      Session session = getSession();
      AgentContext ac = session.getAgentContext();
      Database db = ac.getCurrentDatabase();
      View vw = db.getView("Examples \\ by Chapter");
      int matches = vw.FTSearch("FIELD FORM=\"frmExample\"",50);   ❶
      System.out.println("There were " + matches + " found to meet the criteria.");   ❷
      if (matches > 0)   {   ❸
        ViewEntryCollection vec = vw.getAllEntries();   ❹
        ViewEntry ve = vec.getFirstEntry();
        while (ve != null)   {
          System.out.println("Note ID:  " + ve.getNoteID());
          ve.recycle();
          ve = vec.getNextEntry();    }
        vec.recycle();}
      vw.clear();   ❺
      vw.recycle();
      db.recycle();
      ac.recycle();
      session.recycle();
    } catch(Exception e) {
      e.printStackTrace();}}   }
```

Explanation

❶ Perform a full-text search in our view for all documents created with the `frmExample` form. The backslash is the escape character used to insert quotes in our search string.

❷ Display the number of matches found.

❸ Process all entries found if there are matches found.

❹ Set a `ViewEntryCollection` object to all entries from the view. The view will contain only entries returned from the full-text search.

❺ The `clear` method clears the results of the full-text search. This resets the contents of the view.

Output

```
There were four entries found to meet the criteria.
Note ID:   24AE
Note ID:   24B2
Note ID:   24A6
Note ID:   24AA
```

7.9   DELETING A VIEW

The `remove` method of the `View` class permanently deletes a view from a database:

```
Session s = getSession();
AgentContext ac = s.getAgentContext();
Database db = ac.getCurrentDatabase();
View vw = db.getView("name of view");
vw.remove();
```

7.10   REFRESHING A VIEW

The `refresh` method of the `View` class refreshes the contents of a view (just like the F9 key):

```
Session s = getSession();
AgentContext ac = s.getAgentContext();
Database db = ac.getCurrentDatabase();
View vw = db.getView("name of view");
vw.refresh();
```

7.11   FOLDERS

Folders are no different than a view when you access Domino objects in Java. You can use all of the classes—`View`, `ViewEntry`, `ViewEntryCollection`, and `ViewNavigator`. One property of the `View` class determines whether or not the view is a folder. The property `isFolder` returns *true* if it is a folder and *false* otherwise.

```
Session s = getSession();
AgentContext ac = s.getAgentContext();
```

```
Database db = ac.getCurrentDatabase();
View vw = db.getView("name of view");
if (vw.isFolder())
  System.out.println(vw.getName() + " is a folder.");
```

7.12 CHAPTER REVIEW

The view is the most basic navigational element in a Domino database. It can be thought of as a type of index to an application. A view can be categorized, sorted, totalled, and so much more. The `View` class is the base class for working with views. There are `ViewColumn`, `ViewEntry`, `ViewEntryCollection`, and `ViewNavigator` classes as well.

- The `getView` and `getViews` methods of the `Database` class access views in a Domino application.
- The `View` class contains various methods and properties for working with views.
- The `ViewEntry` class allows access to individual view entries. In addition, it provides access to the vast amount of properties of a view entry.
- The `ViewEntryCollection` class allows you to work with a group of entries from a view.
- The `ViewNavigator` class allows you to access various elements of a view via a number of `get` and `goto` methods.
- The `FTSearch` method of the `View` class assembles a collection of view entries that match a search query.
- The `remove` method of the `View` class permanently deletes a view.
- The `refresh` method of the `View` class refreshes a view's data.
- A folder is handled exactly as a `View` is handled in the Domino Java classes.

CHAPTER 8

Document class

8.1 What is a document? 77

8.2 Syntax 78

8.3 Accessing individual elements/
fields 79

8.4 Other methods 82

8.5 Properties 85

8.6 Working with profile
Documents 90

8.7 Chapter review 92

The document is one of the most frequently used objects in a Domino application. Due to this fact, we will dive deeply into the various aspects (properties and methods) of the Document Java class. It is essential to understand the usage of the Document class to get the desired results from your application.

8.1 WHAT IS A DOCUMENT?

The Document object accesses documents within Domino databases. The document is the manner in which data is stored in a database. On the other hand, the form is used to display, edit, and enter data. Once a handle to a Domino document is obtained, the various fields of data can be retrieved and/or manipulated. Let's take a look at retrieving a document from a database.

8.2 SYNTAX

The `createDocument` method of the `Database` class creates new documents in a database:

```
Document doc = Database.createDocument;
```

Example 8.1   (Domino Agent)

```
import lotus.domino.*;
import java.util.*;

public class Example_8_1 extends AgentBase {
 public void NotesMain() {
   try {
     Session session = getSession();
     AgentContext ac = session.getAgentContext();
     Database db = ac.getCurrentDatabase();
     Document doc = db.createDocument();          ❶
     doc.replaceItemValue("Form","Memo");         ❷
     doc.replaceItemValue("SendTo","Julius Erving");  ❸
     doc.replaceItemValue("Subject","Test");      ❹
     doc.replaceItemValue("SaveOptions","0");     ❺
     doc.send(false, "");                         ❻
     doc.recycle();
     db.recycle();
     ac.recycle();
     session.recycle();
   } catch(Exception e) {
     e.printStackTrace();  } } }
```

Explanation

❶ The `createDocument` method of the `Database` class composes a new document.

❷ The `replaceItemValue` method of the `Document` class populates the `Form` field.

❸ The `replaceItemValue` method of the `Document` class populates the `SendTo` field.

❹ The `replaceItemValue` method of the `Document` class populates the `Subject` field.

❺ The `replaceItemValue` method of the `Document` class populates the `SaveOptions` field. We want to make certain the document is not saved.

❻ The `send` method sends the document via mail. The first parameter is `boolean`, signaling whether or not the form should be included. The second parameter is the recipient list; we don't need it because we created a `SendTo` field.

In addition to creating a document, you can retrieve existing documents through various objects, including a `View`, `DocumentCollection`, and `Database`. We will take advantage of some of these methods in the rest of this chapter. Example 8.1 gave a glimpse of how to work with individual data items (fields) on a Domino document. Let's take a closer look at these items.

8.3 ACCESSING INDIVIDUAL ELEMENTS/FIELDS

We have seen the `getItemValue` method at work in example 7.8, but there are a few other variations of it.

8.3.1 getItemValue

The `getItemValue` method of the `Document` class returns the value for the item/field specified. The data type of the item does not matter. The only parameter accepted by the method is a string representation of the field/item name. The return value for the method is a `Vector` containing all values stored in the item. The values start at an index of zero.

```
Vector = Document.getItemValue("field/item name");
```

8.3.2 getItemValueDouble

The `getItemValueDouble` method of the `Document` class returns the value of an item in a `double` numeric value. A value of zero is returned if the item does not contain a numeric value.

```
double = Document.getItemValueDouble("field/item name");
```

0.3.3 getItemValueInteger

The `getItemValueInteger` method of the `Document` class returns the value of an item in a single numeric `integer` value. A value of zero is returned if the item does not contain a numeric value.

```
int = Document.getItemValueInteger("field/item name");
```

8.3.4 getItemValueString

The `getItemValueString` method of the `Document` class returns the contents of an item in a single string value. The empty string is returned if the item is empty or contains time/date/numeric data. Also, this item returns only the text portion of a rich text field.

```
String = Document.getItemValueString("field/item name");
```

8.3.5 appendItemValue

The `appendItemValue` method of the `Document` class serves the same purpose as the `replaceItemValue` method. It creates a new item with the specified name. If the item already exists, it creates another item with the same name. The appendItem-

Value method accepts two parameters. The first signals the item or field name. The other parameter is the value to be stored in the field.

```
Document.appendItemValue("field/item name",value);
```

8.3.6 replaceItemValue

The `replaceItemValue` method places values into a field on a form. The field is created if it does not already exist; otherwise the contents of the field are replaced. This method accepts two parameters. The first is the item or field name, and the second is the value to be stored in it.

```
Document.replaceItemValue("field/item name",value);
```

NOTE A multi-valued item can be created by passing a `Vector` containing all values as the second parameter of the `replaceItemValue` or `appendItemValue` methods of the `Document` class.

Example 8.2 (Domino Agent)

```
import lotus.domino.*;

import java.util.*;
public class Example_8_2 extends AgentBase {
  public void NotesMain() {
    try {
      Session session = getSession();
      AgentContext ac = session.getAgentContext();
      Database db = ac.getCurrentDatabase();
      Document doc = db.createDocument();                    ❶
      doc.replaceItemValue("Form","Demo");                   ❷
      Double d = new Double(9.00);                           ❸
      doc.replaceItemValue("SalesAmount",d);                 ❹
      Integer i = new Integer(3);                            ❺
      doc.replaceItemValue("UnitsSold",i);                   ❻
      doc.replaceItemValue("SalesPerson","Lenny Dykstra");   ❼
      doc.appendItemValue("Manager","Jim Fregosi");          ❽
      Vector itemsSold = new Vector();                       ❾
      itemsSold.addElement("Toaster");                       ❿
      itemsSold.addElement("Microwave");
      itemsSold.addElement("Television");
      doc.replaceItemValue("ItemsSold",itemsSold);           ⓫
      if (doc.hasItem("flagField"))  {                       ⓬
      doc.replaceItemValue("flagField","0");  }              ⓭
      doc.save();                                            ⓮
      doc.getItemValueString("SalesPerson");                 ⓯
      doc.getItemValueDouble("SalesAmount");                 ⓰
      doc.getItemValueInteger("UnitsSold");                  ⓱
      Vector items = doc.getItemValue("ItemsSold");          ⓲
      doc.recycle();
      db.recycle();
      ac.recycle();
```

```
        session.recycle();
    } catch(Exception e) {
        e.printStackTrace();}    }   }
```

Explanation

❶ Create a new document.

❷ Set the contents of the field named `Form`.

❸ Instantiated a new `Double` object and set it to the value 9.00.

❹ Populate the `SalesAmount` field with the `Double` object.

❺ Instantiated a new `Integer` object and set it to the value of 3.

❻ Populate the `UnitsSold` field with the `Integer` object.

❼ Set the contents of the `SalesPerson` field to a `String` value.

❽ Set the contents of the `Manager` field to a `String` value.

❾ Create a new `Vector` object to hold the items' sold values.

❿ Add elements to the `Vector`.

⓫ Populate the `ItemsSold` field using the newly created `Vector` object. This creates a multi-valued field.

⓬ Determine if the `Document` has a field via the `hasItem` method.

⓭ If the `Document` has the field, set the contents of it.

⓮ Save the `Document` via the `save` method with no arguments.

⓯ Retrieve the `String` value stored in the `SalesPerson` field.

⓰ Retrieve the `Double` value stored in the `SalesAmount` field.

⓱ Retrieve the `Integer` value stored in the `UnitsSold` field.

⓲ Create a new `Vector` object containing the elements from the `ItemsSold` field.

> **NOTE**   The `Vector` object can retrieve values for any field. The `Vector` will have only one element (index of zero) if the field has only one value. Otherwise, it will have as many elements as the item has values.

8.3.7   hasItem

The `hasItem` method was utilized in example 8.2. It allows you to quickly determine whether or not a document has a certain field value. Attempting to access a nonexistent field will result in an exception, so be careful.

8.3.8   getFirstItem

A document can contain multiple instances of the same-named field, so you can use the `getFirstItem` method to retrieve the first occurrence of the field. This method returns an `Item` object. We will not dive into its details at this point. Chapter 9 covers the `Item` class.

```
Item = Document.getFirstItem("Item Name");
```

NOTE   A null value is returned if the item does not exist.

8.4   OTHER METHODS

In addition to the methods already discussed, there are a number of methods that facilitate different tasks related to working with documents.

8.4.1   computeWithForm

The `computeWithForm` method evaluates all of the default values, input translation, and input validation for a document's form. It accepts two parameters. The first is `boolean` and ignored, so set it to true or false with no consequences. The second signals whether or not an error should be raised if validation fails for any field. The return value of the method is true or false, signaling whether or not any errors occurred with form validation/translation.

```
boolean = Document.computeWithForm(boolean, boolean);
```

8.4.2   copyAllItems

The `copyAllItems` method copies all items from one document to another. The first parameter is the destination document, and the second parameter is true or false, signaling whether or not existing fields on the destination document should be replaced.

```
Document.copyAllItems(Document, boolean);
```

Example 8.3   (Domino Agent)

```
import lotus.domino.*;
import java.util.*;
public class Example_8_3 extends AgentBase {
 public void NotesMain() {
   try {
     Session session = getSession();
     AgentContext ac = session.getAgentContext();
     Database db = ac.getCurrentDatabase();
     View vw = db.getView("Examples \\ by Chapter");
     ViewNavigator vn = vw.createViewNav();              ❶
     Document sourceDoc = (Document)vn.getFirstDocument();    ❷
     while (sourceDoc != null)    {    ❸
       Document destDoc = db.createDocument();    ❹
       sourceDoc.copyAllItems(destDoc, true);    ❺
       destDoc.save();    ❻
       sourceDoc.recycle();
       destDoc.recycle();
       sourceDoc = (Document)vn.getNextDocument();        }    ❼
     // Cleanup objects.....
     vn.recycle();
     vw.recycle();
     db.recycle();
     ac.recycle();
```

```
    session.recycle();
  } catch(Exception e) {
    e.printStackTrace();} } }
```

━

Explanation

❶ Create a new `ViewNavigator` object containing all entries from the view.

❷ Retrieve the first document from the `ViewNavigator` object via the `getFirstDocument` method. We must explicitly cast the returned type of the `getFirstDocument` method (`ViewEntry`) to `Document`.

❸ Loop through all documents in the `ViewNavigator` with a `while` loop.

❹ Create a new `Document`.

❺ Copy all items (fields) from one document to the newly created document via the `copyAllItems` method.

❻ Save the new `Document`.

❼ Retrieve the next document from the `ViewNavigator`. Again, we must cast the returned object.

8.4.3   copyItem

The `copyItem` copies an item to the current `Document` from another. It utilizes the `Item` class, which chapter 9 discusses.

```
Document.copyItem(Item, "Optional new name");
```

8.4.4   copyToDatabase

The `copyToDatabase` method copies a document to a specified database. It accepts one and only one parameter, the destination `Database` object.

```
Document.copyToDatabase(Database);
```

8.4.5   createReplyMessage

The `createReplyMessage` method creates a new document that is composed as a reply to the current document. It creates a reply to itself. You may want to use this to facilitate the tracking of versions of a document.

```
Document.createReplyMessage(boolean);
```

The one and only parameter signals true/false as to whether the newly created recipient list for the document contains all of the recipients of the original. The newly created document will get mailed if, and only if, the `send` method is initiated.

8.4.6   createRichTextItem

The `createRichTextItem` method creates a new rich text field on a document. Chapter 10 discusses rich text items. This method accepts only one parameter, the field name for the new item.

```
RichTextItem = Document.createRichTextItem("name");
```

8.4.7   encrypt

The `encrypt` method encrypts the contents of a document. Only the fields with the `isEncrypted` property set to true are encrypted.

```
Document.encrypt();
```

8.4.8   getAttachment

The `getAttachment` method retrieves file attachments from a document. Chapter 10, which covers the `RichTextItem` class, discusses this method.

```
Document.getAttachment("filename");
```

8.4.9   makeResponse

The `makeResponse` method makes one `Document` a response to another. This is useful when you need to chain documents or move responses. Also, you can use this method to version documents as well. The only parameter is a pointer to the main document that will receive the response.

```
Document.makeResponse(Document);
```

8.4.10   putInFolder

The `putInFolder` method moves a `Document` to a specified folder. The name of the folder is the first parameter. The second parameter signals true/false as to whether the folder should be created if it does not currently exist.

```
Document.putInFolder("folder name",true)
```

8.4.11   remove

The `remove` method permanently removes a document from a database. It accepts one boolean parameter that signals whether or not the document should be removed if it has been modified after you opened it. The return value is `boolean` as well; it signals whether or not the deletion was successful.

```
boolean = Document.remove(true);
```

8.4.12   removeFromFolder

The `removeFromFolder` method is the opposite of `putInFolder`. It removes a document from the specified folder.

```
Document.removeFromFolder("folder name");
```

8.4.13   removeItem

The `removeItem` method deletes all instances of a field on a `Document`. It accepts only one parameter, the name of the field to delete.

```
Document.removeItem("Field name");
```

8.4.14   renderToRTItem

The `renderToRTItem` method creates a picture of a `Document` in a rich text field. This may be useful for versioning. It accepts the destination rich text item object as the only parameter and returns true/false signaling whether or not it was successful.

```
boolean = Document.renderToRTItem(RichTextItem);
```

8.4.15   sign

The `sign` method signs a `Document` object. It accepts no parameters and returns no values.

```
Document.sign();
```

8.5   PROPERTIES

In addition to the various methods for manipulating a `Document` object, there are numerous properties as well. Also, a few of the properties have corresponding set methods to manipulate their values. The complete property list is as follows:

- `Authors`: Vector of `String` objects containing all author names
- `ColumnValues`: Vector of objects containing all items corresponding to columns in the document's parent `View`
- `EmbeddedObjects`: Vector of `EmbeddedObject` objects containing all OLE objects in the document
- `EncryptionKeys`: Vector of `String` objects containing all keys used to encrypt the document
- `FolderReferences`: Vector of `String` objects containing the universal Ids for all folders that contain the `Document` object
- `FTSearchScore`: If a `Document` object was returned as part of a full-text search, this property returns the full-text search score. A value of zero is returned if it was not returned as part of a full-text search.
- `hasEmbedded`: Signals true/false depending on whether or not it has embedded objects (attachments, OLE objects)
- `isDeleted`: Signals true/false depending on whether or not an item has been flagged to be deleted. This works in conjunction with the "soft deletes" feature.
- `isEncryptOnSend`: Signals true/false depending on whether or not it is set to be encrypted when mailed
- `isNewNote`: Signals true/false depending on whether or not it is new (has not been saved)

- isProfile: Signals true/false depending on whether or not it is a profile Document
- isResponse: Signals true/false depending on whether or not it is a response document
- isSaveMessageOnSend: Signals true/false depending on whether or not it is set to be automatically saved when mailed
- isSentByAgent: Signals true/false depending on whether or not it was sent (mailed) by a Domino agent
- isSigned: Signals true/false depending on whether or not it is signed
- isSignOnSend: Signals true/false depending on whether or not it is set to be signed when mailed
- isValid: Signals true/false depending on whether or not it represents an existing Document rather than a deletion stub
- Items: Vector of Item objects containing all items in a document
- Key: The key for a profile Document (if it is a profile)
- LastAccessed: A DateTime object representing the last time the Document object was accessed (read or modified)
- LastModified: A DateTime object representing the last time the Document object was saved
- NameOfProfile: The name of a profile Document (if it is a profile Document)
- NoteID: The NoteID of a document
- ParentDatabase: The Database object that contains the Document object
- ParentDocumentUNID: The universal ID of the Document object's parent. A null value is returned if it is not a response document.
- ParentView: The View object that was used when the Document object was opened. A null value is returned if the Document was not retrieved from a View object.
- Responses: DocumentCollection object containing all responses to the document object (if any)
- Signer: The Notes username of the person that created the signature, if it is signed. A null value is returned if it is unsigned.
- Size: The size of the Document object in bytes (int)
- UniversalID: The universal ID for the Document object
- Verifier: If it is signed, the Verifier property returns the certificate that verified it. Otherwise, a null value is returned.

Example 8.4 (Domino Agent)

```
import lotus.domino.*;
import java.util.*;
import java.io.PrintWriter;

public class Example_8_4 extends AgentBase {
 public void NotesMain() {
   try {
     Session session = getSession();
     AgentContext ac = session.getAgentContext();
     Database db = ac.getCurrentDatabase();
     PrintWriter pw = getAgentOutput();
     View vw = db.getView("Examples \\ by Chapter");
     ViewNavigator vn = vw.createViewNav();         ❶
     ViewEntry ve = vn.getFirstDocument();          ❷
     Vector vAuthors;                               ❸
     Vector vColumns;
     while (ve != null)    {                        ❹
       Document doc = (Document)(ve.getDocument());  ❺
       vAuthors = doc.getAuthors();                 ❻
       if (vAuthors != null) {                      ❼
         for (int x = 0; x < vAuthors.size(); x++)    {   ❽
           pw.println("Author:  " + vAuthors.elementAt(x)); } }
         vColumns = doc.getColumnValues();          ❾
         if (vColumns != null)   {                  ❿
           for (int y = 0; y < vColumns.size(); y++) {   ⓫
             pw.print("Column Value " + y + ":  ");
             pw.println(vColumns.elementAt(y));   }   }
           pw.print("Document created:  ");         ⓬
           pw.println(doc.getCreated().getLocalTime());
           pw.print("Document last accessed:  ");   ⓭
           pw.println(doc.getLastAccessed().getLocalTime());
           pw.print("Document last modified:  ");   ⓮
           pw.println(doc.getLastModified().getLocalTime());
           if (doc.hasEmbedded()) {                 ⓯
             pw.println("Document has embedded items.");
           }else {
             pw.println("Document has no embedded items.");   }
           if (doc.getFTSearchScore() == 0) {       ⓰
             pw.println("Document was not returned from a search.");
           }else {
             pw.print("Document FT Search Score:  ");
             pw.println(doc.getFTSearchScore());   }
           pw.print("Encrypt on send is set to:  ");   ⓱
           pw.println(doc.isEncryptOnSend());
           if (doc.isNewNote())   {                 ⓲
             pw.println("Document is new!");
           }else {
             pw.println("Document is not new.");   }
           if (doc.isProfile()) {
             pw.println("Document is a Profile Document.");   ⓳
```

```
     pw.println("The key value is:  " + doc.getKey());    ⑳
     pw.print("The name of the profile is:  ");    ㉑
     pw.println(doc.getNameOfProfile()); }
  if (doc.isResponse()) {
     pw.print("Document is a Response Document to ");    ㉒
     pw.println(doc.getParentDocumentUNID());}
  pw.print("Save on send is set to:  ");    ㉓
  pw.println(doc.isSaveMessageOnSend());
  if (doc.isSentByAgent()) {    ㉔
     pw.print("This document was sent from a");
     pw.println("Domino agent.");    }
  pw.println("Document is signed:  " + doc.isSigned());    ㉕
  pw.print("Sign on send is set to:  ");    ㉖
  pw.println(doc.isSignOnSend());
  if (doc.isValid()) {    ㉗
     pw.println("The Document is not a deletion stub.");
  }else {
     pw.print("The Document does not exist, ");
     pw.println("it is a deletion stub.");    }
  Vector vItems = doc.getItems();    ㉘
  pw.print("There are " + vItems.size());    ㉙
  pw.println(" items on this document.");
  pw.println("Document NoteID:  " + doc.getNoteID());    ㉚
  if (doc.getParentView() != null) {
     View parentView = doc.getParentView();    ㉛
     pw.print("The document was retrieved from a ");    ㉜
     pw.println(" view named " + parentView.getName());
     parentView.recycle();
  }else  {
     pw.print("The document was not retrieved ");
     pw.println("from a view.");    }
  if (doc.getResponses() == null) {    ㉝
     DocumentCollection respDC = doc.getResponses();    ㉞
     pw.print("The document has " + respDC.getCount());    ㉟
     pw.println(" responses.");
     respDC.recycle();
  }else  {
     pw.println("The document has no responses.");    }
  pw.print("The size of the document (in bytes) ");    ㊱
  pw.println(" is " + doc.getSize());
  pw.print("The document universal ID is ");    ㊲
  pw.println(doc.getUniversalID());
  ve.recycle();
  doc.recycle();
  ve = vn.getNextDocument();  }
 vn.recycle();
 vw.recycle();
 db.recycle();
 ac.recycle();
 session.recycle();
} catch(Exception e) {
 e.printStackTrace(); } } }
```

Explanation

❶ Create a new `ViewNavigator` object containing all entries from the view.

❷ Set the `ViewEntry` object to the first document in the `ViewNavigator` object.

❸ Declare `Vector` objects to be used to access `Authors` and `ColumnValues` properties.

❹ Use a `while` loop to access all entries in the `ViewNavigator`.

❺ Retrieve the `Document` object from the current entry. Explicitly cast it to a `Document` object.

❻ Populate the `Vector` with the `Document` authors (if there are any).

❼ We only want to process the elements of the `Vector` if it has been populated.

❽ Use a `for` statement to loop through all elements in the vAuthors `Vector`.

❾ Populate the `Vector` with the `Document` ColumnValues (if there are any).

❿ We only want to process the elements of the `Vector` if it has been populated. We accessed this `Document` without a view, so it will be null.

⓫ Use a `for` statement to loop through all elements in the `Vector`.

⓬ Print the date/time the `Document` was created.

⓭ Print the last accessed time/date for the `Document`. The `getLocalTime` method of the `DateTime` class is utilized. Chapter 16 covers the `DateTime` class in more detail.

⓮ Print the last modified time/date for the `Document`. The `getLocalTime` method of the `DateTime` class is used.

⓯ Determine if the `Document` contains any embedded objects.

⓰ Determine if the `Document` was returned from a full-text search.

⓱ Determine if the `EncryptOnSend` property is enabled.

⓲ Determine if the `Document` is new.

⓳ Determine if a `Document` is a profile.

⓴ If it is a profile `Document`, print its key value.

㉑ If it is a profile `Document`, print its name.

㉒ If the `Document` is a response, get its parent's universal ID.

㉓ Determine if the `isSaveMessageOnSend` property is enabled.

㉔ Determine if a Domino agent sent the `Document`.

㉕ Determine if the `Document` is signed.

㉖ Determine if the `SignOnSend` property is enabled.

㉗ Determine if the `Document` is a deletion stub or normal `Document`.

㉘ Populate a `Vector` of `Item` objects with all `Items` from the `Document`.

㉙ Display the number of items found on the Document.

㉚ Print the NotesID.

㉛ If the Document was retrieved from a View, get a handle on its parent View object.

㉜ Retrieve the Name property of the parent View object.

㉝ Determine if the Document has any responses.

㉞ If the Document does have responses, populate a DocumentCollection object with all its responses.

㉟ Print the number of responses.

㊱ Print the size of the Document.

㊲ Print the universal ID.

Output (for one document)

```
Author:  CN=Tony Patton/O=BaseLine
Document created:  11/07/99 10:05:00 PM EST
Document last accessed:  11/07/99 10:05:46 PM EST
Document last modified:  11/07/99 10:05:46 PM EST
Document has embedded items.
Document was not returned from a search.
Encrypt on send is set to:  false
Document is not new.
Save on send is set to:  false
Document is signed:  false
Sign on send is set to:  false
The Document is not a deletion stub.
There are 7 items on this document.
Document NoteID:  24AA
The document was not retrieved from a view.
The document has not responses.
The size of the document (in bytes) is 7888
The document universal ID is 589F117A312BFD19852568230010F01A
```

8.6 WORKING WITH PROFILE DOCUMENTS

A profile Document is a special type of document used in a Domino database. Profile Documents store configuration information, user information, or any other piece of data specific to a user or database, or whatever else you can dream up. They act as environment variables except for the fact that they travel with the database, so you don't have to worry about a user changing computers and so forth. The profiles are stored in a Domino database but are not displayed in any view. There are special methods, properties, and @Functions/Commands for working with profile Documents.

A key value makes a profile Document unique. Key values must be unique within the database; otherwise they are of no use. How would you retrieve a profile if there were no way to differentiate it from others? A common key value is a user's username, but something like "configuration" could be used for storing database configuration information. The choice is up to you, the developer. Let's take a look at working with profile Documents.

Example 8.5   (Domino Agent)

```
import lotus.domino.*;
import java.util.*;

public class Example_8_5 extends AgentBase {
 public void NotesMain() {
   try {
     Session session = getSession();
     AgentContext ac = session.getAgentContext();
     Database db = ac.getCurrentDatabase();
     Document doc = db.getProfileDocument("Configuration",session.getUserName());   ❶
     doc.replaceItemValue("Default Directory","c:\test");   ❷
     doc.replaceItemValue("Report Title","Test Report");   ❸
     doc.save();   ❹
     doc.recycle();
     db.recycle();
     ac.recycle();
     session.recycle();
   } catch(Exception e) {   ❺
     e.printStackTrace();   } } }   ❻
```

Explanation

❶ Get the profile Document from the Database using the getProfileDocument method. A new profile Document is created if it does not exist.

❷ Populate a field. A profile Document can contain any number and type of fields.

❸ Populate another field.

❹ Save the Document.

The code in example 8.6 retrieves the newly created profile Document.

Example 8.6

```
import lotus.domino.*;
import java.util.*;

public class Example_8_6 extends AgentBase {
 public void NotesMain() {
   try {
     Session session = getSession();
     AgentContext ac = session.getAgentContext();
     Database db = ac.getCurrentDatabase();
     Document doc = db.getProfileDocument("Configuration",session.getUserName());   ❶
     System.out.print("Default Directory:  ");   ❷
     System.out.println(doc.getItemValue("Default Directory"));
```

```
System.out.print("Report Title");
System.out.println(doc.getItemValue("Report Title"));
System.out.println("Key Value:  " + doc.getKey());       ❸
System.out.println("Profile Name:  " + doc.getNameOfProfile());    ❹
doc.recycle();
db.recycle();
ac.recycle();
session.recycle();
} catch(Exception e) {
e.printStackTrace();  }  }  }
```

Explanation

❶ Retrieve the profile Document from the database using the key and name values assigned in example 8.5.

❷ Print the contents of the two fields we created.

❸ Retrieve the key value via the getKey method of the Document object.

❹ Retrieve the profile name value via the getNameOfProfile method of the Document object.

Output

```
Default Directory:  [test]
Report Title[Test Report]
Key Value:  CN=Tony Patton/O=TIS
Profile Name:  Configuration
```

The power offered by profile Documents is endless. They work with the Notes client as well as Web browsers, so database settings and user information can be stored for all of your users. Profile Documents are much cleaner to use than cookies with browsers or environment variables with the Notes client. You don't have to worry about changing computers or users editing or deleting files.

8.7   CHAPTER REVIEW

I made this chapter detailed to make certain that you could achieve a good, thorough understanding of the Document object. Documents are used throughout the rest of the book, so the points in this chapter will be hammered home time and time again.

- The Document is the format in which data is encapsulated and stored in a Domino database.

- A Document can contain items or fields that store specific name/value pairs for data elements.

- The Database object offers the createDocument method to create new documents.

- The `DocumentCollection`, `ViewEntryCollection`, `ViewNavigator`, and `View` objects offer methods to access existing documents.

- The `getItemValue` method of the `Document` class retrieves the contents of a specified field. There are variations for working with `Double`, `Integer`, and `String` values.

- The `replaceItemValue` and `appendItemValue` methods of the `Document` class populate field values.

- There are numerous methods available in the `Document` class for copying items, deleting the document, and so forth.

- There are a variety of properties available for investigating the contents and type of data stored in a `Document`.

- Profile `Document`s offer a clean method for storing user-specific information.

CHAPTER 9

Item class

9.1 What is an Item?   94
9.2 Creating an Item   94
9.3 Getting an existing Item   95
9.4 Removing an Item   96
9.5 is properties   97

9.6 More properties   99
9.7 type and values properties   102
9.8 Other methods   104
9.9 Chapter review   105

9.1   WHAT IS AN ITEM?

An Item represents a single piece of data on a form regardless of whether it has one value or is multivalued. When you create a form in a Domino database, fields are placed on the form for entering and displaying data. Each field has a corresponding Item, and hidden fields (not visible to the user of a form) are available as Item objects as well. Lets take a look at creating a new Item and accessing existing fields on a form.

9.2   CREATING AN ITEM

The replaceItemValue and appendItemValue methods discussed in chapter 8 create new fields or items on a document. You must take care with the appendItemValue method, because it will create another copy of an Item if it already exists. You can use a number of methods to copy existing items as well.

```
Document.replaceItemValue("Item name",value);
Document.appendItemValue("Item name", value);
```

94

The value used to populate an Item can be a `String`, `Vector` of objects, numeric, and so forth.

9.3 GETTING AN EXISTING ITEM

The `getFirstItem` and `getItems` methods of the `Document` class can retrieve a field value from a form as an `Item` object. Before you use these methods, you can use the `hasItem` method to determine if an Item exists. This avoids errors resulting from accessing nonexistent Items.

Example 9.1   (Domino Agent)

```
import lotus.domino.*;
import java.util.*;

public class Example_9_1 extends AgentBase {
 public void NotesMain() {
   try {
     Session session = getSession();
     AgentContext ac = session.getAgentContext();
     Database db = ac.getCurrentDatabase();
     View vw = db.getView("Examples \\ by Chapter");
     ViewNavigator vn = vw.createViewNav();
     ViewEntry ve = vn.getFirstDocument();
     while (ve != null)    {
       Document doc = (Document)ve.getDocument();   ❶
       if (doc.hasItem("SalesPerson"))   {  ❷
         Item field = doc.getFirstItem("SalesPerson");   }  ❸
       ve.recycle();
       ve = vn.getNextDocument();        }
     vn.recycle();
     vw.recycle();
     db.recycle();
     ac.recycle();
     session.recycle();
   } catch(Exception e) {
     e.printStackTrace();  }  }  }
```

Explanation

❶ Retrieve the current `Document` object from the `ViewEntry` object.

❷ We only want to work with the field if it exists; `hasItem` returns true if it does.

❸ Create an `Item` object containing the `SalesPerson` field from the current `Document` object.

9.4 REMOVING AN ITEM

Often you will encounter a situation where you must remove a data Item from all documents in a database. The remove method of the Item class facilitates such a need. It permanently deletes all instances of an Item (and its data) from a Document. The removeItem method of the Document class achieves the same results. You must save the document in order to write the deletion to disk.

Example 9.2 removes the field called Managers from every document in our application.

Example 9.2   (Domino Agent)

```
import lotus.domino.*;
import java.util.*;

public class Example_9_2 extends AgentBase {
 public void NotesMain() {
  try {
   Session session = getSession();
   AgentContext ac = session.getAgentContext();
   Database db = ac.getCurrentDatabase();
   View vw = db.getView("Examples \\ by Chapter");
   ViewNavigator vn = vw.createViewNav();
   ViewEntry ve = vn.getFirstDocument();
   while (ve != null)    {
    Document doc = (Document)ve.getDocument();
    if (doc.hasItem("Manager"))  {  ❶
     Item field = doc.getFirstItem("Manager");  ❷
     field.remove();  ❸
     doc.save();  }  ❹
    doc.recycle();
    ve.recycle();
    ve = vn.getNextDocument();      }
   vn.recycle();
   db.recycle();
   ac.recycle();
   session.recycle();
  } catch(Exception e) {
   e.printStackTrace();} } }
```

Explanation

❶ Determine if the field exists before proceeding with the deletion.

❷ Set the Item object to the field on the Document.

❸ Call the remove method of the Item class to delete all instances of the Item and its data from the Document.

❹ Save the Document to make the deletion permanent.

9.5 IS PROPERTIES

A number of is properties return a boolean value signaling if a certain property of the Item class is true or false. Each of the properties has a corresponding set method for populating the property of an Item.

The following is a list of properties that have corresponding is and set methods for working with them.

- Authors: Signals whether an Item is of the type authors
- Encrypted: Signals whether an Item is encrypted
- Names: Signals whether an Item is of the type names
- Protected: Signals whether an Item is editable only by users with at least editor access
- Readers: Signals whether an Item is of the type readers
- SaveToDisk: Signals whether an Item is saved when the Document is saved. If this is set to false for an existing item, it performs the same operation as a remove.
- Signed: Signals whether an Item contains a signature
- Summary: Signals whether an Item is a summary. This property must be set to true for its data value(s) to appear in a view.

Example 9.3 demonstrates the properties listed above. We will access all documents in a View and disable all of the security settings (readers, authors, protected, and so forth) on all of the Items in every Document. Also, we want to make sure the Item data can be displayed in a View via the Summary property.

Example 9.3   (Domino Agent)

```
import lotus.domino.*;
import java.util.*;
import java.io.PrintWriter;
public class Example_9_3 extends AgentBase {
 public void NotesMain() {
  try {
    Session session = getSession();
    PrintWriter pw = getAgentOutput();
    AgentContext ac = session.getAgentContext();
    Database db = ac.getCurrentDatabase();
    View vw = db.getView("Examples \\ by Chapter");
    ViewNavigator vn = vw.createViewNav();
    ViewEntry ve = vn.getFirstDocument();
    while (ve != null)    {
     Document doc = (Document)ve.getDocument();
     Vector items = doc.getItems();        ❶
     for (int x=0; x < items.size(); x++) {   ❷
       Item cur = (Item)items.elementAt(x);   ❸
```

```
            If (cur.isAuthors()) {  ④
              cur.setAuthors(false);    }
            if (cur.isEncrypted()) {  ⑤
              pw.print("The item " + cur.getName());  ⑥
              pw.println(" is encrypted, it will be disabled.");
              cur.setEncrypted(false); }  ⑦
            else {
              pw.println("The item " + cur.getName());
              pw.println(" is not encrypted.");   }
            if (cur.isNames()) {  ⑧
              cur.setNames(false);    }
            if (cur.isProtected()) {  ⑨
              cur.setProtected(false);    }
            if (cur.isReaders())  {  ⑩
              cur.setReaders(false);    }
            if (!cur.isSaveToDisk()) {  ⑪
              cur.setSaveToDisk(true); }
            if (cur.isSigned()) {  ⑫
              cur.setSigned(false); }
            if (!cur.isSummary()) {  ⑬
              cur.setSummary(true);    } }
          ve.recycle();
          ve = vn.getNextDocument();        }
        vn.recycle();
        vw.recycle();
        db.recycle():
        ac.recycle();
        session.recycle();
      } catch(Exception e) {
        e.printStackTrace(); } } }
```

Explanation

❶ Create a `Vector` object containing all `Item` objects from the `Document`.

❷ Use the `for` statement to loop through all items in the document.

❸ Create an `Item` object from the current element in the `Vector` using the loop variable as the index. The element is explicitly cast to an `Item` object.

❹ If the `Item` is an authors field, disable it.

❺ If the `Item` is encrypted, disable it.

❻ Display the `Item`'s name and details of encryption.

❼ Disable the encryption setting via the `setEncryption` method of the `Item` class.

❽ If the current `Item` is a names field, disable it.

❾ If the current `Item` is protected, disable it.

❿ If the current `Item` is a readers field, disable it.

CHAPTER 9 ITEM CLASS

⓫ If the current Item is not set to be saved with the Document, enable it. The exclamation mark (!) is the logical Not operator in Java.

⓬ If the current Item is signed, disable it.

⓭ If the current Item does not have its summary flag set, enable it. This allows the values stored in the Item to be displayed in a View.

9.6 MORE PROPERTIES

There are a number of other properties available for the Item class. One such property is a pointer to the Document that contains the Item, the name of the Item, and the last modified date for it. A list of these properties follows:

- DateTimeValue: Read/write property that returns or sets a DateTime object representing the Item's value. A null value is returned if the value is not a date or time value.

- LastModified: Read-only property that returns a DateTime object representing the last modified setting for an Item

- Name: Read-only property that returns the name of an Item (field name)

- Parent: Read-only property that returns a Document object representing the Document that contains the Item

- Text: Read-only property that returns a String representation of the contents of the Item

- Type: Read-only property that returns the data type of an Item. An integer value is returned; the constant values are listed later in this chapter.

- ValueDouble: Read/write property that returns/sets the value of an Item using a numeric value

- ValueInteger: Read/write property that returns/sets the value of an item using an integer value

- ValueLength: Read-only property that returns the storage space in bytes required to store the Item as an integer

- Values: Read/write property that returns the value(s) stored in an Item. It returns a Vector containing the values.

- ValueString: Read/write property that returns/sets the value of an Item using a text value

Example 9.4   (Domino Agent)

```
import lotus.domino.*;
import java.util.*;
import java.io.PrintWriter;

public class Example_9_4 extends AgentBase {
```

```java
public void NotesMain() {
 try {
   Session session = getSession();
   PrintWriter pw = getAgentOutput();
   AgentContext ac = session.getAgentContext();
   Database db = ac.getCurrentDatabase();
   View vw = db.getView("Examples \\ by Chapter");
   ViewNavigator vn = vw.createViewNav();
   ViewEntry ve = vn.getFirstDocument();
   while (ve != null)    {
    Document doc = (Document)ve.getDocument(); ❶
    Vector items = doc.getItems(); ❶
    for (int x=0; x < items.size(); x++) { ❷
     Item cur = (Item)items.elementAt(x); ❸
     DateTime dt = cur.getDateTimeValue(); ❹
     if (dt == null){ ❺
      pw.print("Item " + cur.getName());
      pw.println(" is not a date-time value.");  }
     else {
      pw.print("Item " + cur.getName());
      pw.println(" is a date-time value.");  }
     DateTime lm = cur.getLastModified(); ❻
     pw.println("Last modified " + lm.getLocalTime()); ❼
     if (cur.getParent() != null)  {  ❽
      if (cur.getParent().isResponse()) { ❾
       pw.print("The parent document for the ");
       pw.println(cur.getName() + " item is a response document."); }
      else {
       pw.print("The parent document for the " + cur.getName());
       pw.println(" is not a response document."); }}
     pw.println("Text:  " + cur.getText()); ❿
     pw.println("Type:  " + cur.getType()); ⓫
     double dbl = cur.getValueDouble(); ⓬
     if (dbl !== 0) { ⓭
      pw.print("The " + cur.getName());
      pw.println( + " contains a double value.");  }
     else {
      pw.print("The " + cur.getName());
      pw.println(" does not contain a double value.");  }
      int ivalue = cur.getValueInteger(); ⓮
      if (ivalue !==0) { ⓯
      pw.print("The " + cur.getName());
      pw.println(" contains an integer value.");  }
     else {
      pw.print("The " + cur.getName() + " does not ");
      pw.println("contain an integer value.");  }
      pw.print("The length of the " + cur.getName());
      pw.print(" item is " + cur.getValueLength()); ⓰
      pw.println(" in bytes.");
      String vs = cur.getValueString(); ⓱
      if (vs == "") {  ⓲
       pw.print("The " + cur.getName());
```

```
        pw.println(" does not contain a string value.");  }
      else {
        pw.print("The " + cur.getName());
        pw.println(" contains a string value.");  }  }
    ve.recycle();
    ve = vn.getNextDocument();        }
    vn.recycle();
    vw.recycle();
    db.recycle():
    ac.recycle();
    session.recycle();
  } catch(Exception e) {
    e.printStackTrace();  }  }  }
```

Explanation

❶ Create a Vector object containing all Item objects from the current Document.

❷ A for statement is used to loop through all items in the Document.

❸ Retrieve Item from the Vector using the loop index value. The element is explicitly cast to an Item object.

❹ Retrieve the DateTime value from the current Item.

❺ Determine if the Item is a DateTime value or not.

❻ Retrieve the last modified DateTime value for the Item.

❼ Print the last modified text via the getLocalTime method of the DateTime object.

❽ Determine if the parent Document of the current Item exists.

❾ Determine if the parent Document of the current Item is a response Document.

❿ Print the text of the Item.

⓫ Print the type of the Item.

⓬ Retrieve the double value of the Item. A zero is returned if it is not a double.

⓭ Print whether or not the Item is a double.

⓮ Retrieve the integer value of the Item. A zero is returned if it is not an integer value.

⓯ Print whether or not the Item contains an integer value.

⓰ Print the length of the Item in bytes.

⓱ Retrieve the string value of the Item. The empty string is returned if the Item does not contain a string value.

⓲ Determine if the Item contains a string value.

Output

```
Item $FILE is not a date-time value.
Last modified 11/07/99 10:05:46 PM EST
The parent document for the $FILE is not a response document.
```

```
Text:
Type:  1084
The $FILE contains a double value.
The $FILE contains an integer value.
The length of the $FILE item is 70 in bytes.
The $FILE contains a string value.
```

9.7 TYPE AND VALUES PROPERTIES

The type property can be instrumental to working with data in an Item. The values property returns a Vector containing all values contained in an Item. Because the Vector contains objects as its default, accessing values in the Vector requires careful attention so you do not cause an exception. The returned value from the Vector must be cast to the proper type to be properly handled.

9.7.1 List of type constants

The viable types (constants) are as follows:

- Item.ACTIONCD
- Item.ASSISTANTINFO
- Item.ATTACHMENT
- Item.AUTHORS
- Item.COLLATION
- Item.DATETIMES
- Item.EMBEDDEDOBJECT
- Item.ERRORITEM
- Item.FORMULA
- Item.HTML
- Item.ICON
- Item.LSOBJECT
- Item.NAMES
- Item.NOTELINKS
- Item.NOTEREFS
- Item.NUMBERS
- Item.OTHEROBJECT
- Item.QUERYCD
- Item.READERS
- Item.RICHTEXT
- Item.SIGNATURE
- Item.TEXT
- Item.UNAVAILABLE
- Item.UNKNOWN
- Item.USERDATA
- Item.USERID
- Item.VIEWMAPDATA
- Item.VIEWMAPLAYOUT

Example 9.5 includes the corresponding integer values for the constants. It uses a `case` statement to determine the type of data stored in the `Item`.

Example 9.5 (Domino Agent)

```java
import lotus.domino.*;
import java.util.*;
import java.io.PrintWriter;

public class Example_9_5 extends AgentBase {
  public void NotesMain() {
    try {
      Session session = getSession();
      PrintWriter pw = getAgentOutput();
      AgentContext ac = session.getAgentContext();
      Database db = ac.getCurrentDatabase();
      View vw = db.getView("Examples \\ by Chapter");
      ViewNavigator vn = vw.createViewNav();
      ViewEntry ve = vn.getFirstDocument();
      String output;                                      ❶
      while (ve != null)    {
       Document doc = (Document)ve.getDocument();
       Vector items = doc.getItems();   ❷
       for (int x=0; x < items.size(); x++) {  ❸
       Item cur = (Item)items.elementAt(x);  ❹
       output = "";  ❺
       switch (cur.getType())  {  ❻
        case (16) : output = "ActionCD";  break;  ❼
        case (17) : output = "Assistant Info";  break;
        case (1084) : output = "Attachment";  break;
        case (1076) : output = "Authors";  break;
        case (1024) : output = "Date-time";  break;
        case (2) : output = "Collation";  break;
        case (1090) : output = "Embedded Object";  break;
        case (256) : output = "Error Item";  break;
        case (1536) : output = "Formula";  break;
        case (21) : output = "HTML";  break;
        case (6) : output = "Icon";  break;
        case (20) : output = "LotusScript Object";  break;
        case (25) : output = "MIME";  break;
        case (1074) : output = "Names";  break;
        case (7) : output = "Notes Link";  break;
        case (4) : output = "Notes Reference";  break;
        case (768) : output = "Numeric";  break;
        case (1085) : output = "Other object";  break;
        case (15) : output = "QueryCD";  break;
        case (1075) : output = "Readers";  break;
        case (1) : output = "Rich Text";  break;
        case (8) : output = "Signature";  break;
        case (1280) : output = "Text";  break;
        case (512) : output = "Unavailable";  break;
        case (0) : output = "Unknown";  break;
        case (14) : output = "User data";  break;
        case (1792) : output = "UserID";  break;
        case (18) : output = "View Map Data";  break;
        case (19) : output = "View Map Layout";  break;  }
```

```
        pw.print("The item named " + cur.getName());  ❽
        pw.println(" contains " + output);     }
       ve.recycle();
       ve = vn.getNextDocument();        }
      vn.recycle();
      vw.recycle();
      db.recycle():
      ac.recycle();
      session.recycle();
    } catch(Exception e) {
      e.printStackTrace();} } }
```

Explanation

❶ Declare String variable used to store output.

❷ Populate Vector object with all Item objects from the Document.

❸ Loop through all Item objects in the Vector using a for loop.

❹ Retrieve Item from the Vector using the loop index.

❺ Clear the String variable.

❻ A switch/case statement is used to determine the type of the Item.

❼ The case statements use the actual integer value rather than the constant.

❽ Print the results.

Output (for one document)

```
The item named $FILE contains Attachment
The item named Form contains Text
The item named $Fonts contains Rich Text
The item named keyChapter contains Text
The item named keyExample contains Text
The item named rtfCode contains Rich Text
The item named $UpdatedBy contains Names
```

9.8   OTHER METHODS

There are a few additional methods for working with Items.

9.8.1   abstractText

The abstractText method retrieves a portion (or abstract) of text from an Item. The first parameter specifies the length of the returned abstract/text, the second parameter signals whether or not vowels should be dropped, and the last parameter specifies whether or not the table of abbreviations in the file (noteabbr.txt) should be used.

```
String = Item.abstractText(length, boolean, boolean);
```

9.8.2   appendToTextList

The appendToTextList method adds value(s) to an Item that contains a list of strings. It accepts either a String value or a Vector of String values.

```
appendToTextList(String/Vector);
```

9.8.3 containsValue

The `containsValue` method determines if a value is contained in an `Item` or not. It does not search for a text value. Rather, it searches for matches in the list of values for an `Item`. It returns true if a match is found; it accepts an object as a parameter. The object can be a `String`, `Integer`, `Double`, or `DateTime`.

```
boolean = Item.containsValue(Object);
```

9.8.4 copyItemToDocument

The `copyItemToDocument` method copies an `Item` to a specific `Document`. It accepts one required parameter, the destination `Document`. The second parameter is the new name for the `Item` (if required).

```
Item.copyItemToDocument(Document, "newName");
```

9.9   CHAPTER REVIEW

The `Item` class allows you to access individual elements/fields on a `Document` object. There are numerous properties that allow you to access and set various `Item` attributes. In addition, you can use a number of methods to manipulate `Items` as well. You can copy, search for a value, append a value, and delete an `Item` from a `Document`. You can use the `values` and `type` properties to retrieve a value from an `Item` and determine its data type. The `Item` class has a long list of constants that correspond to the type of values stored in an `Item`.

- A handle to an `Item` object can be obtained via `Document` class methods.
- You can use a number of `is` and `set` methods to determine and set an `Item`'s attributes.
- You can use a number of additional properties to retrieve everything from the text stored in the field to the last modified date-time value of the `Item`.
- The `values` and `type` properties can traverse values stored in an `Item` and determine their `type`.
- The `Item` class has a number of constants that correspond to possible data types for an `Item`.
- There are a number of methods available for working with an `Item` object.

C H A P T E R   1 0

The RichTextItem class

10.1 What is the RichTextItem class?   106

10.2 Accessing an existing rich text item   106

10.3 Creating a new rich text item   107

10.4 Adding data   109

10.5 RichTextStyle class   111

10.6 RichTextParagraphStyle class   115

10.7 RichTextTab class   120

10.8 EmbeddedObject class   122

10.9 Chapter review   128

10.1 WHAT IS THE RICHTEXTITEM CLASS?

The `RichTextItem` class works with nonstandard items on a `Document`. These items contain rich text elements such as text longer than 256 bytes, file attachments, OLE objects, `Document` links, and other objects. The `RichTextItem` class is derived from the `Item` class, so all properties and methods available in the `Item` class are available in the `RichTextItem` class.

You should use the `RichTextItem` object when you are unsure of the type of data to be entered and stored in a field. A rich text field can store anything from regular text to file attachments. The flexibility given the user does add more work for the developer.

10.2 ACCESSING AN EXISTING RICH TEXT ITEM

The `getFirstItem` method of the `Document` class retrieves a handle on a `RichTextItem` object from a `Document` object. This is the same method used to retrieve a normal Item object, so the returned object must be explicitly cast to a RichTextItem object.

```
RichTextItem = (RichTextItem)Document.getFirstItem("field name")
```

10.3 CREATING A NEW RICH TEXT ITEM

In addition to working with existing rich text items, you can create new rich text items on a Document using the createRichTextItem method of the Document class. This method accepts one and only one parameter, the name of the new rich text field. It returns the newly created RichTextItem object.

```
RichTextItem = Document.createRichTextItem("Body");
```

Example 10.1 retrieves a handle to a rich text item from a Document object.

Example 10.1   (Domino Agent)

```
import lotus.domino.*;
import java.util.*;
import java.io.PrintWriter;
public class Example_10_1 extends AgentBase {
 public void NotesMain() {
   try {
     Session session = getSession();
     PrintWriter pw = getAgentOutput();
     AgentContext ac = session.getAgentContext();
     Database db = ac.getCurrentDatabase();
     View vw = db.getView("Examples \\ by Chapter");
     ViewNavigator vn = vw.createViewNav();
     ViewEntry ve = vn.getFirstDocument();
     while (ve != null)   {
       Document doc = (Document)ve.getDocument();  ❶
       RichTextItem rtf = (RichTextItem)doc.getFirstItem("rtfCode");  ❷
       if (rtf.getType() == Item.RICHTEXT)  {  ❸
         pw.print("The item named " + rtf.getName());  ❹
         pw.println(" is a rich text item.");   }
       ve.recycle();
       ve = vn.getNextDocument();       }
     vn.recycle();
     vw.recycle();
     db.recycle():
     ac.recycle();
     session.recycle();
   } catch(Exception e) {
     e.printStackTrace();} } }
```

Explanation

❶ Create a `Document` object from the `ViewEntry` object.

❷ Retrieve the specific field from the `Document`. It is stored in a `RichTextItem` object.

❸ Ensure that the type of the `RichTextItem` object is rich text. The `getType` property of the `RichTextItem`'s parent class (`Item`) is used to determine its `type`. The `type` constants from the `Item` class are used as well.

❹ Print the name of the rich text item.

Output

```
The item named rtfCode is a rich text item.
```

Example 10.2 creates a new rich text field on a newly created `Document`.

Example 10.2   (Domino Agent)

```
import lotus.domino.*;
import java.util.*;

public class Example_10_2 extends AgentBase {
  public void NotesMain() {
    try {
      Session session = getSession();
      AgentContext ac = session.getAgentContext();
      Database db = ac.getCurrentDatabase();
      Document doc = db.createDocument();             ❶
      RichTextItem rtf = doc.createRichTextItem("Body");   ❷
      rtf.addNewLine(1);    ❸
      rtf.appendText("This is a new rich text item.");   ❹
      doc.replaceItemValue("Subject","Test");   ❺
      doc.save();
      doc.recycle();
      db.recycle():
      ac.recycle();
      session.recycle();
    } catch(Exception e) {
    e.printStackTrace();} } }
```

Explanation

❶ Create a new `Document` in the `Database`.

❷ Create a new `RichTextItem` field on the `Document`. The field is named body.

❸ Add a new line to the `body` field. The `addNewLine` method is in the `RichTextItem` class.

❹ Add text to the body field. The `appendText` method of the `RichTextItem` class is used.

❺ Create and populate the field named `Subject`.

10.4 ADDING DATA

Example 10.2 gave a glimpse of the methods available for adding data to a `RichTextItem` object. The following methods are available for working with data in a `RichTextItem` object.

10.4.1 addNewLine

The `addNewLine` method can add any number of carriage returns to the body of a `RichTextItem` object. The current point in the object is used as the insertion point for the new line(s). There are three formats of the `addNewLine` method:

- `addNewLine`: Adds one carriage return
- `addNewLine(int)`: Adds the specified number of carriage returns
- `addNewLine(int, boolean)`: Adds the specified number of carriage returns. The second parameter signals true/false depending on whether or not a new paragraph separator is added before the carriage returns.

10.4.2 addPageBreak

The `addPageBreak` method adds a new page break to the body of a `RichTextItem`. There are two formats:

- `addPageBreak`: Adds one page break
- `addPageBreak(RichTextParagraphStyle)`: Adds a page break with the specified style

NOTE   The `RichTextParagraphStyle` class is covered later in this chapter.

10.4.3 addTab

The `addTab` method appends the specified number of tabs to a `RichTextItem` object. There are two formats of `addTab`:

- `addTab`: Appends one tab
- `addTab(int)`: Appends the specified number of tabs

10.4.4 appendDocLink

The `appendDocLink` method adds a doclink to a particular Domino object to the end of a `RichTextItem` object. There are three formats of the `appendDocLink` method:

- `appendDocLink(Object)`: Adds the specified link
- `appendDocLink(Object, String)`: Adds the specified link with the text to appear when a user presses and holds the mouse button on it

- appendDocLink(Object, String, String): Adds the specified link with the text to appear when the user presses and holds the mouse button on it, and the hotspot text that appears when the user actually selects the doclink

10.4.5   appendRTItem

The appendRTItem method appends the contents on one RichTextItem object to the end of another RichTextItem object. It has one format:

- appendRTItem(RichTextItem): Appends the specified RichTextItem to the end of the item

10.4.6   appendText

The appendText method appends the specified text to the end of a RichText-Item object:

```
appendText(String)
```

10.4.7   getFormattedText

The getFormattedText method retrieves the contents of a RichTextItem as plain text. The only format of the getFormattedText function accepts three parameters. The first parameter signals (true/false) depending on whether tabs should be stripped from the text. The second parameter specifies the number of characters at which a line is wrapped; it defaults to zero to be ignored. The last parameter signals the maximum number of characters to be returned; it defaults to zero, which sets the parameter to be ignored.

```
String = RichTextItem.getFormattedText(boolean, int, int)
```

Example 10.3   (Domino Agent)

```
import lotus.domino.*;
import java.util.*;

public class Example_10_3 extends AgentBase {
  public void NotesMain() {
    try {
      Session session = getSession();
      AgentContext ac = session.getAgentContext();
      Database db = ac.getCurrentDatabase();
      Document doc = db.createDocument();
      RichTextItem rtf = doc.createRichTextItem("Body");   ❶
      rtf.addNewLine(1);   ❷
      rtf.appendText("This is another new rich text item.");   ❸
      rtf.addPageBreak();   ❹
      rtf.addTab(1);   ❺
      rtf.appendText("This is a new page.");   ❻
      rtf.addNewLine(1);   ❼
      rtf.appendDocLink(db,"Parent DB Link","Parent DB Link");   ❽
      doc.replaceItemValue("Subject","Test");
```

```
        doc.save();
        doc.recycle();
        db.recycle();
        ac.recycle();
        session.recycle();
    } catch(Exception e) {
        e.printStackTrace();}}   }
```

Explanation

❶ Create a new rich text item on the `Document`.

❷ Add a carriage return to the rich text item.

❸ Append text to the rich text item.

❹ Add a page break to the rich text item.

❺ Add one tab to the rich text item.

❻ Append text following the tab.

❼ Add a carriage return after the text.

❽ Add a doclink to the current database at the end of the `Document`.

10.5   *RichTextStyle class*

Adding text, tabs, and carriage returns is good, but a `RichTextItem` provides so much more functionality. For example, when you compose a mail memo, you can set the font color, font face, and special effects such as bold, italics, or underline. The `RichTextStyle` class facilitates such effects.

Before you can set the attributes using the class, you must create the class. You can create it using the `createRichTextStyle` method of the `Session` class, and the `appendStyle` method of the `RichTextItem` class.

10.5.1   Bold

`Bold` is a read/write property that allows you to enable and disable boldfacing. It has the following possible values:

- RichTextStyle.YES enables bold.
- RichTextStyle.NO disables bold.
- RichTextStyle.STYLE_NO_CHANGE does nothing.
- RichTextStyle.MAYBE maintains the previous setting.

10.5.2   Color

`Color` is a read/write property that allows you to set and retrieve the color of text. It has the following possible values:

- RichTextStyle.COLOR_BLACK
- RichTextStyle.COLOR_BLUE

- RichTextStyle.COLOR_CYAN
- RichTextStyle.COLOR_DARK_BLUE
- RichTextStyle.COLOR_DARK_CYAN
- RichTextStyle.COLOR_DARK_GREEN
- RichTextStyle.COLOR_DARK_MAGENTA
- RichTextStyle.COLOR_DARK_RED
- RichTextStyle.COLOR_DARK_YELLOW
- RichTextStyle.COLOR_GRAY
- RichTextStyle.COLOR_GREEN
- RichTextStyle.COLOR_LIGHT_GRAY
- RichTextStyle.COLOR_MAGENTA
- RichTextStyle.COLOR_RED
- RichTextStyle.COLOR_WHITE
- RichTextStyle.COLOR_YELLOW
- RichTextStyle.COLOR_STYLE_NO_CHANGE does nothing.
- RichTextStyle.COLOR_MAYBE maintains the previous color.

10.5.3   Effects

Effects is a read/write property that can set/get one of a number of effects. It has the following possible values:

- RichTextStyle.EFFECTS_EMBOSS
- RichTextStyle.EFFECTS_EXTRUDE
- RichTextStyle.EFFECTS_NONE
- RichTextStyle.EFFECTS_SHADOW
- RichTextStyle.EFFECTS_SUBSCRIPT
- RichTextStyle.EFFECTS_SUPERSCRIPT
- RichTextStyle.EFFECTS_STYLE_NO_CHANGE does nothing.
- RichTextStyle.EFFECTS_MAYBE maintains previous effect(s).

10.5.4   Font

Font is a read/write property that allows you to set and retrieve the font for text. It has the following possible values:

- RichTextStyle.FONT_COURIER sets the font to Courier.
- RichTextStyle.FONT_HELV sets the font to Helvetica.
- RichTextStyle.FONT_ROMAN sets the font to Times New Roman.
- RichTextStyle.FONT_STYLE_NO_CHANGE does nothing.
- RichTextStyle.FONT_MAYBE maintains the previous font setting.

10.5.5   FontSize

FontSize is a read/write property that allows you to set and retrieve the size of the font. It has the following possible values:

- 1 to 250 is the integer that represents the desired point size.
- RichTextStyle.STYLE_NO_CHANGE does nothing.
- RichTextStyle.MAYBE maintains the previous setting.

10.5.6 Italic

`Italic` is a read/write property that allows you to enable and disable italics. It has the following possible values:

- RichTextStyle.YES enables italics.
- RichTextStyle.NO disables italics.
- RichTextStyle.STYLE_NO_CHANGE does nothing.
- RichTextStyle.MAYBE maintains the previous setting.

10.5.7 Parent

`Parent` is the session object that contains the `RichTextStyle` object.

```
Session = RichTextStyle.Parent
```

10.5.8 StrikeThrough

`StrikeThrough` is a read/write property that allows you to enable and disable strikethrough. It has the following possible values:

- RichTextStyle.YES enables strikethrough.
- RichTextStyle.NO disables strikethrough.
- RichTextStyle.STYLE_NO_CHANGE does nothing.
- RichTextStyle.MAYBE maintains the previous setting.

10.5.9 Underline

`Underline` is a read/write property that allows you to underline text. It has the following possible values:

- RichTextStyle.YES enables underlining.
- RichTextStyle.NO disables underlining.
- RichTextStyle.STYLE_NO_CHANGE does nothing.
- RichTextStyle.MAYBE maintains the previous setting.

Example 10.4 (Domino Agent)

```
import lotus.domino.*;
import java.util.*;

public class Example_10_4 extends AgentBase {
  public void NotesMain() {
    try {
      Session session = getSession();AgentContext ac = session.getAgentContext();
      Database db = ac.getCurrentDatabase();
      Document doc = db.createDocument();
      RichTextItem rtf = doc.createRichTextItem("Body"); ❶
```

```
            RichTextStyle rts = session.createRichTextStyle();  ➋
            rts.setBold(RichTextStyle.YES);  ➌
            rts.setItalic(RichTextStyle.NO);  ➍
            rts.setUnderline(RichTextStyle.YES);  ➎
            rts.setStrikeThrough(RichTextStyle.NO);  ➏
            rts.setColor(RichTextStyle.COLOR_DARK_BLUE);  ➐
            rts.setFont(RichTextStyle.FONT_COURIER);  ➑
            rts.setFontSize(12);  ➒
            rts.setPassThruHTML(RichTextStyle.NO);  ➓
            rtf.appendStyle(rts);  ⑪
            rtf.addNewLine(2);  ⑫
            rtf.appendText("This is more text to be added.");  ⑬
            rts.setColor(RichTextStyle.COLOR_RED);  ⑭
            rts.setFont(RichTextStyle.FONT_HELV);  ⑮
            rts.setItalic(RichTextStyle.YES);  ⑯
            rtf.appendStyle(rts);  ⑰
            rtf.addNewLine(1);  ⑱
            rtf.addTab(1);  ⑲
            rtf.appendText("More text to be added.");  ⑳
            doc.save();
            doc.recycle();
            db.recycle();
            ac.recycle();
            session.recycle();
        } catch(Exception e) {
            e.printStackTrace();}  }  }
```

Explanation

❶ Create a new RichTextItem on the current Document.

❷ Create a new RichTextStyle object using the Session object.

❸ Enable the bold setting of the RichTextStyle object.

❹ Disable the italic setting of the RichTextStyle object.

❺ Enable the underline setting of the RichTextStyle object.

❻ Disable the strikethrough setting of the RichTextStyle object.

❼ Set the color attribute of the RichTextStyle object to dark blue.

❽ Set the font face of the RichTextStyle object to Courier.

❾ Set the font size of the RichTextStyle object to 12.

❿ Disable the Pass-thru HTML attribute of the RichTextStyle object.

⑪ Apply the RichTextStyle object to the RichTextItem. All text after this point will have the specified style.

⑫ Add two carriage returns to the body of the RichTextItem.

⑬ Add text to the end of the RichTextItem.

⑭ Set the color attribute of the RichTextStyle object to red.

⑮ Set the font face of the `RichTextStyle` object to Helvetica.

⑯ Enable the italic setting of the `RichTextStyle` object.

⑰ Apply the changed `RichTextStyle` object to the `RichTextItem`. All text after this point will have the new style.

⑱ Add a carriage return to the end of the `RichTextItem`.

⑲ Add one tab to the current location of the `RichTextItem`.

⑳ Add the text to the end of the `RichTextItem`.

NOTE   Each `set` method has a corresponding `get` method for retrieving the attribute's setting.

10.6   *RICHTEXTPARAGRAPHSTYLE CLASS*

The `RichTextParagraphStyle` class formats the spacing of a paragraph within a rich text item. You can create this class using the `createRichTextParagraphStyle` method of the `Session` class, and apply it to a `RichTextItem` via its `appendParagraphStyle` method.

This class has the following properties that can be read or set via the corresponding `get`/`set` methods.

10.6.1   Alignment

`Alignment` is a read/write property that sets the horizontal alignment of the paragraph. It has the following possible values:

- RichTextParagraphStyle.ALIGN_CENTER
- RichTextParagraphStyle.ALIGN_FULL
- RichTextParagraphStyle.ALIGN_LEFT
- RichTextParagraphStyle.ALIGN_NOWRAP
- RichTextParagraphStyle.ALIGN_RIGHT

10.6.2   FirstLineLeftMargin

`FirstLineLeftMargin` is a read/write property that sets the left margin of the first line of the paragraph. It has the following possible values:

- RichTextParagraphStyle.RULER_ONE_CENTIMETER
- RichTextParagraphStyle.RULER_ONE_INCH

10.6.3   InterLineSpacing

`InterLineSpacing` is a read/write property that sets the spacing between individual lines in the paragraph. It has the following possible values:

- RichTextParagraphStyle.SPACING_DOUBLE
- RichTextParagraphStyle.SPACING_ONE_POINT_50
- RichTextParagraphStyle.SPACING_SINGLE

10.6.4 LeftMargin

`LeftMargin` is a read/write property that sets the left margin of each line in the paragraph. It has the following possible values:

- RichTextParagraphStyle.RULER_ONE_CENTIMETER
- RichTextParagraphStyle.RULER_ONE_INCH

10.6.5 Pagination

`Pagination` is a read/write property that determines how page breaks are handled in a paragraph. It has the following possible values:

- RichTextParagraphStyle.PAGINATE_BEFORE
- RichTextParagraphStyle.PAGINATE_DEFAULT
- RichTextParagraphStyle.PAGINATE_KEEP_TOGETHER
- RichTextParagraphStyle.PAGINATE_KEEP_WITH_NEXT

10.6.6 RightMargin

`RightMargin` is a read/write property that sets the right margin of each line in the paragraph. It has the following possible values:

- RichTextParagraphStyle.RULER_ONE_CENTIMETER
- RichTextParagraphStyle.RULER_ONE_INCH

10.6.7 SpacingAbove

`SpacingAbove` is a read/write property that sets the spacing above each paragraph. It has the following possible values:

- RichTextParagraphStyle.SPACING_DOUBLE
- RichTextParagraphStyle.SPACING_ONE_POINT_50
- RichTextParagraphStyle.SPACING_SINGLE

10.6.8 SpacingBelow

`SpacingBelow` is a read/write property that sets the spacing below each paragraph. It has the following possible values:

- RichTextParagraphStyle.SPACING_DOUBLE
- RichTextParagraphStyle.SPACING_ONE_POINT_50
- RichTextParagraphStyle.SPACING_SINGLE

Example 10.5   (Domino Agent)

```
import lotus.domino.*;
import java.util.*;

public class Example_10_5 extends AgentBase {
  public void NotesMain() {
    try {
      Session session = getSession();
```

```
        AgentContext ac = session.getAgentContext();
        Database db = ac.getCurrentDatabase();
        Document doc = db.createDocument();
        RichTextItem rtf = doc.createRichTextItem("Body");
        RichTextStyle rts = session.createRichTextStyle();        ❶
        rts.setBold(RichTextStyle.YES);        ❷
        rts.setItalic(RichTextStyle.NO);
        rts.setUnderline(RichTextStyle.YES);
        rts.setStrikeThrough(RichTextStyle.NO);
        rts.setColor(RichTextStyle.COLOR_DARK_BLUE);
        rts.setFont(RichTextStyle.FONT_COURIER);
        rts.setFontSize(12);
        rts.setPassThruHTML(RichTextStyle.NO);
        rtf.appendStyle(rts);        ❸
        RichTextParagraphStyle ps = session.createRichTextParagraphStyle();        ❹
        ps.setAlignment(RichTextParagraphStyle.ALIGN_FULL);        ❺
        if (ps.getFirstLineLeftMargin() != RichTextParagraphStyle.RULER_ONE_INCH) {        ❻
        ps.setFirstLineLeftMargin(RichTextParagraphStyle.RULER_ONE_INCH); }
        ps.setInterLineSpacing(RichTextParagraphStyle.SPACING_DOUBLE);        ❼
        ps.setLeftMargin(RichTextParagraphStyle.RULER_ONE_INCH);        ❽
        if (ps.getPagination() != RichTextParagraphStyle.PAGINATE_KEEP_TOGETHER) {        ❾
        ps.setPagination(RichTextParagraphStyle.PAGINATE_KEEP_TOGETHER); }
        ps.setRightMargin(RichTextParagraphStyle.RULER_ONE_INCH);        ❿
        ps.setSpacingAbove(RichTextParagraphStyle.SPACING_SINGLE);        ⓫
        ps.setSpacingBelow(RichTextParagraphStyle.SPACING_SINGLE);        ⓬
        rtf.addNewLine(2);
        rtf.appendParagraphStyle(ps);        ⓭
        rtf.appendText("This is more text to be added.");
        rts.setColor(RichTextStyle.COLOR_RED);
        rts.setFont(RichTextStyle.FONT_HELV);
        rts.setItalic(RichTextStyle.YES);
        rtf.addNewLine(1);
        rtf.addTab(1);
        rtf.appendText("More text to be added.");
        doc.save();
        doc.recycle();
        db.recycle();
        ac.recycle();
        session.recycle();
    } catch(Exception e) {
    e.printStackTrace();  } } }
```

Explanation

❶ Create a new RichTextStyle object for the RichTextItem.

❷ Enable the bold setting for the RichTextStyle class.

❸ Apply RichTextStyle to the RichTextItem.

❹ Create a new RichTextParagraphStyle object via the createRichTextParagraphStyle method of the Session class.

❺ Set the alignment property of `RichTextParagraphStyle` to full.

❻ Determine if the first line of the left margin property of the `RichTextParagraph-Style` object is one inch; if it is not, set it so.

❼ Set the spacing between lines in `RichTextParagraphStyle` to double.

❽ Set the left margin of `RichTextParagraphStyle` to one inch.

❾ Determine if the pagination setting of the `RichTextParagraphStyle` object is set to keep them together. If it is not, set it so.

❿ Set the right margin of the `RichTextParagraphStyle` object to one inch.

⓫ Set the spacing above paragraphs in the `RichTextParagraphStyle` object to single.

⓬ Set the spacing below paragraphs in the `RichTextParagraphStyle` object to single.

⓭ Apply the `RichTextParagraphStyle` object to the `RichTextItem`.

10.6.9 Tabs

Tabs is a `Vector` of `RichTextTab` objects containing all tabs in a paragraph:

```
Vector = RichTextParagraphStyle.getTabs();
```

It has the following methods.

10.6.10 clearAllTabs

The `clearAllTabs` method clears all tabs contained in a `RichTextParagraph-Style` object:

```
RichTextParagraphStyle.clearAllTabs();
```

10.6.11 setTab

The `setTab` method sets a tab in a `RichTextParagraphStyle` object. It accepts two parameters. The first parameter sets the position of the tab, and the second parameter is the type of tab.

```
RichTextParagraphStyle.setTab(position, type);
```

List of position values

- RichTextParagraphStyle.RULER_ONE_CENTIMETER
- RichTextParagraphStyle.RULER_ONE_INCH

List of type values

- RichTextParagraphStyle.TAB_CENTER
- RichTextParagraphStyle.TAB_DECIMAL
- RichTextParagraphStyle.TAB_LEFT
- RichTextParagraphStyle.TAB_RIGHT

10.6.12 setTabs

The setTabs method sets one or more tabs at even intervals throughout a RichTextParagraphStyle object:

```
RichTextParagraphStyle.setTabs(count, starting position, interval, optional type);
```

List of starting position values

- RichTextParagraphStyle.RULER_ONE_CENTIMETER
- RichTextParagraphStyle.RULER_ONE_INCH

List of interval values

- RichTextParagraphStyle.RULER_ONE_CENTIMETER
- RichTextParagraphStyle.RULER_ONE_INCH

List of type values

- RichTextParagraphStyle.TAB_CENTER
- RichTextParagraphStyle.TAB_DECIMAL
- RichTextParagraphStyle.TAB_LEFT
- RichTextParagraphStyle.TAB_RIGHT

Example 10.6 (Domino Agent)

```
import lotus.domino.*;
import java.util.*;
public class Example_10_6 extends AgentBase {
 public void NotesMain() {
   try {
     Session session = getSession();
     AgentContext ac = session.getAgentContext();
     Database db = ac.getCurrentDatabase();
     Document doc = db.createDocument();
     RichTextItem rtf = doc.createRichTextItem("Body");       ❶
     RichTextStyle rts = session.createRichTextStyle();       ❷
     RichTextParagraphStyle ps = session.createRichTextParagraphStyle();   ❸
     ps.clearAllTabs();   ❹
     ps.setTab(RichTextParagraphStyle.RULER_ONE_INCH, RichTextParagraphStyle.TAB_LEFT);   ❺
     rtf.appendParagraphStyle(ps);   ❻
     rtf.tab(1);   ❼
     rtf.appendText("Blah blah blah.......");   ❽
     doc.save();
     doc.recycle();
     db.recycle();
     ac.recycle();
     session.recycle();
   } catch(Exception e) {
     e.printStackTrace();  }  }  }
```

Explanation

❶ Create a new `RichTextItem` on the `Document`.

❷ Create a new `RichTextStyle` object via the `Session` class.

❸ Create a new `RichTextParagraphStyle` object via the `Session` class.

❹ Clear all tabs in the `RichTextParagraphStyle` object.

❺ Set a tab in the `RichTextParagraphStyle` object.

❻ Apply the `RichTextParagraphStyle` object to the `RichTextItem` object. All tabs will exist in the body of the item.

❼ Tab over one tab in the `RichTextItem`.

❽ Add text to the `RichTextItem` at the tabbed location.

10.7 *RICH TEXT TAB CLASS*

The `RichTextTab` class represents a tab in a `RichTextParagraphStyle` object.

You can create a `RichTextTab` object through the `getTabs` method of the `RichTextParagraphStyle` class, and set it via the `setTab` and `setTabs` methods of the `RichTextParagraphStyle` class:

```
RichTextTab = RichTextParagraphStyle.getTabs();
```

10.7.1 Properties

The `RichTextTab` class has only two properties: `position` and `type`.

10.7.2 Position

The `position` property returns the position of a tab as an integer.

10.7.3 Type

The `type` property returns the type of a tab.

List of type values

- RichTextParagraphStyle.TAB_CENTER
- RichTextParagraphStyle.TAB_DECIMAL
- RichTextParagraphStyle.TAB_LEFT
- RichTextParagraphStyle.TAB_RIGHT

10.7.4 Methods

The `RichTextTab` class has only one method: `clear`.

10.7.5 clear

The `clear` method clears a tab.

Example 10.7　(Domino Agent)

```
import lotus.domino.*;
import java.util.*;
public class Example_10_7 extends AgentBase {
 public void NotesMain() {
   try {
     Session session = getSession();
     AgentContext ac = session.getAgentContext();
     Database db = ac.getCurrentDatabase();
     Document doc = db.createDocument();
     RichTextItem rtf = doc.createRichTextItem("Body");
     RichTextStyle rts = session.createRichTextStyle();
     RichTextParagraphStyle ps = session.createRichTextParagraphStyle();   ❶
     ps.clearAllTabs();   ❷
     ps.setTab(RichTextParagraphStyle.RULER_ONE_INCH,
         RichTextParagraphStyle.TAB_LEFT);   ❸
     ps.setTab(RichTextParagraphStyle.RULER_ONE_INCH*10,
         RichTextParagraphStyle.TAB_LEFT);   ❹
     ps.setTab(RichTextParagraphStyle.RULER_ONE_INCH*20,
         RichTextParagraphStyle.TAB_LEFT);   ❺
     Vector tabs = ps.getTabs();   ❻
     System.out.println("There are " + tabs.size() + " tabs in the paragraph.");   ❼
     for (int i = 0; i < tabs.size(); i ++)   {   ❽
       RichTextTab rtt = (RichTextTab)tabs.elementAt(i);   ❾
       double centPosition = (rtt.getPosition() / 537);   ❿
       double inchPosition = (rtt.getPosition() / 1440);   ⓫
       System.out.print("Tab # " + i + " located at ");   ⓬
       System.out.print(centPosition + " centimeters and ");
       System.out.println(inchPosition + " inches.");
       rtt.clear();   }   ⓭
     rtf.appendParagraphStyle(ps);
     rtf.addTab(1);
     rtf.appendText("Blah blah blah...");
     doc.save();
     doc.recycle();
     db.recycle();
     ac.recycle();
     session.recycle();
   } catch(Exception e) {
     e.printStackTrace();} } }
```

Explanation

❶ Create a new RichTextParagraphStyle object via the Session object.

❷ Clear all existing tabs (if any) from the RichTextParagraphStyle object.

❸ Set a tab in the RichTextParagraphStyle object at 1 inch.

❹ Set a tab in the RichTextParagraphStyle object at 10 inches.

❺ Set a tab in the RichTextParagraphStyle object at 20 inches.

❻ Populate a Vector object containing all tabs from the RichTextParagraphStyle object in the form of RichTextTab objects.

❼ Display the number of tabs found in the `RichTextParagraphStyle` object.

❽ Loop through all tab elements via the `for` statement.

❾ Retrieve an element from the `Vector` object; explicitly cast it to a `RichTextTab` object.

❿ Convert the position of the tab to inches.

⓫ Convert the position of the tab to centimeters.

⓬ Display the tab number, position in inches, and position in centimeters.

⓭ Clear all of the tabs that were previously set.

NOTE Tab positions are returned in the form of twips. One centimeter is equal to 537 twips, and one inch is equal to 1440 twips.

Output
```
There are 3 tabs in the paragraph.
Tab # 0 located at 2.0 centimeters and 1.0 inches.
Tab # 1 located at 26.0 centimeters and 10.0 inches.
Tab # 2 located at 53.0 centimeters and 20.0 inches.
```

10.8 *EMBEDDEDOBJECT CLASS*

The `EmbeddedObject` class works with any embedded object in a `RichTextItem`. This can include attachments, OLE objects, Domino object links, and any other object. The class is not available on Unix-, OS/2-, and Macintosh-based systems.

10.8.1 Accessing embedded objects

You can access embedded objects via the `RichTextItem` and `Document` classes:

```
EmbeddedObject = RichTextItem.getEmbeddedObject("Name of the object");
Vector = RichTextItem.getEmbeddedObjects();
Vector = Document.getEmbeddedObjects();
```

10.8.2 Creating embedded objects

The `embedObject` method of the `RichTextItem` class creates new embedded objects in a rich text field:

```
EmbeddedObject = RichTextItem.embedObject(type, class, source, name);
```

List of possible values for the type property

- EmbeddedObject.EMBED_ATTACHMENT
- EmbeddedObject.EMBED_OBJECT
- EmbeddedObject.EMBED_OBJECTLINK

List of class property values

- Specify the name of the application when you embed an empty object (e.g. Microsoft Word).
- Specify an empty string when you embed an attachment or link to an object.

List of source property values

- Specify the name of the file when you embed a file.
- Specify the name of the file to attach or link.

List of name property values

Specify the unique name given to the embedded object. You can use this name later to access it.

10.8.3 Properties

- ClassName: The name of the application used to create the object. A value of null is returned for attachments.
- FileSize: The size of a file attachment in bytes
- Name: The name assigned to the embedded object
- Object: A handle to an embedded OLE object
- Parent: The RichTextItem object that contains the embedded object
- Source: The internal name given to the embedded object; the original file name when accessed for attachments
- Type: Signals whether an embedded object is an object, link, or attachment
- Verbs: Vector of verbs supported by the embedded object; only applicable to OLE objects

10.8.4 Methods

- activate: Loads an OLE object or link
- doVerb: Executes a valid verb for an OLE object. Valid verbs are accessible in the Verbs property.
- extractFile: Saves an attached file to a network or local drive
- remove: Deletes an EmbeddedObject object from a RichTextItem object. The document containing objects must be saved for the deletion to take effect.

10.8.5 OLE

The original support for OLE (Object Linking and Embedding) was introduced in Lotus Notes version 4.0 through the back-end classes before the Domino HTTP server task was introduced in version 4.5. Full support for OLE currently exists on the Microsoft Windows platform when you're using the Notes Client or via the Agent Manager on a server via a background agent. Both executables (on the Notes Client and Domino Server) require special code to make OLE work correctly.

When you invoke an agent through an Internet address (URL), the executable in control of things is the HTTP server task, not the agent manager or the Client. OLE does not work through the back-end Domino Java classes.

10.8.6　Attachments

An attachment is a file that is physically inserted into a document. You can only insert a file attachment into a RichTextItem object. You can insert a file from the Lotus Notes client via the File | Attach drop-down menu. Web users can take advantage of the Web upload control to attach files to a Web document.

You can create attachments through the Domino Java classes as well, using the embedObject method of the RichTextItem class:

```
EmbeddedObject = RichTextItem.embedObject(RichTextItem.EMBED_ATTACHMENT,
"", "filename", "Unique identifying name/title");
```

Example 10.8　(Domino Agent)

```
import lotus.domino.*;
import java.util.*;
public class Example_10_8 extends AgentBase {
 public void NotesMain() {
  try {
    Session session = getSession();
    AgentContext ac = session.getAgentContext();
    Database db = ac.getCurrentDatabase();
    Document doc = db.createDocument();
    doc.replaceItemValue("Form","frmExample");
    doc.replaceItemValue("keyChapter","Test_10_8");
    doc.replaceItemValue("keyExample","Test_10_8");
    RichTextItem rtf = doc.createRichTextItem("rtfCode");    ❶
    int att = EmbeddedObject.EMBED_ATTACHMENT;    ❷
    rtf.embedObject(att,"","d:\\jk\\ch10\\Ex_10_8.java","Java");    ❸
    doc.save();
    doc.recycle();
    db.recycle();
    ac.recycle();
    session.recycle();
  } catch(Exception e) {
    e.printStackTrace();} }  }
```

Explanation

❶ Create a new RichTextItem object.

❷ Store the EMBED_ATTACHMENT value in a variable.

❸ Embed a file in the RichTextItem object via the embedObject method of the RichTextItem class. The escape character (\) is needed to include a backslash in the string.

Example 10.9 shows how to access an embedded object on a Document

Example 10.9   (Domino Agent)

```
import lotus.domino.*;
import java.util.*;
import java.io.PrintWriter;
public class Example_10_9 extends AgentBase {
 public void NotesMain() {
   try {
     Session session = getSession();
     PrintWriter pw = getAgentOutput();
     AgentContext ac = session.getAgentContext();
     Database db = ac.getCurrentDatabase();
     View vw = db.getView("Examples \\ by Chapter");
     ViewNavigator vn = vw.createViewNav();
     ViewEntry ve = vn.getFirstDocument();
     while (ve != null)   {
       Document doc = (Document)ve.getDocument();
       if (doc.hasEmbedded()) {  ❶
         if (doc.hasItem("rtfCode")) {  ❷
           RichTextItem eortf = (RichTextItem)doc.getFirstItem("rtfCode");  ❸
           Vector eoV = eortf.getEmbeddedObjects();  ❹
           for (int i = 0; i < eoV.size(); i ++) {  ❺
             EmbeddedObject eo = (EmbeddedObject)eoV.elementAt(i);  ❻
             if (eo.getType() == EmbeddedObject.EMBED_ATTACHMENT) {  ❼
               RichTextItem rtf = eo.getParent();  ❽
               pw.print("The item named " + rtf.getName());  ❾
               pw.print(" contains an attachment named ");
               pw.print(eo.getName()  + " with a size of ");
               pw.println(eo.getFileSize());
         } } } }
       ve.recycle();
       doc.recycle();
       ve = vn.getNextDocument();      }
     vn.recycle();
     vw.recycle();
     db.recycle();
     ac.recycle();
     session.recycle();
   } catch(Exception e) {
     e.printStackTrace();}   }   }
```

Explanation

❶ Determine if the Document contains any embedded objects before proceeding.

❷ Determine that the field you want exists before proceeding.

❸ Create a RichTextItem object containing the rtfCode field.

❹ Create a Vector containing all embedded objects in the rich text field.

❺ Loop through each object in the Vector.

➏ Retrieve an object from the `Vector` using the loop index. The object is explicitly cast to an `EmbeddedObject`.

➐ Determine if the object is an attachment.

➑ Create a `RichTextItem` containing the parent item of the attachment. This serves no purpose other than demonstration, since we already have the object set.

➒ Print the results of our find.

Output (for one Document)

```
The item named rtfCode contains an attachment named Example_10_8.java with a
size of 790
```

10.8.7 Creating a link object

Creating a linked object is a bit different than creating an attachment. An attachment is stored in the document container, but linked objects are not. With linked objects, changes are made to the actual file, so any changes are reflected when you launch the file via Notes.

```
EmbeddedObject = RichTextItem.embedObject(RichTextItem.EMBED_OBJECTLINK,
"", "filename", "Unique identifying name/title");
```

The format for creating a link is the same as that for an attachment.

Example 10.10   (Domino Agent)

```
import lotus.domino.*;
import java.util.*;
public class Example_10_10 extends AgentBase {
 public void NotesMain() {
   try {
     Session session = getSession();
     AgentContext ac = session.getAgentContext();
     Database db = ac.getCurrentDatabase();
     Document doc = db.createDocument();
     doc.replaceItemValue("Form","frmExample");
     doc.replaceItemValue("keyChapter","Test_10_10");
     doc.replaceItemValue("keyExample","Test_10_10");
     RichTextItem rtf = doc.createRichTextItem("rtfCode");   ➊
     int att = EmbeddedObject.EMBED_OBJECTLINK;   ➋
     rtf.embedObject(att,"","d:\\jk\\ch10\\Ex108.java","Java");   ➌
      doc.save();
     doc.recycle();
     db.recycle();
     ac.recycle();
     session.recycle();
   } catch(Exception e) {
     e.printStackTrace();} } }
```

Explanation

❶ Create a new `RichTextItem` on the `Document`.

❷ Store the object link constant in an integer variable.

❸ Embed a link to a file in the `RichTextItem` object.

10.8.8 Deleting objects

The `remove` method of the `EmbeddedObject` class handles the task of removing embedded objects from a document. Example 10.11 demonstrates how to remove all objects from every document in a view.

Example 10.11   (Domino Agent)

```
import lotus.domino.*;
import java.util.*;
public class Example_10_11 extends AgentBase {
 public void NotesMain() {
  try {
   Session session = getSession();
   AgentContext ac = session.getAgentContext();
   Database db = ac.getCurrentDatabase();
   View vw = db.getView("Examples \\ by Chapter");
   ViewNavigator vn = vw.createViewNav();
   ViewEntry ve = vn.getFirstDocument();
   EmbeddedObject eo;
   Item cur;
   RichTextItem rtf;
   while (ve != null)   {
    Document doc = (Document)ve.getDocument();
    if (doc.hasEmbedded()) {
     Vector items = doc.getItems();       ❶
     for (int x = 0; x < items.size(); x ++) {   ❷
      cur = (Item)items.elementAt(x);     ❸
      if (cur.getType() == RichTextItem.RICHTEXT) {   ❹
       rtf = (RichTextItem)cur;    ❺
       Vector v = rtf.getEmbeddedObjects();   ❻
       for (int i=0; i < v.size(); i ++) {   ❼
        eo = (EmbeddedObject)v.elementAt(i);    ❽
        eo.remove(); } } }   }    ❾
     // Caution using the next line in the sample database.
     // If it is run in the sample database,
     // all attachments (code) will be removed.
     // doc.save();
     // doc.recycle();
     ve.recycle();
     ve = vn.getNextDocument();      }
   vw.recycle();
   vn.recycle();
   db.recycle();
   ac.recycle();
   session.recycle();
  } catch(Exception e) {
   e.printStackTrace();} } }
```

Explanation

❶ Populate a `Vector` object with all `Item` objects from the `Document` object.

❷ Loop through all objects in the `Vector`.

❸ Retrieve an `Item` from the `Vector` using the loop index. The object is explicitly cast to an `Item` object.

❹ Determine if the `Item` object is a `RichTextItem` object.

❺ If it is a `RichTextItem` object, cast it to a `RichTextItem` object.

❻ Populate a `Vector` with all `EmbeddedObject` objects in the `RichTextItem` object.

❼ Loop through all objects in the `Vector`.

❽ Retrieve an `EmbeddedObject` from the `Vector` using the loop index. The object is explicitly cast to a `RichTextItem` object.

❾ Delete the `EmbeddedObject` object from the `RichTextItem` object, thus removing it from the `Document`. You must save the document for the change to take effect.

10.9 CHAPTER REVIEW

A rich text field on a Notes form provides the most flexibility to users. It allows them to type an endless amount of text. Users can format text with such attributes as color, font face, and other special effects. In addition, they can set the spacing of the paragraph and tabs. If that is not enough, they can embed, link, or attach almost any type of file/object to a rich text field as well. This flexibility may provide a user power, but it adds a tremendous overhead for developers when they work with the data stored in these items. Luckily, a number of classes available in the Domino Java classes make the job much easier.

- You should use the `RichTextItem` object when you are unsure of the type of data to be entered and stored in a field. A rich text field can store anything from regular text to file attachments.

- The `RichTextItem` class is derived from the `Item` class, so all methods in it are available in the `RichTextItem` class.

- The `getFirstItem` method of the `Document` class allows access to a `RichTextItem`. The return type should be cast.

- The `RichTextItem` class contains numerous methods for adding text, carriage returns, and so forth to the body of the `RichTextItem` object.

- The `RichTextStyle` class facilitates manipulating of attributes such as font color, font style, and special effects such as boldface, italics, or underlining.

- The `applyStyle` method of the `RichTextItem` class applies a `RichTextStyle` object to the body of a `RichTextItem` object.

- The `RichTextParagraphStyle` class can format the spacing of a paragraph within a rich text item. Apply it to a `RichTextItem` object via the `applyRichTextParagraphStyle` method of the `RichTextItem` class.

- The `RichTextTab` class represents a tab in a `RichTextParagraphStyle` object.

- The `EmbeddedObject` class works with any embedded object in a `RichTextItem`.

- An `EmbeddedObject` object can include attachment, OLE objects, Domino object links, and most any other object.

- You can remove objects from a `RichTextItem` object via the `remove` method of the `EmbeddedObject` class.

C H A P T E R   1 1

Working with collections

11.1 What is a collection? 130

11.2 DocumentCollection class 130

11.3 Creating a DocumentCollection object 131

11.4 Properties 131

11.5 Accessing documents in a collection 132

11.6 Refining a collection 135

11.7 Adding/removing a document to/from a collection 136

11.8 Working with folders 138

11.9 Updating documents in a collection 139

11.10 stampAll 139

11.11 Working with profiled documents 140

11.12 Sorting a collection 140

11.13 Newsletter class 143

11.14 Chapter review 143

11.1   WHAT IS A COLLECTION?

A document collection resembles a `Vector` or `Enumeration` object. It is an object that contains a group of documents assembled using various methods in the Domino Java classes. A collection of documents can be formed with all documents from a database, a subset of documents from a view, a group of profile documents, all of a document's responses, or as the result of a search.

11.2   DOCUMENTCOLLECTION CLASS

The `DocumentCollection` class works with collections of documents in the Domino Java classes. It contains a few properties and a number of methods for working with documents in the collection. You can instantiate a `DocumentCollection` object in any one of a variety of ways.

130

11.3   CREATING A DOCUMENTCOLLECTION OBJECT

The `AgentContext, Database, Document,` and `View` classes all provide the means to create a `DocumentCollection` object. They have the following formats:

* `DocumentCollection = AgentContext.getUnprocessedDocuments();`
* `DocumentCollection=AgentContext.UnprocessedFTSearch` ("Search Query", maximum returned);
* `DocumentCollection = AgentContext.UnprocessedSearch` ("Search formula", DateTime cutoff, maximum returned);
* `DocumentCollection = Document.getResponses();`
* `DocumentCollection = Database.FTSearch` ("Search Query", maximum returned);
* `DocumentCollection = Database.getAllDocuments();`
* `DocumentCollection = Database.getProfileDocCollection` ("Profile name"):
* `DocumentCollection = Database.search` ("Search formula", DateTime cutoff, maximum returned);
* `DocumentCollection = View.getAllDocumentsByKey` (Vector/Object key value, boolean exact match);

We will explore a number of the formats in the various examples in this chapter and throughout the rest of the book.

11.4   PROPERTIES

A number of properties in the `DocumentCollection` class prove invaluable when you work with a collection of documents.

11.4.1   Count

The `getCount` method returns the number of documents in a `DocumentCollection` object:

```
DocumentCollection dc = db.getAllDocuments();
for (int x = 1; x < dc.getCount(); x ++)   {
  Document doc = dc.getNthDocument(x);   }
```

11.4.2   isSorted

The `isSorted` property signals true/false depending on whether or not a `DocumentCollection` object is sorted. It will be sorted only when it is returned as the result of a full text search. The next snippet of code will return "true" for this property:

```
DocumentCollection dc = db.FTSearch("FIELD FORM=\"Test\"", 0);
if (dc.isSorted()) {
  System.out.println("The collection is sorted.");   }
```

11.4.3 Parent

The `parent` property of the `DocumentCollection` object returns a `Database` object containing the `DocumentCollection` object:

```
Session s = getSession();
AgentContext ac = s.getAgentContext();
DocumentCollection dc = ac.getUnprocessedDocuments()
Database dcParent = dc.getParent();
```

11.4.4 Query

The query property of a `DocumentCollection` object represents the query used to assemble a collection. It returns a value for only those `DocumentCollection` objects formed from a full text search or regular search.

```
DocumentCollection dc = db.FTSearch("FIELD FORM=\"Test\"", 0);
String query = dc.getQuery();
```

11.5 ACCESSING DOCUMENTS IN A COLLECTION

You can use a number of methods available in the `DocumentCollection` class to access individual documents in a collection. They allow you to move forward, backward, to the first document, to the last document, and to a specified document in the collection. Let's take a closer look at these methods.

11.5.1 getDocument

The `getDocument` method searches a collection for the specified `Document` object. It accepts only one parameter: the `Document` to find. A null value is returned if the `Document` is not found. This method is useful for comparing collections and determining if documents in one collection are in the other.

```
Document = DocumentCollection.getDocument(Document);
```

11.5.2 getFirstDocument

The `getFirstDocument` method retrieves the first `Document` object from a collection. It accepts no parameters and returns a null value if the collection is empty.

```
Document = DocumentCollection.getFirstDocument();
```

11.5.3 getLastDocument

The `getLastDocument` method retrieves the last `Document` object from a collection. It accepts no parameters and returns a null value if the collection is empty.

```
Document = DocumentCollection.getLastDocument();
```

11.5.4 getNextDocument

The `getNextDocument` method retrieves the next `Document` object from a collection using the `Document` object passed into it as the reference point. A null value is returned if there are no more documents in the collection.

```
Document = DocumentCollection.getNextDocument(Document);
```

Example 11.1 uses the `getDocument`, `getFirstDocument`, and `getNextDocument` methods to determine how many documents are in two different collections.

Example 11.1   (Domino Agent)

```
import lotus.domino.*;
import java.util.*;
import java.io.PrintWriter;
public class Example_11_1 extends AgentBase {
  public void NotesMain() {
    try {
      Session session = getSession();
      PrintWriter pw = getAgentOutput();
      AgentContext ac = session.getAgentContext();
      Database db = ac.getCurrentDatabase();
      DocumentCollection dc1 = db.FTSearch("In Review",0);   ❶
      DocumentCollection dc2 = db.FTSearch("Bobby Abreu",0);
      Document doc1 = dc1.getFirstDocument();   ❷
      int matches = 0;   ❸
      while (doc1 != null)  {  ❹
        Document doc2 = dc2.getDocument(doc1);   ❺
        if (doc2 != null)  {  ❻
          matches += 1;  }  ❼
        doc2.recycle();
        doc1 = dc1.getNextDocument(doc1);  }  ❽
      pw.print("There are " + matches + " documents ");
      pw.println("that are in both collections.");
      dc1.recycle();
      dc2.recycle();
      db.recycle();
      ac.recycle();
      session.recycle();
    } catch(Exception e) {
      e.printStackTrace();}  }  }
```

Explanation

❶ Create a `DocumentCollection` object via the `FTSearch` method of the `Database` class.

❷ Retrieve the first `Document` object from the first `DocumentCollection` object.

❸ Initialize the counter variable to zero.

❹ Loop through all documents in the collection via a `while` loop.

❺ Use the `getDocument` method of the `DocumentCollection` class to determine if the `Document` from the first collection is in the second collection.

❻ A non-null value is returned if a match is found.

❼ Increment our counter of the number of matches found.

❽ Retrieve the next `Document` object from the `DocumentCollection` object.

Output

There are 0 documents that are in both collections.

11.5.5   getNthDocument

The getNthDocument method retrieves a Document object from a collection using its location within the collection. A null value is returned if there is no document at the specified position within the collection. This method is often used with the getCount method and a for loop to traverse all elements of the collection.

```
Document = DocumentCollection.getNthDocument(int);
```

Example 11.2   (Domino Agent)

```
import lotus.domino.*;
import java.util.*;
import java.io.PrintWriter;
public class Example_11_2 extends AgentBase {
  public void NotesMain() {
    try {
      Session session = getSession();
      PrintWriter pw = getAgentOutput();
      AgentContext ac = session.getAgentContext();
      Database db = ac.getCurrentDatabase();
      DocumentCollection dc = db.getAllDocuments();   ❶
      for (int i = 0; i < dc.getCount(); i ++)  {   ❷
        Document doc = dc.getNthDocument(i);   ❸
        pw.println("Document NoteID:  " + doc.getNoteID());   ❹
        doc.recycle();}
      dc.recycle();
      db.recycle():
      ac.recycle();
      session.recycle();
    } catch(Exception e) {
      e.printStackTrace();}  }  }
```

Explanation

❶ Create a DocumentCollection object containing all documents from the database.

❷ Loop through the DocumentCollection object using a for loop and the getCount method.

❸ Retrieve a Document object from the collection via the getNthDocument method and the loop index.

❹ Display the NoteID for the retrieved Document object.

11.5.6 getPrevDocument

The getPrevDocument method retrieves the previous Document object from a collection using the Document object passed into it as the reference point. A null value is returned if there are no more documents in the collection.

```
Document = DocumentCollection.getPrevDocument(Document);
```

11.6 REFINING A COLLECTION

Implementing its FTSearch method can further refine a DocumentCollection object. This method searches a collection for the specified query. After calling the method, the DocumentCollection object will contain only those documents returned as a result of the full-text search.

```
DocumentCollection.FTSearch("Query", optional maximum number of matches to return);
```

Example 11.3 demonstrates the syntax and use of the FTSearch method.

Example 11.3   (Domino Agent)

```
import lotus.domino.*;
import java.util.*;
import java.io.PrintWriter;
public class Example_11_3 extends AgentBase {
  public void NotesMain() {
    try {
      Session session = getSession();
      PrintWriter pw = getAgentOutput();
      AgentContext ac = session.getAgentContext();
      Database db = ac.getCurrentDatabase();
      DocumentCollection dc = db.getAllDocuments();   ❶
      pw.print("There are " + dc.getCount());   ❷
      pw.println(" documents in the database.");
      dc.FTSearch("Julius Erving",0);   ❸
      pw.print("There were " + dc.getCount());   ❹
      pw.println(" documents returned from the search.");
      dc.recycle();
      db.recycle();
      ac.recycle();
      session.recycle();
    } catch(Exception e) {
      e.printStackTrace();}  }  }
```

Explanation

❶ Assemble a DocumentCollection object containing all documents in the database.

❷ Display the number of documents in the database via the getCount method.

❸ Refine the DocumentCollection object via the FTSearch method. This will remove all documents that do not match the search query from the DocumentCollection object.

❹ Display the number of documents left in the DocumentCollection object after the search.

Output

There are 20 documents in the database.
There were 0 documents returned from the search.

11.7 ADDING/REMOVING A DOCUMENT TO/FROM A COLLECTION

The DocumentCollection object provides two methods for adding and/or removing Document objects from it. The FTSearch method allows a collection to be pared down by a search, but you may want to remove only one Document or add one as well. The addDocument method allows a Document object to be added to a DocumentCollection object, and the deleteDocument method deletes a Document object from a DocumentCollection object.

11.7.1 addDocument

The addDocument method accepts one required parameter and one optional parameter. The first specifies the Document object to be added. The second parameter applies to IIOP applications; it is a boolean value that signals whether or not the system should perform an immediate check for duplicates before performing the add procedure.

NOTE An exception is thrown if a duplicate is found in the Document-Collection object.

```
DocumentCollection.addDocument(Document);
```

11.7.2 deleteDocument

The deleteDocument method accepts one and only one parameter, the Document object to be removed. An exception is thrown if the Document cannot be found in the collection or if it has already been deleted. Use the getDocument method to avoid an exception.

```
DocumentCollection.deleteDocument(Document);
```

Example 11.4 illustrates the use of both the deleteDocument and addDocument methods. The code is not of practical use, but it gives a good demonstration of the use and syntax of the methods.

Example 11.4   (Domino Agent)

```
import lotus.domino.*;
import java.util.*;
public class Example_11_4 extends AgentBase {
  public void NotesMain() {
    try {
      Session session = getSession();
      AgentContext ac = session.getAgentContext();
      Database db = ac.getCurrentDatabase();
      View vw = db.getView("Examples \\ by Chapter");
      Document doc = vw.getDocumentByKey("Test",false);    ❶
      DocumentCollection dc = db.getAllDocuments();    ❷
      if (doc != null) {    ❸
        Document docFound = dc.getDocument(doc);    ❹
        if (docFound != null) {    ❺
          dc.deleteDocument(doc);    }
        else   {
          dc.addDocument(doc);    }   }    ❻
      dc.recycle();
      doc.recycle();
      vw.recycle();
      db.recycle();
      ac.recycle();
      session.recycle();
    } catch(Exception e) {
      e.printStackTrace();}    }    }
```

Explanation

❶ Retrieve a Document object from a View.

❷ Create a DocumentCollection object containing all documents in the Database object.

❸ We will proceed only if the Document from the View exists; a null Document object passed to the getDocument method will throw an exception. We want to avoid this.

❹ Search for the Document object from the View in the DocumentCollection object.

❺ Delete the Document object from the DocumentCollection object, if it is found.

❻ Add the Document object to the DocumentCollection object, if it is not found.

11.8 WORKING WITH FOLDERS

I stated earlier that the Domino Java classes treat a View and Folder the same when you work with them in code. This is true, but a number of unique methods exist throughout the classes for use only with a folder. Documents are displayed in a view via a selection formula, whereas a folder has Document objects placed into it either through code or via user interaction. There is no selection formula for a folder.

The DocumentCollection class provides two methods for working with folders. The putAllInFolder method places all Document objects in a DocumentCollection object into a specific folder. The removeAllFromFolder removes all Document objects in a DocumentCollection object from a specific folder. These methods do not delete or add documents to a database; they just place or remove them from a folder. Folders contain pointers to Document objects, not the objects themselves.

The methods' syntax is as follows:

```
DocumentCollection.putAllInFolder("folder name", boolean);
DocumentCollection.removeAllFromFolder("folder name");
```

NOTE The putAllInFolder method accepts an optional second parameter that specifies whether the specified folder should be created if it does not exist. The removeAllFromFolder method does nothing if the folder does not exist or does not contain the documents.

Example 11.5 (Domino Agent)

```
import lotus.domino.*;
import java.util.*;
public class Example_11_5 extends AgentBase {
 public void NotesMain() {
   try {
     Session session = getSession();
     AgentContext ac = session.getAgentContext();
     Database db = ac.getCurrentDatabase();
     DocumentCollection dc = db.getAllDocuments();     ❶
     dc.FTSearch("Chapter 11");     ❷
     dc.putAllInFolder("Chapter 11");     ❸
     dc.removeAllFromFolder("Temp");     ❹
     dc.recycle();
     db.recycle();
     ac.recycle();
     session.recycle();
   } catch(Exception e) {
     e.printStackTrace();}   }   }
```

Explanation

❶ Create a `DocumentCollection` object containing all documents in the database.

❷ Refine the `DocumentCollection` object.

❸ Put all of the `Document` objects in the chapter 11 folder.

❹ Remove all of the `Document` objects from the Temp folder.

11.9 UPDATING DOCUMENTS IN A COLLECTION

Many agents are triggered by specific events, such as new documents being created, edited, or mailed into the database. For this reason, a `Document` object must be marked as processed when an agent "'touches" it. This ensures that the agent will not process the `Document` again and again in an endless loop. The `DocumentCollection` class provides the `updateAll` method to handle this task:

```
DocumentCollection.updateAll();
```

The `updateAll` method marks all `Document` objects in a collection as processed. The `updateProcessedDoc` method in the `AgentContext` class marks a specific `Document` as processed. The next two snippets of code perform the same tasks:

```
Session session = getSession();
AgentContext ac = session.getAgentContext();
DocumentCollection dc = ac.getUnprocessedDocuments();
dc.updateAll();
```

or

```
Session session = getSession();
AgentContext ac = session.getAgentContext();
DocumentCollection dc = ac.getUnprocessedDocuments();
for (int x = 0; x < dc.getCount(); x ++) {
ac.updateProcessedDoc(dc.getNthDocument(x));   }
```

11.10 STAMPALL

The `stampAll` method of the `DocumentCollection` class is a very nice feature for streamlining the updating of a particular field on a set of `Document` objects. It places a value in a specific field on all documents in a collection. The great part is that the documents do not have to be saved for the changes to take effect; changes are handled by the system. Also, the specified field is created if it does not already exist.

```
DocumentCollection.stampAll("field/item name",value);
```

The next two snippets of code perform the same task. Notice how much shorter/cleaner the `stampAll` method is.

```
Session s = getSession();
AgentContext ac = s.getAgentContext();
Database db = ac.getCurrentDatabase();
DocumentCollection dc = db.getAllDocuments();
dc.StampAll("Status","Done");
```

or

```
Session s = getSession();
AgentContext ac = s.getAgentContext();
Database db = ac.getCurrentDatabase();
DocumentCollection dc = db.getAllDocuments();
Document doc = dc.getFirstDocument();
while (doc != null)  {
doc.replaceItemValue("Status","Done");
doc.save();
doc = dc.getNextDocument(doc);   }
```

11.11 WORKING WITH PROFILED DOCUMENTS

The Database class provides a method for working with a collection of profile documents. The method, called getProfileDocCollection, returns a DocumentCollection object. It accepts one parameter, the name of the profile. An empty DocumentCollection object is returned if there are no matching profiles.

Example 11.6   (Domino Agent)

```
import lotus.domino.*;
import java.util.*;
public class Example_11_6 extends AgentBase {
 public void NotesMain() {
   try {
     Session session = getSession();
     AgentContext ac = session.getAgentContext();
     Database db = ac.getCurrentDatabase();
     DocumentCollection dc = db.getProfileDocCollection("User Profile"); ❶
     if (dc.getCount() > 0) { ❷
       dc.stampAll("ExpiresDate","1/1/2001"); } ❸
     dc.recycle();
     db.recycle();
     ac.recycle();
     session.recycle();
   } catch(Exception e) {
     e.printStackTrace();} } }
```

Explanation

❶ Create a DocumentCollection object containing all "User Profile" profile documents from the Database.

❷ Proceed only if the DocumentCollection object is not empty.

❸ Populate/create the field called ExpiresDate on each Document object in the collection.

11.12 SORTING A COLLECTION

A DocumentCollection object is sorted only when it is returned from a full-text search. There is no built-in method for sorting it, so we must create our own routine.

Example 11.7 will sort Document objects in a collection using a field called LastName. You can change the sort field and utilize it for your own needs. The example takes advantage of the Vector, DocumentCollection, and Document objects. Let's take a look at the code.

Example 11.7   (Domino Agent)

```
import lotus.domino.*;
import java.util.*;
import java.io.PrintWriter;
public class Example_11_7 extends AgentBase {
 public void NotesMain() {
  try {
   Session session = getSession();
   PrintWriter pw = getAgentOutput();
   AgentContext ac = session.getAgentContext();
   Database db = ac.getCurrentDatabase();
   DocumentCollection dc = db.getAllDocuments();
   if (dc.getCount() > 0)  {
    Document[] adocs = new Document[dc.getCount()];    ❶
    int count = 0;    ❷
    Document doc = dc.getFirstDocument();    ❸
    pw.println("-----------------------------------------");
    pw.println("                  Before Sorting              ");
    pw.println("-----------------------------------------");
    while (doc != null) {
     adocs[count] = doc;    ❹
     count++;    ❺
     pw.print("Last Name:   ");
     pw.println(doc.getItemValueString("LastName"));
     doc = dc.getNextDocument(doc);  }    ❻
    // Start Bubble Sort Routine    ❼
    for (int y = 0; y < adocs.length; y ++) {
     for (int x = 0; x < (adocs.length - y - 1); x++) {
      Document temp1 = (Document)adocs[x];
      Document temp2 = (Document)adocs[x+1];
      String temp3 = temp1.getItemValueString("LastName");
      String temp4 = temp2.getItemValueString("LastName");
      if (temp4.toString().compareTo(temp3.toString()) < 0)  {
       adocs[x] = temp2;
       adocs[x + 1] = temp1;  } } }
     // End Bubble Sort Routine
     pw.println("-----------------------------------------");
     pw.println("                  After Sorting               ");
     pw.println("-----------------------------------------");
     for (int i = 0; i < adocs.length; i ++)  {
      pw.print("Last Name:   ");    ❽
      pw.println(adocs[i].getItemValueString("LastName"));}  }
    dc.recycle();
    db.recycle();
    ac.recycle();
    session.recycle();
   }catch(Exception e) {
    e.printStackTrace();}  }  }
```

Explanation

❶ Create a new array of Document objects. The size of the array is set to the size of the
DocumentCollection object.

❷ Initialize our count variable to zero.

❸ Retrieve the first Document object from the DocumentCollection object.

❹ Add the Document object to the array using the count variable as the index.

❺ Increment the count variable.

❻ Retrieve the next Document object.

❼ The bubble routine code is placed between the two comment lines. Java comment
lines can start with double forward slashes. The bubble sort is not the most efficient
sort routine, so it could easily be replaced by other routines, such as the quicksort.
The bubble sort compares adjacent values in the array with the smaller values "bub-
bling" to the top of the array.

❽ Use a for loop to print the sorted contents of the array.

Output

```
- - - - - - - - - - - - - - - - - - - - - - - - - - - - - - - - - - - - - - - - - - - - - - - -
        Before Sorting            .
- - - - - - - - - - - - - - - - - - - - - - - - - - - - - - - - - - - - - - - - - - - - - - - -

Last Name:   Jones
Last Name:   Patton
Last Name:   Hamilton
Last Name:   Zeus
Last Name:   Ackerman
Last Name:   Williams
Last Name:   Smith
Last Name:   Hall
Last Name:   Spotts
Last Name:   Erving


- - - - - - - - - - - - - - - - - - - - - - - - - - - - - - - - - - - - - - - - - - - - - - - -
        After Sorting
- - - - - - - - - - - - - - - - - - - - - - - - - - - - - - - - - - - - - - - - - - - - - - - -

Last Name:   Ackerman
Last Name:   Erving
Last Name:   Hall
Last Name:   Hamilton
Last Name:   Jones
Last Name:   Patton
Last Name:   Smith
Last Name:   Spotts
Last Name:   Williams
Last Name:   Zeus
```

CHAPTER 11   WORKING WITH COLLECTIONS

11.13 NEWSLETTER CLASS

Another topic that deserves a bit of attention in a discussion of the `DocumentCollection` class is the `Newsletter` class. The `Newsletter` class allows a group of related documents to be sent via email to a user's mailbox. The `Newsletter` class takes a collection and mails a document with details about all documents in the collection. The group of documents is in the form of a `DocumentCollection` object. It is created using the `createNewsletter` method of the `Session` class and returns the newly created `Newsletter` object.

```
Newsletter = Session.createNewsletter(DocumentCollection);
```

Chapter 19 covers the `Newsletter` class in greater detail.

11.14 CHAPTER REVIEW

The `DocumentCollection` class offers a quick way to work with a bunch of documents from a database. It can be formed through a search from a view, unprocessed documents for an agent, or just plain all documents from a database. Once you have a `DocumentCollection` object created, you can get its size, remove documents from it, add documents to it, and traverse it. You can go to a specific document within it, or move to the previous, next, last, or first document. You can use the position number to navigate through documents as well. Finally, you can move all the contents to a folder or remove them from a folder. Sorting the contents of a `DocumentCollection` is not easy; there is no built-in function for it. The results of a full-text search are returned in sorted order (by score). You must write your own routine if you want results returned unsorted.

- You can create `DocumentCollection` objects from the `Database`, `View`, and `AgentContext` objects.
- The `getNextDocument`, `getLastDocument`, `getFirstDocument`, `getPrevDocument`, `getDocument`, and `getNthDocument` methods can access and manipulate separate entries.
- The `deleteDocument` method removes a `Document` from the collection, while the `addDocument` method adds one.
- All contents of a `DocumentCollection` object can be removed from a folder (`removeAllFromFolder`) or added to a folder (`PutAllInFolder`).
- The `stampAll` method creates and/or populates a field on all elements in the collection.
- The `updateAll` method stamps the contents of a collection as processed, so an agent won't hit them again mistakenly.
- You can perform a full-text search on a collection to refine the contents.
- Sorting a collection can be cumbersome, but algorithms like the bubble sort and quicksort offer some help.

C H A P T E R   1 2

Activity logging

12.1 Overview   144

12.2 Creating   144

12.3 Properties   145

12.4 logAction   145

12.5 logError   145

12.6 Using the agent log   146

12.7 Logging to a file   148

12.8 Logging via Email   148

12.9 Logging to a Domino database   151

12.10 Chapter review   152

12.1   OVERVIEW

The Log class allows you to record actions and errors. You can record them via an email message to a Domino database, text file, or agent log. You can create a Log object using the createLog method of the Session class. The syntax is listed next.

12.2   CREATING

```
Log = Session.createLog(String);
```

The createLog method accepts one and only one parameter, the name assigned to the Log object. Once you create the object, you must specify the type of Log through the corresponding open method. This includes openMailLog, openFileLog, openAgentLog, and openNotesLog. Each of these open methods will be covered in detail throughout this chapter.

12.3 PROPERTIES

Let's take a look at the Log class properties before we cover the various methods for working with the different type of logs:

- **IsLogActions**: Read/write property that signals if action logging is set or not. It is set through the setLogActions method.

- **IsLogErrors**: Read/write property that signals if error logging is set or not. It is set through the setLogErrors method.

- **IsOverwriteFile**: Read/write property for file logging; it signals whether or not an existing log file should be overwritten. It is set through the setOverwriteFile method.

- **NumActions**: Returns the number of actions logged so far as an integer value

- **NumErrors**: Returns the number of errors logged so far as an integer value

- **Parent**: Returns the Session object used to create the Log

- **ProgramName**: Read/write property representing the name of the program or agent whose activity is being logged

There are three methods related to logging information to a Log object: logAction, logError, and logEvent. We will cover only the logAction and logError methods.

12.4 LOGACTION

The logAction method records actions you specify to a Log object. It accepts one String parameter containing the text to be recorded as an action in the Log object. The logAction method creates a new document when you use it with a Domino log database. A line containing the description is added to the body of the memo when you use mail logging. The ProgramName property, date/time, and description are added to the text file when you use text file logging, and to the Agent Log window when you use agent logging.

```
Log.logAction("Description");
```

12.5 LOGERROR

The logError method records errors to a Log object. It accepts two parameters: an integer representing the error code, and a text description of the error.

```
Log.logError(Error_Code, "Description");
```

The logError method creates a new document when you use it with a Domino log database. A line containing the code and description is added to the body of the memo when you use mail logging. The ProgramName property, date/time, code, and description are added to the text file when you use text file logging, and to the Agent log window when you use agent logging.

12.6 USING THE AGENT LOG

One of the four techniques available for logging is using an agent's log. You can view the agent's log by right-clicking on an agent in the Domino Designer. Figure 12.1 shows the log for an existing agent.

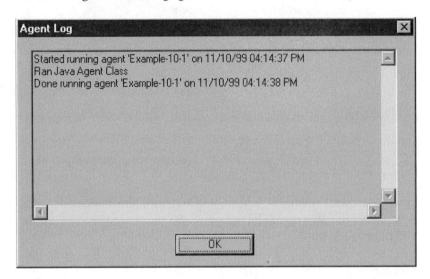

Figure 12.1   Agent log

The openAgentLog method of the Log class starts logging to an agent's log. The openAgentLog method is called, followed by logAction or logError to record data, and the close method to close the log.

Example 12.1   (Domino Agent)

```
import lotus.domino.*;
import java.util.*;
public class Example_12_1 extends AgentBase {
  public void NotesMain() {
    try {
      Session session = getSession();
      AgentContext ac = session.getAgentContext();
        Log aLog = session.createLog("Agent Log Example");   ❶
        aLog.openAgentLog();   ❷
      Database db = ac.getCurrentDatabase();
      DocumentCollection dc1 = db.FTSearch("In Review",0);
        aLog.logAction(dc1.getCount() + " In Review docs found.");   ❸
      DocumentCollection dc2 = db.FTSearch("Proposed",0);
        aLog.logAction(dc2.getCount() + " Proposed docs found.");   ❹
      Document doc1 = dc1.getFirstDocument();
      int matches = 0;
```

```
      while (doc1 != null)  {
        Document doc2 = dc2.getDocument(doc1);
        if (doc2 != null)  {
          matches += 1;  }
        doc2.recycle();
        doc1 = dc1.getNextDocument(doc1);  }
        aLog.logAction("There are " + matches);  ❺
        aLog.close();  ❻
      aLog.recycle();
      dc1.recycle();
      dc2.recycle();
      db.recycle();
      ac.recycle();
      session.recycle();
    } catch(Exception e) {
    e.printStackTrace();}  }  }
```

Explanation

❶ Create a new Log object using the current Session object. We assign it a name as well.

❷ Open an agent log via the openAgentLog method.

❸ Log an action to the agent log.

❹ Log another action to the agent log.

❺ Log an action to the agent log.

❻ Close the agent log.

Output

Figure 12.2 shows the results via the Agent Log pop-up window.

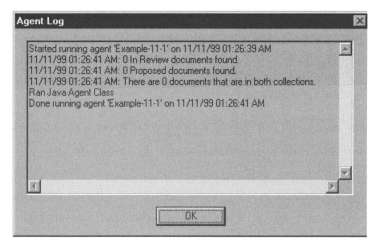

Figure 12.2 Agent Log window

12.7 LOGGING TO A FILE

The process of logging to a text file is similar to logging to an agent log, but the method does accept a parameter—the path and name of the file to store the log:

```
Log.openFileLog("log file/path");
```

Example 12.2 uses the code from example 11.2.

Example 12.2   (Domino Agent)

```
import lotus.domino.*;
import java.util.*;
public class Example_12_2 extends AgentBase {
 public void NotesMain() {
   try {
     Session session = getSession();
      Log fLog = session.createLog("Text file log example.");   ❶
     AgentContext ac = session.getAgentContext();
      fLog.openFileLog("c:\\notes\\data\\log.txt");   ❷
     Database db = ac.getCurrentDatabase();
     DocumentCollection dc = db.getAllDocuments();
     for (int i = 0; i < dc.getCount(); i ++)   {
      Document doc = dc.getNthDocument(i);
       fLog.logAction("Document NoteID:   " + doc.getNoteID());   ❸
      doc.recycle(); }
       fLog.close();   ❹
     fLog.recycle();
     dc.recycle();
     db.recycle();
     ac.recycle();
     session.recycle();
   } catch(Exception e) {
     e.printStackTrace();}   }   }
```

Explanation

❶ Create a new Log object.

❷ Create a new text file for logging.

❸ Send action to the text file.

❹ Close the log.

12.8 LOGGING VIA EMAIL

The process of logging via Email is similar to the other methods, but it accepts two parameters. The first parameter is a Vector of recipient addresses, and the second is the subject of the message.

```
Log.openMailLog(Vector, "Subject");
```

Example 12.3 uses the code from example 11.7.

Example 12.3   (Domino Agent)

```java
import lotus.domino.*;
import java.util.*;
public class Example_12_3 extends AgentBase {
 public void NotesMain() {
  try {
    Session session = getSession();
    AgentContext ac = session.getAgentContext();
     Log eLog = session.createLog("Sorting Example");   ❶
     Vector recipients = new Vector();   ❷
    recipients.addElement("Julius Erving");   ❸
    recipients.addElement("Moses Malone");
     eLog.openMailLog(recipients, "Sorting Results");   ❹
    Database db = ac.getCurrentDatabase();
    View vw = db.getView("Examples \\ by Chapter");
    DocumentCollection dc = db.getAllDocuments();
    if (dc.getCount() > 0)   {
     Document[] adocs = new Document[dc.getCount()];
     int count = 0;
     Document doc = dc.getFirstDocument();
     eLog.logAction("-------------------------------------");   ❺
     eLog.logAction("-------   Before Sorting    ----------");
     eLog.logAction("-------------------------------------");
     while (doc != null) {
      adocs[count] = doc;
      count++;
       eLog.logAction("Last Name:  " + doc.getItemValueString("LastName"));   ❻
      doc = dc.getNextDocument(doc); }
     // Bubble sort
     for (int y = 0; y < adocs.length; y ++) {
      for (int x = 0; x < (adocs.length - y - 1); x++) {
       Document temp1 = (Document)adocs[x];
       Document temp2 = (Document)adocs[x+1];
       String temp3 = temp1.getItemValueString("LastName");
       String temp4 = temp2.getItemValueString("LastName");
       if (temp4.toString().compareTo(temp3.toString()) < 0)   {
       adocs[x] = temp2;
       adocs[x + 1] = temp1;  } } }
      eLog.logAction("-----------------------------------------");
      eLog.logAction("----------   After Sorting    ----------");
      eLog.logAction("-----------------------------------------");
      for (int i = 0; i < adocs.length; i ++)   {
     eLog.logAction("Last Name:  " + adocs[i].getItemValueString("LastName"));}   ❼
     eLog.close(); }
     eLog.recycle();
     db.recycle();
     vw.recycle();
     dc.recycle();
     ac.recycle();
```

```
        session.recycle();
    } catch(Exception e) {
        e.printStackTrace();}  }  }
```

Explanation

❶ Create a new Log object.

❷ Create a new Vector object for the recipient names.

❸ Add a user mail name to the Vector.

❹ Create an email log.

❺ Send an action description to the log.

❻ Send an action description to the log.

❼ Send an action description to the log.

Output (email message)

```
Subject:Sorting Results
11/11/99 02:04:26 AM Sorting Example starting
11/11/99 02:04:26 AM -------------------------------------------
11/11/99 02:04:26 AM ---------    Before Sorting    -------------
11/11/99 02:04:26 AM -------------------------------------------
11/11/99 02:04:26 AM Last Name:  Jones
11/11/99 02:04:26 AM Last Name:  Patton
11/11/99 02:04:26 AM Last Name:  Hamilton
11/11/99 02:04:26 AM Last Name:  Zeus
11/11/99 02:04:26 AM Last Name:  Ackerman
11/11/99 02:04:26 AM Last Name:  Williams
11/11/99 02:04:26 AM Last Name:  Smith
11/11/99 02:04:26 AM Last Name:  Hall
11/11/99 02:04:26 AM Last Name:  Spotts
11/11/99 02:04:26 AM Last Name:  Erving
11/11/99 02:04:26 AM -------------------------------------------
11/11/99 02:04:26 AM --------    After Sorting    ---------------
11/11/99 02:04:26 AM -------------------------------------------
11/11/99 02:04:26 AM Last Name:  Ackerman
11/11/99 02:04:26 AM Last Name:  Erving
11/11/99 02:04:26 AM Last Name:  Hall
11/11/99 02:04:26 AM Last Name:  Hamilton
11/11/99 02:04:26 AM Last Name:  Jones
11/11/99 02:04:26 AM Last Name:  Patton
11/11/99 02:04:26 AM Last Name:  Smith
11/11/99 02:04:26 AM Last Name:  Spotts
11/11/99 02:04:26 AM Last Name:  Williams
11/11/99 02:04:26 AM Last Name:  Zeus
```

12.9 Logging to a Domino database

The process of logging to a Domino database is just like the other methods. It accepts two parameters. The first parameter is a server containing the log database, and the second is the database filename.

NOTE   You should use the Agent Log template file (`alog4.ntf`) to create your log database. It contains all of the required forms and views to display the log documents.

```
Log.openNotesLog("Server", "database filename");
```

Example 12.4 shows how to log activity to a local log database.

Example 12.4   (Domino Agent)

```
import lotus.domino.*;
import java.util.*;
public class Example_12_4 extends AgentBase {
 public void NotesMain() {
   try {
     Session session = getSession();
     AgentContext ac = session.getAgentContext();
     Log dbLog = session.createLog("Agent Log Example");  ❶
     dbLog.openNotesLog("","log12.nsf");  ❷
     Database db = ac.getCurrentDatabase();
     DocumentCollection dc1 = db.FTSearch("In Review",0);
     dbLog.logAction(dc1.getCount() + " In Review documents found.");  ❸
     DocumentCollection dc2 = db.FTSearch("Proposed",0);
     dbLog.logAction(dc2.getCount() + " Proposed documents found.");
     Document doc1 = dc1.getFirstDocument();
     int matches = 0;
     while (doc1 != null)  {
       Document doc2 = dc2.getDocument(doc1);
       if (doc2 != null)  {
         matches += 1;  }
       doc2.recycle();
       doc1 = dc1.getNextDocument(doc1);  }
       if (matches == 0) {
         dbLog.logError(0,"There were no matches found.");  }  ❹
       else {
         dbLog.logAction("There are " + matches + " documents that are
            in both collections."); }
     dbLog.close();  ❺
     dbLog.recycle();
     dc1.recycle();
     dc2.recycle();
     db.recycle();
     ac.recycle();
     session.recycle();
   } catch(Exception e) {
     e.printStackTrace();}  }  }
```

Explanation

❶ Create a new `Log` object.

❷ Set up the `Log` to use a local Domino database.

❸ Send an action to the `Log`.

❹ Send an error to the `Log` if no matches were found.

❺ Close the `Log` object.

Output (the resulting main view in the log database)

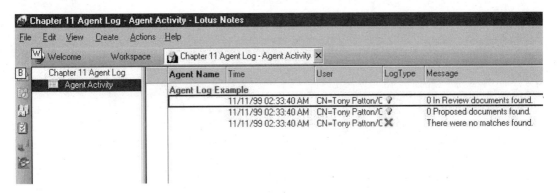

Figure 12.3   Example 12.4 output

12.10 *Chapter Review*

The `Log` class logs agent activity and errors to a variety of formats: Domino database, email message, text file, or agent log. You create the `Log` object using the `createLog` method in the `Session` class. There are a number of methods and properties available for access via Java.

- The `Log` class provides a vehicle for logging activity and errors.

- The `createLog` method of the `Session` class creates an instance of the `Log` class.

- The `openMailLog`, `openNotesLog`, `openAgentLog`, and `openFileLog` methods of the `Log` class are available for working with the different `Log` output formats.

- You can use a number of properties in the `Log` class to access numerous attributes of the `Log`.

Working with the ACL

13.1 What is the ACL?   153

13.2 Seven access levels   154

13.3 ACL class   156

13.4 Properties   157

13.5 Save   158

13.6 ACLEntry class   158

13.7 Working with roles   165

13.8 Chapter review   168

13.1   WHAT IS THE ACL?

The access control list (ACL) is one of the most important aspects of a Domino database. It determines who can (or cannot) access the application. In addition, it determines what tasks a user (or server) can perform in a database. You can list users by their names in the ACL or as part of a group. You define groups in the Domino Directory (formerly called the name and address book), the groups allow multiple users to be combined for easy maintenance. The ACL is just one aspect of security implemented in Domino.

13.2 SEVEN ACCESS LEVELS

There are seven levels of access to a database in Domino. Here is a description of each.

13.2.1 Manager

Users with manager access can modify ACL settings, encrypt a database for local security, modify replication settings, and delete a database—tasks permitted by no other access level. Managers can also perform all tasks allowed by other access levels. Domino requires each database to have at least one manager. It is best to assign at least two people manager access in case one of them is absent or unavailable. Also, the server is usually listed as a manager so it can perform all of its necessary tasks with no security problems.

13.2.2 Designer

Users with designer access can modify all database design elements (fields, forms, views, public agents, the database icon, Using and About documents, and so on), can modify replication formulas, and can create a full-text index. Also, designers can perform all tasks allowed by lower access levels. Assign designer access to the original developer of the database or to a user responsible for maintaining and updating the design after the database is in production.

13.2.3 Editor

Users assigned editor access can create documents and edit all documents, even those created by others. Assign editor access to users responsible for maintaining the data in an application.

13.2.4 Author

Users assigned author access can create documents and edit those documents that they create. Assign author access to allow users to contribute to a database but not edit documents created by others. When possible, use author access rather than editor access to reduce replication and save conflicts.

13.2.5 Reader

Users assigned reader access can read documents in a database, but they cannot create or edit documents, no matter who created them. Assign reader access to users who must be able to read an application's data, such as a company policy database.

Anyone with at least reader access to a database can create personal agents in the database if the database manager selects the ACL "Create personal agents" option. However, users can only run agents that perform tasks allowed by their access level. For example, someone with reader access can create a personal (private) agent that deletes documents, but the agent will not actually delete any documents when it is run.

13.2.6 Depositor

Users assigned depositor access can create documents, but they cannot see any documents in the database. This includes documents created by them. Assign depositor access to allow users to contribute to a mail-in database. For example, a ballot-box type of application would require only depositor access to facilitate anonymity.

13.2.7 No access

Users assigned no access cannot do anything with a database. Assign no access as the default setting in the ACL to prevent unauthorized users from accessing an application.

You can access the database ACL from the Notes workspace by right-clicking the mouse on the database icon (select Access Control under the highlighted Database option), or from the file pull-down menu (File | Database | Access Control). Figure 13.1 shows the ACL window. The window shows who has access to the database and the level of their access. The ACL can contain users, groups, or servers. Server access determines which servers can replicate the application.

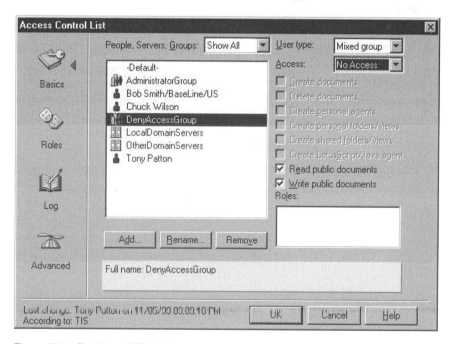

Figure 13.1   Database ACL window

Accessing a database ACL via the Domino Java classes involves the Database, ACL, and ACLEntry classes. The Database class provides the getACL method that returns the ACL property as an ACL object.

13.3   ACL CLASS

The syntax for obtaining a database's ACL is as follows:

```
ACL = Database.getACL();
```

Example 13.1   (Domino Agent)

```java
import lotus.domino.*;
import java.util.*;
import java.io.PrintWriter;
public class Example_13_1 extends AgentBase {
 public void NotesMain() {
   try {
     Session session = getSession();
     PrintWriter pw = getAgentOutput();
     AgentContext ac = session.getAgentContext();
     Database db = ac.getCurrentDatabase();
     ACL dbACL = db.getACL();  ❶
     pw.print("The current user, " + session.getCommonUserName());  ❷
     pw.print(", level of access is ");
     pw.println(db.getCurrentAccessLevel());
     String output = "The maximum access level for Internet access to the database, ";  ❸
     output += db.getTitle() + " is ";
     switch (dbACL.getInternetLevel())  {  ❹
       case (0) :  pw.println(output + " No Access");  break;
       case (1) :  pw.println(output + " Depositor");  break;
       case (2) :  pw.println(output + " Reader");  break;
       case (3) :  pw.println(output + " Author");  break;
       case (4) :  pw.println(output + " Editor");  break;
       case (5) :  pw.println(output + " Designer");  break;
       case (6) :  pw.println(output + " Manager");  break; }
     dbACL.recycle();
     db.recycle();
     ac.recycle();
     session.recycle();
   } catch(Exception e) {
     e.printStackTrace();} }  }
```

Explanation

❶ Set ACL object to the ACL of the current Database object.

❷ Display the current user's username and access level using properties of the Session and Database objects.

❸ String variable to be used in all output.

❹ A switch/case block is used to determine the access level and display a message accordingly. The level of access starts at the bottom at zero with No Access, up to a level of Manager, which is six.

Output

The current user, Tony Patton, level of access is 6
The maximum access level for Internet access to the database, Domino Java Examples is Editor

13.4 PROPERTIES

Example 13.1 illustrated the use of the `InternetLevel` property of the `ACL` class. The integer values were used in the code, but there are constants available in the `ACL` class to make the code more legible. In addition to the `InternetLevel` property, there are properties for uniform access, the parent `Database` object, and to obtain the roles.

13.4.1 InternetLevel

The `getInternetLevel` and `setInternetLevel` methods allow you to retrieve and set this property. It contains the maximum Internet (browser client) access for the database.

Following is a list of constants defined in the `ACL` class for each possible access level:

- ACL.LEVEL_NOACCESS
- ACL.LEVEL_DEPOSITOR
- ACL.LEVEL_READER
- ACL.LEVEL_AUTHOR
- ACL.LEVEL_EDITOR
- ACL.LEVEL_DESIGNER
- ACL.LEVEL_MANAGER

You could rewrite the `switch/case` block from example 13.1 as follows:

```
switch (dbACL.getInternetLevel())  {
case (ACL.LEVEL_NOACCESS): pw.println(output + " No Access");  break;
case (ACL.LEVEL_DEPOSITOR): pw.println(output + " Depositor");  break;
case (ACL.LEVEL_READER): pw.println(output + " Reader");  break;
case (ACL.LEVEL_AUTHOR): pw.println(output + " Author");  break;
case (ACL.LEVEL_EDITOR): pw.println(output + " Editor");  break;
case (ACL.LEVEL_DESIGNER): pw.println(output + " Designer");  break;
case (ACL.LEVEL_MANAGER): pw.println(output + " Manager");  break; }
```

13.4.2 IsUniformAccess

The `isUniformAccess` and `setUniformAccess` methods allow you to retrieve and set this property. It signals whether or not a consistent `ACL` is enforced across all replicas of the database.

```
ACL dbACL = db.getACL();
if (dbACL.isUniformAccess()) {
  dbACL.setUniformAccess(false); }
```

13.4.3 Parent

The getParent method allows you to access the Parent property of the ACL class. It returns a Database object representing the ACL container.

```
Database db = ACL.getParent();
```

13.4.4 Roles

The getRoles method returns a Vector of String objects representing all roles defined in the database that contains the ACL.

```
ACL dbACL = db.getACL();
Vector roles = dbACL.getRoles();
for (int x=0; x < roles.size(); x ++) {
System.out.println("Role:  " + roles.elementAt(x)); }
```

13.5 SAVE

If you change a value of one of the properties of an ACL object, you must save the ACL object. You achieve this via the save method of the ACL class.

```
ACL.save();
```

13.6 ACLENTRY CLASS

A number of additional methods allow you to work with roles and individual entries in the ACL.

Each entry in an ACL object is called an entry. The ACL class contains methods to access entries. These methods return ACLEntry objects. The ACLEntry class represents individual entries in an ACL object. This class offers more power when you work with an ACL object and its entries.

13.6.1 Accessing ACL Entries

```
ACLEntry = ACL.getEntry("username");
ACLEntry = ACL.getFirstEntry();
ACLEntry = ACL.getNextEntry();
ACLEntry = ACL.createACLEntry("username",access_level);
ACLEntry = ACL.removeACLEntry("username");
```

The create/remove methods allow you to add and delete entries. The getEntry method retrieves a specific entry. The getFirstEntry and getNextEntry methods allow an ACL to be traversed similar to working with a Document-Collection object.

Example 13.2   (Domino Agent)

```
import lotus.domino.*;
import java.util.*;
import java.io.PrintWriter;
public class Example_13_2 extends AgentBase {
```

```
public void NotesMain() {
  try {
    Session session = getSession();
    PrintWriter pw = getAgentOutput();
    AgentContext ac = session.getAgentContext();
    Database db = ac.getCurrentDatabase();
    ACL dbACL = db.getACL();                              ❶
    ACLEntry entry = dbACL.getFirstEntry();       ❷
    while (entry != null) {                  ❸
     pw.println("Username: " + entry.getName());       ❹
     pw.println("Access Level:  " + entry.getLevel());   ❺
     pw.println("Roles:  " + entry.getRoles());  ❻
     pw.print("AdminReaderAuthor?  ");       ❼
     pw.println(entry.isAdminReaderAuthor());
     pw.println("AdminServer?  " + entry.isAdminServer());  ❽
     pw.print("Allowed to create documents? ");   ❾
     pw.println(entry.isCanCreateDocuments());
     pw.print("Allowed to delete documents? ");   ❿
     pw.println(entry.isCanDeleteDocuments());
     pw.print("Allowed to create personal agents? ");  ⓫
     pw.println(entry.isCanCreatePersonalAgent());
     pw.print("Allowed to create person folders? ");  ⓬
     pw.println(entry.isCanCreatePersonalFolder());
     pw.print("Allowed to create shared folders? ");  ⓭
     pw.println(entry.isCanCreateSharedFolder());
     pw.print("Create LScript/Java agents? ");  ⓮
     pw.println(entry.isCanCreateLSOrJavaAgent());
     pw.println("Entry is a group?  " + entry.isGroup());  ⓯
     pw.println("Entry is a person?  " + entry.isPerson());  ⓰
     pw.println("Entry is a server?  " + entry.isServer());  ⓱
     pw.println("Public reader?  " + entry.isPublicReader());  ⓲
     pw.println("Public writer?  " + entry.isPublicWriter());  ⓳
     pw.println("User type:  " + entry.getUserType());  ⓴
     entry = dbACL.getNextEntry(entry);    }  ㉑
    entry.recycle();
    dbACL.recycle();
    db.recycle();
    ac.recycle();
    session.recycle();
  } catch(Exception e) {
    e.printStackTrace();}  }  }
```

Explanation

❶ Retrieve the ACL object from the Database object.

❷ Retrieve the first entry from the ACL object.

❸ Loop through all entries in the ACL object via a while loop.

❹ Display the name property of the entry.

❺ Display the name access level (corresponds to constants) of the entry.

❻ Display the entry's roles enclosed in square brackets.

❼ Display IsAdminAuthor property.

❽ Display IsAdminServer property.

❾ Display whether or not the entry can create documents.

❿ Display whether or not the entry can delete documents.

⓫ Display whether or not the entry can create personal agents.

⓬ Display whether or not the entry can create personal folders.

⓭ Display whether or not the entry can create shared folders.

⓮ Display whether or not the entry is allowed to create LotusScript or Java agents.

⓯ Display whether or not the entry is a group.

⓰ Display whether or not the entry is a person.

⓱ Display whether or not the entry is a server.

⓲ Display whether the public reader setting is enabled or disabled.

⓳ Display whether the public writer setting is enabled or disabled.

⓴ Display the user type of the entry.

㉑ Retrieve the next entry from the ACL using the current entry as the pointer.

Output (one entry)

```
Username:  -Default-
Access Level:  5
Roles:  []
AdminReaderAuthor?  false
AdminServer?  false
Allowed to create documents?  true
Allowed to delete documents?  true
Allowed to create personal agents?  true
Allowed to create person folders?  true
Allowed to create shared folders?  true
Allowed to create LotusScript/Java agents?  false
Entry is a group?  false
Entry is a person?  false
Entry is a server?  false
Public reader?  true
Public writer?  true
User type:  0
```

You can set all of the properties accessed in example 13.2 as well. Example 13.3 retrieves a specific entry from an ACL and resets its various properties.

Example 13.3 (Domino Agent)

```
import lotus.domino.*;
import java.util.*;
public class Example_13_3 extends AgentBase {
  public void NotesMain() {
    try {
```

```
          Session session = getSession();
          AgentContext ac = session.getAgentContext();
          Database db = ac.getCurrentDatabase();
          ACL dbACL = db.getACL(); ❶
          setEntrySettings(dbACL, "Bob Smith/Organization"); ❷
          dbACL.recycle();
          db.recycle();
          ac.recycle();
          session.recycle();
        } catch(Exception e) {
          e.printStackTrace();   } }

    public void setEntrySettings (ACL passedACL, String passedUsername) throws NotesException ❸
    {
     ACLEntry entry = passedACL.getEntry(passedUsername); ❹
     if (entry != null) { ❺
      entry.setLevel(ACL.LEVEL_EDITOR); ❻
      entry.setAdminReaderAuthor(false);
      entry.setAdminServer(false);
      entry.setCanCreateDocuments(true);
      entry.setCanDeleteDocuments(true);
      entry.setCanCreatePersonalAgent(true);
      entry.setCanCreatePersonalFolder(true);
      entry.setCanCreateSharedFolder(false);
      entry.setCanCreateLSOrJavaAgent(false);
      entry.setGroup(false);
      entry.setPerson(true);
      entry.setServer(false);
      entry.setPublicReader(true);
      entry.setPublicWriter(true);
      entry.setUserType(ACLEntry.TYPE_PERSON); ❼
      passedACL.save(); ❽
      entry.recycle();
      passedACL.recycle(); } } }
```

Explanation

❶ Create a new ACL object from the current Database object.

❷ Call the setEntrySettings method; we pass the ACL object and username into the method.

❸ Declare our setEntrySettings method. We accept two parameters. We must declare that it throws a NotesException from the ACLEntry class.

❹ Retrieve the ACLEntry object for the username passed into the method.

❺ Proceed only if the entry was found.

❻ Set the level of the user, and then set other properties.

❼ Set the user type of the user via an ACLEntry constant.

❽ Save the ACL object; the settings will not take effect until the object is saved.

Example 13.3 takes advantage of constants defined in the ACLEntry class for use with the UserType property. Here is a full list of the constants:

- ACLEntry.TYPE_MIXED_GROUP
- ACLEntry.TYPE_PERSON
- ACLEntry.TYPE_PERSON_GROUP
- ACLEntry.TYPE_SERVER
- ACLEntry.TYPE_SERVER_GROUP
- ACLEntry.TYPE_UNSPECIFIED

NOTE All the properties of an ACLEntry object are accessible via the Access Control List for a database via the Domino workspace. Figure 13.1 shows the window; notice the various checkboxes (grayed for the selection) and other settings for each entry.

13.6.2 Removing an Entry

The remove method of the ACLEntry class facilitates the removal of an entry from a database's ACL. Example 13.4 demonstrates a Domino agent that automates the removal of users from all databases on a server. A group called Terminations from the Name and Address Book is used to get the list of users to be removed.

Example 13.4   (Domino Agent)

```
import lotus.domino.*;
import java.util.*;
public class Example_13_4 extends AgentBase {
 public void NotesMain() {
  try {
   Session session = getSession();
   AgentContext ac = session.getAgentContext();
   Log aLog = session.createLog("Remove Terminations Agent");    ❶
   aLog.openAgentLog();    ❷
   Document group = getGroupDocument(session, null, "Terminations");    ❸
   if (group != null) {
    Item members = group.getFirstItem("Members");    ❹
    if (members != null) {    ❺
     Vector users = members.getValues();    ❻
     aLog.logAction(users.size() + " terminated users.");    ❼
     DbDirectory dbDir = session.getDbDirectory(null);    ❽
     if (dbDir != null) {    ❾
      Database db = dbDir.getFirstDatabase(DbDirectory.DATABASE);    ❿
      while (db != null) {    ⓫
      for (int x = 0; x < users.size(); x ++) {    ⓬
       ACL dbACL = db.getACL();    ⓭
       if (deleteEntry(dbACL, (String)users.elementAt(x))) {    ⓮
        Log.logAction((String)users.elementAt(x) + " removed
           from " + db.getTitle()); }
       else { aLog.logAction((String)users.elementAt(x) + " not
           found in " + db.getTitle()); }
       db = dbDir.getNextDatabase();}    ⓯
      dbDir.recycle();}
     else { aLog.logError(0,"Database directory not found."); }    ⓰
```

```
            else { aLog.logError(1,"The members field on the group document not found."); }
        else { aLog.logError(2,"Group document not found."); }
        aLog.recycle();
        db.recycle();
        ac.recycle();
        session.recycle();
    } catch (NotesException n) {    ⓗ
        System.out.println("Notes error#" + n.id + ", named:   " + n.text);
    } catch(Exception e) {
        e.printStackTrace(); } }

public boolean deleteEntry (ACL passedACL, String passedUsername) throws NotesException    ⓘ
{
    ACLEntry entry = passedACL.getEntry(passedUsername);    ⓙ
    if (entry != null) {    ⓴
        entry.remove();    ㉑
        passedACL.save();    ㉒
        return true;    ㉓
    } else { return false;} }

public Document getGroupDocument (Session passedSession, String passedServer,
        String passedGroupName) throws NotesException    ㉔
{
    if ((passedSession != null) & (passedGroupName != "")) {    ㉕
        Database nab = passedSession.getDatabase(passedServer, "names.nsf");    ㉖
        if (nab != null) {    ㉗
            View nabView = nab.getView("Groups");    ㉘
            if (nabView != null) {    ㉙
                Document groupDoc = nabView.getDocumentByKey(passedGroupName.trim());    ㉚
                return groupDoc;    }    ㉛
            else {
                return null;   }}    ㉜
        else {
            return null; }}
    else { return null; }}}
```

Explanation

❶ Create a new Log object for the current agent.

❷ The Log object will use the agent log.

❸ Retrieve the group document from the NAB on the specified server. The get-GroupDocument method of our agent is used. We specify null for the server name because we are working locally. We are working with the group named Terminations.

❹ If the group document is found, retrieve the member Item (field) object from it. This contains all users in the group.

❺ Proceed only if the members field is found.

❻ Retrieve all values from the member's Item object and place them into a Vector object.

❼ Send the number of users in the group to the Log object via an action.

❽ Set the DbDirectory object to the specified server. We use null for local.

9 Continue only if the directory is found.

10 Set the `Database` object to the first `Database` object in the `DbDirectory` object. We use the `getFirstDirectory` method of the `DbDirectory` class.

11 Loop through all `Database` objects in the `DbDirectory` object.

12 Use a `for` loop to process every user in the Terminations group (from the `members` field).

13 Set the `ACL` object to the current `Database` object's ACL.

14 Call the `deleteEntry` method in your agent. It returns true if the deletion was successful; otherwise it returns false. Log the result.

15 Retrieve the next `Database` object from the `DbDirectory` object via the `getNextDatabase` method of the `DbDirectory` class.

16 All `if` statements in the code have a corresponding `else` statement that logs the error.

17 We catch a Notes/Domino-specific error in our `try/catch` block. The `NotesException` class is defined in the Domino Java classes. It has the `id` property that returns the error number, and the corresponding `text` property represents the error message. We record the error in the log, if it is encountered.

18 This is the declaration for the `deleteEntry` method. It returns a boolean value and accepts two parameters: an `ACL` object and the username to delete.

19 Instantiate an `ACLEntry` object to the first entry of the `ACL` object passed into the method. The `getFirstEntry` method of the `ACL` class is used.

20 Proceed only if an entry is found.

21 Remove the `ACLEntry` from the `ACL` object via the `remove` method of the `ACLEntry` object.

22 Save the `ACL` object so the deletion will be permanent.

23 Return a true value to the calling code; this signals a successful deletion.

24 The declaration for the `getGroupDocument` method. It accepts three parameters: `Session` object, server name, and group name. It returns no value (void).

25 Continue only if the `Session` and group name parameters are valid.

26 Retrieve the NAB `Database` object from the specified server. We use the default NAB: `names.nsf`.

27 Proceed only if the NAB `Database` object is found.

28 Set a `View` object to the Groups view in the NAB.

29 Proceed only if the `View` exists.

30 Set the `Document` object to the specified parameter.

31 Return the located `Document` object to the calling code.

32 If an error occurs, return a null value to signal it.

13.7 WORKING WITH ROLES

Roles are an enhancement to the access control list. They allow database-specific sub-grouping within the ACL; that is, they allow a type of group specific to a database. Roles are defined in the ACL and are not listed in the name and address book. In figure 13.1, the Roles button on the left side of the window allows you to view all roles defined for a database. Also, roles can be accessed via the Domino Java classes. The ACL and ACLEntry objects provide various methods and properties for working with a database's roles. The ACL class allows you to add, remove, and rename roles.

Example 13.5   (Domino Agent)

```
import lotus.domino.*;
import java.util.*;
import java.io.PrintWriter;
public class Example_13_5 extends AgentBase {
 public void NotesMain() {
   try {
     Session session = getSession();
     PrintWriter pw = getAgentOutput();
     AgentContext ac = session.getAgentContext();
     Database db = ac.getCurrentDatabase();
     ACL dbACL = db.getACL();  ❶
     Vector rolesList = dbACL.getRoles();  ❷
     pw.println("---  Roles  --------------------------");
     for (int i = 0; i < rolesList.size(); i ++) {  ❸
       pw.println("---  " + rolesList.elementAt(i));;}  ❹
     dbACL.addRole("Chapter13");  ❺
     dbACL.save();
     dbACL.recycle();
     db.recycle();
     ac.recycle();
     session.recycle();
   } catch(Exception e) {
     e.printStackTrace();}}}
```

Explanation

❶ Set the ACL object to the Database object's ACL.

❷ Retrieve a list of roles from the ACL object and place it into a Vector of String.

❸ Traverse the list of roles from the Vector object.

❹ Print the name of the role. (It will be enclosed in square brackets.)

❺ Add a new role to the ACL object via the ACL class' addRole method.

Output

```
---  Roles  ----------------------------
---  [Administrators]
---  [Editors]
```

13.7.1 ACL Class Methods

There are three methods available in the ACL class:

- addRole ("name of role");
- deleteRole ("name of role");
- renameRole ("old name of role", "new name of role");

Example 13.6 (Domino Agent)

```
import lotus.domino.*;
import java.util.*;
public class Example_13_6 extends AgentBase {
 public void NotesMain() {
  try {
    Session session = getSession();
    AgentContext ac = session.getAgentContext();
    Database db = ac.getCurrentDatabase();
    ACL dbACL = db.getACL();  ❶
    dbACL.renameRole("Administrator","Admin");  ❷
    dbACL.deleteRole("Chapter13");  ❸
    dbACL.save();  ❹
    dbACL.recycle();
    db.recycle();
    ac.recycle();
    session.recycle();
  } catch(NotesException n) {
    System.out.println("Error, id#" + n.id + ", text:  " + n.text);
  } catch(Exception e) {
    e.printStackTrace(); }}}
```

Explanation

❶ Retrieve the ACL object from the Database object.

❷ Rename the role Administrator to Admin.

❸ Delete the role from the ACL object.

❹ Save the ACL changes.

13.7.2 ACLEntry Class Methods

The ACLEntry class contains a list of roles for individual entries. Its format mimics the roles of the ACL class. In addition, there are methods for determining if a role is enabled (isRoleEnabled) for an entry, and you can turn a role on and off through the enableRole/disableRole methods. Example 13.7 illustrates these methods' syntax and use.

Example 13.7　(Domino Agent)

```java
import lotus.domino.*;
import java.util.*;
public class Example_13_7 extends AgentBase {
 public void NotesMain() {
   try {
     Session session = getSession();
     AgentContext ac = session.getAgentContext();
     Database db = ac.getCurrentDatabase();
     ACL dbACL = db.getACL();  ❶
     ACLEntry entry = dbACL.getFirstEntry();  ❷
     while (entry != null) {  ❸
       Vector entries = entry.getRoles();  ❹
       System.out.println("Entry:  " + entry.getName());  ❺
       System.out.println("Roles");
       for (int x=0; x < entries.size(); x ++) {  ❻
         System.out.println(entries.elementAt(x)); }
       if (entry.isRoleEnabled("Admin")) {  ❼
         System.out.println("User is listed as an administrator."); }
       entry.disableRole("Test");  ❽
       entry.enableRole("Editor");  ❾
         dbACL.save();  ❿
       entry.recycle();
         entry = dbACL.getNextEntry();}  ⓫
     entry.recycle();
     dbACL.recycle();
     db.recycle();
     ac.recycle();
     session.recycle();
   } catch(NotesException n) {
     System.out.println("Error, id#" + n.id + ", text:  " + n.text);
   } catch(Exception e) {
     e.printStackTrace();} } }
```

Explanation

❶ Retrieve the ACL from the Database object.

❷ Get the first entry from the ACL object.

❸ Loop through all ACLEntry objects in the ACL.

❹ Retrieve all roles for the ACLEntry object.

❺ Display the username associated with the ACLEntry.

❻ Display all role names for the ACLEntry.

❼ Determine if the entry is in the Admin role or not.

❽ Remove the entry from the Test role.

❾ Add the user to the Editor role.

❿ Save the ACL object for the changes to take effect.

⓫ Get the next ACLEntry object from the ACL.

Output

```
Entry:  -Default-
Roles
Entry:  Julius Erving
Roles
[Admin]
[Test]
User is listed as an administrator.
```

13.8 CHAPTER REVIEW

The ACL and ACLEntry classes allow you to access the various settings for the ACL as well as individual entries in the ACL. Methods in the ACL class facilitate traversing the entries in it, much like a DocumentCollection object. Roles are like special groups that are specific to a database. Each entry in an ACL can belong to one or more groups or none at all. The ACL and ACLEntry classes allow you to add, delete, or rename roles. In addition, you can add or remove entries from a role.

- The ACL class represents a database access control list.
- The Database class contains the getACL method, which allows an ACL object to be set.
- The ACL object contains many settings that are accessible via its properties.
- No changes made to an ACL are permanent until you call the save method.
- The ACLEntry class allows you to access individual entries in an ACL.
- Individual entries in an ACL object have various attributes that you can read or set via properties and methods in the ACLEntry class.
- The getEntry, getFirstEntry, and getLastEntry methods of the ACL class allow you to quickly access entries in an ACL object.
- The roles property of the ACL class returns a Vector containing all roles defined in its Database container.
- The roles property of the ACLEntry class returns a Vector containing all roles enabled for a specific entry.

C H A P T E R   1 4

Agent class

14.1 Overview   169
14.2 Syntax   169
14.3 Properties   171
14.4 Methods   177

14.5 Passing parameters   179
14.6 AgentContext class   181
14.7 Processing documents   182
14.8 Chapter review   186

14.1 OVERVIEW

Agents allow you to automate tasks within the Domino environment. Any number of events can be configured to trigger and run them, such as the creation of new documents or new mail arriving. Also, users can run agents manually or call them via a Domino URL or the WebQueryOpen/WebQuerySave form events. The Agent class provides the means to work with agents within Java.

14.2 SYNTAX

You can obtain an Agent object from one of two classes: Database or AgentContext. We have seen in the examples up to this point the syntax for obtaining a handle to the current Agent from within a Domino agent via the AgentContext class. The syntax is as follows:

```
Agent = AgentContext.getCurrentAgent();
```

The getCurrentAgent method of the AgentContext class cannot be used unless you are already working with an agent. If you want to work with an existing agent that is not currently running, the Database class provides two methods to access any agent contained in the Database (whether that agent is running or not).

The first method (getAgent) allows you to access a specific agent. It accepts only one parameter: the name of the agent.

```
Agent = Database.getAgent(nString);
```

The other way to access an agent is through the Agents property of the Database class. This property returns a Vector of all Agent objects within a Database object.

```
Vector = Database.getAgents();
```

Example 14.1 demonstrates the use of the Agents property.

Example 14.1 (Domino Agent)

```
import lotus.domino.*;
import java.io.PrintWriter;
import java.util.Vector;
public class Example_14_1 extends AgentBase {
  public void NotesMain() {
    try {
      Session session = getSession();
      Database db = session.getDatabase(null,"names.nsf");    ❶
      PrintWriter pw = getAgentOutput();
      pw.println("List of agents in " + db.getTitle());    ❷
      Vector agnts = db.getAgents();    ❸
      for (int x = 0; x < agnts.size(); x ++) {    ❹
        Agent cur = (Agent)agnts.elementAt(x);    ❺
        pw.print("Agent:   " + cur.getName());    ❻
        pw.println(" was last run on " + cur.getLastRun());
        cur.recycle();}
      db. .recycle();
      session.recycle();
    } catch(Exception e) {
      e.printStackTrace(); } } }
```

Explanation

❶ Retrieve the local Domino Directory Database object.

❷ Display the title line with the name of the Database object.

❸ Populate Vector with all Agent objects.

❹ Traverse the list of Agent objects.

❺ Retrieve the Agent object from Vector; the element must be explicitly cast to an Agent object.

❻ Display the Agent's name and last run date. A last run date of null will be displayed if the agent has never been run.

Output

```
List of agents in Patton's Address Book
Agent:   CreateMailMemo was last run on null
Agent:   ScheduleMeeting was last run on null
Agent:   Edit Address Book Profile was last run on null
Agent:   Copy to Personal Address Book was last run on null
```

14.3 PROPERTIES

Example 14.1 took advantage of the LastRun and Name properties of the Agent class. The following is a complete list of the properties:

- Comment: Any comments entered concerning an agent. You can enter comments for an agent via the Options button in the Designer window.

- CommonOwner: The Notes common name of the userid that was last used to modify/save the agent

- IsEnabled: Read/write property signaling whether a scheduled agent is enabled or disabled

- IsNotesAgent: Signals whether or not the agent is designed for the Notes environment. The other option is a Web agent. This is the next-to-last column in the list of agents in a database.

- IsPublic: Signals whether or not an agent is available to all users. You can share an agent by checking the Shared Agent checkbox in the Properties InfoBox during the design of an agent. If you do not check this checkbox, the agent is personal and only available to the person who created it.

- IsWebAgent: Signals whether or not an agent is designed to be viewed using a web browser

- LastRun: The date that an agent last ran/executed

- Name: The agent's name/title

- Owner: The Notes name of the userid that was last used to modify/save the agent

- Parent: The Database object container of the agent

- Query: The query search string defined for an agent. Set this via the Add Search button in the design of the agent. An empty string is returned if the query search string has not been used

- ServerName: The name of the server on which the agent is set to run

- Target: The type of documents the agent will process

- Trigger: The trigger for the agent; when it will run

> **NOTE** You can set only the ServerName and IsEnabled properties via Java. All other properties are available for viewing only.

The `Target` property has the following list of `Agent` class constants:

- Agent.TARGET_ALL_DOCS
- Agent.TARGET_ALL_DOCS_IN_VIEW
- Agent.TARGET_NEW_DOCS
- Agent.TARGET_NEW_OR_MODIFIED_DOCS
- Agent.TARGET_NONE
- Agent.TARGET_SELECTED_DOCS
- Agent.TARGET_UNREAD_DOCS_IN_VIEW

The `Trigger` property has the following list of possible `Agent` class constants:

- Agent.TRIGGER_AFTER_MAIL_DELIVERY
- Agent.TRIGGER_BEFORE_MAIL_DELIVERY
- Agent.TRIGGER_DOC_PASTED
- Agent.TRIGGER_DOC_UPDATE
- Agent.TRIGGER_MANUAL
- Agent.TRIGGER_NONE
- Agent.TRIGGER_SCHEDULED

Example 14.2 displays the use of a variety of the properties.

Example 14.2   (Domino Agent)

```
import lotus.domino.*;
import java.io.PrintWriter;
import java.util.Vector;
public class Example_14_2 extends AgentBase {
  public void NotesMain() {
    try {
      Session session = getSession();
      Database db = session.getDatabase(null,"names.nsf");
      PrintWriter pw = getAgentOutput();
      pw.println("List of agents in " + db.getTitle());
      Vector aqnts = db.getAgents();                            ❶
      for (int x = 0; x < agnts.size(); x ++) {                 ❷
        Agent cur = (Agent)agnts.elementAt(x);                  ❸
        pw.println("Agent:  " + cur.getName());                 ❹
        pw.println("Comment:  " + cur.getComment());            ❺
        pw.println("Common Owner:  " + cur.getCommonOwner());   ❻
        pw.println("Owner:  " + cur.getOwner());                ❼
        pw.println("Enabled?  " + cur.isEnabled());             ❽
        if (cur.isPublic()) {                                   ❾
          pw.println("The agent is shared");}
        else  {
          pw.println("The agent is private."); }
        pw.println("Notes Agent?  " + cur.isNotesAgent());      ❿
        pw.println("Web Agent?  " + cur.isWebAgent());          ⓫
        pw.println("Last Run:  " + cur.getLastRun());           ⓬
        pw.println("Query:  " + cur.getQuery());                ⓭
```

```
        pw.println("Run on server:   " + cur.getServerName());  ⓮
        pw.println("Target documents:  " + cur.getTarget());  ⓯
        pw.println("Triggered by:  " + cur.getTrigger() + "\n");  }  ⓰
    db.recycle();
    cur.recycle();
    session.recycle();
} catch(Exception e) {
  e.printStackTrace();}}}
```

Explanation

❶ Fill the Vector object with all Agent objects from the Database object.

❷ Loop through all objects in the Vector object.

❸ Retrieve an Agent object from the Vector object. The element must be explicitly cast to an Agent object.

❹ Display the name.

❺ Display the comments.

❻ Display the common name of the owner.

❼ Display the full hierarchical owner's name.

❽ Display if it is turned on or off.

❾ Determine if it is shared or private.

❿ Determine if it is a Notes agent.

⓫ Determine if it is a Web agent.

⓬ Display the last run date.

⓭ Display the query (if there is any) for it.

⓮ Display the server on which it is set to run. It will be blank for local agents.

⓯ Display the target property as an integer.

⓰ Display the trigger property as an integer.

Output

```
List of agents in Patton's Address Book
Agent:  TestPersonal
Comment:
Common Owner: Tony Patton
Owner:  CN=Tony Patton/O=TIS
Enabled?  true
The agent is private.
Notes Agent?  true
Web Agent?  true
Last Run:  null
Query:  ("Tony")
Run on server:
Target documents:  4
Triggered by:  4
```

Example 14.2 took advantage of the `Trigger` and `Target` properties, but the results were integer values that mean nothing to you and me. Example 14.3 uses a `switch/case` directive to display more meaningful results. Also, it takes advantage of the constants.

Example 14.3   (Domino Agent)

```
import lotus.domino.*;
import java.io.PrintWriter;
import java.util.Vector;
public class Example_14_3 extends AgentBase {
  public void NotesMain() {
    try {
      Session session = getSession();
      Database db = session.getDatabase(null,"names.nsf");
      PrintWriter pw = getAgentOutput();
      pw.println("List of agents in " + db.getTitle());      ❶
      Vector agnts = db.getAgents();      ❷
      for (int x = 0; x < agnts.size(); x ++) {      ❸
       Agent cur = (Agent)agnts.elementAt(x);      ❹
       String triggerOut = "Triggered ";      ❺
       switch (cur.getTrigger()) {      ❻
        case (Agent.TRIGGER_AFTER_MAIL_DELIVERY) :      ❼
         triggerOut += " after mail is delivered.";      ❽
         break;      ❾
        case (Agent.TRIGGER_BEFORE_MAIL_DELIVERY) :
         triggerOut += " before mail is delivered.";
         break;
        case (Agent.TRIGGER_DOC_PASTED) :
         triggerOut += " when documents are pasted into database.";
         break;
        case (Agent.TRIGGER_DOC_UPDATE) :
         triggerOut += " when documents are created/modified.";
         break;
        case (Agent.TRIGGER_MANUAL) :
         triggerOut += " manually.";
         break;
        case (Agent.TRIGGER_NONE) :
         triggerOut += " is not set.";
         break;
        case (Agent.TRIGGER_SCHEDULED) :
         triggerOut += " via a schedule.";
         break;
        default :      ❿
         triggerOut += " is not set.";
         break;}
       String targetOut = "Targeted:   ";      ⓫
       switch (cur.getTarget()) {      ⓬
        case (Agent.TARGET_ALL_DOCS) :      ⓭
          targetOut += " all documents in the database.";      ⓮
          break;      ⓯
        case (Agent.TARGET_ALL_DOCS_IN_VIEW) :
         targetOut += " all documents in a view.";
```

```
      break;
     case (Agent.TARGET_NEW_DOCS) :
      targetOut += " all newly created documents.";
      break;
     case (Agent.TARGET_NEW_OR_MODIFIED_DOCS) :
      targetOut += " all new or modifed documents.";
      break;
     case (Agent.TARGET_NONE) :
      targetOut += " no target is set..";
      break;
     case (Agent.TARGET_SELECTED_DOCS) :
      targetOut += " selected documents..";
      break;
     case (Agent.TARGET_UNREAD_DOCS_IN_VIEW) :
      targetOut += " all unread documents in a view.";
      break;
     default :
      targetOut += " no target is set.";
      break;  }
    pw.println("Agent:  " + cur.getName());   ⓰
    pw.println(targetOut);   ⓱
    pw.println(triggerOut);   ⓲
    pw.println();   }
   db.recycle();
   session.recycle();
   } catch(Exception e) {
    e.printStackTrace();}}}
```

Explanation

❶ Display the agent's name/title.

❷ Populate `Vector` with all `Agent` objects from the `Database` object.

❸ Loop through all objects in the `Vector` object.

❹ Access the object in `Vector` via a loop index. The object must be explicitly cast to an `Agent` object.

❺ Set the first part of our `String` used for output.

❻ Use a switch/case block to process the `Trigger` property.

❼ Use the Trigger constants defined in the `Agent` class.

❽ Set the output `String` accordingly.

❾ We must break out of the switch/case block if our condition has been satisfied.

❿ The default setting for the switch/case block. This is accessed if the value is not found by any of the `case` statements.

⓫ Set up our `String` object for the `Target` property.

⓬ Use a `switch/case` block to process the `Target` property.

⓭ Use Target constants defined in the `Agent` class.

⓮ Set the output string accordingly.

⓯ We must break out of the switch/case block if our condition has been satisfied.

⓰ Display the Agent's name.

⓱ Display the Target String variable.

⓲ Display the Trigger String variable.

Output

```
Agent:  Copy to Personal Address Book
Targeted:   selected documents.
Triggered  manually.


Agent:  Test
Targeted:   no target is set.
Triggered after mail is delivered.


Agent:  Test2
Targeted:   all new or modified documents.
Triggered via a schedule.
```

Example 14.4 disables all agents in the current database.

Example 14.4   (Domino Agent)

```
import lotus.domino.*;
import java.util.Vector;
public class Example_14_4 extends AgentBase {
  public void NotesMain() {
    try {
      Session session = getSession();
      AgentContext ac = session.getAgentContext();
      Database db = ac.getCurrentDatabase();   ❶
      Vector agnts = db.getAgents();   ❷
      for (int x = 0; x < agnts.size(); x ++) {   ❸
        Agent cur = (Agent)agnts.elementAt(x);   ❹
        cur.setEnabled(false);   ❺
        cur.save();   ❻
        cur.recycle();}
      db.recycle();
      ac.recycle();
      session.recycle();
    } catch(Exception e) {
      e.printStackTrace();}}}
```

Explanation

❶ Retrieve the Agent's Database container object.

❷ Populate Vector with all Agent objects in the Database object.

❸ Loop through all objects in the `Vector`.

❹ Retrieve the `Agent` object from the `Vector` object using a loop index. The object must be explicitly cast to an `Agent` object.

❺ Disable the `Agent` object; it will not run as scheduled.

❻ Save the changes to the `Agent`. Changes will not take affect until it is saved.

Example 14.5 sets the server name and enables a specific agent via the `Database` `getAgent` method.

Example 14.5   (Domino Agent)

```
import lotus.domino.*;
import java.util.Vector;
public class Example_14_5 extends AgentBase {
  public void NotesMain() {
    try {
      Session session = getSession();
      AgentContext ac = session.getAgentContext();
      Database db = ac.getCurrentDatabase();
      Agent agnt = db.getAgent("TestPersonal");   ❶
      if (agnt != null) {   ❷
        agnt.setEnabled(true);   ❸
        agnt.setServerName("BaseLine/US");   ❹
        agnt.save();    }   ❺
      agnt.recycle();
      db.recycle();
      ac.recycle();
      session.recycle();
    } catch(Exception e) {
      e.printStackTrace();}}}
```

Explanation

❶ Retrieve a specific `Agent` object from the current `Database` object.

❷ Proceed only if the `Agent` object was found.

❸ Enable the agent to run.

❹ Set the name of the server on which the agent will run.

❺ Save the agent so the new settings will take effect.

14.4   METHODS

Example 14.5 takes advantage of the `save` method in the `Agent` class; you must call this method for any changes made to it to be implemented. There are three other methods available.

14.4.1　run

The run method allows you to run one agent from another. An agent cannot run on its own.

```
Agent.run();
```

14.4.2　runOnServer

The runOnServer method runs an agent on the server on which it is located. This method is a godsend for testing agents manually without having to work on the server itself. An agent cannot call this method for itself.

```
Agent.runOnServer();
```

14.4.3　remove

The remove method deletes an agent permanently.

```
Agent.remove();
```

Example 14.6　(Domino Agent)

```
import lotus.domino.*;
import java.util.Vector;
public class Example_14_6 extends AgentBase {
 public void NotesMain() {
  try {
   Session session = getSession();
   Database db1 = session.getDatabase(null, "names.nsf");   ❶
   if (db1 != null) {   ❷
    Agent agnt1 = db1.getAgent("TestPersonal");   ❸
    if (agnt1 != null) {   ❹
     agnt1.run();   }   ❺
    agnt.recycle();}
   Database db2 = session.getDatabase(null, "dom27.nsf");
   if (db2 != null) {
    Agent agnt2 = db2.getAgent("Cleanup");
    if (agnt2 != null) {
     agnt2.remove(); }   ❻
    agnt2.recycle();}
   Database db3 = session.getDatabase(null, "praclsc.nsf");
    if (db3 != null)  {
    Agent agnt3 = db3.getAgent("Purge");
     if (agnt3 != null) {
      agnt3.runOnServer(); }   ❼
     agnt3.recycle();}
   db3.recycle();
   db2.recycle();
   db1.recycle();
   session.recycle();
  } catch(Exception e) {
   e.printStackTrace(); }}}
```

Explanation

❶ Retrieve the local `Database` object.

❷ Proceed only if the `Database` object was found.

❸ Retrieve a specific `Agent` object from the `Database` object.

❹ Proceed only if the `Agent` object was found.

❺ Run the `Agent`; it will be run locally.

❻ Remove the `Agent` object from the `Database` object.

❼ Run the `Agent` object on the server.

14.5   PASSING PARAMETERS

Passing data into an agent has always been a wish of Domino developers. Domino 5.02 adds this functionality by allowing NoteIDs to be passed to and from agents. The NoteID refers to a document in the Domino database so this document can be used to store information needed by the agent. The NoteID is passed as a single parameter to an agent, and it is accessed via the `getParameterDocID` method of the `Agent` class.

If we have a `Document` object set up as `doc`, we can pass its NoteID to agents using the following syntax:

```
agent.run(doc.getNoteID());
```

or

```
agent.runOnServer(doc.getNoteID());
```

Once we pass the NoteID, we can access it in the agent body as follows:

```
String tempNoteID = agent.getParameterDocID();
```

You may wonder how and when you would need to do this. Example 14.7 shows how a scheduled agent runs other agents depending on a field value. The document containing the field value is passed into the other agents for their use.

Example 14.7   (Domino Agent)

```
import lotus.domino.*;

public class Example extends AgentBase {
  public void NotesMain() {
    try {
      Session s = this.getSession();
      AgentContext ac = s.getAgentContext();
      Database db = ac.getCurrentDatabase();
      View vw = db.getView("ItemsToProcess");   ❶
      Agent agt = null;   ❷
      if (vw != null) {
```

```
        Document doc = vw.getFirstDocument();  ❸
        while (doc != null){  ❹
          String keyValue = doc.getItemValueString("Status");
          String noteID = doc.getNoteID();  ❺
          if ((keyValue != null) & (keyValue != "")){
            if (keyValue == "new") {
              agt = db.getAgent("NewAgent");  ❻
              if (agt != null)
                agt.run(noteID); }  ❼
            else if (keyValue == "old") {
              agt = db.getAgent("OldAgent");
              if (agt != null)
                agt.run(noteID);  }  ❽
            doc = vw.getNextDocument(doc);  } }}
      vw.recycle();
      db.recycle();
      ac.recycle();
      s.recycle();
    } catch(NotesException n) {
      System.out.print("Domino error#" + n.id);
      System.out.println(" (" + n.text + ")");
    } catch(Exception e) {
      e.printStackTrace(); } } }
```

Explanation

❶ Get the view that contains documents to be processed.

❷ Create the Agent object.

❸ Retrieve the first document from the view.

❹ Loop through all documents in the view.

❺ Retrieve the NoteID of the current document.

❻ Get the Agent object from the database.

❼ Run the Agent object passing the NoteID to it.

❽ Run the Agent object passing the NoteID to it.

Once you pass the NoteID into an agent, you can easily access it. The next few lines of code use the NoteID parameter to retrieve the associated document and use fields from it to create a mail memo message:

Example 14.8   (Domino Agent)

```
import lotus.domino.*;
import java.util.Vector;
public class NewAgent extends AgentBase {
  public void NotesMain() {
    try {
      Session s = this.getSession();
```

```
AgentContext ac = s.getAgentContext();
Database db = ac.getCurrentDatabase();
Agent curAgent = ac.getCurrentAgent();  ❶
Document memo = null;  ❷
String noteid = curAgent.getParameterDocID();  ❸
if ((noteid != "") & (noteid != null)) {  ❹
  Document pDoc = db.getDocumentByID(noteid);  ❺
  if (pDoc != null) {  ❻
    memo = db.createDocument();  ❼
    memo.replaceItemValue("Form","Memo");
    String pSendTo = pDoc.getItemValueString("SendTo");  ❽
    Vector sendTo = new Vector();  ❾
    sendTo.addElement(pSendTo);
    String pSubject = pDoc.getItemValueString("Subject");
    memo.replaceItemValue("Subject",pSubject);
    memo.send(false, sendTo); } }  ❿
curAgent.recycle();
db.recycle();
ac.recycle();
s.recycle();
} catch(NotesException n) {
System.out.print("Domino error #" + n.id);
System.out.println(" (" + n.text + ")");
} catch(Exception e) {
e.printStackTrace(); } } }
```

Explanation

❶ Set the Agent object to the current agent.

❷ Create a Document object for creating a mail message.

❸ Retrieve the parameter passed to the agent.

❹ Proceed only if the parameter was properly passed.

❺ Retrieve the Document object from the database via the NoteID passed to the agent.

❻ Proceed only if the document exists.

❼ Create a new Document object for the memo.

❽ Retrieve a field value from the document; it is used to populate field value on mail message.

❾ Create a Vector object to hold recipient names for the memo.

❿ Send the memo using the Vector object for recipients.

14.0   AGENTCONTEXT CLASS

Up to this point we have used the AgentContext class extensively in most of the examples. An AgentContext object represents the environment in which an agent is running. You obtain a handle to it via the `Session` class. You have seen the following lines used constantly to get a handle to the `AgentContext` object:

```
Session session = getSession();
AgentContext ac = session.getAgentContext();
```

14.6.1 getCurrentDatabase

Once you initialize an `AgentContext` object, you can use various properties and methods of its class. The one method we have used repeatedly is the `getCurrentDatabase` method. This method returns a `Database` object representing the `Database` in which the agent resides. Here is the code used to get it:

```
Session session = getSession();
AgentContext ac = session.getAgentContext();
Database db = ac.getCurrentDatabase();
```

14.6.2 getCurrentAgent

The `getCurrentAgent` method works just like the `getCurrentDatabase` method, but it returns an `Agent` object representing the current agent.

```
Session session = getSession();
AgentContext ac = session.getAgentContext();
Agent agnt = ac.getCurrentAgent();
```

14.7 PROCESSING DOCUMENTS

As discussed earlier, a certain event can trigger agents to run. For instance, the creation of a new document or modification of an existing document can trigger an agent to run. The documents handled by the agent must be flagged as processed so they will not be processed again. The `AgentContext` class provides methods for accessing the documents to be processed by the agent, and flagging the documents once they have been processed.

14.7.1 unProcessedFTSearch/unProcessedSearch

The `unProcessedFTSearch` method performs a full-text search on all documents not yet processed by an agent. It returns a subset of the documents that match the search criteria. The `unProcessedSearch` method works the same way, but it performs a normal search. Both methods return a `DocumentCollection` object containing all documents found.

Example 14.9   (Domino Agent)

```
import lotus.domino.*;
public class Example_14_9 extends AgentBase {
  public void NotesMain() {
    try {
      Session s = getSession();
      AgentContext ac = s.getAgentContext();   ❶
```

```
DocumentCollection udc = ac.unprocessedFTSearch("Unprocessed", 0);   ❷
Document doc;   ❸
if (udc.getCount() > 0) {   ❹
  for (int x=0; x < udc.getCount(); x++){   ❺
    doc = udc.getNthDocument(x);   ❻
    doc.replaceItemValue("Flag","Processed");   ❼
    doc.save();   ❽
    ac.updateProcessedDoc(doc); } }   ❾
doc.recycle();
db.recycle();
ac.recycle();
session.recycle();
} catch(Exception e) {
e.printStackTrace();}}}
```

Explanation

❶ Create an AgentContext object for the current agent.

❷ Assemble a DocumentCollection object containing all Documents that match the search criteria and have not been processed by the agent.

❸ Create a Document object to retrieve individual Document objects from the collection.

❹ Proceed only if the DocumentCollection object is not empty.

❺ Loop through all Document objects.

❻ Retrieve the Document object from the DocumentCollection object using the getNthDocument method and the loop index value.

❼ Set the contents of a field on the Document object.

❽ Save the Document object.

❾ Mark the Document object as processed by the Agent object. This ensures that the Agent object will not inadvertently process it again.

If you have read about the DocumentCollection class in chapter 11, you may be aware of a quicker, streamlined way to code example 14.5. You can use the updateAll and stampAll methods of the DocumentCollection class. Example 14.10 illustrates their use.

Example 14.10   (Domino Agent)

```
import lotus.domino.*;
public class Example_14_10 extends AgentBase {
  public void NotesMain() {
    try {
      Session s = getSession();
      AgentContext ac = s.getAgentContext();
      DocumentCollection udc = ac.unprocessedFTSearch("Unprocessed", 0);
```

```
        udc.stampAll("Flag","Processed");  ❶
        udc.updateAll();  ❷
        udc.recycle();
        ac.recycle();
        s.recycle();
    } catch(Exception e) {
        e.printStackTrace();}}}
```

Explanation

❶ Populate the specified field on all documents with the value.

❷ Mark all documents in the collection as processed by the Agent.

Now, that is much smoother. The system takes care of saving the changes.

14.7.2   SavedData

The SavedData property of the AgentContext class is fascinating. A Domino agent has its own document in the Database, but it is never visible to the user (or developer) in any form. You can save and retrieve data to and from the Document between calls to the Agent. The only problem is that the Document is wiped clean every time it is saved/modified. A modification includes enabling or disabling. One simple piece of data to save is the number of times an Agent has run (been called). Example 14.11 illustrates this.

Example 14.11   (Domino Agent)

```
import lotus.domino.*;
import java.io.PrintWriter;
public class Example_14_11 extends AgentBase {
  public void NotesMain() {
     try {
     Session s = getSession();
     PrintWriter pw = getAgentOutput();
     AgentContext ac = s.getAgentContext();
     Document adoc = ac.getSavedData();  ❶
     int curCount = 0;  ❷
     if (adoc.hasItem("count")) {  ❸
       Item countItem = adoc.getFirstItem("count");  ❹
       pw.println("Number of times ran:  " + countItem.getValueInteger());  ❺
       curCount = countItem.getValueInteger() + 1;}  ❻
       else {
       pw.println("Number of times ran:  0");
     curCount = 1; }  ❼
    if (adoc.hasItem("user")) {
       pw.println("User name:  " + adoc.getItemValue("user")); }  ❽
     else {
       pw.println("User name field is empty."); }
       Integer cur = new Integer(curCount);  ❾
       adoc.replaceItemValue("user", ac.getEffectiveUserName());  ❿
```

```
        adoc.replaceItemValue("count", cur);  ⑪
        adoc.save();  ⑫
        adoc.recycle();
        adoc.recycle();
        s.recycle();
    } catch(Exception e) {
        e.printStackTrace();}}}
```

Explanation

❶ Retrieve the Agent Document object.

❷ Initialize our counter variable.

❸ Determine if the field exists.

❹ Retrieve the count variable from the Document object and place it into an Item object.

❺ Display the current count.

❻ Increment the counter.

❼ Initialize the counter to one; this is executed if the field has not been created yet.

❽ Display the last user to run or access the Agent.

❾ Create an Integer object with our count variable. The replaceItemValue method of the Document class requires the value parameter (second parameter) to be an object. For this reason, the primitive data type int will not work.

❿ Set the contents of the user field. You could use the appendItemValue method of the Document class to maintain a list of all users.

⑪ Set the contents of the count field.

⑫ Save the Agent Document.

Run the agent once or more and you will notice the counter rise. The output reflects running it five times.

Output

```
Number of times ran:  0
User name field is empty.
Number of times ran:  1
User name:  [CN=Tony Patton/O=TIS]
Number of times ran:  2
User name:  [CN=Tony Patton/O=TIS]
Number of times ran:  3
User name:  [CN=Tony Patton/O=TIS]
Number of times ran:  4
User name:  [CN=Tony Patton/O=TIS]
```

14.7.3 DocumentContext

The `DocumentContext` property of the `AgentContext` class is very important when you work with Web clients. It represents the in-memory `Document` when an agent is called. Non-Domino programs create a `Document` in memory, and they can call an agent to work with it. When a Web client submits a document to a Domino server, the `DocumentContext` property of the `AgentContext` class retrieves and processes it.

The `DocumentContext` property returns a `Document` object. Once you have a handle on it, you can work with it just like any other document. Chapter 21 covers this property in more detail.

```
Document = AgentContext.getDocumentContext;
```

14.7.4 PrintWriter class

I want to conclude this chapter with a brief description of the `PrintWriter` class. I expect most developers to ask, "Why is it needed? You can use the `System.out.println` command to achieve the same results." When you work with Domino agents and the Notes client only, `System.out.println` suffices. On the other hand, if your intended audience is Web-based, you must use the `PrintWriter` class. No ifs, ands, or buts. That is the way Lotus designed it, so you must stick to the program. Many examples in this book take advantage of the `PrintWriter` class to send output to the Java Console Window. Also, chapter 21, which covers working with the Web, includes more examples of using the `PrintWriter` class with browser clients.

14.8 CHAPTER REVIEW

The `Agent` class is the most important vehicle when you work with Java in the Domino Designer environment. It is the only place where you can use Java code. Java standalone applications and applets can access Domino objects remotely, but within Domino, the `Agent` is it. For this reason it is very important to understand just how an agent works and the various methods and properties available in the `Agent` class. A thorough understanding of the Domino server agent manager task could not hurt as well, but it is beyond the scope of this book. In addition, the `AgentContext` class allows access to the current environment for a running agent.

- The Domino agent is the one and only place to run Java code within the Domino Designer.

- You can obtain an `Agent` object through the `Database` and/or `AgentContext` classes.

- Numerous properties in the `Agent` class allow you to access everything from the server on which it runs, including the last time it ran and what triggers its execution.

- You can edit only two properties of the `Agent` class: `IsEnabled` and `ServerName`. You must call the save method for the changes to take effect.

- The `runOnServer` and `run` methods of the `Agent` class allow agents to be started from another agent. An agent cannot use these methods on itself.

- The `remove` method of the `Agent` class permanently deletes an `Agent` from a `Database`.

- The `AgentContext` class allows access to an agent's environment when it is running. It allows access to itself and its database container.

- The `DocumentContext` property of the `AgentContext` class retrieves documents from memory. It is very important when you work with Web clients.

- The `SavedData` property of the `AgentContext` class allows access to an `Agent`'s `Document`. You can store and retrieve data to and from an `Agent`'s `Document` between calls to the agent.

- You must use the `PrintWriter` class when you send data to a Web client, but it is optional for Notes clients.

C H A P T E R   1 5

Name class

15.1 Overview   188
15.2 Syntax   189
15.3 Creation   190
15.4 Properties   191
15.5 Putting it to use   193
15.6 Chapter review   195

15.1   OVERVIEW

The Name class represents a Domino user/server name. The use of this class allows access to the various attributes of a Domino username. Many classes in the Domino Java hierarchy allow access to the current user's common name. This is true in the Session and AgentContext classes. The Name class differs in the fact that it allows access to individual portions of a name and other attributes. A Domino user name is contained in a hierarchical format, such as this:

CN=Tony Patton/OU1=Help Desk/OU=IS/OU=Corporate/O=BaseLine/C=US

The elements are defined as follows:

- CN: Common Name
- OU: Organizational Unit within Organization (There can be from one to four of these specified as OU1, OU2, OU3, and OU4.)
- O: Organization Name, usually the company name for the user
- C: Country

15.2 SYNTAX

The syntax for the implementation of the Name class is very straightforward. You can obtain a handle to a Name object for the current user via the Session class.

15.2.1 getUserNameObject method

The getUserNameObject method of the Session class returns a Name object representing the current user.

```
Name = Session.getUserNameObject();
```

Example 15.1 (Domino Agent)

```
import lotus.domino.*;
import java.io.PrintWriter;
import java.util.Vector;
public class Example_15_1 extends AgentBase {
  public void NotesMain() {
    try {
      Session s = getSession();
      PrintWriter pw = getAgentOutput();
      Name curName = s.getUserNameObject();       ❶
      pw.println("Current user:  " + curName.getCommon());   ❷
      s.recycle();
    } catch(Exception e) {
      e.printStackTrace();}}}
```

Explanation

❶ Retrieve the Name object representing the current user.

❷ Display the common name of the user via the Common property of the Name class.

Output

```
Current user:  Tony Patton
```

15.2.2 getUserNameList

The getUserNameList method returns a Vector of Name objects representing the primary and alternate (if it exists) user name for the current user.

```
Vector = Session.getUserNameList();
```

Example 15.2 (Domino Agent)

```
import lotus.domino.*;
import java.io.PrintWriter;
import java.util.Vector;
public class Example_15_2 extends AgentBase {
  public void NotesMain() {
    try {
```

```
      Session s = getSession();
      PrintWriter pw = getAgentOutput();
        Vector names = s.getUserNameList();        ❶
        for (int x = 0; x<names.size(); x++) {     ❷
          Name curName = (Name)names.elementAt(x);  ❸
          pw.println("Name " + x + " is "+ curName.getCommon());}  ❹
      s.recycle();
      } catch(Exception e) {
        e.printStackTrace();}}}
```

Explanation

❶ Populate a Vector object of Name objects for the current user. It will contain the primary name and alternate name, if it exists.

❷ Loop through all Name objects in the Vector.

❸ Retrieve the current Name object using a loop index variable. The returned object must be cast to a Name object.

❹ Display the common user name for the entry via the Common property of the Name class.

Output

```
Name 0 is Tony Patton
```

15.3   CREATION

You can create a new Name object via the createName method of the Session class. This method has one required parameter: the user's name. The second parameter is optional; it specifies the language. You should use the second parameter for alternate names only.

```
Name = Session.createName(String, Optional_String);
```

Example 15.3 uses the EffectiveUserName property of the AgentContext class to create a new Name object that represents it.

Example 15.3   (Domino Agent)

```
import lotus.domino.*;
import java.io.PrintWriter;
public class Example_15_3 extends AgentBase {
  public void NotesMain() {
    try {
      Session s = getSession();
      PrintWriter pw = getAgentOutput();
      AgentContext ac = s.getAgentContext();
      Name curName = s.createName(ac.getEffectiveUserName());  ❶
      if (curName != null) {  ❷
        pw.println("Effective name:  " + ac.getEffectiveUserName());  ❸
```

CHAPTER 15   NAME CLASS

```
        pw.println("Common name:   " + curName.getCommon()); ❹
        pw.println("Country:   " + curName.getCountry()); ❺
        pw.println("Initials:  " + curName.getInitials()); ❻
        pw.println("Organization:  " + curName.getOrganization()); ❼
        pw.println("Surname:  " + curName.getSurname()); } ❽
    curName.recycle();
    ac.recycle();
    s.recycle();
  } catch(Exception e) {
    e.printStackTrace();}}}
```

Explanation

❶ Create a Name object from the user name retrieved via the
getEffectiveUserName method of the AgentContext class.

❷ Proceed only if the Name object is valid.

❸ Display the effective user name.

❹ Display the common name for the user.

❺ Display the user's country (if it is set).

❻ Display the user's initials (if they are set).

❼ Display the user's organization name (if it is set).

❽ Display the user's surname (if it is set).

Output

```
Effective name: CN=Tony Patton/O=BaseLine/C=US
Common name: Tony Patton
Country:  US
Initials:
Organization: TIS
Surname:
```

A number of the properties of a Domino user name are optional. It is up to the discretion of the Domino server administrator (or whoever creates users) as to what
information gets entered for a user. Such information as the country, initials, and surname are not required.

15.4 PROPERTIES

We have seen various properties of the Name class in action, but here is a complete list
of all of them. Many of the properties correspond to aspects of the hierarchical name,
as described in section 15.1. Also, all property values are read-only and accessible via
a corresponding get method.

- Abbreviated: The hierarchical name in an abbreviated form
- Addr821: Internet address in Internet standard RFC 821 Address Format Syntax

- `Addr822Comment1`: Comment1 portion of RFC 822 address
- `Addr822Comment2`: Comment2 portion of RFC 822 address
- `Addr822Comment3`: Comment3 portion of RFC 822 address
- `Addr822LocalPart`: LocalPart portion of RFC 822 Address Format Syntax
- `Addr822Phrase`: Phrase portion of RFC 822 Address Format Syntax
- `ADMD`: Administration management domain name portion of a hierarchical name
- `Canonical`: Hierarchical name in canonical format
- `Common`: Common name portion of a hierarchical name
- `Country`: Country portion of a hierarchical name
- `Generation`: Generation portion of a hierarchical name
- `Given`: Given portion of a hierarchical name
- `Initials`: The initials portion of a hierarchical name
- `IsHierarchical`: Signals (true/false) whether name is hierarchical
- `Keyword`: All components of a name except the user name
- `Language`: Language tag associated with name
- `Organization`: Organization portion of a hierarchical name
- `OrgUnit1`: First organizational unit of a hierarchical name
- `OrgUnit2`: Second organizational unit of a hierarchical name
- `OrgUnit3`: Third organizational unit of a hierarchical name
- `OrgUnit4`: Fourth organizational unit of a hierarchical name
- `Parent`: `Session` object that contains the `Name` object
- `PRMD`: Private management domain name portion of a hierarchical name
- `Surname`: The surname portion of a hierarchical name

Example 15.4 retrieves and displays all properties for the current user.

Example 15.4   (Domino Agent)

```
import lotus.domino.*;
import java.io.PrintWriter;
public class Example_15_4 extends AgentBase {
  public void NotesMain() {
    try {
      Session s = getSession();
      PrintWriter pw = getAgentOutput();
      AgentContext ac = s.getAgentContext();
      Name curName = s.getUserNameObject();
      if (curName != null) {
        pw.println("Abbreviated:   " + curName.getAbbreviated());
```

```
pw.println("Addr821:   " + curName.getAddr821());
pw.println("Addr822Comment1:   " + curName.getAddr822Comment1());
pw.println("Addr822Comment2:   " + curName.getAddr822Comment2());
pw.println("Addr822Comment3:   " + curName.getAddr822Comment3());
pw.println("Addr822LocalPart:   " + curName.getAddr822LocalPart());
pw.println("Addr822Phrase:   " + curName.getAddr822Phrase());
pw.println("Canonical:   " + curName.getCanonical());
pw.println("Common name:   " + curName.getCommon());
pw.println("Country:   " + curName.getCountry());
pw.println("Generation:   " + curName.getGeneration());
pw.println("Given:   " + curName.getGiven());
pw.println("Initials:   " + curName.getInitials());
pw.println("Hierarchical?   " + curName.isHierarchical());
pw.println("Keyword:   " + curName.getKeyword());
pw.println("Language:   " + curName.getLanguage());
pw.println("Organization:   " + curName.getOrganization());
pw.println("OrgUnit1:   " + curName.getOrgUnit1());
pw.println("OrgUnit2:   " + curName.getOrgUnit2());
pw.println("OrgUnit3:   " + curName.getOrgUnit3());
pw.println("OrgUnit4:   " + curName.getOrgUnit4());
pw.println("PRMD:   " + curName.getPRMD());
pw.println("Surname:   " + curName.getSurname()); }
curName.recycle();
ac.recycle();
s.recycle();
} catch(Exception e) {
e.printStackTrace();}}}
```

15.5   PUTTING IT TO USE

Now we have looked at the inner workings of the Name class; it does provide a lot of
information regarding a user's name. It serves the same purpose as the @Name function in the Notes formula language. You can always get a user's name via the
Session or AgentContext classes, but it may not be in the format that you desire.
For instance, you may want to populate a field on a form using the user's name. In
this case you don't want the fully hierarchical name used, because it appears garbled
when it is displayed to the user. Example 15.5 achieves this.

Example 15.5   (Domino Agent)

```
import lotus.domino.*;
public class Example_15_5 extends AgentBase {
 public void NotesMain() {
   try {
     Session s = getSession();
     AgentContext ac = s.getAgentContext();
     Database db = ac.getCurrentDatabase();
     Document doc = db.createDocument();      ❶
     Name user = s.getUserNameObject();      ❷
```

```
        doc.replaceItemValue("Form","Demo");
        doc.replaceItemValue("Title", "Test");
         doc.replaceItemValue("Name", user.getCommon());   ❸
        doc.save();
        doc.recycle();
        user.recycle();
        db.recycle();
        ac.recycle();
        s.recycle();
      } catch(Exception e) {
        e.printStackTrace();}}}
```

Explanation

❶ Create a new Document object.

❷ Obtain the Name object that represents the current user.

❸ Populate the Name field with the user's common name.

Another use for the Name class could be searching for all documents for a certain user. Example 15.6 illustrates this use. It searches for all documents containing instances of a certain name and then deletes them.

Example 15.6   (Domino Agent)

```
import lotus.domino.*;
public class Example_15_6 extends AgentBase {
 public void NotesMain() {
   try {
     Session s = getSession();
     AgentContext ac = s.getAgentContext();
     removeDocs(s, "Mike Jones/Finance/BaseLine/US", null, "test.nsf");   ❶
     ac.recycle();
     s.recycle();
   } catch(NotesException n) {
     System.out.println("Notes exception #" + n.id + ", " + n.text);   ❷
   } catch(Exception e) {
     e.printStackTrace();}}

public void removeDocs(Session pSession, String pName, String pServer, String pDB)
     throws NotesException {   ❸
   Database db = pSession.getDatabase(pServer, pDB);   ❹
   Name user = pSession.createName(pName);   ❺
   DocumentCollection dc = db.FTSearch(user.getCommon(),0);   ❻
   if (dc.getCount() > 0) {   ❼
     dc.removeAll(true); }   ❽
 db.recycle();
 user.recycle();
 dc.recycle();} }
```

Explanation

❶ Call the `removeDocs` method. It accepts four parameters: `Session` object, user name, server name, and database filename/path.

❷ Display details of the Notes exception, if it occurs.

❸ The `removeDocs` method declaration. It returns no value (void) and is available to the world (public). It may throw a `NotesException` object, so we must specify exceptions via the `Throws` keyword.

❹ Create `Database` object via server name and database filename/path passed into method.

❺ Create a new `Name` object for the user name passed into the method.

❻ Create a `DocumentCollection` object containing all documents found that contain the user name.

❼ Proceed only if documents were returned via the search.

❽ Delete all documents via the `removeAll` method of the `DocumentCollection` class.

15.6 CHAPTER REVIEW

The `Session` and `AgentContext` classes provide access to the current user's name, and there is a wealth of information regarding it. The `Name` class provides access to all properties of a user's name. You can create a new `Name` object via the `createName` method of the `Session` class and the name passed into it. The `Name` class can be useful in various places in an application; it mimics the functionality of @Name in the Notes formula language.

- The `Name` class contains numerous properties for a user name.
- You can retrieve a `Name` object using the `Session` object's `getUserNameObject` and `getUserNameList` methods.
- The `createName` function of the `Session` class creates a `Name` object that represents the user name passed into it.
- You can use the `getEffectiveUserName` method of the `AgentContext` class with the `Session`'s `createName` function to create a `Name` object for the current user.
- The `Name` class provides some of the same functionality as @Name in the Notes formula language.

C H A P T E R   1 6

Date-time values

16.1 Overview   196
16.2 Creating   196
16.3 Special identifiers   197
16.4 Properties   198
16.5 Adjusting   200
16.6 More methods   201
16.7 Finding the difference between two
      Date-Time objects   204

16.8 Searching using date-time
      values   205
16.9 DateRange class   205
16.10 Free-time search   207
16.11 International class   208
16.12 Working with Date-Time fields   213
16.13 GregorianCalendar class   216
16.14 Chapter review   218

16.1 OVERVIEW

The Java `DateTime` class allows you to work with date-time values in the Domino format. The format is slightly different from the `java.util.Date` class. You can create a new `DateTime` object via the `Session` class, and retrieve existing `DateTime` objects from the `AgentContext`, `Database`, `DateRange`, `DateTime`, `Document`, and `View` classes.

16.2 CREATING

The `Session` class creates a new `DateTime` object. It has two formats: the first one accepts a `String` value representing a date-time value, and the other accepts a `java.util.Date` object.

```
DateTime = Session.createDateTime(String);
```

and

```
DateTime = Session.createDateTime(java.util.Date);
```

196

16.3   SPECIAL IDENTIFIERS

The `createDateTime` method of the `Session` class accepts three special values: today, tomorrow, and yesterday. These identifiers initiate the `DateTime` object accordingly. Example 16.1 illustrates their use, as well as the `createDateTime` method.

Example 16.1   (Domino Agent)

```
import lotus.domino.*;
import java.io.PrintWriter;
public class Example_16_1 extends AgentBase {
  public void NotesMain() {
    try {
      Session s = getSession();
      PrintWriter pw = getAgentOutput();
      AgentContext ac = s.getAgentContext();
      DateTime dt1 = s.createDateTime("6/1/2000 01:00:00 PM");   ❶
      DateTime dt2 = s.createDateTime("Today");   ❷
      DateTime dt3 = s.createDateTime("Tomorrow");   ❸
      DateTime dt4 = s.createDateTime("Yesterday");   ❹
      DateTime dt5 = s.createDateTime("06:30:00 AM");   ❺
      DateTime dt6 = s.createDateTime("4/15/1999");   ❻
      pw.println("dt1:   " + dt1.getLocalTime());   ❼
      pw.println("dt2:   " + dt2.getLocalTime());
      pw.println("dt3:   " + dt3.getLocalTime());
      pw.println("dt4:   " + dt4.getLocalTime());
      pw.println("dt5:   " + dt5.getLocalTime());
      pw.println("dt6:   " + dt6.getLocalTime());
      dt1.recycle();
      dt2.recycle();
      dt3.recycle();
      dt4.recycle();
      dt5.recycle();
      dt6.recycle();
      ac.recycle();
      s.recycle();
    } catch(NotesException n) {
      System.out.println("Notes exception #" + n.id + ", " + n.text);
    } catch(Exception e) {
      e.printStackTrace();}}}
```

Explanation

❶ Create a new `DateTime` object using the specified date and time.

❷ Create a new `DateTime` object using today's date.

❸ Create a new `DateTime` object using tomorrow's date.

❹ Create a new `DateTime` object using yesterday's date.

❺ Create a new `DateTime` object using the specified time.

❻ Create a new `DateTime` object using the specified date.

❼ Display the contents of each `DateTime` object.

Output

```
dt1:   06/01/2000 01:00:00 PM EDT
dt2:   11/15/99
dt3:   11/16/99
dt4:   11/14/99
dt5:   06:30:00 AM
dt6:   04/15/99
```

16.4   PROPERTIES

Numerous properties available in the `DateTime` class can access certain portions of the date-time value.

16.4.1   DateOnly

The `DateOnly` property returns only the date portion of its value.

16.4.2   GMTTime

The `GMTTime` property returns the date-time value converted to Greenwich Mean Time.

16.4.3   IsDST

The `IsDST` property returns true or false signaling whether or not the date-time value represents daylight savings time.

16.4.4   LocalTime

The `LocalTime` property returns the date-time value in the local time zone.

16.4.5   Parent

The `Parent` property returns the `Session` object that contains the `DateTime` object.

16.4.6   TimeOnly

The `TimeOnly` property returns only the time portion of its value.

16.4.7   TimeZone

The `TimeZone` property returns the time zone of the date-time value as an integer value. The number indicates the number of hours that must be added to the value to get the Greenwich Mean Time when the `IsDST` property is false.

16.4.8 ZoneTime

The ZoneTime property returns the time portion of the date-time value adjusted for the TimeZone and IsDST properties. Example 16.2 takes advantage of the properties.

Example 16.2   (Domino Agent)

```
import lotus.domino.*;
import java.io.PrintWriter;
public class Example_16_2 extends AgentBase {
  public void NotesMain() {
    try {
      Session s = getSession();
      PrintWriter pw = getAgentOutput();
      AgentContext ac = s.getAgentContext();
      DateTime dt = s.createDateTime("Yesterday 01:01:00 PM");   ❶
      pw.println("Local Time: " + dt.getLocalTime());   ❷
      pw.println("Date:   " + dt.getDateOnly());   ❸
      pw.println("Time:   " + dt.getTimeOnly());   ❹
      pw.println("GMT:   " + dt.getGMTTime());   ❺
      pw.println("Time Zone:   " + dt.getTimeZone());   ❻
      pw.println("Zone Time:   " + dt.getZoneTime());   ❼
      pw.println("Daylight Savings Time?   " + dt.isDST());   ❽
      dt.recycle();
      ac.recycle();
      s.recycle();
    } catch(NotesException n) {
      System.out.println("Notes exception #" + n.id + ", " + n.text);
    } catch(Exception e) {
      e.printStackTrace();}}}
```

Explanation

❶ Create a new DateTime object that represents the given time for yesterday.

❷ Display the local time.

❸ Display the date portion.

❹ Display the time portion.

❺ Display the Greenwich Mean Time.

❻ Display the time zone.

❼ Display the zone time.

❽ Display whether or not daylight savings time has been applied.

Output

```
Local Time:  11/14/99 01:01:00 PM EST
Date:  11/14/99
Time:  01:01:00 PM
GMT:  11/14/99 06:01:00 PM GMT
Time Zone:  5
Zone Time:  11/14/99 01:01:00 PM EST
Daylight Savings Time?  false
```

16.5 ADJUSTING

In addition to the properties, a variety of methods available in the DateTime class work with the value stored in it. They allow you to adjust various aspects of the date-time value. All these methods accept an integer value that can be negative or positive:

- adjustDay: Adjusts only the day portion of a date value
- adjustHour: Adjusts only the hour portion of the time value
- adjustMinute: Adjusts only the minute portion of the time value
- adjustMonth: Adjusts only the month portion of the date value
- adjustSecond: Adjusts only the seconds portion of the time value
- adjustYear: Adjusts only the year portion of the date value

Let's take a look at these methods in action in example 16.3.

Example 16.3   (Domino Agent)

```
import lotus.domino.*;
import java.io.PrintWriter;
public class Example_16_3 extends AgentBase {
 public void NotesMain() {
  try {
   Session s = getSession();
   PrintWriter pw = getAgentOutput();
   AgentContext ac = s.getAgentContext();
   DateTime dt = s.createDateTime("Tomorrow 12:00:00 PM");  ❶
   pw.println("Local Time:  " + dt.getLocalTime());  ❷
   dt.adjustDay(15);  ❸
   pw.println("Local Time:  " + dt.getLocalTime());
   dt.adjustHour(-48);  ❹
   pw.println("Local Time:  " + dt.getLocalTime());
   dt.adjustMinute(600);  ❺
   pw.println("Local Time:  " + dt.getLocalTime());
   dt.adjustMonth(6);  ❻
   pw.println("Local Time:  " + dt.getLocalTime());
   dt.adjustSecond(-360);  ❼
   pw.println("Local Time:  " + dt.getLocalTime());
   dt.adjustYear(-2);  ❽
   pw.println("Local Time:  " + dt.getLocalTime());
   dt.recycle();
   ac.recycle();
   s.recycle();
  } catch(NotesException n) {
   System.out.println("Notes exception #" + n.id + ", " + n.text);
  } catch(Exception e) {
   e.printStackTrace();}}}
```

Explanation

❶ Create a new `DateTime` object for noon tomorrow.

❷ Display the local time.

❸ Add 15 days to the date-time value.

❹ Subtract 48 hours from the date-time value.

❺ Add 600 minutes (10 hours) to the date-time value.

❻ Add 6 months to the date-time value.

❼ Subtract 360 seconds (6 minutes) from the date-time value.

❽ Subtract 2 years from the date-time value.

Output

```
Local Time: 11/16/99 12:00:00 PM EST
Local Time: 12/01/99 12:00:00 PM EST
Local Time: 11/29/99 12:00:00 PM EST
Local Time: 11/29/99 10:00:00 PM EST
Local Time: 05/29/2000 10:00:00 PM EDT
Local Time: 05/29/2000 09:54:00 PM EDT
Local Time: 05/29/98 09:54:00 PM EDT
```

16.6 MORE METHODS

There are a number of methods in addition to the adjustment-related methods.

16.6.1 convertToZone

The `convertToZone` method alters the time zone and daylight savings time settings for the `DateTime` object.

```
DateTime.convertToZone(time_zone_integer, boolean_dst);
```

16.6.2 setAnyDate

The `setAnyDate` method sets the date portion of a `DateTime` object to a random date value.

```
DateTime.setAnyDate();
```

16.6.3 setAnyHour

The `setAnyHour` method sets the time portion of a `DateTime` object to a random time value.

```
DateTime.setAnyTime();
```

16.6.4 setLocalDate

The `setLocalDate` method sets the local date portion of the `DateTime` object to the value passed into it.

```
DateTime.setLocalDate("Date");
```

16.6.5 setLocalTime

The setLocalTime method sets the local time portion of the DateTime object to the value passed into it.

```
DateTime.setLocalTime("Time");
```

NOTE   The time is in the form of minutes:hours:seconds AM/PM (xx:xx:xx XM).

16.6.6 setNow

The setNow method sets the date and time values of the DateTime object to the current time and date.

```
DateTime.setNow();
```

16.6.7 timeDifference

The timeDifference method finds the difference in seconds between two DateTime objects.

16.6.8 toJavaDate

The toJavaDate method converts a DateTime object value to a java.util.Date object.

```
java.util.Date = DateTime.toJavaDate();
```

Example 16.4 takes advantage of some of these methods.

Example 16.4   (Domino Agent)

```
import lotus.domino.*;
import java.io.PrintWriter;
import java.util.Date;
public class Example_16_4 extends AgentBase {
  public void NotesMain() {
    try {
      Session s = getSession();
      PrintWriter pw = getAgentOutput();
      DateTime dt = s.createDateTime("1/1/1998 12:00:00 PM");    ❶
      pw.println("Local Time:   " + dt.getLocalTime());    ❷
      dt.setAnyDate();    ❸
      pw.println("Local Time:   " + dt.getLocalTime());    ❹
      dt.setAnyDate();    ❺
      pw.println("Local Time:   " + dt.getLocalTime());
      dt.setAnyTime();    ❻
      pw.println("Local Time:   " + dt.getLocalTime());
      dt.setNow();    ❼
      pw.println("Local Date/Time:   " + dt.getLocalTime());
      dt.setLocalTime(8,45,0,0);    ❽
      pw.println("Local Time:   " + dt.getLocalTime());
      dt.setLocalDate(1969,4,15);    ❾
      pw.println("Local Time:   " + dt.getLocalTime());
      Date javaDate1 = new Date();    ❿
```

```
        Date javaDate2 = dt.toJavaDate();  ⑪
        pw.println("Java date/time:  " + javaDate2.toString());
        pw.println("Java date/time:  " + javaDate1.toString());  ⑫
        javaDate1.setDate(15);  ⑬
        javaDate1.setMonth(4);  ⑭
        javaDate1.setYear(1969);  ⑮
        pw.println("Java date/time:  " + javaDate1.getMonth());  ⑯
        dt.recycle();
        s.recycle();
    } catch(NotesException n) {
        System.out.println("Notes exception #" + n.id + ", " + n.text);
    } catch(Exception e) {
        e.printStackTrace();}}}
```

Explanation

❶ Create a new DateTime object with the specified date and time.

❷ Display the local date-time for the DateTime object.

❸ Set the date portion of the DateTime object to a random date value.

❹ Display the local date-time for the DateTime object.

❺ Set the time portion of the DateTime object to a random time value.

❻ Set the time portion of the DateTime object to a random time value.

❼ Set the date-time value of the DateTime object to the current date and time.

❽ Set the local time portion of the DateTime object to 8:45 a.m.

❾ Set the local date portion of the DateTime object to April 15, 1969.

❿ Create a new Java Date object.

⑪ Create a new Java Date object using the Domino DateTime object.

⑫ Display the Java date-time property of the Java Date object.

⑬ Set the date portion of the Java Date object.

⑭ Set the month portion of the Java Date object.

⑮ Set the year portion of the Java Date object.

⑯ Display the month setting of the Java Date object.

Output

```
Local Time:  01/01/98 12:00:00 PM EST
Local Time:  12:00:00 PM
Local Time:  12:00:00 PM
Local Time:
Local Date/Time:  11/15/99 01:33:34 AM EST
Local Time:  11/15/99 08:45:00 AM EST
Local Time:  04/15/69 09:45:00 AM EDT
Java date/time:  Tue Apr 15 09:45:00 EDT 1969
Java date/time:  Mon Nov 15 01:33:31 EST 1999
Java date/time:  4
```

16.7 FINDING THE DIFFERENCE BETWEEN TWO DATE-TIME OBJECTS

The timeDifference method of the DateTime class was discussed previously, but example 16.5 puts it to use.

Example 16.5   (Domino Agent)

```
import lotus.domino.*;
import java.io.PrintWriter;
import java.util.Date;
public class Example_16_5 extends AgentBase {
  public void NotesMain() {
    try {
      Session s = getSession();
      PrintWriter pw = getAgentOutput();
      DateTime dt1 = s.createDateTime("01/01/2001 12:00:00 AM");    ❶
      DateTime dt2 = s.createDateTime("Today");    ❷
      dt2.setNow();    ❸
      int diff = dt1.timeDifference(dt2);    ❹
      int minutes = (diff / 60);    ❺
      int hours = (diff / 3600);    ❻
      int days = (diff / 86400);    ❼
      pw.println("----------------------------------------------");
      pw.println("              Countdown");
      pw.println("----------------------------------------------");
      pw.println("There are " + diff + " seconds until 2001.");    ❽
      pw.println("There are " + minutes + " minutes until 2001.");    ❾
      pw.println("There are " + days + " days until 2001.");    ❿
      pw.println("----------------------------------------------");
      dt2.recycle();
      dt1.recycle();
      s.recycle();
    } catch(NotesException n) {
      System.out.println("Notes exception #" + n.id + ", " + n.text);
    } catch(Exception e) {
      e.printStackTrace();}}}
```

Explanation

❶ Create a new DateTime object for January 1, 2001.

❷ Create a new DateTime object for today.

❸ Set the date-time of the DateTime object to the current date and time.

❹ Calculate the difference in seconds between the two date-time values.

❺ Convert the difference in seconds to minutes.

❻ Convert the difference in seconds to hours.

❼ Convert the difference in seconds to days.

8 Display the number of seconds until January 1, 2001.

9 Display the number of hours until January 1, 2001.

10 Display the number of days until January 1, 2001.

Output

```
-------------------------------------------
Countdown
-------------------------------------------
There are 4054142 seconds until 2001.
There are 67569 minutes until 2001.
There are 46 days until 2001.
-------------------------------------------
```

16.8 SEARCHING USING DATE-TIME VALUES

The `DateTime` class is used to search via the `search` method of the `Database` class and the `unprocessedSearch` method of the `AgentContext` class. It is used as the cutoff date for the searches. The searches return only documents created after the date-time value in the `DateTime` object.

The `search` method of the `Database` object searches all documents in the database:

```
Session s = getSession();
AgentContext ac = s.getAgentContext();
Database db = ac.getCurrentDatabase();
DateTime dt = new DateTime("01/01/1996");
DocumentCollection dc = db.Search("Java",dt,0);
```

The `unprocessedSearch` method of the `AgentContext` class searches all documents not yet processed by the agent:

```
Session s = getSession();
AgentContext ac = s.getAgentContext();
DateTime dt = new DateTime("01/01/1996");
DocumentCollection dc = ac.unprocessedSearch("Java", dt, 0);
```

16.9 DATERANGE CLASS

The `DateRange` class is another date-time-related Domino Java class. This class represents a range of date-times. It has only four properties, which you can retrieve and set via the respective `get` and `set` methods:

- `EndDateTime`: The ending date-time of the range. A `DateTime` object represents it.
- `StartDateTime`: The starting date-time of the range. A `DateTime` object represents it.
- `Text`: The starting and ending date-time of the `DateRange` object returned as a string
- `Parent`: The `Session` object used to create the `DateRange` object

You can create a DateRange object via the createDateRange method of the Session class:

```
DateRange = Session.createDateRange();
```

Example 16.6   (Domino Agent)

```
import lotus.domino.*;
import java.io.PrintWriter;
public class Example_16_6 extends AgentBase {
 public void NotesMain() {
   try {
     Session s = getSession();
     PrintWriter pw = getAgentOutput();
     DateRange dr = s.createDateRange();                           ❶
     DateTime sdt = s.createDateTime("04/15/1999 12:00:00 PM");    ❷
     DateTime edt = s.createDateTime("04/17/1999 12:00:00 PM");    ❸
     dr.setStartDateTime(sdt);        ❹
     dr.setEndDateTime(edt);          ❺
     pw.println("Start date-time: " + dr.getStartDateTime());      ❻
     pw.println("End date-time: " + dr.getEndDateTime());          ❼
     pw.println("Text:   " + dr.getText());       ❽
     int diff = edt.timeDifference(sdt);        ❾
     int minutes = (diff / 60);
     int hours = (diff / 3600);
     int days = (diff / 86400);
     pw.println("The date range is " + diff + " seconds.");        ❿
     pw.println("The date range is " + minutes + " minutes.");     ⓫
     pw.println("The date range is " + days + " days.");           ⓬
     edt.recycle();
     sdt.recycle();
     dr.recycle();
     s.recycle();
   } catch(NotesException n) {
     System.out.println("Notes exception #" + n.id + ", " + n.text);
   } catch(Exception e) {
     e.printStackTrace();}}}
```

Explanation

❶ Create a new DateRange object.

❷ Create a new DateTime object for the start date-time of the DateRange object.

❸ Create a new DateTime object for the end date-time of the DateRange object.

❹ Set the start date-time of the DateRange object using a DateTime object.

❺ Set the end date-time of the DateRange object using a DateTime object.

❻ Display the start date-time.

❼ Display the end date-time.

❽ Display the start and end date-times as text.

❾ Compute the difference of the start and end date-times in seconds.

❿ Display the difference in seconds.

⓫ Display the difference in minutes.

⓬ Display the difference in days.

Output

```
Start date-time: 04/15/99 12:00:00 PM EDT
End date-time: 04/17/99 12:00:00 PM EDT
Text:  04/15/99 12:00:00 PM EDT - 04/17/99 12:00:00 PM EDT
The date range is 172800 seconds.
The date range is 2880 minutes.
The date range is 2 days.
```

16.10 FREE-TIME SEARCH

The freeTimeSearch method of the Session class searches for free time slots for calendaring and scheduling. Of course, you must use and enable calendaring and scheduling in the Domino server. The method returns a Vector of DateRange objects containing matches. It has the following format:

```
Vector = Session.freeTimeSearch(DateRange, int, Vector, boolean);
```

- DateRange: The date-time range to find
- int: The length in minutes of the free-time interval to find
- String/Vector: List of Domino names or single name to be used in free time search
- boolean: Signals true if you only want the first match, or false if you want all matches

You can put the freeTimeSearch method to use in any calendar and scheduling applications. Example 16.7 illustrates its use.

Example 16.7   (Domino Agent)

```
import lotus.domino.*;
import java.io.PrintWriter;
import java.util.Vector;
public class Example_16_7 extends AgentBase {
  public void NotesMain() {
    try {
      Session s = getSession();
      PrintWriter pw = getAgentOutput();
      DateRange dr = s.createDateRange();              ❶
      DateTime sdt = s.createDateTime("04/16/1999 12:00:00 PM");   ❷
      DateTime edt = s.createDateTime("04/17/1999 12:00:00 PM");   ❸
      dr.setStartDateTime(sdt);     ❹
      dr.setEndDateTime(edt);    ❺
```

```
        Vector namesToFind = new Vector();  ❻
        namesToFind.addElement("Julius Erving");  ❼
        namesToFind.addElement("Len Dykstra");
        namesToFind.addElement("Charles Barkley");
        int diff = edt.timeDifference(sdt);  ❽
        int minutes = (diff / 60);  ❾
        Vector freeFind = s.freeTimeSearch(dr, minutes, namesToFind, false);  ❿
        if (freeFind == null) {  ⓫
        pw.println("No matching slots found."); }
    else {
        for (int x=0; x < freeFind.size(); x ++) {  ⓬
          DateRange cur = (DateRange)freeFind.elementAt(x);  ⓭
        pw.println("Match:  " + cur.getText());
        cur.recycle();}}
    edt.recycle();
    sdt.recycle();
    dr.recycle();
    s.recycle();
  } catch(NotesException n) {
    System.out.println("Notes exception #" + n.id + ", " + n.text);
  } catch(Exception e) {
    e.printStackTrace();}}}
```

Explanation

❶ Create a new `DateRange` object.

❷ Create a `DateTime` object to use for the start date-time of the `DateRange` object.

❸ Create a `DateTime` object to use for the end date-time of the `DateRange` object.

❹ Set the start date-time of the `DateRange` object.

❺ Set the end date-time of the `DateRange` object.

❻ Create a `Vector` object for the names to find.

❼ Add names to the `Vector` object.

❽ Retrieve the difference in seconds between the start and end date-times.

❾ Calculate the difference in minutes between the start and end date-times.

❿ Populate the `Vector` object with `DateRange` objects found during the free-time search.

⓫ Proceed only if the search was successful.

⓬ Loop through all elements in the `Vector` object of matches.

⓭ Retrieve the `DateRange` element from `Vector`; the element must be explicitly cast to the `DateRange` type.

16.11 INTERNATIONAL CLASS

With the new global economy upon us, we have to keep in mind that our applications may be used outside of the country in which they were designed. The

`International` class provides a way to work with some of the date-time issues (as well as others). It represents the international settings for the operating system on which the code runs. In Windows 3.x/95/98/NT you can find these settings via the Control Panel.

16.11.1 Accessing

You can access an `International` object via the `getInternational` method of the `Session` class.

```
International = Session.getInternational();
```

16.11.2 Properties

All properties of the `International` class are read-only; you cannot set them in any way through code. You must execute the changes at the operating-system level.

- `AMString`: The string used to denote a.m. time. For English, this will be "AM".
- `CurrencyDigits`: The number of decimal digits in numbers
- `CurrencySymbol`: The character used to represent currency. For the United States, this will be "$".
- `DateSep`: The character used to separate months, days, and years
- `DecimalSep`: The character used as the decimal separator in numbers
- `IsCurrencySpace`: Boolean flag that signals if currency numbers have a space between the currency symbol and the number
- `IsCurrencySuffix`: Boolean flag that signals if the currency symbol follows the number (true) or precedes it (false)
- `IsCurrencyZero`: Boolean flag that signals if fractional numbers have zero before the decimal separator
- `IsDateDMY`: Boolean flag that signals if the date format is day-month-year
- `IsDateMDY`: Boolean flag that signals if the date format is month-day-year
- `IsDateYMD`: Boolean flag that signals if the date format is year-month-day
- `IsDST`: Boolean flag that signals whether or not daylight savings time is in effect
- `IsTime24Hour`: Boolean flag that signals if the time format is 24 hours
- `Parent`: The `Session` object used to create the `International` object
- `PMString`: The string used to denote p.m. entries. For English, this will be "PM",
- `ThousandsSep`: The character used to separate thousands in numbers. A comma is commonly used.
- `TimeSep`: The character used to separate hours, minutes, and seconds in a time value
- `TimeZone`: An integer denoting the time zone. Lotus Help states that this number represents the number of hours that must be added (positive or negative value) to get the Greenwich Mean Time for a time value.

- Today: The string that means "Today" in a date-time specification. Remember that you can use this string to instantiate a `DateTime` object to today's date.

- Tomorrow: The string that means "Tomorrow." You can use this string to instantiate a `DateTime` object to tomorrow's date.

- Yesterday: The string that means "Yesterday." You can use this string to instantiate a `DateTime` object to yesterday's date.

Example 16.8 accesses the various properties of an `International` object running on a Windows 98 platform in the Eastern Time Zone of the United States.

Example 16.8   (Domino Agent)

```
import lotus.domino.*;
import java.io.PrintWriter;
import java.util.Vector;
public class Example_16_8 extends AgentBase {
 public void NotesMain() {
   try {
     Session s = getSession();
     PrintWriter pw = getAgentOutput();
     International intl = s.getInternational();
     pw.println("AM string: " + intl.getAMString());
     pw.println("PM string: " + intl.getPMString());
     pw.println("Currency digits: " + intl.getCurrencyDigits());
     pw.println("Currency symbol: " + intl.getCurrencySymbol());
     pw.println("Currency space before number? " + intl.isCurrencySpace());
     pw.println("Currency symbol after number? " + intl.isCurrencySuffix());
     pw.println("Zero before decimal point in currency? " + intl.isCurrencyZero());
     pw.println("Thousands separator: " + intl.getThousandsSep());
     pw.println("Date format day-month-year? " + intl.isDateDMY());
     pw.println("Date format month-day-year? " + intl.isDateMDY());
     pw.println("Date format year-month-day? " + intl.isDateYMD());
     pw.println("Daylight savings time? " + intl.isDST());
     pw.println("24 hour day? " + intl.isTime24Hour());
     pw.println("Time separator: " + intl.getTimeSep());
     pw.println("Time zone: " + intl.getTimeZone());
     pw.println("Today text value: " + intl.getToday());
     pw.println("Tomorrow text value: " + intl.getTomorrow());
     pw.println("Yesterday text value: " + intl.getYesterday());
     intl.recycle();
     s.recycle();
   } catch(NotesException n) {
     System.out.println("Notes exception #" + n.id + ", " + n.text);
   } catch(Exception e) {
     e.printStackTrace();}}}
```

Output

```
AM string: AM
PM string: PM
Currency digits: 2
```

```
Currency symbol: $
Currency space before number? false
Currency symbol after number? false
Zero before decimal point in currency? true
Thousands separator: ,
Date format day-month-year? false
Date format month-day-year? true
Date format year-month-day? false
Daylight savings time? true
24 hour day? false
Time separator: :
Time zone: 5
Today text value: Today
Tomorrow text value: Tomorrow
Yesterday text value: Yesterday
```

You can use the getTomorrow, getToday, and getYesterday methods in conjunction with the DateTime class to create DateTime objects.

Example 16.9   (Domino Agent)

```
import lotus.domino.*;
import java.io.PrintWriter;
public class Example_16_9 extends AgentBase {
 public void NotesMain() {
   try {
     Session s = getSession();
     PrintWriter pw = getAgentOutput();
      International intl = s.getInternational();      ❶
      String pm = intl.getPMString();      ❷
      String tsep = intl.getTimeSep();      ❸
      String dsep = intl.getDateSep();      ❹
     DateTime dt1 = s.createDateTime(intl.getToday());      ❺
     DateTime dt2 = s.createDateTime(intl.getTomorrow());      ❻
     DateTime dt3 = s.createDateTime(intl.getYesterday());      ❼
     DateTime dt4;
     if (intl.isDateDMY()) {      ❽
      dt4 = s.createDateTime("15"+dsep+"4"+dsep+"1969"+"
         "+tsep+"00"+tsep+"00 "+pm);      ❾
     } else if (intl.isDateMDY()) {      ❿
       dt4 = s.createDateTime("4"+dsep+"15"+dsep+"1969"+"
         "+tsep+"00"+tsep+"00 "+pm);
     } else if (intl.isDateYMD()) {      ⓫
       dt4 = s.createDateTime("1969"+dsep+"4"+dsep+"15"+"
         "+tsep+"00"+tsep+"00 "+pm);
     } else {
       dt4 = s.createDateTime("4/15/1969 12:00:00 PM"); }
       pw.print("dt1:   " + dt1.getDateOnly() + " ");      ⓬
       pw.println(dt1.getTimeOnly());
     pw.print("dt2:   " + dt2.getDateOnly() + " ");
     pw.println(dt2.getTimeOnly());
     pw.print("dt3:   " + dt3.getDateOnly() + " ");
     pw.println(dt3.getTimeOnly());
     pw.print("dt4:   " + dt4.getDateOnly() + " ");
     pw.println(dt4.getTimeOnly());
```

```
        dt1.recycle();
        dt2.recycle();
        dt3.recycle();
        dt4.recycle();
        intl.recycle();
        s.recycle();
    } catch(NotesException n) {
        System.out.println("Notes exception #" + n.id + ", " + n.text);
    } catch(Exception e) {
        e.printStackTrace();}}}
```

Explanation

❶ Create an International object.

❷ Retrieve the p.m. setting for the International object.

❸ Retrieve the time separator for the International object.

❹ Retrieve the date separator for the International object.

❺ Create a DateTime object using the Today property of the International object. This ensures that no error occurs when/if the application is run on a different system.

❻ Create a DateTime object using the Tomorrow property of the International object.

❼ Create a DateTime object using the Yesterday property of the International object.

❽ Determine if the format of dates for the International object is day-month-year. If so, set our Date object's value accordingly.

❾ Populate our DateTime object using the day-month-year format. We utilize the time separator, date separator, and PM string of the International class to ensure no runtime errors.

❿ Determine if the format of dates for the International object is month-day-year. If so, set our Date object's value accordingly.

⓫ Determine if the format of dates for the International object is year-month-day.

⓬ Display the values of all our Date objects to ensure that they were properly created.

Output

```
dt1:  11/15/99
dt2:  11/16/99
dt3:  11/14/99
dt4:  04/15/69 12:00:00 PM
```

16.12 Working with Date-Time fields

You can designate fields on a Domino form as Date-Time fields. There is no method of the Document class available to easily access these values in Domino Java. For this reason, you must use a Vector object and casting. The Vector object retrieves the Date-Time field, and the Vector element(s) must be cast to a DateTime object. Once this is done, you can manipulate the values as a DateTime object. Example 16.10 illustrates the point by searching in the database for all documents that are overdue. A mail memo is sent if an item is overdue.

Example 16.10 (Domino Agent)

```
import lotus.domino.*;
import java.io.PrintWriter;
import java.util.Vector;
public class Example_16_10 extends AgentBase {
PrintWriter pw = this.getAgentOutput();
 public void NotesMain() {
   try {
     Session s = getSession();
     AgentContext ac = s.getAgentContext();
     Database db = ac.getCurrentDatabase();
     DocumentCollection dc = db.getAllDocuments();
     if (dc.getCount() > 0){
       Document doc = dc.getFirstDocument();
       DateTime rightNow = s.createDateTime("01/01/1987");    1
       rightNow.setNow();    2
       while (doc != null) {
         Vector dtValues = new Vector();    3
         dtValues = doc.getItemValue("DueDate");    4
         if (dtValues != null)  {    5
           if (dtValues.size() > 0){    6
             DateTime dtValue = (DateTime)dtValues.elementAt(0);    7
             int diff = dtValue.timeDifference(rightNow);    8
             if (diff < 0) {    9
               Document memo = db.createDocument();    10
               memo.replaceItemValue("Form", "Memo");
               Vector recipients = new Vector();
               recipients.addElement(doc.getItemValue("CheckedOutBy"));
               String title = doc.getItemValueString("BookTitle");
               String subject = "Your book " + title + " is overdue.";
               memo.replaceItemValue("Subject", subject);
               String body = "Please return as soon as possible.";
               memo.replaceItemValue("Body",body);
               memo.send(false, recipients);
               memo.recycle();} } } } }
     dc.recycle();
     db.recycle();
     ac.recycle();
     s.recycle();
```

```
  } catch(NotesException n) {
  pw.print("Domino error#" + n.id);
  pw.println(" (" + n.text + ")");
  } catch(Exception e) {
  e.printStackTrace(); } } }
```

Explanation

❶ Create a new `DateTime` object via the `Session` object.

❷ Set the value to the current date and time.

❸ Create a new `Vector` object to hold values from the Date/Time field.

❹ Retrieve the Date/Time field from the current `Document` object.

❺ Proceed only if the `Vector` object exists.

❻ Proceed only if the `Vector` object has elements.

❼ Our Date/Time field has only one value, so it is at element zero of the `Vector` object. The object in the `Vector` object must be cast to the type we are retrieving, thus `DateTime`.

❽ Compute the difference between the current date and time and the value stored on the document.

❾ Proceed only if the value is less than the current day.

❿ Create a new `Document` object for the mail memo.

Example 16.11 utilizes both the `International` and `DateTime` classes. The script extracts the day portion of the date value and determines if the day value is equal to the current day value. The script sends an email memo if they are the same. This technique is useful for performing tasks on a certain day of the month, such as the first day of the month.

Example 16.11   (Domino Agent)

```
import lotus.domino.*;
import java.util.Vector;
import java.util.Date;
public class Example_16_11 extends AgentBase {
  public void NotesMain() {
    try {
      Session s = this.getSession();
      AgentContext ac = s.getAgentContext();
      Database db = ac.getCurrentDatabase();
      DocumentCollection dc = db.getAllDocuments();
      Document doc = null;
      if (dc.getCount() > 0){
        for (int i = 1; i <= dc.getCount(); i++)  {
          doc = dc.getNthDocument(i);
          Vector monthDayV = new Vector();
```

```
        monthDayV = doc.getItemValue("DayDue");  ❶
        if (monthDayV != null) {
          if (monthDayV.size() > 0)  {
            DateTime rNowDT = s.createDateTime("01/01/1987");  ❷
            rNowDT.setNow();  ❸
            DateTime mDayDT = (DateTime)monthDayV.elementAt(0);  ❹
            International inter = s.getInternational();  ❺
            String dateSep = inter.getDateSep();  ❻
            String rNowS = rNowDT.getDateOnly();  ❼
            String mDayS = mDayDT.getDateOnly();
            int sepD1 = rNowS.indexOf(dateSep);  ❽
            int sepD2 = rNowS.lastIndexOf(dateSep);  ❾
            int sepD3 = mDayS.indexOf(dateSep);
            int sepD4 = mDayS.lastIndexOf(dateSep);
            String tempDayN = null;
            String tempDayM = null;
            if (inter.isDateDMY()){
              tempDayN = rNowS.substring(0, (sepD1-1));  ❿
              tempDayM = mDayS.substring(0, (sepD3-1));}
            else if (inter.isDateMDY())  {
              tempDayN = rNowS.substring((sepD1+1), sepD2);
              tempDayM = mDayS.substring((sepD3+1), sepD4);   }
            else if (inter.isDateYMD())  {
              tempDayN = rNowS.substring((sepD2+1),(rNowS.length()-1));
              tempDayM = mDayS.substring((sepD4+1), (mDayS.length()-1));}
            if (tempDayN == tempDayM)  {  ⓫
              Document memo = db.createDocument();
              memo.replaceItemValue("Form","Memo");
              memo.replaceItemValue("Subject","Items are due today.");
              memo.replaceItemValue("Body","You have items due.");
              Vector recipients = new Vector();
              recipients.addElement("Graham Greene");
              memo.send(false, recipients);
              memo.recycle(); } } } } }
    dc.recycle();
    db.recycle();
    ac.recycle();
    s.recycle();
  } catch(NotesException n) {
  System.out.print("Domino error#" + n.id);
  System.out.println(" ( " + n.text + ")");
  } catch(Exception n) {
  e.printStackTrace();} } }
```

Explanation

❶ Retrieve the Date-Time field from the form.

❷ Create a new `DateTime` object.

❸ Set the date-time value property of the `DateTime` object to the current date and time.

❹ Get the DateTime object from the Vector object.

❺ Create a new International object.

❻ Get the date separator setting for the current machine.

❼ Convert the DateTime value to the String object.

❽ Find the first occurrence of the date separator character in the String object.

❾ Find the last occurrence of the date separator character in the String object.

❿ If the format of the date for the current machine is day-month-year, then extract the date portion using the substring method of the String class.

⓫ If the days are equal, send an email memo.

16.13 GREGORIANCALENDAR CLASS

The Java language provides its own classes for working with date and time values. These include the GregorianCalendar, Calendar, and Date classes. You can find them in the java.util package. When you work with Domino date-time values, you can use the toJavaDate method to obtain a Date object. Once you have a Date object, you can use it to create a GregorianCalendar object to work with the values, as follows:

```
Session s = new NotesSession();
DateTime dt = s.createDateTime("01/01/1987");
dt.setNow();
java.util.Date javaDT = dt.toJavaDate();
GregorianCalendar gc = new GregorianCalendar();
gc.setTime(javaDT);
```

The combination of the Calendar and GregorianCalendar classes allows you to work with many facets of a date-time, such as the year, day, month, hour, and minutes. You can retrieve these properties by utilizing the Calendar class, thus:

```
int dayPortion = gc.get(java.util.Calendar.DAY);
int hourPortion = gc.get(java.util.Calendar.HOUR_OF_DAY);
int yearPortion = gc.get(java.util.Calendar.YEAR);
int minutePortion = gc.get(java.util.Calendar.MINUTE);
```

NOTE   The Year property is Y2K compliant, so it does return four-digit values.

The DAY property of the Calendar class returns the day portion of a date value. Also, you can retrieve the day of the week and the day of the year. The DAY_OF_WEEK property returns the day of the week, starting at zero for Sunday and ending with six for Saturday. The DAY_OF_YEAR property returns from 1 to 365 for the day of the year; January 1 would return 1. Example 16.12 takes advantage of these properties in an application for checking out books; the code determines if the book is due or not.

Example 16.12   (Domino Agent)

```
import java.util.*;
public class Example_16_12 extends AgentBase {
 public void NotesMain() {
  try {
    Session s = getSession();
    AgentContext ac = s.getAgentContext();
    Database db = ac.getCurrentDatabase();
    Vector duedate = new Vector();
    DateTime rightNowDT = s.createDateTime("01/01/1987");   ❶
    DateTime duedateDT = s.createDateTime("01/01/1987");    ❷
    GregorianCalendar rightNowGC = new GregorianCalendar();  ❸
    GregorianCalendar duedateGC = new GregorianCalendar();   ❹
    View vw = db.getView("CheckedOut");
    if (vw != null) {
     Document doc = vw.getFirstDocument();
     while (doc != null) {
      dueDate = sched.getItemValue("DueDate");   ❺
      if (duedate != null) {
       if (duedate.size() > 0) {   ❻
        duedateDT = (DateTime)lastRunV.elementAt(0);   ❼
        rightNowDT.setNow();   ❽
        rightNowGC.setTime(rightNowDT.toJavaDate());   ❾
        duedateGC.setTime(duedateDT.toJavaDate());
        int nowYear = rightNowGC.get(Calendar.YEAR);   ❿
        int dueYear = duedateGC.get(Calendar.YEAR);
        int nowMonth = rightNowGC.get(Calendar.MONTH);   ⓫
        int dueMonth = duedateGC.get(Calendar.MONTH);
        int nowDay = rightNowGC.get(Calendar.DAY_OF_YEAR);   ⓬
        int dueDay = duedateGC.get(Calendar.DAY_OF_YEAR);
        int nowHour = rightNowGC.get(Calendar.HOUR_OF_DAY);   ⓭
        int dueHour = duedateGC.get(Calendar.HOUR_OF_DAY);
        int nowMin = rightNowGC.get(Calendar.MINUTE);   ⓮
        int dueMin = duedateGC.get(Calendar.MINUTE);
        if (dueYear <= nowYear) {   ⓯
         if (dueMonth <= nowMonth) {   ⓰
          if (dueDay <= nowDay) {   ⓱
           doc.replaceItemValue("Status","Overdue");   ⓲
           doc.save();} } } } } } }
  } catch (NotesException n) {
   System.out.print("Notes error#" + n.id);
   System.out.println(" (" + n.text + ")");
  } catch(Exception e) {
   e.printStackTrace(); } } }
```

Explanation

❶ Create a new `DateTime` object for later use.

❷ Create a new `DateTime` object for later use.

❸ Create a new `GregorianCalendar` object for later use.

❹ Create a new `GregorianCalendar` object for later use.

❺ Retrieve the due date field in a `Vector` object.

❻ Proceed only if the `Vector` object contains values.

❼ Retrieve the `DateTime` object from the `Vector` object.

❽ Set the value of the `DateTime` object to the current date and time.

❾ Instantiate the `GregorianCalendar` object using a `Date` object.

❿ Retrieve the year portion of the `GregorianCalendar` object.

⓫ Retrieve the month portion of the `GregorianCalendar` object.

⓬ Retrieve the day portion of the `GregorianCalendar` object.

⓭ Retrieve the hour portion of the `GregorianCalendar` object.

⓮ Retrieve the minute portion of the `GregorianCalendar` object.

⓯ Determine if the due year is less than or equal to the current year.

⓰ Determine if the due month is less than or equal to the current month.

⓱ Determine if the due day is less than or equal to the current day.

⓲ Set the status field of the `Document` object to overdue.

16.14 CHAPTER REVIEW

The `DateTime`, `DateRange`, and `International` classes facilitate the use of Domino date-time values in our applications. The format of a Domino date-time is a little different than that used in the Core Java `java.lang.Date` class. The `Session` object creates instances of all three Domino Java classes. The `International` class is very powerful. It allows access to system settings for date, time, and numeric and currency values. The settings are specific to the operating system. You can use these settings to create Domino date-time values to ensure no errors occur when you run the code on other systems.

- The `DateTime` class works with Domino date-time values.
- The `DateTime` class has various methods for accessing properties of it. These include retrieving only the date and/or time portions of its value.
- There are a number of *adjust* methods for adjusting the time and/or date value contained in a `DateTime` object.
- You can use the `timeDifference` method of the `DateTime` class to retrieve the difference (in seconds) between two `DateTime` objects.
- The `DateRange` object represents a range of objects denoted by a start date-time and an end date-time.
- `DateTime` objects can create `DateRange` objects.
- You will use the `DateRange` object extensively when you perform Domino calendaring and schedule free-time searches.
- The `International` class allows access to various system settings, including time, date, numeric, and currency settings. You can use these attributes when you create `DateTime` values to ensure system mobility.

C H A P T E R   1 7

Working with outlines

17.1 Overview   219
17.2 Syntax   220
17.3 Properties   220
17.4 Traversing an outline   221

17.5 Other methods   224
17.6 OutlineEntry class   225
17.7 Chapter review   230

17.1   OVERVIEW

The outline is a feature added to the Domino environment starting with version five. It is a tool for providing navigation in a Domino application. It is a custom navigation structure. An outline can contain links to all of the views, folders, or pages in a database, and you can arrange the entries in a hierarchy with twisties to expand and collapse them. In addition, you can include actions such as creating a document or links to Internet addresses (URLs) as well. Figure 17.1 shows an outline for the accompanying Java source code database in a frameset.

NOTE   You utilize outlines in an application by embedding them on a page.

In figure 17.1, the outline is located in the left frame of the frameset. The outline has been embedded in a page element, which is set to load in the frameset. The right-hand frame contains a page element.

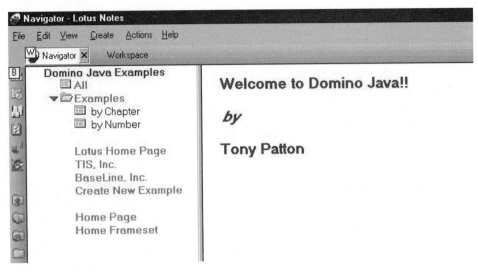

Figure 17.1   Sample outline

The Java Outline class provides programming access and control over `Outline` elements and their individual entries. There is a separate class, `OutlineEntry`, for working with individual entries. We will cover it later in this chapter.

17.2   SYNTAX

You access and create an `Outline` object via the `Database` class. The `Database` class contains `createOutline` and `getOutline` methods.

To access an existing `Outline` object, use the following:

```
Outline = Database.getOutline("name of outline");
```

To create a new `Outline` object, use the following:

```
Outline = Database.createOutline("name of new outline");
```

17.3   PROPERTIES

The `Outline` class contains three properties pertaining to the `Outline` object. All three are read-only, so they have only a *get* method.

- `Alias`: The assigned alias name of the `Outline`. You can use this for programming access. It behaves the same as aliases for Views and/or Forms. It is optional.
- `Comment`: Text description of the `Outline` entered by its developer. It is entirely optional.
- `Name`: The name assigned to an `Outline`. It is required.

Example 17.1 displays all three properties for the outline displayed in figure 17.1.

Example 17.1 (Domino Agent)

```
import lotus.domino.*;
import java.io.PrintWriter;
public class Example_17_1 extends AgentBase {
 public void NotesMain() {
  try {
    Session session = getSession();
    AgentContext ac = session.getAgentContext();
    PrintWriter pw = getAgentOutput();
    Database db = ac.getCurrentDatabase();
    Outline out = db.getOutline("Test");        ❶
    if (out != null) {  ❷
      pw.println("Outline name:  " + out.getName());        ❸
      pw.println("Outline alias:  " + out.getAlias());        ❹
      pw.println("Outline comments:  " + out.getComment()); }   ❺
    else {
      pw.println("Outline does not exist."); }
    out.recycle();
    db.recycle();
    ac.recycle();
    session.recycle();
  } catch(Exception e) {
    e.printStackTrace();}}}
```

Explanation

❶ Retrieve the specified Outline object from the current Database object.

❷ Proceed only if the Outline object was found.

❸ Display the name of the Outline object.

❹ Display the alias for the Outline object.

❺ Display any comments for the Outline object.

Output

```
Outline name:  Test
Outline alias:  outNav
Outline comments: This outline provides basic navigation for the database.
```

17.4   TRAVERSING AN OUTLINE

Numerous methods in the Outline class allow you to traverse its entries. The functionality is similar to working with View or DocumentCollection objects. The method names and their descriptions are as follows:

- getFirst: Retrieves the first entry in an Outline object
- getNext: Retrieves the next entry in the Outline using a specific entry as a point of reference
- getNextSibling: Retrieves the next entry from the Outline at the same level as the specified entry
- getParent: Retrieves the parent entry of the current entry
- getPrev: Retrieves the previous entry in the Outline using a specific entry as a point of reference
- getPrevSibling: Retrieves the previous entry from the Outline at the same level as the specified entry

Each of the *get* methods returns the entry as an OutlineEntry object, or the null value if nothing is found. Let's take a look at putting these methods to use.

Example 17.2 *walks* through an Outline object, accessing every entry in it.

Example 17.2   (Domino Agent)

```
import lotus.domino.*;
import java.io.PrintWriter;
public class Example_17_2 extends AgentBase {
  public void NotesMain() {
    try {
      Session session = getSession();
      AgentContext ac = session.getAgentContext();
      PrintWriter pw = getAgentOutput();
      Database db = ac.getCurrentDatabase();
      Outline out = db.getOutline("Test");  ❶
      if (out != null) {  ❷
        pw.println("Outline name:  " + out.getName());  ❸
        OutlineEntry outent = out.getFirst();  ❹
        while (outent != null) {  ❺
          pw.println("Entry:  " + outent.getLabel() + ", level:  " + outent.getLevel());  ❻
          outent = out.getNext(outent); } }  ❼
      else {
        pw.println("Outline does not exist."); }
      out.recycle();
      db.recycle();
      ac.recycle();
      session.recycle();
    } catch(Exception e) {
      e.printStackTrace();}}}
```

Explanation

❶ Get the specified Outline object from the current Database object.

❷ Proceed only if the Outline object was found.

❸ Display the name property of the `Outline` object.

❹ Get the first `OutlineEntry` object from the `Outline` object.

❺ Loop through all entries in the `Outline` object.

❻ Display the title and level of the `OutlineEntry` object.

❼ Get the next `OutlineEntry` object from the `Outline` object.

NOTE The output shows all first-level entries as level zero (0); entries with a level of one (1) are children to the zero-level entries above them.

Output

```
Outline name: Test
Entry: All, level: 0
Entry: Examples, level: 0
Entry:   by Chapter, level: 1
Entry:   by Number, level: 1
Entry: Other Views, level  0
Entry:   , level: 0
Entry: Lotus Home Page, level: 0
Entry: TIS, Inc., level: 0
Entry: BaseLine, Inc., level: 0
Entry: Create New Example, level: 0
Entry:   , level: 0
Entry: Home Page, level: 0
Entry: Home Frameset, level: 0
```

Example 17.3 *walks* through an `Outline` object, accessing all first-level entries in it.

Example 17.3   (Domino Agent)

```
import lotus.domino.*;
import java.io.PrintWriter;
public class Example_17_3 extends AgentBase {
  public void NotesMain() {
    try {
      Session session = getSession();
      AgentContext ac = session.getAgentContext();
      PrintWriter pw = getAgentOutput();
      Database db = ac.getCurrentDatabase();
      Outline out = db.getOutline("Navigator");     ❶
      if (out != null) {     ❷
        pw.println("Outline name:  " + out.getName());     ❸
        OutlineEntry outent = out.getFirst();     ❹
        while (outent != null) {     ❺
          pw.print("Entry:  " + outent.getLabel());     ❻
          pw.println(", level:  " + outent.getLevel());
          outent = out.getNextSibling(outent); } }     ❼
      else {
        pw.println("Outline does not exist."); }
      out.recycle();
      db.recycle();
      ac.recycle();
```

```
        session.recycle();
    } catch(Exception e) {
    e.printStackTrace();}}}
```

Explanation

❶ Retrieve the specified `Outline` object.

❷ Proceed only if the `Outline` object was found.

❸ Display the name of the `Outline` object.

❹ Get the first `OutlineEntry` object from the `Outline` object.

❺ Loop through all `OutlineEntry` objects in the `Outline` object.

❻ Display the label and level of the `OutlineEntry` object.

❼ Get the next sibling `OutlineEntry` object; this will get the next entry (if there is any) at the same level.

NOTE   The output shows that only first-level (zero) entries were retrieved. The first entry is used as the base for getting siblings in this example.

Output

```
Outline name: Navigator
Entry: All, level: 0
Entry: Examples, level: 0
Entry: Other Views, level: 0
Entry:  , level: 0
Entry: Lotus Home Page, level: 0
Entry: TIS, Inc., level: 0
Entry: BaseLine, Inc., level: 0
Entry: Create New Example, level: 0
Entry:  , level: 0
Entry: Home Page, level: 0
Entry: Home Frameset, level: 0
```

17.5   OTHER METHODS

In addition to the *get*-related methods, a few other methods achieve various results.

17.5.1   addEntry

The `addEntry` method adds a new `OutlineEntry` object to an `Outline` object. It accepts the new entry as the first parameter, and the second parameter signals the entry to use as the reference (by default the new entry is placed after it). A third parameter is optional; it is a boolean to signal whether the new entry it should appear after (true) or before (false) the reference entry. The last parameter is optional as well; it signals whether the entry should be created as a child (true) to the reference entry. If the fourth parameter is true, the third parameter is ignored.

```
Outline.addEntry(OutlineEntry, OutlineEntry, boolean, boolean);
```

17.5.2 removeEntry

The `removeEntry` method deletes an `OutlineEntry` object from an `Outline` object.

```
Outline.removeEntry(OutlineEntry);
```

17.5.3 moveEntry

The `moveEntry` method moves an `OutlineEntry` object from one place in the `Outline` object to another. Its parameters match those described for the `addEntry` method.

```
Outline.moveEntry(OutlineEntry, OutlineEntry, boolean, boolean);
```

17.5.4 createEntry

The `createEntry` method creates a brand new `OutlineEntry` object. It accepts one parameter, the name of the entry. It returns the newly created `OutlineEntry` object. You must use the `addEntry` method to actually insert the new entry into an `Outline` object.

```
OutlineEntry = Outline.createEntry(String);
```

17.5.5 save

The `save` method saves any/all changes made to the `Outline`. You must call this method for any changes made to take effect.

```
Outline.save();
```

17.6 OUTLINEENTRY CLASS

As you have seen, the `OutlineEntry` class works with individual entries in an `Outline` object. A handle to an `OutlineEntry` object is obtained through the `Outline` class, as seen in the last section.

17.6.1 Properties

The `OutlineEntry` class has a number of methods that allow you to access various attributes on an entry as well as populate some of the values:

- `Alias`: Read/write property that returns any aliases defined for the entry.
- `Database`: Read-only property that returns the `Database` object that is the source for the entry. This only returns a non-null object if the entry points to a valid `Database` object.
- `Document`: Read-only property that returns the `Document` object that is the source of the entry. This only returns a non-null object if the entry points to a valid `Document` object.
- `EntryClass`: Read-only property that returns the type of the entry (see the following list). You should use this method before you attempt to access the element's resource. It has the following possible values:

- `OutlineEntry.OUTLINE_CLASS_DATABASE`
- `OutlineEntry.OUTLINE_CLASS_DOCUMENT`
- `OutlineEntry.OUTLINE_CLASS_FORM`
- `OutlineEntry.OUTLINE_CLASS_FOLDER`
- `OutlineEntry.OUTLINE_CLASS_FRAMESET`
- `OutlineEntry.OUTLINE_CLASS_NAVIGATOR`
- `OutlineEntry.OUTLINE_CLASS_PAGE`
- `OutlineEntry.OUTLINE_CLASS_UNKNOWN`
- `OutlineEntry.OUTLINE_CLASS_VIEW`

- `Formula`: Read-only property that returns the formula for an action entry; if no formula is defined, the empty string is returned.
- `FrameText`: Read/write property that returns the target frame name (if it is defined) for the entry
- `HasChildren`: Read-only property signaling whether or not an entry has child entries linked to it
- `ImagesText`: Read/write property that returns the name of the image file used as an icon for the entry
- `isHidden`: Read/write property that signals whether or not an entry is hidden
- `isInThisDB`: Read-only property that signals whether or not the entry points to a resource that is in its Database container
- `isPrivate`: Read-only property that signals whether or not an entry is private (only for a certain individual)
- `Label`: Read/write property that represents the text displayed on an entry
- `Level`: Read-only property that returns the level of the entry within the `Outline` object. The topmost level is zero.
- `NamedElement`: Read-only property that returns the named element referenced by the entry. A named element is a Page, FrameSet, Navigator, or another entity within a Domino database.
- `Type`: Read-only property that returns the type of entry. It has the following list of possible values:
    - `OutlineEntry.OUTLINE_OTHER_FOLDERS_TYPE`
    - `OutlineEntry.OUTLINE_OTHER_UNKNOWN_TYPE`
    - `OutlineEntry.OUTLINE_OTHER_VIEWS_TYPE`
    - `OutlineEntry.OUTLINE_TYPE_ACTION`
    - `OutlineEntry.OUTLINE_TYPE_NAMEDELEMENT`
    - `OutlineEntry.OUTLINE_TYPE_NOTELINK`
    - `OutlineEntry.OUTLINE_TYPE_URL`
- `URL`: Read-only property that returns the URL of an entry
- `View`: Read-only property that returns the `View` object that is the source of the entry

17.6.2 Methods

In addition to the properties, there are a few methods you can use in performing tasks on an `OutlineEntry` object:

- setAction: Sets a formula for an entry
- setNamedElement: Sets a named element (Page, Frameset, Navigator, View) for an entry
- setNoteLink: Sets the resource link (Document, Database, or View) for an entry
- setURL: Sets the Internet address (URL) for an entry

Example 17.4   (Domino Agent)

```java
import lotus.domino.*;
import java.io.PrintWriter;
public class Example_17_4 extends AgentBase {
 public void NotesMain() {
  try {
    Session session = getSession();
    AgentContext ac = session.getAgentContext();
    PrintWriter pw = getAgentOutput();
    Database db = ac.getCurrentDatabase();
    Outline out = db.getOutline("Navigator");
    if (out != null) {
     pw.println("Outline name:  " + out.getName());        [1]
     pw.println("---------------------------------");
     OutlineEntry outent = out.getFirst();                 [2]
     while (outent != null) {                              [3]
     switch (outent.getType()) {                           [4]
      case (OutlineEntry.OUTLINE_OTHER_FOLDERS_TYPE):      [5]
      if (outent.isInThisDB()) {                           [6]
       if (outent.getEntryClass() == OutlineEntry.OUTLINE_CLASS_VIEW) {  [7]
        View vw = outent.getView();                        [8]
        pw.println("View: " + vw.getName()); }             [9]
       else {
        pw.println("View: unknown.");} }
       else {
        pw.println("View: unknown.");}
        break;                                             [10]
      case (OutlineEntry.OUTLINE_OTHER_UNKNOWN_TYPE) :
       pw.println("Unknown type for the element.");
       break;
      case (OutlineEntry.OUTLINE_OTHER_VIEWS_TYPE) :
       if (outent.isInThisDB()) {
        if (outent.getEntryClass() == OutlineEntry.OUTLINE_CLASS_VIEW) {
         View vw = outent.getView();
         pw.println("View: " + vw.getName()); }
        else {
         pw.println("View: unknown.");} }
       else {
         pw.println("View: unknown.");}
       break;
      case (OutlineEntry.OUTLINE_TYPE_ACTION) :
       pw.println("Action: " + outent.getFormula());
       break;
      case (OutlineEntry.OUTLINE_TYPE_NAMEDELEMENT) :
       type = "";
```

```
      switch (outent.getEntryClass()) {  ⑪
       case (OutlineEntry.OUTLINE_CLASS_DATABASE) :  ⑫
        type = "Database";  ⑬
       break;
      case (OutlineEntry.OUTLINE_CLASS_DOCUMENT) :
       type = "Document";
       break;
      case (OutlineEntry.OUTLINE_CLASS_FORM) :
       type = "Form";
       break;
      case (OutlineEntry.OUTLINE_CLASS_FOLDER) :
       type = "Folder";
       break;
      case (OutlineEntry.OUTLINE_CLASS_FRAMESET) :
       type = "Frameset";
       break;
      case (OutlineEntry.OUTLINE_CLASS_NAVIGATOR) :
       type = "Navigator";
       break;
      case (OutlineEntry.OUTLINE_CLASS_PAGE) :
       type = "Page";
       break;
      case (OutlineEntry.OUTLINE_CLASS_UNKNOWN) :
       type = "Unknown";
       break;
      case (OutlineEntry.OUTLINE_CLASS_VIEW) :
       type = "View";
       break;
      default :
       type = "Unknown"; }
     pw.println("Named Element: " + type);  ⑭
     case (OutlineEntry.OUTLINE_TYPE_NOTELINK) :  ⑮
      pw.println("Link" + outent.getNamedElement());  ⑯
     break;
    case (OutlineEntry.OUTLINE_TYPE_URL) :
     pw.println("URL: " + outent.getURL());
     break;
    default:
     pw.println("Unknown type for the element."); }
     outent = out.getNext(outent); } }  ⑰
   else {
    pw.println("Outline does not exist."); }
   out.recycle();
   db.recycle();
   ac.recycle();
   session.recycle();
  } catch(Exception e) {
   e.printStackTrace();}}}
```

Explanation

❶ Display the Outline object name.

❷ Get the first OutlineEntry object from the Outline object.

❸ Loop through all `OutlineEntry` objects in the `Outline` object.

❹ Retrieve the type attribute and use a `switch/case` block to handle it accordingly using the built-in constants in the `OutlineEntry` class.

❺ Determine if the type of entry is a folder.

❻ If it is a folder, determine if it is in the current database.

❼ Retrieve the `EntryClass` property of the `OutlineEntry` object; use a `switch/case` block to display its class. The constants in the `OutlineEntry` class are used.

❽ Retrieve the `View` object for the `View` reference link of the entry.

❾ Display the name of the view.

❿ The break command is necessary to ensure that control doesn't spill over to the next case statement and default statement.

⓫ Use the `EntryClass` property of the `OutlineEntry` object in a `switch/case` block.

⓬ Determine if the current entry is a reference to a `Database` object.

⓭ If it is a database, set the output string accordingly.

⓮ Display the type for the element.

⓯ Determine if the current entry is a reference to a Notes link.

⓰ If it is a link, display it via the `NamedElement` property.

⓱ Retrieve the next `OutlineEntry` object from the `Outline` object.

Output

```
Outline name:  Navigator
-------------------------------------------------
Named Element: View
Unknown type for the element.
Named Element: View
Named Element: View
View: unknown.
Unknown type for the element.
URL: http://www.lotus.com/
URL: http://www.tisny.com/
URL: http://www.baselineinc.com/
Action: @SetTargetFrame("Main");
@Command([Compose];"frmExample")
Unknown type for the element.
Named Element: Page
Named Element: Frameset
```

17.7   CHAPTER REVIEW

The Outline design element was added to the Domino environment with release five. It allows you, the developer, to add custom navigation for your Domino application. The Java `Outline` and `OutlineEntry` classes provide programming access to the `Outline` object and its elements. Individual elements in an `Outline` object can contain static text, references to named elements (such as a page view or frameset), action links views (@Functions/@Commands), or Internet links (URLs).

- The Outline is a design element that provides custom navigation to your application.
- The Outline can have a hierarchical structure, and an element can expand and collapse to show its child elements.
- The Java `Outline` class provides programmatic control over a `Database` outline.
- The `Outline` class provides methods for adding, moving, or deleting individual entries.
- The `Outline` class provides numerous methods for traversing its entries. This is much like working with a `DocumentCollection` or `View` object.
- The `OutlineEntry` class provides access to individual elements of an `Outline`.
- The `OutlineEntry` class provides numerous properties. Because you can set some of these in code, you can set the type and reference element of an entry.

C H A P T E R   1 8

Working with your classes

18.1 Overview   231
18.2 Designing classes   231
18.3 this   232
18.4 Creating a class   232

18.5 Constructors   234
18.6 Multiple objects   237
18.7 Script libraries   239
18.8 Chapter review   243

18.1 OVERVIEW

The use of object-oriented principles in the software development cycle has gained momentum over the last few years. The introduction of the Java language has fueled this growth. Java is an object-oriented language much like C++; it supports object-oriented principles as well as procedural development.

The Domino database can be described as a database of objects. The objects are represented by the database container, forms, fields, agents, and so forth. Up to this point, you have seen each of the Domino objects described in detail. This chapter turns your attention to creating your own classes.

18.2 DESIGNING CLASSES

The work involved in designing good object-oriented applications goes far beyond the scope of this book. There are a great number of methodologies in place today that foster object-oriented design. The uniform modeling language (UML) has gained

231

popularity recently. These methodologies help create solid reusable classes. The examples in this chapter are fairly straightforward, but proper planning and design go a long way toward a good application.

18.3   THIS

Use the keyword this within an object (class instance) to access its attributes. This is a real timesaver, because you do not have to repeatedly type a class name when you use a class within itself.

18.4   CREATING A CLASS

Example 18.1 defines a simple Java class.

Example 18.1

```
public class Report    ❶
{  ❷
  private String title;    ❸
  public void setTitle(String passedVariable)    ❹
  {  ❺
    this.title = passedVariable;    ❻
  }  ❼
  public String getTitle()    ❽
  {  ❾
    return this.title;    ❿
  }  ⓫
}  ⓬
```

Explanation

❶ A class named Report is declared. The public identifier says it is available to all.

❷ This is the opening brace for the Report class definition.

❸ The property title is declared. It is visible only within the class. The   private identifier denotes this.

❹ The method setTitle is declared as available to the world (public). It sets the property called title to the value passed into it. The void identifier signals that the method returns no value.

❺ The opening brace designates the beginning of the setTitle method.

❻ Populate the title property with the value passed into the method.

❼ The ending brace designates the end of the setTitle method.

❽ The method getTitle is declared as available to the world (public). The String identifier signals that a String value is returned from this method. The value stored in the title property is returned.

⑨ The opening brace designates the beginning of the `getTitle` method.

⑩ The `return` statement identifies the value to return. In this case the `title` property is returned.

⑪ The ending brace designates the end of the `getTitle` method.

⑫ The ending brace designates the end of the `Report` class definition.

The keywords `public` and `private` in example 18.1 denote the scope of the variables and/or methods; that is, they define who can see and/or access the objects being created. `Public` says that the whole world can use it. `Private` states that only the object containing it can use it. In example 18.1, only the `Report` class can access the `title` property. The methods `setTitle` and `getTitle` are available to the world, so other objects can reach the `title` property through these methods. The methods assure that the `title` property is used the way it was designed. The *get* and *set* methods encapsulate the data in the class.

Now that we have created the base `Report` class, it has the title, which is common to all of our reports. We will use this class to create our Sales report. Our `sales` class contains the properties `SalesToDate`, `ProjectedSales`, and `PastSales`.

Example 18.2

```
public class Sales extends Report    ❶
{
  private double SalesToDate;    ❷
  private double ProjectedSales;    ❸
  private double PastSales;    ❹
  public void setSalesToDate(double passedSales)    ❺
{
    this.SalesToDate = passedSales;
  }
  public double getSalesToDate()    ❻
  {
    return this.SalesToDate;
  }
  public void setProjectedSales(double passedProjected)
  {
    this.ProjectedSales = passedProjected;
  }
  public double getProjectedSales()
  {
    return this.ProjectedSales;
  }
  public void setPastSales(double passedPast)
  {
    this.PastSales = passedPast;
  }
  public double getPastSales()
  {
    return this.PastSales;
  }
}
```

Explanation

❶ Create the Sales class. It inherits design from the Report class; this means that all attributes of the Report class are available within the new Sales class.

❷ The property SalesToDate is declared. It is visible only within the class. The private identifier denotes this.

❸ The property ProjectedDate is declared. It is visible only within the class.

❹ The property PastDate is declared. It is visible only within the class.

❺ The method setSalesToDate is declared as available to the world (public). It sets the property called SalesToDate to the value passed into it. The void identifier signals that the method returns no value.

❻ The method getSalesToDate is declared as available to the world (public). The double identifier signals that a double value is returned from this method. The value stored in the SalesToDate property is returned.

18.5   CONSTRUCTORS

Chapter 3 described constructors, and this section presents some code. A constructor is a method that is automatically called when a class instance (object) is created. It can be overloaded to *construct* the object using a variety of parameters. Example 18.3 uses a constructor to initialize property values. Notice that the constructor has two formats.

Example 18.3

```
public class Example_18_3 {  ❶
  private String FirstName;   ❷
  private String LastName;   ❸
  private int count;   ❹
  Example_18_3() {   ❺
    this.FirstName = "";
    this.LastName = "";
    this.count = 1; }
  Example_18_3(int pCount) {   ❻
    this.FirstName = "";
    this.LastName = "";
    this.count = pCount; }
  Example_18_3(int pCount, String pFirst,String pLast) {   ❼
    this.FirstName = pFirst;
    this.LastName = pLast;
    this.count = pCount; }
  public void setFirstName(String passedName) {
    this.FirstName = passedName; }
  public String getFirstName() {
    return this.FirstName; }
  public void setLastName(String passedName) {
    this.LastName = passedName; }
  public String getLastName() {
    return this.LastName; }
  public void setCount(int pCount) {
```

```
  this.count = pCount; }
public int getCount() {
  return this.count; } }
```

NOTE   The constructor has no return type or scope identifiers.

Figure 18.1 shows the Domino Designer client with classes from all three of the previous examples defined in it. A script library stores the custom classes.

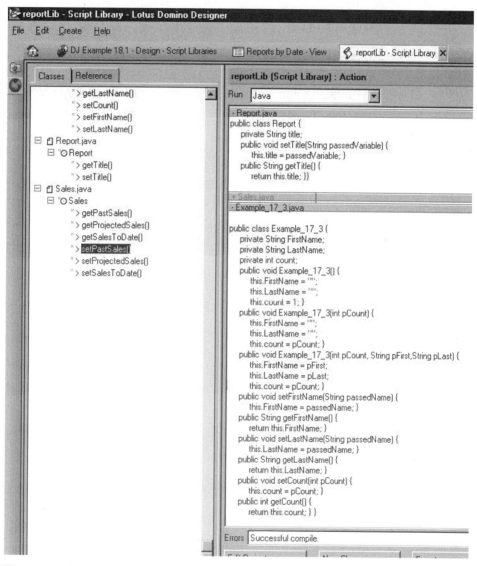

Figure 18.1   Script library with three classes

Explanation

❶ Declare the new class.

❷ Declare the FirstName property as a String.

❸ Declare the LastName property as a String.

❹ Declare the count property as a String.

❺ The first constructor accepts no parameters and sets the properties as such.

❻ The second constructor accepts an integer value that is used to set the count property.

❼ The third constructor accepts three parameters that are used to set alL three properties.

Let's take advantage of the last class and see what the constructors yield.

Example 18.4   (Domino Agent)

```
import lotus.domino.*;
import java.io.PrintWriter;
public class Example_18_4 extends AgentBase {
  public void NotesMain() {
    try {
      Session session = getSession();
      AgentContext ac = session.getAgentContext();
      PrintWriter pw = getAgentOutput();
      Example_18_3 test1 = new Example_18_3();           ❶
      pw.println("test1.count: " + test1.getCount());    ❷
      pw.println("test1.FirstName: " + test1.getFirstName());  ❸
      pw.println("test1.LastName: " + test1.getLastName());    ❹
      Example_18_3 test2 = new Example_18_3(20);         ❺
      pw.println("test2.count: " + test2.getCount());    ❻
      pw.println("test2.FirstName: " + test2.getFirstName());
      pw.println("test2.LastName: " + test2.getLastName());
      Example_18_3 test3 = new Example_18_3(5,"Tony","Patton");  ❼
      pw.println("test3.count: " + test3.getCount());
      pw.println("test3.FirstName: " + test3.getFirstName());
      pw.println("test3.LastName: " + test3.getLastName());
      ac.recycle();
      session.recycle();
    } catch(Exception e) {
      e.printStackTrace();}}}
```

Explanation

❶ Create a new object using the class from example 18.3. We pass no parameters to it.

❷ Display the count property when no parameters are used to initialize it.

❸ Display the FirstName property when no parameters are used to initialize it.

❹ Display the LastName property when no parameters are used to initialize it.

❺ Create a new object using the class from example 18.3. We pass one integer value into it.

❻ Display the properties of the object when the constructor with one integer parameter is called.

❼ Create a new object using the three-parameter constructor.

Output

```
test1.count: 1
test1.FirstName:
test1.LastName:
test2.count: 20
test2.FirstName:
test2.LastName:
test3.count: 5
test3.FirstName: Tony
test3.LastName: Patton
```

The output shows the results of our code. It verifies that different constructors are called depending on how the object is instantiated. If you browse through the Domino Java classes, you will notice that a number of the methods (this can include constructors) are overloaded.

One example of an overloaded method is the FTSearch method of the Database class. It has the following three formats:

```
public DocumentCollection FTSearch(String query)
public DocumentCollection FTSearch(String query, int max)
public DocumentCollection FTSearch(String query, int max, int sortopt, int otheropt)
```

The correct FTSearch method is called, depending on the parameters passed into the method.

18.6   MULTIPLE OBJECTS

You have seen the Vector class used extensively in the other chapters up to this point. Let's take one more look using a Vector to deal with our own classes.

By default a Vector can contain only objects. The objects can be of any type, but you must take care when you access individual objects within a Vector. Usually, an object is cast to a certain type when you access it as a Vector element. Example 18.5 creates a Vector element of our objects from example 18.3.

Example 18.5   (Domino Agent)

```
import lotus.domino.*;
import java.io.PrintWriter;
import java.util.Vector;
public class Example_18_5 extends AgentBase {
  public void NotesMain() {
    try {
      Session session = getSession();
      AgentContext ac = session.getAgentContext();
      PrintWriter pw = getAgentOutput();
```

```
        Vector myObjects = new Vector();  ❶
        Example_18_3 test1 = new Example_18_3();  ❷
        myObjects.addElement(test1);  ❸
        Example_18_3 test2 = new Example_18_3(20);  ❹
        myObjects.addElement(test2);  ❺
        Example_18_3 test3 = new Example_18_3(1,"Tony","Patton");  ❻
        myObjects.addElement(test3);  ❼
        Example_18_3 test4 = new Example_18_3(32,"Joe","Smith");
        myObjects.addElement(test4);
        Example_18_3 test5 = new Example_18_3(6,"Julius","Erving");
        myObjects.addElement(test5);
        Example_18_3 test6 = new Example_18_3(4,"Len","Dykstra");
        myObjects.addElement(test6);
        Example_18_3 test7 = new Example_18_3();
        test7.setLastName("Cunningham");  ❽
        test7.setFirstName("Randall");  ❾
        test7.setCount(12);  ❿
        myObjects.addElement(test7);
        Example_18_3 test8 = new Example_18_3(1,"Vicke","Hamilton");
        myObjects.addElement(test8);
        for (int x=0;x < myObjects.size(); x++) {  ⓫
          Example_18_3 test9 = (Example_18_3)myObjects.elementAt(x);  ⓬
          pw.println("Object# " + x + " count: " + test9.getCount());  ⓭
          pw.println("Object# " + x + " First Name: " + test9.getFirstName());
          pw.println("Object# " + x + " Last Name: " + test9.getLastName());}
        ac.recycle();
        session.recycle();
      } catch(Exception e) {
        e.printStackTrace();}}}
```

Explanation

❶ Create a new Vector object to store multiple instances of our class.

❷ Create a new instance of our class using the no argument constructor.

❸ Add the newly created object to our Vector object.

❹ Create another instance of our class with one parameter.

❺ Add the newly created object to our Vector object.

❻ Create another instance of our class with three parameters.

❼ Add the newly created object to our Vector object.

❽ Call the setLastName method of our class to populate the LastName property.

❾ Call the setFirstName method of our class to populate the FirstName property.

❿ Call the setCount method of our class to populate the count property.

⓫ Loop through all elements in the Vector object.

⑫ Retrieve an object from the Vector using the loop index. The returned object must be explicitly cast to the appropriate type.

⑬ Display the properties of the object retrieved from the Vector.

Output

```
Object# 0 count: 1
Object# 0 First Name:
Object# 0 Last Name:
Object# 1 count: 20
Object# 1 First Name:
Object# 1 Last Name:
Object# 2 count: 1
Object# 2 First Name: Tony
Object# 2 Last Name: Patton
Object# 3 count: 32
Object# 3 First Name: Joe
Object# 3 Last Name: Smith
Object# 4 count: 6
Object# 4 First Name: Julius
Object# 4 Last Name: Erving
Object# 5 count: 4
Object# 5 First Name: Len
Object# 5 Last Name: Dykstra
Object# 6 count: 12
Object# 6 First Name: Randall
Object# 6 Last Name: Cunningham
Object# 7 count: 1
Object# 7 First Name: Vicke
Object# 7 Last Name: Hamilton
```

Example 18.5 took advantage of a very important design feature in Domino Designer: a script library.

18.7   SCRIPT LIBRARIES

Many applications use common routines and functions extensively. Other programming languages such as C (#include) provide a mechanism for code sharing and reuse. Java has the import statement as well, which places code in one location where many different scripts can access it. This reduces the likelihood of errors; there is only one place where you must edit code if you find bugs or need to make changes.

The Domino Designer development environment has provided the Script Library. Script libraries allow code to be shared among many elements in a database and across different databases (if it is properly set up). You can use script libraries across several databases by copying the script library from one database (set up as a design template) to another, and then selecting yes in response to the question of whether the script library design should be inherited to receive future changes.

Script libraries are listed under Resources for a database. Figure 18.2 shows their location. You can create a new script library by selecting script libraries from the Design pane (in figure 18.2) or by using the drop-down menu (see figure 18.3). Once you create a script library in Java, you can use the New Script Library button (see figure 18.4) to create a new one.

Figure 18.2
Location of script libraries in Domino Designer

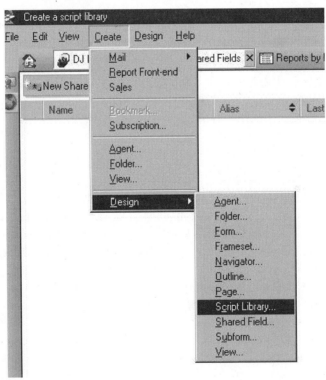

Figure 18.3 Creating a new script library via the drop-down menu

CHAPTER 18 WORKING WITH YOUR CLASSES

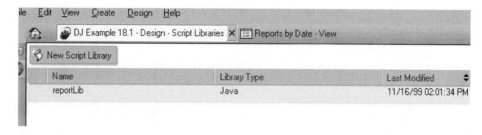

Figure 18.4   Creating a new script library via the script library pane

Selecting the New Script Library button displays a blank script library. You must select Java as the type before proceeding (see figure 18.5).

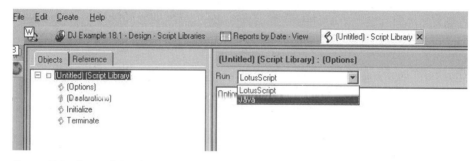

Figure 18.5   A new (blank) script library

Once you select Java, you can begin to create one or more Java classes for use in other code. Figure 18.1 displayed the script library created for use in the examples. Once you create a Java script library, you can include it in an agent via the Edit Project button displayed in figure 18.6.

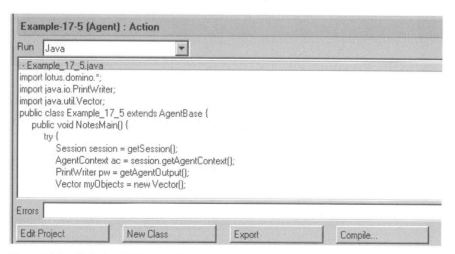

Figure 18.6   Click the Edit Project Button in the agent pane to use a script library.

Selecting the Edit Project button displays the Organize Java Agent Files window, which allows you to add and remove class files from the agent. Selecting an item from the Browse box signals the system to use the local filing system or shared Java libraries. You must select Shared Java Libraries to take advantage of script libraries.

Figure 18.7 shows this option being selected.

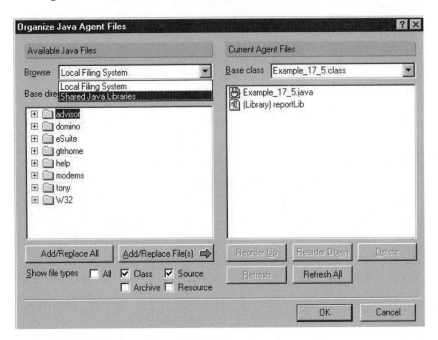

Figure 18.7   Organize Java Agent Files window

Once you select Shared Java Libraries, you can select a script library from a list of available script libraries. Figure 18.8 shows the possible choices, with the script library highlighted and added via the Add/Replace File(s) button.

Once you add your script library, it appears in the right pane with "(Library)" added to the beginning of its name.

NOTE   The contents of a script library are seen as part of your agent/code, so no two classes can have the same name. The system will not allow your code to be saved if conflicts exist.

Once your script library is added to your agent, the classes in the library are available for use in your code. You cannot view the classes within the library from the agent.

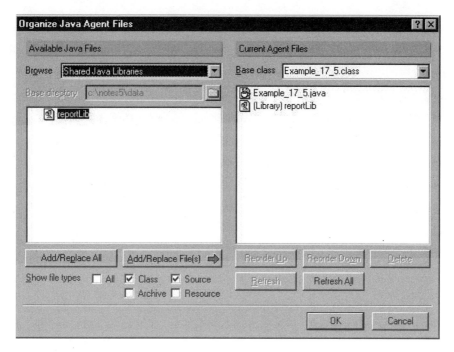

Figure 18.8   List of shared Java libraries

18.8   CHAPTER REVIEW

Java is a very powerful object-oriented language. It allows you to create your own classes. Your classes can have any number of properties and/or methods. You should declare properties as private and accessible via *set* and *get* methods. This is commonly called encapsulation. You can use a constructor to initialize a class, and you can overload it to provide numerous ways to create an object. Script libraries facilitate code sharing and reuse within the Domino developer community.

- The `class` keyword signals a class declaration.
- The `public` identifier signals that the class/property/method is available to the world.
- The `private` identifier signals that a property/method is only available to its class.
- The `extends` keyword implements class inheritance.
- Declaring properties as `private` enforces data encapsulation when the corresponding *set* and *get* methods for accessing the property are provided.
- The `this` keyword in an object can refer to itself.
- The `Vector` object can store multiple instances of an object or disparate objects.
- Script libraries allow code to be shared and reused across applications.

C H A P T E R   1 9

Reports

19.1 Overview   244
19.2 Reports as documents   245
19.3 Newsletter class   256
19.4 Chapter review   260

19.1 OVERVIEW

Reporting is one area where users continually want more. Products such as Crystal Reports, Microsoft Access, Lotus Approach, and Notes Reporter provide very powerful reporting capabilities. On the other hand, separate products require more time for installation, setup, distribution, and learning.

Views provide a rudimentary type of report with categorization, sorting, and total columns. As the number of documents in a database increases, so does the data. Consequently, it becomes more difficult to get a grasp on the data. Also, large views can take a very long amount of time to load. The Domino Java classes can address some of these issues.

The power provided by Domino Java allows the generation of custom reports within the Domino environment using either a Web client or the Lotus Notes client. You can create reports from a view or button, or on a scheduled basis when you use the Lotus Notes client. You can use scheduled agents and the form-based events

(WebQueryOpen and WebQuerySave) with a Web browser client. Also, the format of a report may take the form of an email message, Domino document, or just a pop-up window.

NOTE   This chapter is heavily dependent on concepts from the previous.

19.2   REPORTS AS DOCUMENTS

When discussing reporting possibilities, the document is one step above a view. You can create the report data/content in the back end via the Domino Java classes and save it in the form of a document. Once you save the document(s), users can view them via their preferred client.

Let's take a look at a simple example. In the scenario in example 19.1, a database contains sales records for six divisions: One, Two, Three, Four, Five, and Six. The manager wants a monthly report that summarizes sales for the six divisions.

Example 19.1   (Domino Agent)

```
import lotus.domino.*;
import java.util.Vector;
public class Example_19_1 extends AgentBase {
 public void NotesMain() {
   try {
     Session session = getSession();
     AgentContext ac = session.getAgentContext();
     Database db = ac.getCurrentDatabase();
     DocumentCollection dc = db.getAllDocuments();        ❶
     dc.FTSearch("FIELD FORM = \"salesRecord\"",0);        ❷
     Document doc = dc.getFirstDocument();        ❸
     double dSales[] = new double[6];        ❹
     Vector divisions = new Vector();        ❺
     while (doc != null) {        ❻
       if (doc.hasItem("divisionName") & doc.hasItem("divisionSales")) {        ❼
         String divisionName = doc.getItemValueString("divisionName");        ❽
         double divisionSales = doc.getItemValueDouble("divisionSales");        ❾
         int location;
         if (divisions.contains(divisionName)) {        ❿
           location = divisions.indexOf(divisionName);        ⓫
           dSales[location] += divisionSales;        ⓬
         } else {
           divisions.addElement(divisionName);        ⓭
           dSales[divisions.size() - 1] = divisionSales; }}        ⓮
         doc = dc.getNextDocument(doc);}        ⓯
         if (divisions != null) {        ⓰
           Document newDoc = db.createDocument();        ⓱
           newDoc.replaceItemValue("Form","frmDivisionSales");        ⓲
           newDoc.appendItemValue("divisionNames",divisions);        ⓳
           Vector temp1 = new Vector();        ⓴
         Double temp2;
           for (int i=0; i < dSales.length; i++) {        ㉑
```

```
        temp2 = new Double(dSales[i]);  ㉒
        temp1.addElement(temp2.toString());}  ㉓
      newDoc.appendItemValue("salesTotal", temp1);  ㉔
      newDoc.save();  ㉕
    newDoc.recycle();}
  doc.recycle();
  dc.recycle();
  ac.recycle();
  session.recycle();
} catch(Exception e) {
  e.printStackTrace();}}}
```
■

Explanation

❶ Create a new `DocumentCollection` object containing all documents from the current `Database` object.

❷ Refine the `DocumentCollection` through the `FTSearch` method. We want only those created using the salesRecord form.

❸ Retrieve the first `Document` object in the collection.

❹ Declare a new array of double values to store the totals for each division.

❺ Create a new `Vector` object to store division names found.

❻ Loop through all `Document` objects in the collection.

❼ Determine if the `Document` object contains the required fields before proceeding.

❽ Retrieve the division name from the current `Document` object.

❾ Retrieve the sales amount from the current `Document` object.

❿ Determine if the `Vector` object already contains the division name; if it does, we have already processed it, so we should just increment its sales total.

⓫ Retrieve the current location of the division within the `Vector` object.

⓬ Use the location number to retrieve the corresponding sales amount fro its array and increment its value with the number retrieved from the `Document` object.

⓭ If the division has not been processed (not found in the `Vector` object), add it to the `Vector` object and add its sales amount to the array.

⓮ We use the index value of the newly added item of the `Vector` object (the size property, because it was the last one added) for the index value for its corresponding sales amount.

⓯ Retrieve the next `Document` object from the collection.

⓰ Proceed with creating the report `Document` object only if the `Vector` object is not empty.

⓱ Create a new `Document` object for the report.

⓲ Set the form value for the report `Document` object.

⑲ Populate the multi-valued division's field with the Vector object.

⑳ Create a new Vector object to be used for processing the list of sales amounts.

㉑ Loop through each element in the array of sales amounts.

㉒ Retrieve an element from the array in the form of a Double object.

㉓ Convert the Double object value to a String value and add it to the Vector object.

㉔ Populate the multi-valued sales amount field with the Vector object.

㉕ Save the new report Document object.

Output

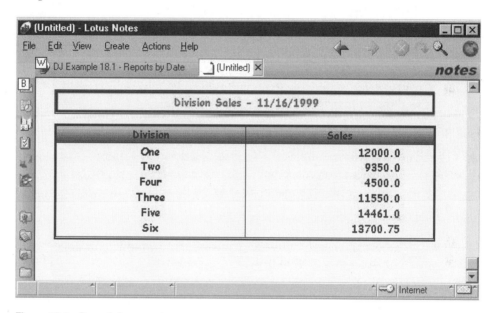

Figure 19.1   Report document

19.2.1   Email

Example 19.1 stored the reports in the database where there was a view for reviewing the reports by date. Alternatively, the reports could have been emailed to the appropriate person(s). You must include the report form in the database with the mailed document so the user can properly open and view it. The first parameter of the Send method of the Document class allows you to set this. A value of true indicates to send the form with the document. Also, you will find fields needed for emailing added to the document. These include a SendTo and a Subject field, at a minimum. You can use the CopyTo and BlindCopyTo fields as well. Otherwise, you can pass a Vector object of recipient names as the second parameter of the send method. You will also find a SaveOptions field added. A value of zero (0) signals the system to *never* save documents created with the form, and a value of one (1) has the opposite effect. You can use the MailOptions field as well; it signals whether a document is automatically mailed (value of one) or never mailed (value of zero).

You could insert the following lines of code in place of the call to the save method (item #25) from example 19.1:

```
Vector recipients = new Vector();
recipients.addElement("tpatton@tisny.com");
recipients.addElement("aspatton@bellsouth.net");
newDoc.replaceItemValue("SaveOptions","0");
newDoc.replaceItemValue("Subject", "Report");
newDoc.send(true, recipients);
```

19.2.2 Scheduled

You could place the code from example 19.1 into a scheduled Domino agent and set the schedule to run at the interval defined by you. This would automate the creation of reports either through the creation of documents or by sending them via email. A manager may want a report every morning, so you could set the schedule to run and send the report at a certain time every morning.

19.2.3 Selective/custom reports

The code from example 19.1 processes all documents in the database, but you could easily change it to process only those documents not yet processed by the agent. Item #1 from the example could be changed to the following:

```
DocumentCollection dc = ac.getUnprocessedDocuments();
```

This line forms a collection of documents that have not been processed by the agent. They may be new or modified.

19.2.4 Form as a front end

If your reporting requires a lot of user input, then you need to create a number of custom reports. The criteria for the report vary according to the user. You can use a form as a type of reporting front end. The form will have a SaveOptions field set to zero (0) so that it is never saved. It is never saved because you only use it to create reports. The user enters his/her criteria and selects a button in the Notes client (or submits it from a Web client) to trigger report generation.

Example 19.2 allows the user to select the divisions to include in the report via the Notes form and a keyword list. The front-end form in the Notes client looks like figure 19.2, and the Web client's front-end form appears in figure 19.3.

There are two Generate Report buttons on the form. One is visible to Web clients only, and the other is only visible to Lotus Notes clients. Clicking the button for Lotus Notes clients calls the agent (see the code in example 19.2) directly. Clicking the button for the Web clients places the name of the agent in its WebQuerySave form event.

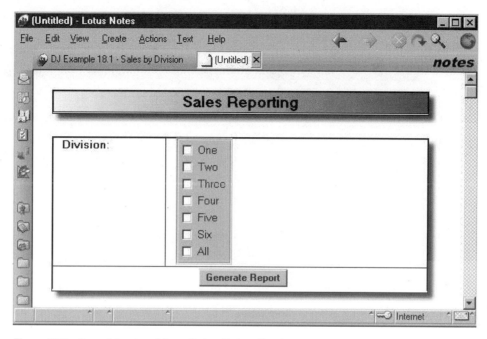

Figure 19.2 Report front-end form (Lotus Notes client)

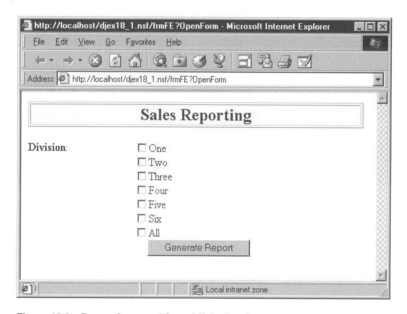

Figure 19.3 Report front-end form (Web client)

Example 19.2 shows the code for processing input from the front-end form. The script library portion of the example is listed first, with an explanation.

Example 19.2   (Domino Agent)

```
public class Sales{  ❶
  private String DivisionName;  ❷
  private double SalesAmount;  ❸
  private double ReturnsAmount;  ❹
  private int Count;  ❺
  public void setDivisionName(String pName)  {  ❻
    if (pName.trim() != "") {  ❼
      this.DivisionName = pName; }}  ❽
  public String getDivisionName()  {  ❾
    return this.DivisionName; }
    public void setSalesAmount(double pAmount)  {  ❿
      if (pAmount != 0.0) {  ⓫
        this.SalesAmount = pAmount; }}  ⓬
    public double getSalesAmount()  {  ⓭
      return this.SalesAmount; }
  public void setReturnsAmount(double pReturns)  {
    if (pReturns != 0.0) {
      this.ReturnsAmount = pReturns; }}
public double getReturnsAmount()  {
    return this.ReturnsAmount; }
  public void setCount(int pAmount)  {
    this.Count = pAmount; }
  public int getCount()  {
    return this.Count; }
    public void incCount(int i) {  ⓮
    if (i > 0) {
      this.Count += i;}}
  public void incReturnsAmount(double d) {
    if (d > 0.0) {
      this.ReturnsAmount += d; }}
  public void incSalesAmount(double d) {
    if (d > 0.0) {
      this.SalesAmount += d;}}}

import lotus.domino.*;
import java.util.Vector;
  public class Utils {  ⓯
    public boolean oneFlag = false;  ⓰
  public boolean twoFlag = false;
  public boolean threeFlag = false;
  public boolean fourFlag = false;
  public boolean fiveFlag = false;
  public boolean sixFlag = false;
  public boolean allFlag = false;
    public String setSearchString() {  ⓱
      String oneString = "(FIELD divisionName = \"One\")";  ⓲
```

```
        String twoString = "(FIELD divisionName = \"Two\")";
        String threeString = "(FIELD divisionName = \"Three\")";
        String fourString = "(FIELD divisionName = \"Four\")";
        String fiveString = "(FIELD divisionName = \"Five\")";
        String sixString = "(FIELD divisionName = \"Six\")";
         boolean firstTime = true;        ⑲
        String orString = " OR ";
         String rString="";        ⑳
         if (this.oneFlag==true) {        ㉑
          rString = oneString;        ㉒
          firstTime = false;}        ㉓
        if (this.twoFlag==true) {
         if (firstTime==true) {
          rString += orString + twoString;
          firstTime = false;}
         else {
          rString = twoString; }}
        if (this.threeFlag==true) {
         if (firstTime==true) {
          rString += orString + threeString;
          firstTime = false;}
         else {
          rString = threeString; }}
        if (this.fourFlag==true) {
         if (firstTime==true) {
          rString += orString + fourString;
          firstTime = false;}
         else {
          rString = fourString; }}
        if (this.fiveFlag == true) {
         if (firstTime==false) {
          rString += orString + fiveString;
          firstTime = false;}
         else {
          rString = fiveString; }}
         if (this.sixFlag == true) {
          if (firstTime == true) {
           rString += orString + sixString;
           firstTime = false;}
          else {
           rString = sixString; }}
      return rString; }

   public void setFlags(Document pDoc) throws NotesException {    ㉔
     Item selection = pDoc.getFirstItem("division");    ㉕
     if (selection != null) {    ㉖
      Vector divisions = selection.getValues();    ㉗
      for (int x=0; x<divisions.size(); x++) {    ㉘
        String temp = (String)divisions.elementAt(x);    ㉙
        if (temp.toUpperCase() =="ONE") {    ㉚
          oneFlag = true;}    ㉛
        else if (temp.toUpperCase() =="TWO") {
```

```
        twoFlag = true; }
    else if (temp.toUpperCase() =="THREE") {
      threeFlag = true;}
    else if (temp.toUpperCase() =="FOUR") {
      fourFlag = true;}
    else if (temp.toUpperCase() =="FIVE") {
      fiveFlag = true;}
    else if (temp.toUpperCase() =="SIX") {
      sixFlag = true; }
    else if (temp.toUpperCase() =="ALL") {
      allFlag = true; }}}}}
```

Explanation

❶ Declare a new class called `Sales`.

❷ Declare a `private String` property named `DivisionName`.

❸ Declare a `private double` property named `SalesAmount`.

❹ Declare a `private double` property named `ReturnsAmount`.

❺ Declare a `private integer` property named `Count`.

❻ Create a method to set the contents of the `DivisionName` property. It accepts one `String` parameter.

❼ Proceed only if the parameter is not empty.

❽ Set the `DivisionName` property using the parameter.

❾ Create a method to retrieve the contents of the `DivisionName` property.

❿ Create a method to set the contents of the `SalesAmount` property. It accepts one `double` parameter.

⓫ Proceed only if the parameter's value is not zero (0).

⓬ Set the `SalesAmount` property value.

⓭ Create a method to retrieve the contents `SalesAmount` property.

⓮ Create a method to increment the contents of the `Count` property. It accepts one parameter, the value to add.

⓯ Declare a new class called `Utils`.

⓰ Declare `boolean` flag variables to signal the divisions to process, the divisions selected by the user.

⓱ Declare a `setSearchString` method that formulates the string used to conduct a full-text search.

⓲ Create String variables for each division's search criteria. These will create a search string to be used for the divisions selected.

⓳ Create a boolean variable that signals whether or not it is the first item processed .

⓴ Initialize the return string to the empty string.

㉑ Determine if division one has been selected. Construct the search string accordingly.

㉒ Set the return string to the search criteria for division one.

㉓ Reset the boolean variable to false to signal that an item has been processed.

㉔ Declare the `setFlags` method; it accepts one parameter, the `Document` object to process.

㉕ Retrieve the division field from the passed `Document` object in the form of an `Item` object.

㉖ Proceed only if the division `Item` object was found.

㉗ Populate the `Vector` object with all values from the division field.

㉘ Loop through all elements in the `Vector` object.

㉙ Retrieve the current element from `Vector`; cast it to a `String` type.

㉚ Determine if division one has been selected.

㉛ Set its corresponding boolean flag if it has one.

Example 19.3 is the Domino agent that takes advantage of the script library:

Example 19.3   (Domino Agent)

```
import lotus.domino.*;
import java.util.Hashtable;
import java.util.Vector;
import java.util.Enumeration;
import java.io.PrintWriter;
public class Example_19_3 extends AgentBase {
  public void NotesMain() {
    try {
      Session s = getSession();
      AgentContext ac = s.getAgentContext();
      PrintWriter pw = getAgentOutput();
      Document doc = ac.getDocumentContext();
      Database db = ac.getCurrentDatabase();
      DocumentCollection dc = db.getAllDocuments();
      String searchString = "";        ❶
      Utils u = new Utils();            ❷
      Hashtable table = new Hashtable();   ❸
      if (doc != null) {
       u.setFlags(doc);       ❹
       searchString = u.setSearchString();    ❺
       dc.FTSearch("(FIELD FORM=\"salesRecord\")",0);    ❻
       dc.FTSearch(searchString,0);    ❼
       Document dcDoc = dc.getFirstDocument();    ❽
       Sales sale;    ❾
        while (dcDoc != null) {    ❿
         if ((dcDoc.hasItem("divisionName")) & (dcDoc.hasItem("sales")) &
            (dcDoc.hasItem("count")) & (dcDoc.hasItem("returns"))){    ⓫
          sale = new Sales();    ⓬
          if (table.isEmpty()) {    ⓭
```

```
        sale.setDivisionName(dcDoc.getItemValueString("divisionName"));  ⑭
        sale.setSalesAmount(dcDoc.getItemValueDouble("sales"));  ⑮
        sale.setReturnsAmount(dcDoc.getItemValueDouble("returns"));  ⑯
        sale.setCount(dcDoc.getItemValueInteger("count"));  ⑰
        Object val = table.put(dcDoc.getItemValueString("divisionName"),sale);}  ⑱
    else {
        if (table.containsKey(dcDoc.getItemValueString("divisionName"))) {  ⑲
          Sales temp = (Sales)table.get(dcDoc.getItemValueString("divisionName"));  ⑳
          temp.incSalesAmount(dcDoc.getItemValueDouble("sales"));  ㉑
          temp.incReturnsAmount(dcDoc.getItemValueDouble("returns"));  ㉒
          temp.incCount(dcDoc.getItemValueInteger("count"));}  ㉓
        else {
          sale.setDivisionName(dcDoc.getItemValueString("divisionName"));
          sale.setSalesAmount(dcDoc.getItemValueDouble("sales"));
          sale.setReturnsAmount(dcDoc.getItemValueDouble("returns"));
          sale.setCount(dcDoc.getItemValueInteger("count"));
          Object val = table.put(dcDoc.getItemValueString("divisionName"),sale); }} }
    dcDoc = dc.getNextDocument(dcDoc);} } ㉔
    if (table.size() != 0) {  ㉕
      Document reportDoc = db.createDocument();  ㉖
      reportDoc.replaceItemValue("Form","frmDivisionReport");  ㉗
      Enumeration enum = table.elements();  ㉘
      Vector v1 = new Vector();  ㉙
    Vector v2 = new Vector();
    Vector v3 = new Vector();
    Vector v4 = new Vector();
    Double d1, d2, d3, d4;
      while (enum.hasMoreElements()) {  ㉚
        Sales current = (Sales)enum.nextElement();  ㉛
        d1 = new Double(current.getSalesAmount());  ㉜
        v1.addElement(d1);  ㉝
      d2 = new Double(current.getReturnsAmount());
      v2.addElement(d2);
      d3 = new Double(current.getCount());
      v3.addElement(d3);
      v4.addElement(current.getDivisionName());}
        reportDoc.replaceItemValue("salesTotal",v1);  ㉞
      reportDoc.replaceItemValue("returnsTotal",v2);
      reportDoc.replaceItemValue("countTotal",v3);
      reportDoc.replaceItemValue("divisionNames",v4);
        reportDoc.save();  ㉟
      reportDoc.recycle();}
    dc.recycle();
    doc.recycle();
    db.recycle();
    ac.recycle();
    s.recycle();
  } catch(Exception e) {
    e.printStackTrace();}}}
```

Explanation

❶ Initialize the variable used in the searches.

❷ Create a new instance of the `Utils` class. Its methods will be utilized.

❸ Create a new `Hashtable` object to store the `Sales` objects.

❹ Call the `setFlags` method of the `Utils` class using the current `Document` object.

❺ Set the search string variable using the `setSearchString` method of the `Utils` class.

❻ Refine the collection to only those documents created with a certain form.

❼ Refine the collection more using the string constructed by the `setSearchString` method.

❽ Retrieve the first `Document` object from the `DocumentCollection` object.

❾ Declare a new `Sales` object.

❿ Loop through all documents in the collection.

⓫ Proceed only if the document has the required fields.

⓬ Instantiate a new `Sales` object.

⓭ Check if the `Hashtable` object is empty; this signals the first time.

⓮ Populate the `DivisionName` property of the `Sales` object.

⓯ Populate the `SalesAmount` property of the `Sales` object.

⓰ Populate the `ReturnsAmount` property of the `Sales` object.

⓱ Populate the `Count` property of the `Sales` object.

⓲ Insert the `Sales` object into the `Hashtable` object.

⓳ Determine if the division from the document exists in the `Hashtable` object.

⓴ Retrieve the matching element from the `Hashtable` object so we can work with it.

㉑ Increment the `SalesAmount` property of the `Sales` object.

㉒ Increment the `ReturnsAmount` property of the `Sales` object.

㉓ Increment the `Count` property of the `Sales` object.

㉔ Retrieve the next `Document` object from the `DocumentCollection` object.

㉕ The report Document will be created only if the `Hashtable` object is not empty.

㉖ Create the new report `Document` object.

㉗ Populate the form field of the report Document.

㉘ Populate an `Enumeration` object with all objects from the `Hashtable` object.

㉙ Declare `Vector` objects to be used to populate multi-valued fields on the report Document.

㉚ Loop through all objects in the `Enumeration` object.

㉛ Retrieve the current object; it must be explicitly cast to a `Sales` object.

㉜ Declare a new `Double` object using the `SalesAmount` property of the `Sales` object. This is necessary because the `Vector` class accepts only objects. The `SalesAmount` property is the primitive `double` type, so it must be converted.

㉝ Add the `Double` object to the `Vector` object.

㉞ Populate the `SalesTotal` field using the appropriate `Vector` object. Passing a `Vector` object into the `replaceItemValue` method automatically inserts multiple values (for multi-valued fields only).

㉟ Save the newly created report `Document` object.

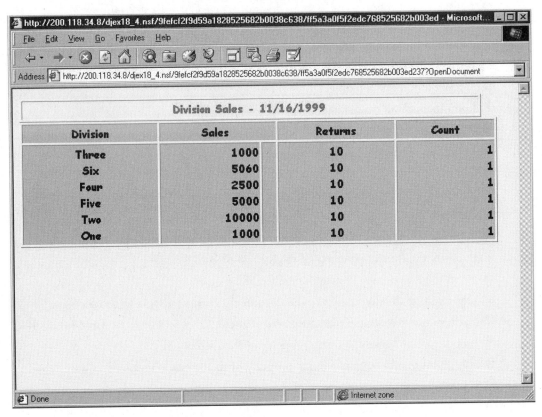

Figure 19.4   Report document created by example 19.3

19.3   NEWSLETTER CLASS

The `Newsletter` class allows you to send a group of related documents via Email to a user's mailbox. The `Newsletter` class takes a collection and mails a document with details about all documents in the collection. The group of documents is in the form of a `DocumentCollection` object. You create it using the `createNewsletter` method of the `Session` class; it returns the newly created `Newsletter` object.

```
Newsletter = Session.createNewsletter(DocumentCollection);
```

19.3.1 Properties

The Newsletter class has three important properties:

- IsDoScore: Read/write boolean property that signals whether or not the relevance score should be included. The relevance score applies to Document-Collection objects created by searching (full-text or normal). These objects are sorted according to their relevance to the search criteria. This property is applicable to the formatMsgWithDoclinks method only.

- IsDocSubject: Read/write boolean property that signals whether a subject line is included next to each doclink in the body of the newsletter. The field used for the subject content is the SubjectItemName property. The isDocSubject property is only applicable to the formatMsgWithDoclinks method (it is required with it).

- SubjectItemName: Read/write property used in conjunction with the isDoSubject property. It sets the field to be used as the subject tag next to the doclinks.

19.3.2 Methods

The Newsletter class has only two methods, and they deal with the creation of the Newsletter:

- formatDocument: This method creates a Document object that contains the rendering of a Document object in the Newsletter DocumentCollection object. This method is similar to forwarding a document, which displays a rendering of the forwarded document in the body of it.

```
Document = Newsletter.formatDocument(Database,
document_index_value_in_collection);
```

- formatMsgWithDoclinks: This method creates a Document object that contains a link to each Document within the Newsletter DocumentCollection object. It accepts only one parameter, which signals the Database in which it is created; a null value signals the user's mail database.

```
Document = Newsletter.formatMsgWithDoclinks(Database);
```

Listing 19.4   (Domino Agent)

```
import lotus.domino.*;
public class Example_19_3 extends AgentBase {
  public void NotesMain() {
    try {
      Session s = getSession();
      AgentContext ac = s.getAgentContext();
      Database db = ac.getCurrentDatabase();
      DocumentCollection dc = db.getAllDocuments();   ❶
      dc.FTSearch("Tony",0);   ❷
```

```
    if (dc.getCount() > 0) {  ❸
      Newsletter nw = s.createNewsletter(dc);  ❹
      nw.setSubjectItemName("divisionName");  ❺
      nw.setDoSubject(true);  ❻
      nw.setDoScore(true);  ❼
      Document memo = nw.formatMsgWithDoclinks(db);  ❽
      memo.replaceItemValue("Form","memo");  ❾
      memo.send(false, "Tony Patton");  ❿
      memo.recycle();
      nw.recycle();}
    dc.recycle();
    db.recycle();
    ac.recycle();
    s.recycle();
  } catch(Exception e) {
    e.printStackTrace();}}}
```

Explanation

❶ Create a DocumentCollection object with all documents.

❷ Refine the DocumentCollection via a full-text search.

❸ Proceed only if the DocumentCollection object is not empty.

❹ The createNewsletter method of the Session class is used to create a new Newsletter object with the DocumentCollection object.

❺ Set the field name on the Document objects in the DocumentCollection object to be used in the subject line for each doclink in the Newsletter object.

❻ Signal the script to use the subject line.

❼ Signal the script to use the full-text score.

❽ Create a new Document object for the Newsletter memo.

❾ Set the form to the mail memo form.

❿ Send the Newsletter document to the specified user. The first boolean parameter is set to false to signal that the form does not have to be sent with it. This is due to the fact that all users have the memo form in the mailbox.

Output

Figure 19.5 displays the result of our script. It is the email received/sent by the code.

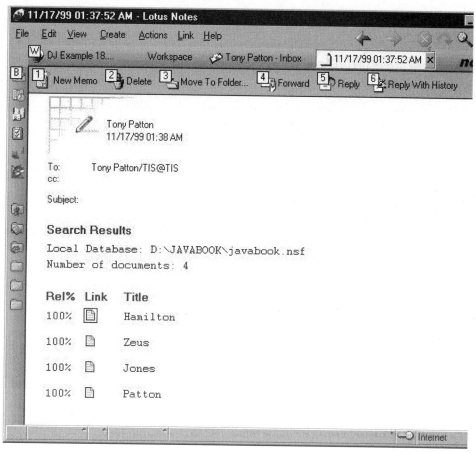

Figure 19.5 Newsletter mail message from example 19.3

Listing 19.5 (Domino Agent)

```
import lotus.domino.*;
public class Example_19_5 extends AgentBase {
 public void NotesMain() {
  try {
   Session s = getSession();
   AgentContext ac = s.getAgentContext();
   Database db = ac.getCurrentDatabase();
   DocumentCollection dc = db.getAllDocuments();
   dc.FTSearch("Tony",0);
   if (dc.getCount() > 0) {
    Newsletter nw = s.createNewsletter(dc);      ❶
    Document memo;      ❷
    for (int x = 0; x < dc.getCount(); x++) {
     memo = nw.formatDocument(db, x + 1);      ❸
     memo.replaceItemValue("Form", "memo");
     memo.replaceItemValue("Subject", "Newsletter Demo");      ❹
```

```
      memo.send(false, "Tony Patton");
      memo.recycle();}
   nw.recycle(); }
 dc.recycle();
 db.recycle();
 ac.recycle();
 s.recycle();
 } catch(Exception e) {
  e.printStackTrace();}}}
```

Explanation

❶ Create a `Newsletter` object.

❷ Create a new `Document` object for the mail memo.

❸ Call the `formatDocument` method of the `Newsletter` class to create a copy of the document contents (much like forwarding). The second parameter provides the index value of the document to render—the index starts at 1 instead of 0 for collections, so 1 must be added to the current index value.

❹ Set the subject of the email.

19.4   CHAPTER REVIEW

Reporting is one of the most discussed weaknesses of the Domino Application Server development platform. You can use third-party tools such as Microsoft Access or Crystal Reports to create reports using Domino data via an ODBC connection to Domino. This can be time-consuming to set up, and it adds another layer of product(s) to support and learn. The Domino Java classes provide an excellent development environment for building custom reporting solutions within the Domino environment. The reports can include views, documents, newsletters, emails, and custom input screens. You can view the results via the Lotus Notes or a Web client.

- Views are the simplest form of a report in Domino.
- You can use documents to create reports; tables are important to properly format the data.
- Schedule, user input, or both can trigger report generation.
- The `Newsletter` class provides a vehicle for quickly creating summary/overview documents.
- You can view reports via both the Lotus Notes and Web-based clients if you designed the reports properly.

C H A P T E R 2 0

Searching

20.1 Full-text indexing databases 261
20.2 Logical search operators 263
20.3 Searching a view 264
20.4 Searching a database 266
20.5 Creating a full-text index 267
20.6 Chapter review 268

As a database grows, the need to locate a certain document or subset of documents grows as well. Thankfully, searching is a standard feature of Domino. In addition, Domino Java exposes the power of searching in your applications.

20.1 FULL-TEXT INDEXING DATABASES

Full-text indexing a database adds more power to your searching capabilities for that database. A tab in the database properties pop-up window (see figure 20.1) contains the index settings for the database.

The `Database` object contains a property, `isFTIndexed`, for determining if a database is full-text indexed or not. This read-only property returns true if the database is full-text indexed, false if it is not.

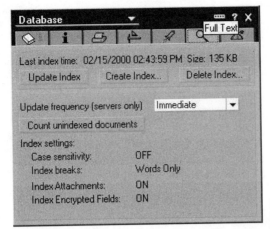

Figure 20.1
Database Properties Full-Text tab

Example 20.1 (Domino Agent)

```
import lotus.domino.*;
public class JavaAgent extends AgentBase {
 public void NotesMain() {
  try {
    Session s = getSession();
    AgentContext ac = s.getAgentContext();
    Database db = ac.getCurrentDatabase();
    if (db.isFTIndexed()) { ❶
      System.out.println("Database " + db.getTitle() + " is full-text indexed."); }
    else {
      System.out.println("Database " + db.getTitle() + " is not full-text indexed."); }
    db.recycle();
    ac.recycle();
    s.recycle();
  } catch(Exception e) {
    e.printStackTrace();}}}
```

Explanation

❶ Access the `isFTIndexed` property of the `Database` object to determine if it is full-text indexed. Display the appropriate message.

Output

```
Database Domino Java Examples is full-text indexed.
```

The results of most searches are returned as a `DocumentCollection` object. This object may be empty or contain thousands of `Document` objects. The `DocumentCollection` object does contain a `FTSearch` method that you can use to trim and refine the collection by performing a search on it. Many of the previous examples have shown this, but let's take one more look in example 20.2.

Example 20.2   (Domino Agent)

```
import lotus.domino.*;
public class Example_20_2 extends AgentBase {
  public void NotesMain() {
    try {
      Session s = getSession();
      AgentContext ac = s.getAgentContext();
      Database db = ac.getCurrentDatabase();
      DocumentCollection dc = db.getAllDocuments();      ❶
      dc.FTSearch("Whatever",0);      ❷
      dc.recycle();
      db.recycle();
      ac.recycle();
      s.recycle();
    } catch(Exception e) {
      e.printStackTrace();}}}
```

Explanation

❶ Create a `DocumentCollection` object containing all documents in the database.

❷ Refine the `DocumentCollection` through the full-text search method of the `DocumentCollection` object.

20.2   *LOGICAL SEARCH OPERATORS*

Logical operators allow you to include multiple conditions in a search. The OR operator returns true if one or more of the conditions are true. The AND operator returns true if and only if all conditions are met. The NOT operator returns the opposite of a condition. You can include these keywords (OR, AND, and NOT) in a search string.

The Java language uses different operators for these logical operators. The AND operator is represented by the ampersand (&). The OR operator is represented by the pipe (|). The NOT operator is represented by the exclamation mark (!). Example 20.3 shows their use.

Example 20.3   (Domino Agent)

```
import lotus.domino.*;
public class Example_20_3 extends AgentBase {
  public void NotesMain() {
    try {
      boolean condition1 = true;
      boolean condition2 = true;
      boolean condition3 = false;
```

```
boolean condition4 = false;
boolean and1 = (condition1) & (condition2);
boolean and2 = (condition2) & (condition4);
boolean and3 = (condition1) & (condition3);
boolean and4 = (condition3) & (condition4);
boolean or1 = (condition1) | (condition2);
boolean or2 = (condition2) | (condition4);
boolean or3 = (condition1) | (condition3);
boolean or4 = (condition3) | (condition4);
boolean not1 = !condition1;
boolean not2 = !condition2;
System.out.println(and1);
System.out.println(and2);
System.out.println(and3);
System.out.println(and4);
System.out.println(or1);
System.out.println(or2);
System.out.println(or3);
System.out.println(or4);
System.out.println(not1);
System.out.println(not2);
} catch(Exception e) {
e.printStackTrace();}}}
```

Output

```
true
false
false
false
true
true
true
false
false
false
```

20.3 SEARCHING A VIEW

You can search a View in a variety of ways: FTSearch, getAllDocumentsByKey,
and getDocumentByKey methods. All methods reduce the number of documents
in the View to those that match the search criteria.

Let's take a look at the FTSearch method first.

Example 20.4 (Domino Agent)

```
import lotus.domino.*;
public class Example_20_4 extends AgentBase {
  public void NotesMain() {
    try {
      Session s = getSession();
      AgentContext ac = s.getAgentContext();
      Database db = ac.getCurrentDatabase();
      View vw = db.getView("Test"); ❶
      Document doc; ❷
      if (vw != null) { ❸
        String searchString = "(FIELD FirstName = \"Barkley\")"; ❹
        int numdocs = vw.FTSearch(searchString,0); ❺
        for (int x=1; x < numdocs; x++) { ❻
          doc = vw.getNthDocument(x); ❼
          doc.recycle();} }
      vw.recycle();
      db.recycle();
      ac.recycle();
      s.recycle();
    } catch(Exception e) {
      e.printStackTrace();}}}
```

Explanation

❶ Retrieve the View object from the current database.

❷ Declare the Document object to be used later.

❸ Proceed only if the View object exists.

❹ Create the search string to be used in the FTSearch method of the View object.

❺ Perform a full-text search on the View object. It returns the number of matches found.

❻ Loop through all Document objects in the refined View object.

❼ Access each Document object via the loop index.

The getAllDocumentsByKey method accepts a Vector object that contains the values to find. The search starts with the first column and first element in the Vector object, and so forth, through the columns and elements. This is shown in example 20.5.

Example 20.5 (Domino Agent)

```
import lotus.domino.*;
import java.util.Vector;
public class Example_20_5 extends AgentBase {
```

```
public void NotesMain() {
  try {
    Session s = getSession();
    AgentContext ac = s.getAgentContext();
    Database db = ac.getCurrentDatabase();
    View vw = db.getView("Test");
    Document doc;
    if (vw != null) {
      Vector searchV = new Vector();           ❶
      searchV.addElement("Charles");            ❷
      searchV.addElement("Barkley");
      DocumentCollection dc = vw.getAllDocumentsByKey(searchV, true);  ❸
      for (int x=1; x < dc.getCount(); x++) {   ❹
        doc = vw.getNthDocument(x);
        //process documents
        doc.recycle();}
      dc.recycle();}
    vw.recycle();
    db.recycle();
    ac.recycle();
    s.recycle();
  } catch(Exception e) {
    e.printStackTrace(); } } }
```

Explanation

❶ Create a new `Vector` object to use as the key values in the search of the `View` object.

❷ Add search values to the `Vector` object.

❸ Populate a `DocumentCollection` object that contains all matching documents from the view. The second parameter signals whether or not a case-sensitive search is performed.

❹ Loop through all `Document` objects in the `DocumentCollection` object.

The `getDocumentByKey` method of the `View` class has the same format as the `getAllDocumentsByKey` method except that it returns only the first match in the first sorted column in the view. The `getDocumentByKey` method returns a `Document` object instead of a `DocumentCollection` object. You could replace Item #3 from example 20.5 with this line (and the `for` loop would not be needed as well):

```
Document doc = vw.getDocumentByKey("Charles",true);
```

20.4   SEARCHING A DATABASE

The `Database` class facilitates searching its whole structure. It contains two methods: `search` and `FTSearch`. You have seen the `FTSearch` method used throughout the book, so let's turn our attention to the `search` method. The difference between the two methods is that the `search` method allows the use of @Functions for the selection criteria. It accepts the search criteria as the first parameter, an optional `DateTime` object for the cutoff date for the search, and an optional third parameter that signals the maximum number of documents to find (zero means find all).

Example 20.6   (Domino Agent)

```
import lotus.domino.*;
public class Example_20_6 extends AgentBase {
  public void NotesMain() {
    try {
      Session s = getSession();
      AgentContext ac = s.getAgentContext();
      Database db = ac.getCurrentDatabase();
      Document doc;
      String searchString = "@Contains(\"Subject\",\"Test\")";   ❶
      DateTime dt = s.createDateTime("01/01/2087");   ❷
      DocumentCollection dc = db.search(searchString, dt, 0);   ❸
      doc = dc.getFirstDocument();   ❹
      while (doc != null) {   ❺
        // process the documents
        doc = dc.getNextDocument(doc); }
      doc.recycle();
      dt.recycle();
      db.recycle();
      ac.recycle();
      s.recycle();
    } catch(Exception e) {
      e.printStackTrace();}}}
```

Explanation

❶ Create the `String` to use for the search. The @Contains formula states that we want all documents with a subject of test.

❷ Create a new `DateTime` object to use as the cutoff date of the search of the database.

❸ Create a `DocumentCollection` object that contains all matches to the search.

❹ Retrieve the first `Document` object from the collection.

❺ Loop through all `Document` objects in the `DocumentCollection` object.

20.5 CREATING A FULL-TEXT INDEX

You can use the `updateFTIndex` method of the `Database` class to update the class' full-text index or create a new one if it does not already exist. This method accepts one parameter that is used to tell the system to create a new index (true) if it does not currently exist, or not to create it (false). The only problem with this method is that it only works for local databases. An error is returned if you attempt to create an index on the database that is not local.

Example 20.7 (Domino Agent)

```
import lotus.domino.*;
public class Example_20_7 extends AgentBase {
 public void NotesMain() {
   try {
     Session s = getSession();
     AgentContext ac = s.getAgentContext();
     Database db = ac.getCurrentDatabase();  ❶
     if (db.isFTIndexed()) {  ❷
       db.updateFTIndex(false);  ❸
       System.out.print("The database is already full-text ");
       System.out.println("indexed, so it has been updated"); }
     else {
       db.updateFTIndex(true);  ❹
       System.out.print("The database is not already full-text ");
       System.out.println(" indexed, so it has been created"); }
     db.recycle();
     ac.recycle();
     s.recycle();
   } catch(NotesException n) {
     System.out.println("Notes error (" + n.id + ") - " + n.text);
   } catch(Exception e) {
     e.printStackTrace();}}}
```

Explanation

❶ Create a `Database` object for the current database.

❷ Determine if the `Database` object has a full-text index.

❸ If it is full-text indexed, update it.

❹ If it is not full-text indexed, create it.

Output

```
The database is already full-text indexed, so it has been updated
```

20.6   CHAPTER REVIEW

The searching capability of Domino is one of its strongest attributes, and the Domino Java classes make it available to the developer in many ways. You can search views, databases, and document collections. A database does not have to have a full-text index to be searched, but having one does make the search much more efficient. Giving the users the power to perform their own searches expands the power of an application.

- You can search collections, databases, and views.
- Search strings for full-text searches can contain logical operators (AND, OR, and NOT).
- You can use the `FTSearch` methods on databases with or without a full-text index.
- Java uses the ampersand (&) as a logical AND, the exclamation mark (!) for the NOT operator, and the pipe (|) for the logical OR.
- The `search` method of the `Database` class allows the use of @Functions.
- The `isFTIndexed` property of the `Database` class returns true if it is full-text indexed and false otherwise.
- You can create or update a full-text index via the `updateFTIndex` method of the `Database` class.

C H A P T E R   2 1

Working with the Web

21.1 Overview 270

21.2 PrintWriter class 271

21.3 Browsers 273

21.4 Environment variables 273

21.5 DocumentContext 274

21.6 Events 277

21.7 Executing agents 278

21.8 Tracking session data 279

21.9 Working with URLs 283

21.10 Chapter review 287

21.1 OVERVIEW

There is a variety of scripting languages available for working with the Web browser environment. JavaScript is the most popular and most widely supported. Microsoft has its own version of it called Jscript, and it also has a scripting derivative of Visual Basic called VBScript. Java is supported in most of the browsers in the form of an applet, but the browser software cannot interpret Java code itself. Java is supported in the browser by the Java Virtual Machine (JVM). Newer technologies such as Java Server Pages (JSPs) can handle inline Java in the HTML page. Chapter 27 discusses Java Server Pages.

You can compile Java code in a Domino agent and call it from a generated Domino page or via a URL on a normal HTML page. This chapter focuses on calling Java agents.

21.2 PRINTWRITER CLASS

Most examples so far have used the `PrintWriter` class. The Lotus documentation states that you must use the `PrintWriter` class when you send output to a Web client. The `PrintWriter` class is contained in the Java Input/Output package. Use the following import statement to access all classes in the IO package (including the `PrintWriter` class):

```
import java.io.*;
```

If you just want the `PrintWriter` class, use the following import statement:

```
import java.io.PrintWriter;
```

> **NOTE**   Remember that case is important; Java is a case-sensitive programming language.

You can obtain a `PrintWriter` object via the `getAgentOutput` method of the `AgentBase` class. You have seen this in various examples; here is another look:

```
import lotus.domino.*;
import java.io.PrintWriter;
public class PWExample extends AgentBase {
  public void NotesMain() {
    try {
      Session s = getSession();
      AgentContext ac = s.getAgentContext();
      PrintWriter pw = this.getAgentOutput();
      ac.recycle();
      s.recycle();
    } catch (Exception e)
      { e.printStackTrace(); } }
```

The line declaring the `PrinterWriter` class uses the `this` keyword to declare it. The line signals the `PrinterWriter` class to use the current class, which inherits its design from `AgentBase`. The `this` keyword is optional, so it could be declared as follows:

```
PrintWriter pw = getAgentOutput();
```

The `PrintWriter` class contains `print` and `println` methods. The `print` method sends output to the browser without a carriage return/new line. The print position is moved to the end of the line following the text. The `println` method sends output with a carriage return/new line appended to it. The print position is moved to the beginning of the next line.

Example 21.1 sends the HTML to the browser when the code is called from a browser.

Example 21.1   (Domino Agent)

```
import lotus.domino.*;
import java.io.PrintWriter;
```

```
public class Example_21_1 extends AgentBase {
 public void NotesMain() {
  try {
    Session s = getSession();
    AgentContext ac = s.getAgentContext();
    PrintWriter pw = this.getAgentOutput();  ❶
    pw.print("<HTML>");  ❷
    pw.println("<HEAD><TITLE>Java Agent Output Test</TITLE></HEAD>");
    pw.println("<BR>");
    pw.println("<H1>Domino Agent Test</H1>");
    pw.println("</HTML>");
    ac.recycle();
    s.recycle();
  } catch(Exception e) {
    e.printStackTrace();}}}
```

Explanation

❶ Create a new `PrintWriter` object.

❷ Send HTML output to the calling client.

Output

Figure 21.1 shows the output in Internet Explorer.

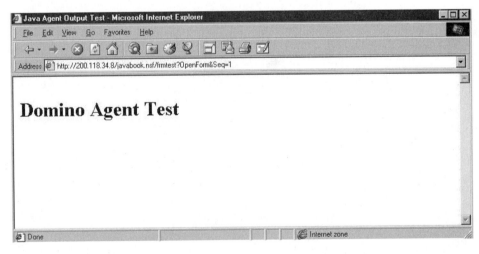

Figure 21.1   Example 21.1 output

The Domino agent illustrated in example 21.1 functions in similar ways to a Java servlet running in a Java-enabled web application server—each fragment of the HTML page is built up with print and println statements. You can probably see how cumbersome it would be to use multiple print and println statements to create a web page using this method. That practical issue is one reason that Java Server Pages (JSPs) were invented. Servlets and JSPs are covered in chapter 25.

21.3 BROWSERS

The connection made between a Web client such as Netscape Navigator and a Web server is not permanent. It is *stateless*. That is, information is sent to and from the browser, and then the connection is closed. For this reason, you must keep track of everything or maintain state. There are a number of techniques for achieving this type of tracking; one of the most popular is cookies.

Basically, a cookie is a file stored on the client PC. It stores information (whatever information is deemed relevant). Another method is passing hidden fields between Web pages. Later, this chapter covers this technique by using the document ID that is unique to the Domino environment. Another method that this chapter covers is the use of profile documents. This is unique to the Domino environment as well. Before you learn about these techniques, take a look at information that is readily available.

21.4 ENVIRONMENT VARIABLES

A number of invaluable pieces of information are made available about the Web client by the HTTP protocol. This information takes the form of environment variables. Now, environment variables can be used in Domino development, but Web environment variables are a separate entity. These variables include information about the client, server, user, or form data. Form data is data that is entered by the user and sent to the Web server. Table 21.1 contains a list of the variables.

Table 21.1 HTTP environment variables

Web Environment Variable	Description
AUTH_TYPE	The authentication method used to validate the user (if there is any)
CONTENT_LENGTH	The length of the data in bytes
CONTENT_TYPE	The MIME type of the data
GATEWAY_INTERFACE	The revision of the Common Gateway Interface that the server uses
HTTP_ACCEPT	A list of the MIME types that the client can accept
HTTP_REFERER	The URL of the document that the client accessed before accessing the current page
HTTPS	Signals whether or not Secure Sockets Layer (SSL) is enabled on the server
HTTP_USER_AGENT	The browser used by the client
PATH_INFO	Extra path information
PATH_TRANSLATED	The translated version of the path given by the PATH_INFO variable
QUERY_STRING	The query information submitted; it is appended to a question mark (?) in the URL
REMOTE_ADDR	The IP address of the client

Table 21.1   HTTP environment variables (continued)

Web Environment Variable	Description
REMOTE_HOST	The host name of the client
REMOTE_IDENT	The user making the request, not supported by most browsers
REMOTE_USER	The authenticated name of the user. This contains a value only if the site/page has security enabled so that the user must enter a valid username/password pair to enter/view
REQUEST_METHOD	The method used by the request (POST/GET)
SCRIPT_NAME	The virtual path of the script being executed
SERVER_NAME	The server's hostname or IP address
SERVER_PORT	The port number of the host on which the server is running, usually 80
SERVER_PROTOCOL	The name and revision of the information protocol that the request accompanied
SERVER_SOFTWARE	The name and version of the server software that is answering the client's request

You can use environment variables on a Domino form by creating a computed-when-composed field with the same name as the environment variable. Also, the field's computed value should be the same name as the environment variable, and they should be hidden at all times. Once you set them up, you can access the Web environment variables as in any other field on a Domino document submitted by a Web client. The DocumentContext property of the AgentContext class gives a handle on the document submitted.

We set up fields on a form for use in Example 21.2. Figure 21.2 shows the field setup; the fields are hidden, but the form design is shown.

21.5   DOCUMENTCONTEXT

The DocumentContext property of the AgentContext class is a read-only property that returns a Document object representing the document submitted. It allows access to the Document and all of its contents through the use of the rest of the Domino Java classes. Use the getDocumentContext method of the AgentContext class to access it. The hidden fields would be useful on all pages where you want to track information about the user visiting your Domino web site. Placing the hidden fields in a subform would allow efficient use in a practical setting.

```
Document = AgentContext.getDocumentContext();
```

Example 21.2 makes use of this method to access the Web environment variables.

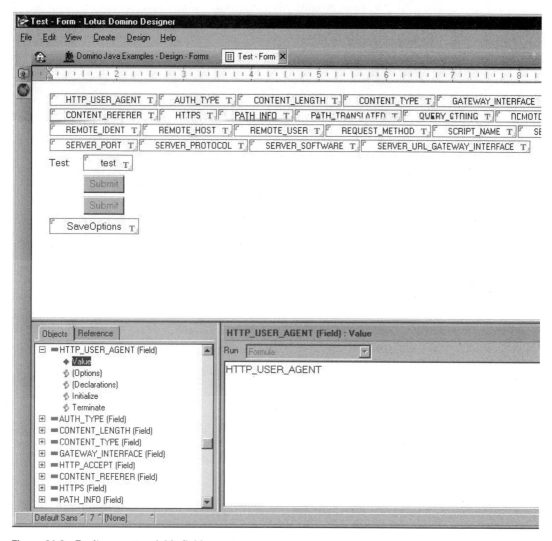

Figure 21.2   Environment variable fields put to use

Example 21.2   (Domino Agent)

```
import lotus.domino.*;
import java.io.PrintWriter;
public class Example_21_2 extends AgentBase {
 public void NotesMain() {
   try {
     Session s = getSession();
     AgentContext ac = s.getAgentContext();
     PrintWriter pw = getAgentOutput();        ❶
     Document doc = ac.getDocumentContext();    ❷
```

DOCUMENTCONTEXT

```
pw.print("<HTML>");
pw.println("<HEAD><TITLE>Example 21.2 - Environment Variables</TITLE></HEAD>");
pw.println("<BODY>");
pw.println("<BR>");
pw.println("<H1>Environment Variables</H1>");
pw.println("AUTH_TYPE :   " + doc.HTTP_AUTH_TYPE + "<BR>");          ❸
pw.println("CONTENT_LENGTH :   " + doc.getItemValue("HTTP_CONTENT_LENGTH") + "<BR>");
pw.println("CONTENT_TYPE :   " + doc.getItemValue("HTTP_CONTENT_TYPE") + "<BR>");
pw.println("GATEWAY_INTERFACE :   " + doc.getItemValue("HTTP_GATEWAY_INTERFACE") + "<BR>");
pw.println("HTTP_ACCEPT :   " + doc.getItemValue("HTTP_ACCEPT") + "<BR>");
pw.println("HTTP_REFERER :   " + doc.getItemValue("HTTP_REFERER") + "<BR>");
pw.println("HTTPS :   " + doc.getItemValue("HTTP_HTTPS") + "<BR>");
pw.println("HTTP_USER_AGENT :   " + doc.getItemValue("HTTP_USER_AGENT") + "<BR>");
pw.println("PATH_INFO :   " + doc.getItemValue("HTTP_PATH_INFO") + "<BR>");
pw.println("PATH_TRANSLATED :   " + doc.getItemValue("HTTP_PATH_TRANSLATED") + "<BR>");
pw.println("QUERY_STRING :   " + doc.getItemValue("HTTP_QUERY_STRING") + "<BR>");
pw.println("REMOTE_ADDR :   " + doc.getItemValue("HTTP_REMOTE_ADDR") + "<BR>");
pw.println("REMOTE_HOST :   " + doc.getItemValue("HTTP_REMOTE_HOST") + "<BR>");
pw.println("REMOTE_IDENT :   " + doc.getItemValue("HTTP_REMOTE_IDENT") + "<BR>");
pw.println("REMOTE_USER :   " + doc.getItemValue("HTTP_REMOTE_USER") + "<BR>");
pw.println("REQUEST_METHOD :   " + doc.getItemValue("HTTP_REQUEST_METHOD") + "<BR>");
pw.println("SCRIPT_NAME :   " + doc.getItemValue("HTTP_SCRIPT_NAME") + "<BR>");
pw.println("SERVER_NAME :   " + doc.getItemValue("HTTP_SERVER_NAME") + "<BR>");
pw.println("SERVER_PORT :   " + doc.getItemValue("HTTP_SERVER_PORT") + "<BR>");
pw.println("SERVER_PROTOCOL :   " + doc.getItemValue("HTTP_SERVER_PROTOCOL") + "<BR>");
pw.println("SERVER_SOFTWARE :   " + doc.getItemValue("HTTP_SERVER_SOFTWARE") + "<BR>");
pw.println("SERVER_URL_GATEWAY_INTERFACE :   " + doc.getItemValue
    ("HTTP_SERVER_URL_GATEWAY_INTERFACE") + "<BR>");
pw.println("</BODY>");
pw.println("</HTML>");
doc.recycle();
ac.recycle();
s.recycle();
} catch(Exception e) {
e.printStackTrace();}}}
```

Explanation

❶ Create the `PrintWriter` object.

❷ Get the `Document` object created by the Web client.

❸ Display the environment variables.

Output

See figure 21.3.

NOTE   The `DocumentContext` property behaves exactly the same way with a Lotus Notes client. The Notes client can call a Java agent via a button, and the agent accesses the data from the document using the same approach. This allows you to use the same code with both Notes and browser clients.

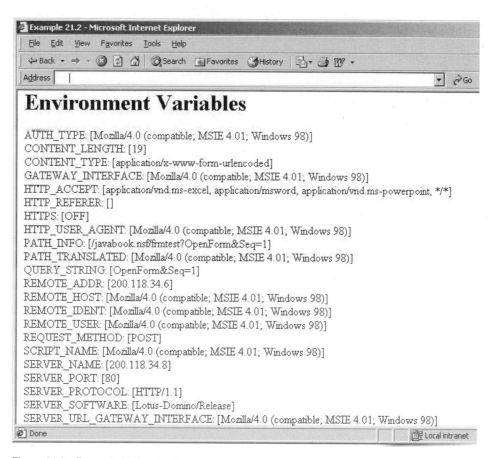

Environment Variables

AUTH_TYPE: [Mozilla/4.0 (compatible; MSIE 4.01; Windows 98)]
CONTENT_LENGTH: [19]
CONTENT_TYPE: [application/x-www-form-urlencoded]
GATEWAY_INTERFACE: [Mozilla/4.0 (compatible; MSIE 4.01; Windows 98)]
HTTP_ACCEPT: [application/vnd.ms-excel, application/msword, application/vnd.ms-powerpoint, */*]
HTTP_REFERER: []
HTTPS: [OFF]
HTTP_USER_AGENT: [Mozilla/4.0 (compatible; MSIE 4.01; Windows 98)]
PATH_INFO: [/javabook.nsf/frmtest?OpenForm&Seq=1]
PATH_TRANSLATED: [Mozilla/4.0 (compatible; MSIE 4.01; Windows 98)]
QUERY_STRING: [OpenForm&Seq=1]
REMOTE_ADDR: [200.118.34.6]
REMOTE_HOST: [Mozilla/4.0 (compatible; MSIE 4.01; Windows 98)]
REMOTE_IDENT: [Mozilla/4.0 (compatible; MSIE 4.01; Windows 98)]
REMOTE_USER: [Mozilla/4.0 (compatible; MSIE 4.01; Windows 98)]
REQUEST_METHOD: [POST]
SCRIPT_NAME: [Mozilla/4.0 (compatible; MSIE 4.01; Windows 98)]
SERVER_NAME: [200.118.34.8]
SERVER_PORT: [80]
SERVER_PROTOCOL: [HTTP/1.1]
SERVER_SOFTWARE: [Lotus-Domino/Release]
SERVER_URL_GATEWAY_INTERFACE: [Mozilla/4.0 (compatible; MSIE 4.01; Windows 98)]

Figure 21.3   Example 21.2 output

21.6 EVENTS

You need to be concerned with two events when you deal with Web clients: WebQueryOpen and WebQuerySave. The format for both events is as follows:

```
@Command([ToolsRunMacro]; "<Your agent goes here.>");
```

This is the default setup of the events, so the name of your agent should be inserted in the quotation marks.

21.6.1 WebQueryOpen

The WebQueryOpen event is fired before the page is presented to the user, that is, before the Domino server converts it to HTML for viewing by the browser. You cannot access and/or modify the document data. Also, any output (such as print statements) is ignored.

NOTE   You can use this event on a Domino 4.5 Server through the use of a hidden field named $$WebQueryOpen or $$WebQuerySave. The agent name is the value of the field. Java is not supported in version 4.5, so you must use LotusScript for your agent(s).

21.6.2   WebQuerySave

The WebQuerySave event is fired when the document is sent to the Domino Server but before it is saved. You can access or modify the document and its data. Output from this event is sent back to the browser via print statements and the `PrintWriter` object. We took advantage of these methods in example 21.2. Figure 21.4 shows the location of the events in the Designer pane for a form.

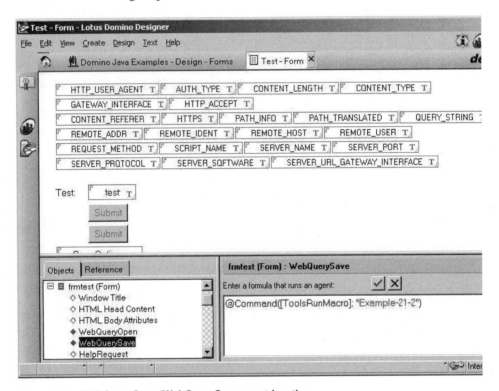

Figure 21.4   WebQueryOpen/WebQuerySave event location

21.7   EXECUTING AGENTS

You can execute Java agents using the database URL from the browser in five ways:

1   ?OpenAgent
   - The command is appended to the server/database URL. The name of the agent to run precedes the ?OpenAgent command. Any values to pass into the agent (via Query_String) should follow the ?OpenAgent command.

2 `?CreateDocument`
- This command takes advantage of the WebQuerySave event. The name of the form precedes the command. When you use this command, the Domino server creates a document and executes the agent specified in the event.

3 `?OpenDocument`
- The use of this command takes advantage of the WebQueryOpen event. When you use it, the Domino server opens the specified document and executes the agent specified in the event. The document identifier precedes the command.

4 Submit button
- When a document is saved/submitted on a Domino server, an agent specified in the WebQuerySave event will be executed.

5 `?OpenForm`
- The use of this command takes advantage of the WebQueryOpen event. When you use it, the Domino server composes a new document using the specified form and presents it in the browser window. The WebQueryOpen event is fired when it is composed. The form name precedes the command in the URL.

Example 21.1 could have been run with the following URL (your IP address may be different); this would have resulted in the document being composed and submitted:

http://200.118.34.8/javabook.nsf/Example-21-1?OpenAgent

Also, the following URL could have been used to compose the document and allow the user to submit it:

http://200.118.34.8/javabook.nsf/frmtest?OpenForm

21.8 TRACKING SESSION DATA

Cookies are the most widely accepted format for tracking user data during a Web client session. The techniques for working with cookies are covered in great detail in the countless number of Web development books on the market, so this book does not cover them.

This book does cover the use of profile documents, which is unique to the Domino environment. Profile documents are a special type of document used in a Domino database. You use them to store configuration information, user information, or any other piece of data. Chapter 8 covered profile documents.

You can use the WebQueryOpen and WebQuerySave form events with profile documents to store user information. The profile document is created based upon the user name of the user, so the user must log in to use the process in this section. An edit-user-settings link can be provided on the site to allow you to enter and edit your settings. Once you enter data, you can use it whenever necessary. Example 21.3 is the code listing for the WebQueryOpen event of the form used to enter and edit user settings.

Example 21.3 (Domino Agent)

```
import lotus.domino.*;
public class Example_21_3 extends AgentBase {
  public void NotesMain() {
    try {
      Session s = getSession();
      AgentContext ac = s.getAgentContext();
      Database db = ac.getCurrentDatabase();
      Document doc = ac.getDocumentContext();        ❶
      if (doc != null) {
        Document pdoc = db.getProfileDocument("UserSettings",s.getUserName());  ❷
        doc.replaceItemValue("FirstName", pdoc.getItemValue("FirstName"));      ❸
        doc.replaceItemValue("LastName", pdoc.getItemValue("LastName"));        ❹
        doc.replaceItemValue("Address", pdoc.getItemValue("Address"));          ❺
        doc.replaceItemValue("City", pdoc.getItemValue("City"));                ❻
        doc.replaceItemValue("State", pdoc.getItemValue("State"));              ❼
        doc.replaceItemValue("ZipCode", pdoc.getItemValue("ZipCode"));          ❽
        doc.replaceItemValue("Country", pdoc.getItemValue("Country"));          ❾
        pdoc recycle();}
      doc.recycle();
      db.recycle();
      ac recycle();
      s recycle();
    } catch(Exception e) {
      e.printStackTrace();}}}
```

Explanation

❶ Retrieve the Web document before it is presented to the user in the browser.

❷ Retrieve the profile document for the user. The user name is the key value used. If it does not exist, a new profile document is created for the user.

❸ Retrieve the first name from the profile and populate the corresponding field in the Web document.

❹ Retrieve the last name from the profile and populate the corresponding field in the Web document.

❺ Retrieve the address from the profile and populate the corresponding field in the Web document.

❻ Retrieve the city from the profile and populate the corresponding field in the Web document.

❼ Retrieve the state from the profile and populate the corresponding field in the Web document.

❽ Retrieve the zip code from the profile and populate the corresponding field in the Web document.

❾ Retrieve the county from the profile and populate the corresponding field in the Web document.

Example 21.4 is the code listing for the WebQuerySave event of the form used to enter and edit user settings. The script saves the user settings for future user. The saved values are reloaded the next time by the code from example 21.3.

Example 21.4   (Domino Agent)

```
import lotus.domino.*;
public class Example_21_4 extends AgentBase {
 public void NotesMain() {
   try {
     Session s = getSession();
     AgentContext ac = s.getAgentContext();
     Database db = ac.getCurrentDatabase();
     Document doc = ac.getDocumentContext();  ❶
     if (doc != null) {
       Document pdoc = db.getProfileDocument("UserSettings",s.getUserName());  ❷
       pdoc.replaceItemValue("FirstName", doc.getItemValue("FirstName"));  ❸
       pdoc.replaceItemValue("LastName", doc.getItemValue("LastName"));
       pdoc.replaceItemValue("Address", doc.getItemValue("Address"));
       pdoc.replaceItemValue("City", doc.getItemValue("City"));
       pdoc.replaceItemValue("State", doc.getItemValue("State"));
       pdoc.replaceItemValue("ZipCode", doc.getItemValue("ZipCode"));
       pdoc.replaceItemValue("Country", doc.getItemValue("Country"));
       pdoc.save();  ❹
       pdoc.recycle();}
     doc recycle();
     db recycle();
     ac recycle();
     s recycle();
   } catch(Exception e) {
     e.printStackTrace();}}}
```

Explanation

❶ Retrieve the document submitted by the browser.

❷ Retrieve the profile document for the user; it is created if it does not exist.

❸ Populate the profile document with the values from the document submitted.

❹ Save the changes to the profile document.

Figure 21.5 shows a form with a link to edit your settings.

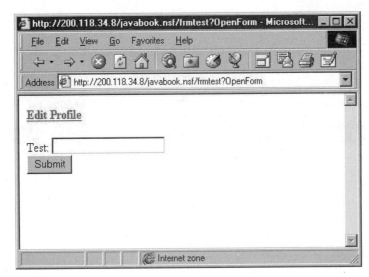

Figure 21.5
Form with a link to edit your settings

Figure 21.6 shows the editing of profile document values.

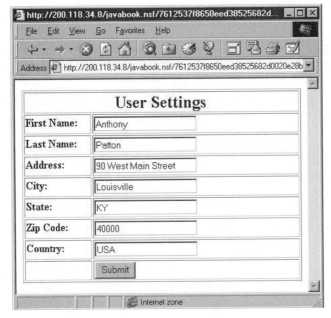

Figure 21.6
Editing User Settings held in a profile document

Figure 21.7 shows the message displayed once you save the profile.

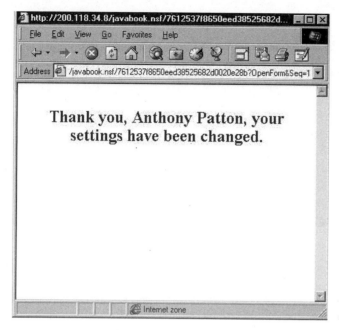

Figure 21.7
Message displayed after a successful profile edit

NOTE You can also use the @Functions, @GetProfileField, and @SetProfileField to retrieve and save profile information when you work with Web clients.

You can use all of the Domino Java classes covered in the previous chapters with Web documents. Once you retrieve the Web document via the `DocumentContext` class, you can manipulate it in any way necessary. You can present information to the user via the `PrintWriter` object.

21.9 WORKING WITH URLS

Java is an excellent language for developing Domino applications. You ultimately realize certain powers when non-Domino aspects of the language are utilized. One example is the net package. This package contains classes for working with Internet addresses and so forth. Example 21.5 takes advantage of the net package to retrieve properties of a URL, and figure 21.8 shows the output.

Example 21.5 (Domino Agent)

```
import lotus.domino.*;
import java.io.PrintWriter;
import java.net.*;
public class Example_21_5 extends AgentBase {
  public void NotesMain() {
    try {
      PrintWriter pw = this.getAgentOutput();
```

```
    String newline = "<BR>";
    URL url = new URL("http://200.118.34.8/javabook.nsf");   ❶
    pw.println("Protocol: " + url.getProtocol()+ newline);   ❷
    pw.println("Host: " + url.getHost()+ newline);   ❸
    pw.println("File name: " + url.getFile()+ newline);   ❹
    pw.println("Port: " + url.getPort()+ newline);   ❺
    pw.println("External form: " + url.toExternalForm()+ newline);   ❻
} catch(Exception e) {
    e.printStackTrace();}}}
```

Explanation

❶ Create a new URL object for the specified address.

❷ Display the protocol used in the URL with an HTML newline appended to it.

❸ Display the host name of the URL.

❹ Display the file name associated with the URL.

❺ Display the port used to get the URL.

❻ Display the address used to retrieve the URL.

The script was executed using the URL:

http://200.118.34.8/javabook.nsf/Example-21-5?OpenAgent.

Output

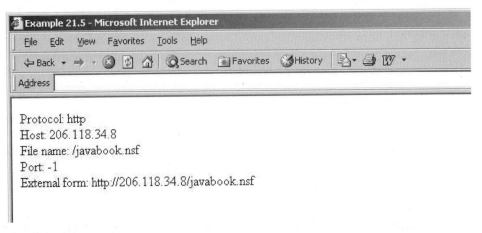

Figure 21.8   Example 21.5 output

Example 21.6 makes a direct connection to the Domino HTTP Server, issues an HTTP command, saves the results in a local file, and sends the file via email.

CHAPTER 21   WORKING WITH THE WEB

Example 21.6   (Domino Agent)

```
import lotus.domino.*;
import java.io.*;
import java.net.*;
public class Example_21_6 extends AgentBase {
 public void NotesMain() {
  InputStream in = null;  ❶
  OutputStream out = null;  ❷
  try {
    Session session = getSession();
    PrintWriter pw = getAgentOutput();
    AgentContext ac = session.getAgentContext();
    Database db = ac.getCurrentDatabase();
    URL url = new URL("http://200.118.34.8:80/");  ❸
    String protocol = url.getProtocol();  ❹
    String host = url.getHost();  ❺
    int port = url.getPort();  ❻
    if (port == -1) { port = 80; }  ❼
    Socket socket = new Socket(host, port);  ❽
    InputStream fromServer = socket.getInputStream();  ❾
    PrintWriter pw2 = new PrintWriter(new OutputStreamWriter(socket.getOutputStream()));  ❿
    pw2.println("POST javabook.nsf/Example-21-2?OpenAgent");  ⓫
    pw2.flush();  ⓬
    out = new FileOutputStream("c:\\example217.txt");  ⓭
  byte[] buffer = new byte[4096];
  int bytes_read;
    while ((bytes_read = fromServer.read(buffer)) != -1) {  ⓮
      out.write(buffer, 0, bytes_read); }  ⓯
  socket.close();  ⓰
  pw2.close();  ⓱
Document doc = db.createDocument();
doc.replaceItemValue("Form","Memo");  ⓲
doc.replaceItemValue("Subject","Check this out:  " + url.toExternalForm());
  RichTextItem rtf = doc.createRichTextItem( "Body");  ⓳
  rtf.appendText("Address:  " + url.toExternalForm());  ⓴
  rtf.addNewLine(1);  ㉑
  rtf.appendText("Server port:  " + port);
  rtf.addNewLine(1);
  rtf.appendText("Host:  " + host);
  rtf.addNewLine(2);
  rtf.embedObject(EmbeddedObject.EMBED_ATTACHMENT,"","c:\\example217.txt","Test");  ㉒
   doc.send(false, "Tony Patton");  ㉓
  doc.recycle();
  rtf.recycle();
  ac.recycle();
  db.recycle();
  session recycle();
} catch(Exception e) {
  e.printStackTrace();}}}
```

Explanation

❶ Create an `InputStream` object to be used with the socket.

❷ Create an `OutputStream` object to be used to create a local file.

❸ Create a new URL object using the test server IP address.

❹ Get the protocol used on the server.

❺ Get the host property of the server.

❻ Get the port number used by the server.

❼ If a port number of −1 is returned, it means it is not specified, so let's use the default http port of 80.

❽ Create a new socket connection to the server.

❾ Instantiate the InputStream object to the socket input.

❿ Create a PrintWriter object to be used to send a command to the server.

⓫ Send a POST command to the server. It runs the specified agent.

⓬ Flush the PrintWriter object to send it now.

⓭ Assign the OutputStream object to a local file.

⓮ Loop through the output (response) from the HTTP command.

⓯ Write the response from the HTTP command to the file.

⓰ Close the socket.

⓱ Close the PrintWriter object.

⓲ Set the form to be used (the mail memo form).

⓳ Create a new RichTextItem on the mail memo form using the body field.

⓴ Add text to the body field using properties of the URL object.

㉑ Add a carriage return to the body field.

㉒ Attach the newly created file to the body field.

㉓ Send the memo.

Output

Figure 21.9 shows the resulting email from example 21.6.

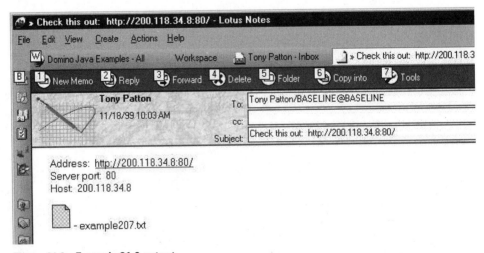

Figure 21.9   Example 21.6 output

21.10 CHAPTER REVIEW

Interacting with Web clients is imperative to successful application development in our Web-centric world. Everything these days is Web-ified, or is in the process of converting. The browser is the killer app, so it must be supported. The DocumentContext property of the AgentContext class facilitates working with Web-created documents. You can send informative messages to the browser from a Java agent via the PrintWriter class. The Java language is robust with built-in support for networking. You can include these features in your agents/application as well.

- Java agents work with browser clients with no problems.

- You can use the DocumentContext property of the AgentContext class to access documents submitted via a Web client.

- Web browsers have a number of environment variables. You can access them and use them in your Java agents. These differ from Domino environment variables.

- The WebQueryOpen and WebQuerySave events are the only events supported by Web clients.

- You can use profile documents to store application-specific and user-specific data.

- Use the PrintWriter object to send output to browser clients. The output can contain HTML, XML, JavaScript, and more.

- The Java language inherently supports networking. This includes working with URLs, and you can easily incorporate these features into your applications.

CHAPTER 22

Developing outside the Domino IDE

22.1 Domino IDE weaknesses 288
22.2 Required files 289
22.3 Version 290
22.4 AgentRunner 290

22.5 Working with the Sun JDK 292
22.6 VisualAge for Java 296
22.7 Other environments 304
22.8 Chapter review 305

This chapter focuses outside of the Domino Designer IDE and takes a look at developing Domino Java code in other development environments. There are a number of excellent integrated development environments (IDE) in today's market. These range from high-end, enterprise development environments to the command-line Java Development Kit (JDK) that is free from the Sun Microsystems Web site (java.sun.com).

22.1 DOMINO *IDE* WEAKNESSES

The Domino Designer Java IDE is very powerful. It allows you to browse the Domino Java classes and the core Java classes so you can quickly locate methods for use in your code. After all, who can remember the syntax for all of the classes? The syntax checking is very powerful as well. It quickly points out nonexistent methods that you have called, missing curly braces, and so forth. The environment provides nice features for managing class files as well. This is where the features seem to end. There is no integrated debugger that allows you to inspect what is actually happening while

288

the Java code is executing, and the Domino Designer Java IDE is limited to the development of Domino agents only. When you need to work outside of the Domino server (servlets, applets, or standalone applications), you must move to another development environment.

22.2   REQUIRED FILES

The Domino Designer IDE takes the pain out of properly configuring the location of files so that you can use them. It takes care of locating the class files that you are using. You must know which files to use when you move out of this environment. Two important files contain the Domino Java classes needed to access the Domino objects: notes.jar and ncso.jar.

22.2.1   notes.jar

The notes.jar file is a Java archive file. This is the Java format for compressed files. It is similar to compressing files with Pkzip or WinZip. Microsoft has a similar technology called cab (cabinet) files. The notes.jar file contains all of the Domino Java classes for accessing Domino resources locally. It is located in the root directory of your Lotus Notes/Domino installation. For an installation that uses the directory named R5 on the C drive, the complete path to the file is as follows:

```
C:\r5\notes.jar
```

22.2.2   ncso.jar

The ncso.jar file is a Java archive file as well. It contains all of the Domino Java classes necessary to access Domino resources/objects remotely (CORBA). It is located in the java subdirectory off of the domino subdirectory of your Domino data directory. That is a bit confusing, so assuming that Notes are installed in the r5 directory on the C drive, the path to the ncso.jar file is as follows:

```
C:\r5\data\domino\java\ncso.jar
```

22.2.3   ncsoc.jar

The ncsoc.jar file is a compressed version of the ncso.jar file described in the previous section. It contains all files that must be downloaded to the client (browser) to allow you to access Domino resources/objects remotely. You should use this file in the archive parameter for applets that will access Domino objects remotely, because its smaller size reduces download time. The ncsoc.jar file is located in the same directory as the ncso.jar file.

22.2.4   CLASSPATH

Both required files (ncso.jar and notes.jar) must be available to your development environment when you develop Domino Java code. You achieve this through the CLASSPATH setting on your system. You should properly set up the CLASSPATH environment variable for your IDE. The documentation for your environment will explain how to access nonstandard Java code (such as Domino).

22.3 VERSION

Lotus Notes/Domino R5 supports JDK 1.1.x. The JDK is a part of the Domino environment, so it cannot be updated separately from the rest of the software (client, server, designer, and so on). For this reason, Lotus/IBM will handle all updates to the JDK included with Domino when it issues updates to the Domino application. Support for Java 2 (JDK 1.2) is expected with the next major release of Domino.

22.4 AGENTRUNNER

AgentRunner is a set of Java classes that allow you to develop and debug Domino Agent code in your favorite IDE. It creates a pseudo-Domino runtime environment. It is included as a standard part of the Domino Java classes (notes.jar file) beginning with Domino version 5, but it was available for use with version 4.6 in the Domino Toolkit for Java. The AgentRunner Java class files are included in a file (AgentRunner.jar) that is part of the core Domino Java classes.

AgentRunner allows you to write your own Domino Java agents in your favorite development environment. Thus, you can take advantage of a more powerful debugger or editor. This may result in faster development time. A normal Domino Java agent extends the `AgentBase` class, but use the `DebugAgentBase` class for Java programs that exist outside of the Domino Designer IDE. The `DebugAgentBase` class allows you to take advantage of the AgentRunner code.

22.4.1 Syntax

Take another look at some code we used in example 7.1. After you review the code, we will look at how the same functionality can be obtained with the Domino Designer IDE.

```
import lotus.domino.*;
public class Example extends AgentBase {
  public void NotesMain() {
    try {
      Session session = getSession();
      AgentContext ac = session.getAgentContext();
      Database db = ac.getCurrentDatabase();
      java.util.Vector v = db.getViews();
      System.out.print("Number of views in " + db.getTitle());
      System.out.println(" is " + v.size());
      for (int x=0; x < v.size(); x ++) {
        View currentView =(View)v.elementAt(x);
        System.out.println("View:   " + currentView.getName());
        currentView recycle();}
      db recycle();
      ac recycle();
```

```
      session recycle();
  } catch(Exception e) {
    e.printStackTrace();  } }  }
```

The code displays the number of views and their names in a database. Here is the code reworked to take advantage of the AgentRunner class:

```
import lotus.domino.*;
public class Example extends DebugAgentBase {
 public void NotesMain() {
   try {
     Session session = getSession();
     AgentContext ac = session.getAgentContext();
     Database db = ac.getCurrentDatabase();
     java.util.Vector v = db.getViews();
     System.out.print("Number of views in " + db.getTitle());
     System.out.println(" is " + v.size());
     for (int x=0; x < v.size(); x ++) {
      View currentView = (View)v.elementAt(x);
       System.out.println("View:  " + currentView.getName());
       currentView recycle(); }
     db recycle();
     ac recycle();
     session recycle();
   } catch(Exception e) {
     e.printStackTrace();  } }  }
```

You will notice that the only major change to the code is the parent class declaration. The code that takes advantage of the AgentRunner class uses the DebugAgentBase class as its parent, while a normal Domino Java agent takes advantage of the AgentBase class.

22.4.2   Lotus Domino Toolkit for Java

The *Lotus Domino Toolkit for Java* contains numerous samples and code for developing Domino Java as agents, servlets, and/or applets. It is available from the Lotus Web site; follow the developer's link (www.lotus.com/home.nsf/welcome/developernetwork). Previous versions of Domino included the AgentRunner classes for installation with the Toolkit for Java. This stopped when the AgentRunner classes were incorporated into the core Domino Java classes in R5.

22.4.3   AgentRunner setup

If you want to use the AgentRunner class in your IDE, you must follow a few steps. We will take a closer look at VisualAge later in the chapter, but here are the steps for proper setup and use:

1 Make the notes.jar file available to your Java IDE. This involves importing or editing a classpath variable; it depends upon your environment.

2 Put the installation directory for your Domino install in the System PATH variable. This is c:\notes\data for standard Domino installations. This is necessary for you to access the lsxbe.dll file, which is required when you utilize the `AgentRunner` class.

3 Write your Java agent extending the `DebugAgentBase` class as the parent class.

4 Test for a valid `Session` object in your code.

AgentRunner takes advantage of a database named AgentRunner.nsf, which is installed in your Domino data directory (c:\notes by default). Every time you use the `AgentRunner` class, a document is created in this database. The process for taking advantage of the `AgentRunner` class is a bit confusing, but here are the steps:

1 Create your Domino Java Agent (extending `DebugAgentBase`).

2 Compile the code in your Java IDE.

3 Import the resulting Java class file into your Domino database.

4 Run the agent from the Domino database. This will create a document for the agent in the AgentRunner database (AgentRunner.nsf). The document must exist in the AgentRunner database in order for the agent to be executed outside of the Domino environment. The Java Console will display the message "Agent-Context dumped to file AgentRunner.nsf for agent": plus the agent and database. Figure 22.1 shows the message format.

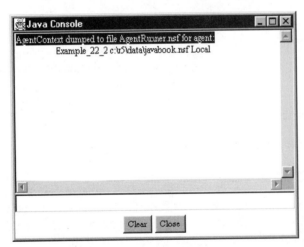

**Figure 22.1
A successfully created
AgentRunner document**

5 This step is optional. Check the AgentRunner database to make certain that the document does exist. Figure 22.2 shows a document in the database.

6 You can now run and debug the agent from your Java IDE.

22.5 WORKING WITH THE SUN JDK

The Java Development Kit from Sun Microsystems is the lowest level of development environment, but that does not mean it is not powerful or very capable. It has no

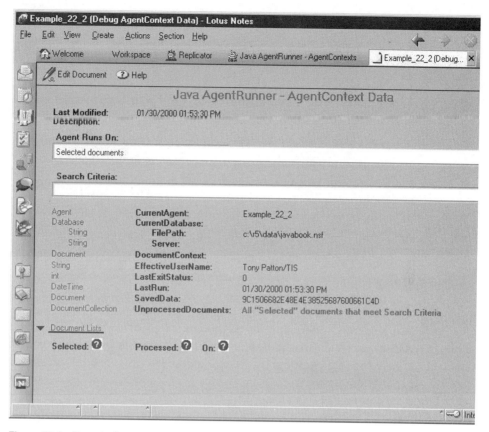

Figure 22.2 Sample AgentRunner database document

fancy graphical interface, so everything is accomplished at the command line. You accomplish all editing of your source code in your favorite text editor. Many developers have their preferences, with the vi editor, Windows Wordpad, and the DOS editor as a few possible choices.

The installation of the Sun JDK creates a number of directories on your system. You specify the root directory, and subdirectories are created off of it. Here is how the directory structure is set up:

```
|--------bin -contains Java programs:  javac, java, jar, jdb, ...
|
JDK ------|--------lib - core java class packages
|
|--------....
```

The bin subdirectory off of the root directory of your JDK installation contains all of the Java programs. Here is a list of these programs:

- javac: Java compiler. Use this to compile your java source files into bytecode.
- java: Java interpreter. Use this to execute your compiled java classes.
- jar: Java archive utility; compresses and decompresses files into the jar format.
- jdb: Java debugger
- appletviewer: Applet viewer for running and testing applets

The lib subdirectory off of the root directory of your JDK installation contains the core Java packages. The most important file is classes.zip. This file contains all of the Java class files. You should place it in the system classpath variable.

On a Windows platform, you should set up the CLASSPATH variable for the Sun JDK in the autoexec.bat file. This makes it available to all applications. Once you have properly configured it on the system, all other applications (like the JDK) can take advantage of it. In addition, you should place the Java programs directory (bin) in the PATH system variable. This makes the Java programs available from any command/system prompt.

You can run the SYSEDIT program from Windows to edit the system files. Figure 22.3 shows the result of running SYSEDIT from the RUN window on a Windows 98 system.

You will notice that the Notes/Domino installation directory was added to the path, and the Domino Java classes were added to the classpath variable.

Your autoexec.bat file should contain the following lines:

```
set classpath=.;c:\r5\notes.jar;c:\r5\data\domino\java\ncso.jar;d:\
     jdk1.1.6\lib\classes.zip  ❶
set path=c:\windows\command;c:\windows;d:\jdk1.1.6\bin;c:\r5\data  ❷
doskey  ❸
```

NOTE   If you use this setup, make certain you specify the proper Domino and JDK paths.

Explanation

❶   The first line sets the classpath variable for use by the JDK. This tells it where to look for referenced class files (in your code) when it compiles into bytecode. Lotus Notes/Domino is installed in the r5 directory on the C drive, and the JDK is installed in the JDK1.1.6 directory on the D drive. The CORBA Domino classes (ncso.jar) are added to the classpath system variable along with the core Domino Java classes (notes.jar).

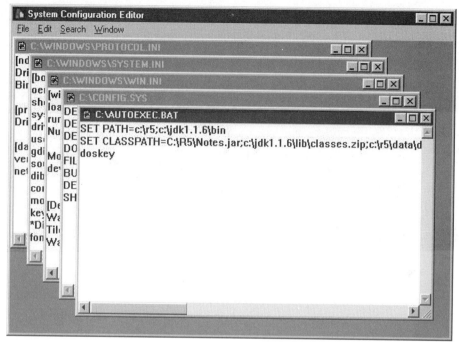

Figure 22.3   Running SYSEDIT in Windows to set CLASSPATH and PATH variables

❷   This line sets the path variable. The system will look in the directories listed for any commands issued at the command line. This saves you the time of specifying the complete path to the Java compiler (javac).

❸   This line loads the doskey program, which keeps a history of commands entered at the command line (DOS prompt). You can scroll through the history using the arrow keys (up and down) on your keyboard. This is a great time saver when you are continuously compiling and running the same class file (making changes in between). Instead of retyping the command each time, scroll to it and press Enter.

NOTE   This setup works on (my) Windows 95/98/NT machines. I am not a Unix, Linux, Macintosh, Be, or OS/2 (or any other system) developer. I assume those environments will require a different approach.

Once you have your environment set up, you can compile and run your Java code from the command line. The program for compiling your Java source file into a Java class file is javac. The command line for it is as follows:

```
javac path\your_Java_filename.java
```

This will compile your Java source file into Java bytecode. The result is the corresponding class file(s)—i.e., if you compile MyFirstTest.java, the resulting class file will be called MyFirstText.class. The command java runs the class file. Omit the .class extension when you call the java command:

```
java class_name
```

Use appletviewer to run an applet:

```
appletviewer class_name
```

The Java Development Kit is the cheapest (free) way to develop Java applications. Proper setup of your environment is required, and the interface is not very user-friendly. We live in a world where most applications make it easy for the user to perform routine or complex tasks through the use of a mouse. Well, the JDK command-line interface is not mouse-supported. The rise in popularity of Java has led to the development of numerous high-end development systems. This includes offerings from major players such as Microsoft and IBM, as well as many others. Let's take a look at IBM's offering.

22.6   VISUALAGE FOR JAVA

VisualAge for Java (currently in version 3) is IBM's premier Java development environment. It can be used in conjunction with the IBM WebSphere Studio development environment and/or WebSphere Application Server to create advanced applications that take advantage of JDBC, Swing classes, and Java Server Pages. It includes a full-featured debugger that allows on-the-fly code changes, extensive help including pop-up help for quick access to object properties and methods, versioning, team development, project/package management, and more.

You can use VisualAge to develop standalone Domino applications, applets for inclusion in Domino documents, Domino agents (with AgentRunner), and servlets. The VisualAge environment is so robust that you may never want to return to the Domino Designer Java IDE. You can develop your code in VisualAge and export/paste it into your Domino agent body. Figure 22.4 shows the VisualAge for Java workspace. This is where you can view all projects/packages.

Figure 22.4 shows all projects in the current workspace. In addition, there are tabs for viewing specific packages, classes, and interfaces, and a problem tab for viewing errors. You can import the Domino Java archive files (jar) into the workspace for use in your applications.

Figure 22.5 shows the VisualAge import window. It allows you to easily view all available methods for the classes/interfaces. You should import two packages into the VisualAge environment:

- Domino Java library (lotus.domino package in the notes.jar file)
- Domino CORBA library (lotus.domino.CORBA package in the ncso.jar file)

Once you have imported the Domino classes, you can view the classes in the VisualAge workspace. Figure 22.6 demonstrates browsing the lotus.notes package after it has been imported.

Once you develop code in VisualAge, you can easily export (or copy or paste) it and then import it into your Domino Java agent IDE.

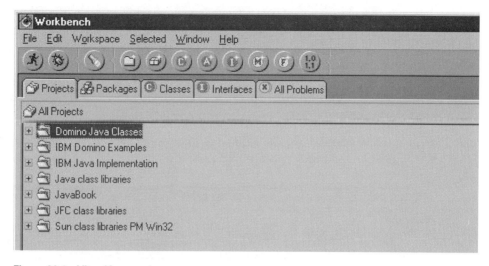

Figure 22.4 VisualAge workspace

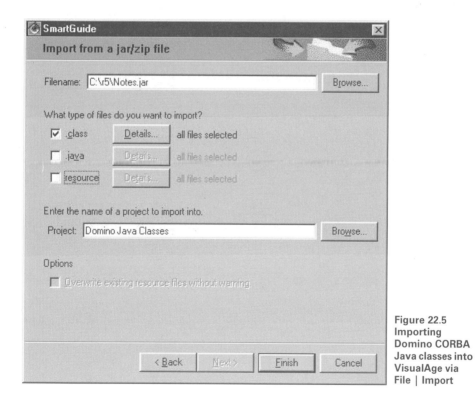

Figure 22.5
Importing
Domino CORBA
Java classes into
VisualAge via
File | Import

NOTE   IBM VisualAge for Java has an excellent feature called code lookup that allows you to quickly and easily view an object's available methods when you enter Java code. When you enter the object name plus the period, and then depress the ALT button and SPACEBAR at the same time, a window appears showing valid selections. The same functionality is provided in Visual Basic.

Another technique for utilizing the Domino Java classes in VisualAge is to specify an external classpath for the VisualAge workspace. You can accomplish this via the Windows | Options drop-down menu selection. Figure 22.7 shows the options list.

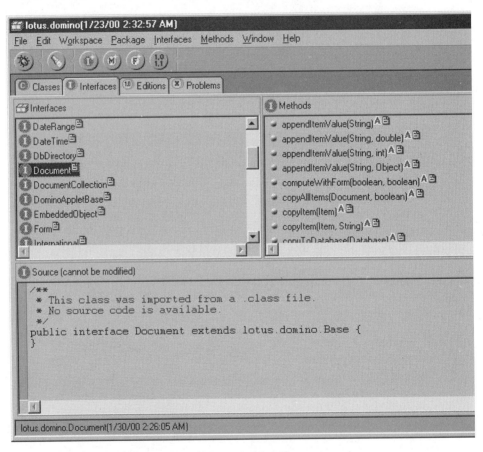

Figure 22.6   Browsing the lotus.notes package in VisualAge

The resources selection allows you to specify a path to external Java classes. Figure 22.8 shows the window that appears when you click on the Edit button. It allows you to add a whole directory or specific jar files.

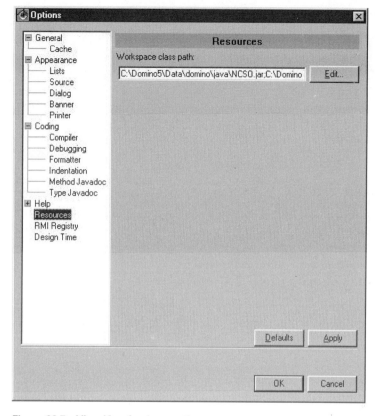

Figure 22.7 VisualAge for Java options

Once you have specified external class references for the workspace, they are available in your Java code. The only drawback is the lack of ability to browse the Domino Java packages in the VisualAge workspace.

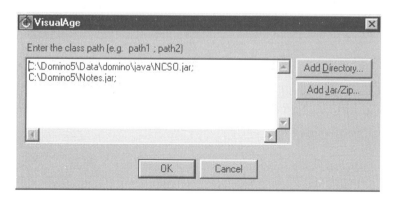

Figure 22.8 Specifying external Java classes in VisualAge

22.6.1 Developing a Java application in VisualAge

Let's take a look at developing a standalone Domino Java application in VisualAge. It is a simple application; we will access the Domino Directory on a Domino server. The code in example 22.1 establishes a session, and then displays the total number of documents in the database.

Example 22.1 (Standalone)

```java
package Chapter22Examples;
/**
 * This type was created in VisualAge.
 */
import lotus.domino.*;
public class Example_22_1 {
/**
 * This method was created in VisualAge.
 * @param args java.lang.String[]
 */
public static void main(java.lang.String[] args) {
  Session s;
  Database db;
  DocumentCollection dc;
  try {
   NotesThread.sinitThread();
   s = NotesFactory.createSession("207.60.107.158","Anthony Patton","password");
   if (s == null) {
     System.out.println("Session could not be established."); }
   else {
     db = s.getDatabase(s.getServerName(), "names.nsf");
     if (db == null) {
      System.out.println("Error accessing database.");
     } else {
      dc = db.getAllDocuments();
      System.out.println("There are " + dc.getCount() + " in " + db.getTitle()); } }
   dc recycle();
   db recycle();
   s recycle();
  } catch (NoClassDefFoundError e) {
   e.printStackTrace();
  } catch (NotesException n) {
   n.printStackTrace();
  } finally {
   NotesThread.stermThread(); } } }
```

Figure 22.9 shows this Java code in the VisualAge workspace.

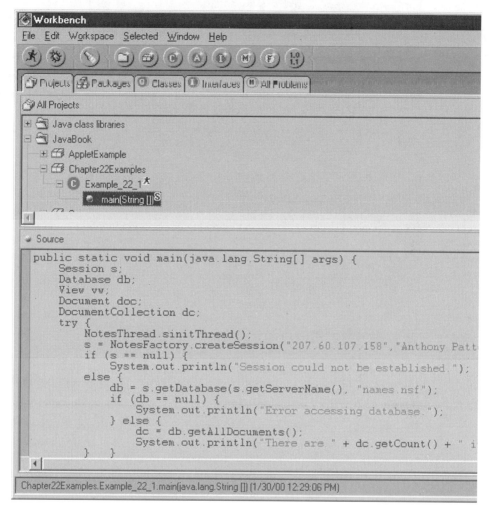

Figure 22.9   Example 22.1 in VisualAge

Running the code in example 22.1 displays the output in the VisualAge Console window, as shown in figure 22.10.

NOTE   Example 22.1 requires that you start the DIIOP server task on the Domino server. This task facilitates remote access to the Domino objects. You can load it via the command LOAD DIIOP from the server console window.

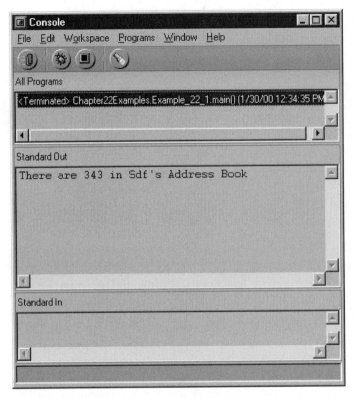

Figure 22.10   Example 22.1 in the VisualAge for Java console output

22.6.2   Using AgentRunner with VisualAge

The AgentRunner class allows you to develop, test, and run Domino Java agents within your favorite Java development environment. If you are developing via 4.6, the AgentRunner is available for download from Lotus' Web site (www.lotus.com). Beginning with version 5, the AgentRunner class is distributed with the Domino Java classes (notes.jar) and is included with a Domino Designer installation. The steps required to utilize AgentRunner in VisualAge are as follows:

1 Successfully enter and compile your Domino Agent code in VisualAge. Make sure the class extends the `DebugAgentBase` class.

2 Export the class file to a local drive.

3 Create the agent in your Domino database. The type is Imported Java.

4 Import the Java class file into your Domino Agent.

5 Run the agent. You should receive a message similar to that shown in figure 22.1.

6 You can optionally check the AgentRunner database (located in your Domino data directory) for a document for the agent. The document will be similar to that shown in figure 22.2.

7 You can now run the agent code from VisualAge via AgentRunner. Highlight the agent class in the VisualAge workspace. From the drop-down menus choose Selected | Tools | Domino AgentRunner.

There are two options available: Run and Properties (see figure 22.11).

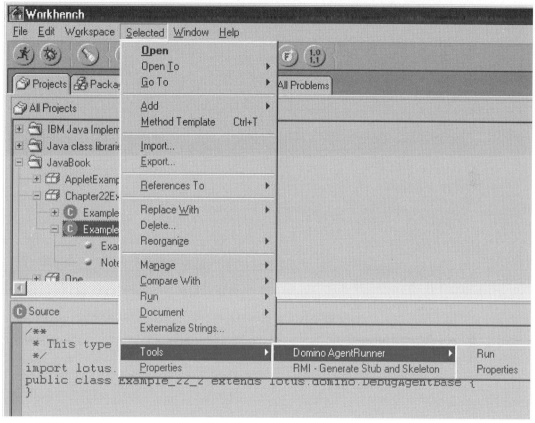

Figure 22.11 AgentRunner options from VisualAge workspace

Selecting Properties opens the window displayed in figure 22.12. It allows you to run the agent, update the context document in the AgentRunner database, or save the changes.

Clicking the Update Agent Context button or double-clicking on an agent opens the window displayed in figure 22.13. It allows you to enter or edit a description, agent criteria, and search criteria. It is the same as editing the AgentContext document in the AgentRunner database. Clicking the Update Agent Context Document button saves the changes to the AgentRunner database.

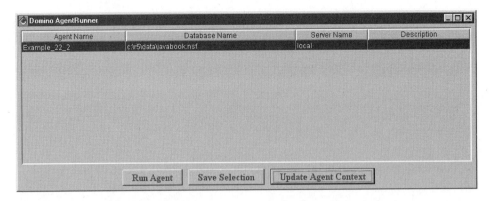

Figure 22.12   AgentRunner properties

xample_22_2   DATABASE=c:\r5\data\javabook.nsf   SERVER=local

Description:

Agent Runs On:
All documents in database
All new and modified documents since last run
All unread documents in view
All documents in view
Selected documents
Run once

Agent Runs On View:

Search Criteria:

Update Agent Context Document

Figure 22.13   Editing Agent properties in VisualAge

22.7   *OTHER ENVIRONMENTS*

VisualAge is not the only tool available in the market, but it is a personal favorite. Symantec's Visual Café, Borland's JBuilder, and PowerJ from Sybase are a few of the others. Microsoft's offering, J++, uses its own version of the JVM. You cannot use it to develop Domino Java applications at this time. You can properly set up all of the other environments to use the Domino Java classes and the AgentRunner to build powerful applications.

22.8   CHAPTER REVIEW

The Domino Designer IDE introduced in R5 is leaps and bounds above its predecessors, but it is still lacking in features when compared to full-featured Java IDEs on the market. The Domino IDE offers syntax checking, importing, exporting, and online help, plus other features. On the other hand, robust environments such as VisualAge for Java and Symantec's Visual Café offer full-featured debuggers, project management, and versioning. These are excellent additions for developing large-scale applications. The Domino Designer IDE will suffice for developing small agents. On the flip side, bigger applications beg for a dedicated Java development environment. VisualAge for Java is just one solution.

C H A P T E R   2 3

Applets

23.1 What is an applet? 306
23.2 Issues 306
23.3 Structure of an applet 307
23.4 Security 307
23.5 Referencing applets in HTML 307

23.6 AppletBase class 309
23.7 Accessing a Domino server 310
23.8 Standard Domino applets 321
23.9 Installing applets locally 322
23.10 Chapter review 323

23.1 WHAT IS AN APPLET?

Applets can be described as programs that run inside of a Web browser. You should keep the size of the programs as small as possible, because you download the applets to the browser from a Web server. Most users have relatively slow connections, so you should take their download time into consideration. On the other hand, Intranet applications may have higher bandwidth available.

23.2 ISSUES

In Lotus Notes/Domino 4.6, Java applets were not allowed to access Domino objects/ data through the back end. Access was restricted to the use of URLs. This changed with the introduction of version 5.

Domino 5 added CORBA/IIOP support, so Java applets can access Domino data/ objects. This is facilitated through the `AppletBase` class. We will take a look at the `AppletBase` class by first surveying the structure of an applet.

23.3 STRUCTURE OF AN APPLET

Typical Java applets inherit design from the `Applet` class found in the java.applet package, and they implement the required methods. These methods included the following:

- `init`: The `init` method is called when an applet is first created. It carries out the first-time initialization of the applet.
- `start`: The `start` method is called every time a browser views the applet. If the user scrolls off the applet and scrolls back, the `start` method is called. This method is called after the `init` method.
- `paint`: The `paint` method is called to do special painting in the applet. This can include anything from the `Graphics` class.
- `stop`: The `stop` method is called every time an applet moves out of sight of the Web browser window.
- `destroy`: The `destroy` method is called when the applet is no longer being utilized. It is called immediately after the `stop` method. The user may go to another page, or close the browser.

The best way to understand when and how these methods are called is through an example, but let's take a look at accessing applets from a Web page first.

23.4 SECURITY

Applets have security restrictions. They cannot read or write data to or from a local drive. This restriction includes running applications on the local file system. An applet is restricted to communicating directly with the Web server on which it originated.

23.5 REFERENCING APPLETS IN HTML

The HTML applet tag brings an applet into an HTML page. It has the following format:

```
<APPLET
   CODE = Applet_class_file
   WIDTH = Width_of_applet_in_pixels
   HEIGHT = Height_of_applet_in_pixels>
</APPLET>
```

The <APPLET> tag has many more attributes which I will not cover here. In HTML 4.0, the <OBJECT> tag was introduced. The <APPLET> tag is now officially deprecated.

You can see that the HTML applet tag includes values that specify the applet's class filename specified by the code parameter. The width and height values specify the display area of the applet within the browser window.

In addition, you can pass parameters into the applet via the param tag within the applet tag. The param signals its name and a value passed in quotation marks.

```
<PARAM NAME=parameter_name VALUE="parameter_value">
```

Let's take a look at a basic applet and the order of the execution of the methods.

Example 23.1   (Applet)

```
import java.applet.*;
import java.awt.*;
public class Example_23_1 extends Applet {   ❶
  public void init() {   ❷
    super.init();   ❸
    System.out.println("Init method"); }   ❹
  public void paint(Graphics g) {   ❺
    System.out.println("Paint method");}
  public void start() {   ❻
    System.out.println("Start method");}
  public void stop() {   ❼
    System.out.println("Stop method");}}
```

Explanation

❶ Declare the class that inherits design from the Applet class.

❷ Declare the init method.

❸ Call the init method of its parent class.

❹ Display a message to the standard out.

❺ Declare the paint method.

❻ Declare the start method.

❼ Declare the stop method.

Figure 23.1 shows the simple applet.

The println statements in the code will send their messages to the standard out, which will be the DOS window from which the appletviewer was initialized.

Output

Here is the output when the applet is first loaded:

```
Init method
Start method
Paint method
```

Run the applet, restart, stop, and so forth to see how and when the different methods are triggered.

Figure 23.1
Example 23.1 applet

23.6   *APPLETBASE CLASS*

Applets that make use of the Domino Java classes must extend the `AppletBase` class. Example 23.1 showed that non-Domino applets must extend the `Applet` class, while the `AppletBase` class extends the `Applet` class. You must create a session with the Domino server before you can access any of the Domino Java objects.

Applets are restricted to accessing the Domino server on which they originate.

23.6.1   Domino session

The `AppletBase` class contains two methods for creating a `Session` object:

- `AppletBase.createSession();`
- `AppletBase.createSession ("username", "password");`

  The session is closed with the `closeSession` method.

`AppletBase.closeSession(Session_object_to_close);`

23.6.2   Methods

The `AppletBase` class includes methods for each corresponding method in the `Applet` class. The name of each method is preceded by `notesApplet`. Here is a list of some of those methods:

- `notesAppletInit`: Takes the place of the standard `init` method of a regular applet
- `notesAppletStart`: Takes the place of the standard `start` method of a regular applet

- `notesAppletStop`: Takes the place of the standard `stop` method of a regular applet
- `notesAppletDestroy`: Takes the place of the standard `destroy` method of a regular applet

Example 23.2 alters Example 23.1 so that it works with Domino.

Example 23.2 (Applet)

```
import lotus.domino.*;
import java.awt.*;
import java.applet.*;
public class Example_23_2 extends AppletBase {
 public void notesAppletInit() {
  super.init();
  System.out.println("NotesAppletInit method"); }
 public void notesAppletDestroy() {
  System.out.println("NotesAppletDestroy method");}
 public void notesAppletStart() {
  System.out.println("NotesAppletStart method");}
 public void notesAppletStop() {
  System.out.println("NotesAppletStop method");}}
```

23.7 ACCESSING A DOMINO SERVER

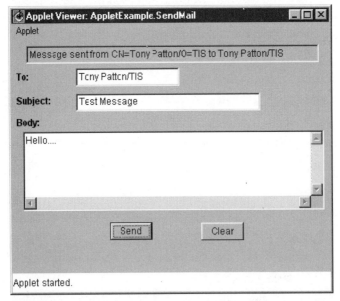

Figure 23.2
SendMail applet

Once you have the structure of an applet down, accessing a Domino server is not much different than other methods. The main aspect of an applet is the construction of the user interface (UI); you must plan out the overall look and feel of your applet.

Popular development environment applications such as VisualAge for Java provide a visual development tool to aid the layout of an applet's user interface.

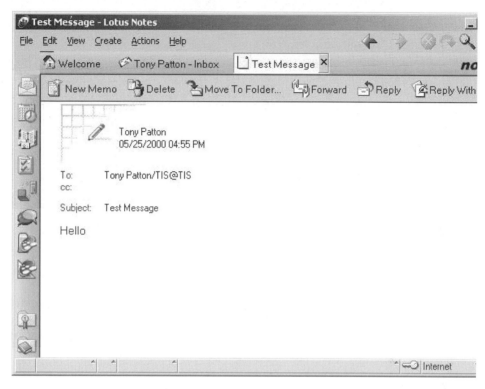

Figure 23.3 Email received

In example 23.3, we construct a simple applet to send an email message. The applet has fields for the recipient's name, subject, and body of the email message. In addition, there is a status field for displaying information regarding the status of the memo. There are two buttons: Send and Clear. Clicking the Clear button clears the contents of all of the fields, and clicking the Send button creates the email message using the applet fields. Figure 23.2 shows the applet.

Figure 23.2 shows an email composed to myself. The status field located at the top of the applet signals that the message has been sent. Figure 23.3 shows the email message opened in my Notes client.

Now let's take a look at the code in example 23.3. The code was generated using VisualAge for Java 2.0.

Example 23.3 (Applet)

```
import java.applet.*;
import java.awt.*;
import lotus.domino.*;
```

```
public class SendMail extends AppletBase implements java.awt.event.ActionListener {
  private Button ivjbtnClear = null;  ❶
  private Button ivjbtnSend = null;
  private Label ivjlblTo = null;  ❷
  private Label ivjlibBody = null;
  private Label ivjlibSubject = null;
  private TextArea ivjtxtBody = null;  ❸
  private TextField ivjtxtSubject = null;  ❹
  private TextField ivjtxtTo = null;
  private TextField ivjtxtStatus = null;
  public void actionPerformed(java.awt.event.ActionEvent e) {  ❺
    if ((e.getSource() == getbtnClear()) ) {  ❻
     connEtoM1(e); }
    if ((e.getSource() == getbtnClear()) ) {
     connEtoM2(e); }
    if ((e.getSource() == getbtnClear()) ) {
     connEtoM3(e); }
    if ((e.getSource() == getbtnSend()) ) {  ❼
     connEtoC1(e); }
    if ((e.getSource() == getbtnClear()) ) {
     connEtoM4(e); } }
    private void connEtoC1(java.awt.event.ActionEvent arg1) {
     try {
       this.sendIt();  ❽
      } catch (java.lang.Throwable ivjExc) {
       handleException(ivjExc); } }
    private void connEtoM1(java.awt.event.ActionEvent arg1) {
     try {
       gettxtBody().setText("");  ❾
      } catch (java.lang.Throwable ivjExc) {
       handleException(ivjExc); } }
    private void connEtoM2(java.awt.event.ActionEvent arg1) {
     try {
       gettxtSubject().setText("");
      } catch (java.lang.Throwable ivjExc) {
       handleException(ivjExc); } }
    private void connEtoM3(java.awt.event.ActionEvent arg1) {
     try {
       gettxtTo().setText("");
      } catch (java.lang.Throwable ivjExc) {
       handleException(ivjExc); } }
    private void connEtoM4(java.awt.event.ActionEvent arg1) {
     try {
       gettxtStatus().setText("");
      } catch (java.lang.Throwable ivjExc) {
       handleException(ivjExc); } }
    private Button getbtnClear() {
     if (ivjbtnClear == null) {
       try {
        ivjbtnClear = new java.awt.Button();
        ivjbtnClear.setName("btnClear");
        ivjbtnClear.setBounds(251, 236, 56, 23);
```

```
      ivjbtnClear.setLabel("Clear");
    } catch (java.lang.Throwable ivjExc) {
      handleException(ivjExc); } }
  return ivjbtnClear; }
private Button getbtnSend() {   ❿
  if (ivjbtnSend == null) {
    try {
      ivjbtnSend = new java.awt.Button();
      ivjbtnSend.setName("btnSend");
      ivjbtnSend.setBounds(130, 235, 56, 23);
      ivjbtnSend.setLabel("Send");
    } catch (java.lang.Throwable ivjExc) {
      handleException(ivjExc); } }
    return ivjbtnSend; }
private Label getlblTo() {
  if (ivjlblTo == null) {
    try {
      ivjlblTo = new java.awt.Label();
      ivjlblTo.setName("lblTo");
      ivjlblTo.setFont(new java.awt.Font("dialog", 1, 12));
      ivjlblTo.setText("To:");
      ivjlblTo.setBounds(6, 39, 74, 20);
    } catch (java.lang.Throwable ivjExc) {
      handleException(ivjExc); } }
    return ivjlblTo; }
  private Label getlibBody() {
    if (ivjlibBody == null) {
      try {
        ivjlibBody = new java.awt.Label();
        ivjlibBody.setName("libBody");
        ivjlibBody.setFont(new java.awt.Font("dialog", 1, 12));
        ivjlibBody.setText("Body:");
        ivjlibBody.setBounds(6, 97, 74, 20);
      } catch (java.lang.Throwable ivjExc) {
        handleException(ivjExc); } }
    return ivjlibBody; }
  private Label getlibSubject() {
    if (ivjlibSubject == null) {
      try {
        ivjlibSubject = new java.awt.Label();
        ivjlibSubject.setName("libSubject");
        ivjlibSubject.setFont(new java.awt.Font("dialog", 1, 12));
        ivjlibSubject.setText("Subject:");
        ivjlibSubject.setBounds(6, 70, 74, 20);
      } catch (java.lang.Throwable ivjExc) {
        handleException(ivjExc); } }
    return ivjlibSubject; }
  private TextArea gettxtBody() {   ⓫
    if (ivjtxtBody == null) {
      try {
        ivjtxtBody = new java.awt.TextArea();
        ivjtxtBody.setName("txtBody");
```

```
      ivjtxtBody.setBackground(java.awt.Color.white);
      ivjtxtBody.setBounds(14, 119, 399, 101);
    } catch (java.lang.Throwable ivjExc) {
      handleException(ivjExc); } }
  return ivjtxtBody; }
private TextField gettxtStatus() {  ⑫
  if (ivjtxtStatus == null) {
    try {
      ivjtxtStatus = new java.awt.TextField();
      ivjtxtStatus.setName("txtStatus");
      ivjtxtStatus.setBounds(20, 9, 387, 23);
    } catch (java.lang.Throwable ivjExc) {
      handleException(ivjExc); } }
  return ivjtxtStatus;  }
private TextField gettxtSubject() {
  if (ivjtxtSubject == null) {
    try {
      ivjtxtSubject = new java.awt.TextField();
      ivjtxtSubject.setName("txtSubject");
      ivjtxtSubject.setBackground(java.awt.Color.white);
      ivjtxtSubject.setBounds(86, 70, 244, 23);
    } catch (java.lang.Throwable ivjExc) {
      handleException(ivjExc); } }
  return ivjtxtSubject; }
private TextField gettxtTo() {  ⑬
  if (ivjtxtTo == null) {
    try {
      ivjtxtTo = new java.awt.TextField();
      ivjtxtTo.setName("txtTo");
      ivjtxtTo.setBackground(java.awt.Color.white);
      ivjtxtTo.setBounds(86, 38, 137, 23);
    } catch (java.lang.Throwable ivjExc) {
      handleException(ivjExc); } }
  return ivjtxtTo; }
private void handleException(Throwable exception) {  ⑭
  System.out.println("--------- UNCAUGHT EXCEPTION ---------");
  exception.printStackTrace(System.out);   }
  public void notesAppletInit() {  ⑮
    super.notesAppletInit();  ⑯
  try {
    setName("SendMail");  ⑰
    setLayout(null);
    setBackground(java.awt.Color.lightGray);  ⑱
    setSize(426, 279);  ⑲
    add(getlblTo(), getlblTo().getName());  ⑳
    add(getlibBody(), getlibBody().getName());
    add(getlibSubject(), getlibSubject().getName());
    add(gettxtTo(), gettxtTo().getName());  ㉑
    add(gettxtBody(), gettxtBody().getName());
    add(gettxtSubject(), gettxtSubject().getName());
    add(getbtnSend(), getbtnSend().getName());  ㉒
    add(getbtnClear(), getbtnClear().getName());
```

```
        add(gettxtStatus(), gettxtStatus().getName());
        initConnections();  ㉓
    } catch (java.lang.Throwable ivjExc) {
        handleException(ivjExc); } }
    private void initConnections() {
      getbtnClear().addActionListener(this);
      getbtnSend().addActionListener(this); }
      public void sendIt() {  ㉔
        String sendTo = gettxtTo().getText();  ㉕
        String subject = gettxtSubject().getText();  ㉖
        String body = gettxtBody().getText();  ㉗
      try {
        NotesThread.sinitThread();  ㉘
        Session s = NotesFactory.createSession();  ㉙
        Database db = s.getDatabase("","names.nsf");  ㉚
        Document memo = db.createDocument();  ㉛
        memo.replaceItemValue("Subject",subject);  ㉜
        memo.replaceItemValue("Body",body);  ㉝
        memo.replaceItemValue("Form","memo");  ㉞
        memo.send(sendTo);  ㉟
        gettxtStatus().setText("Message sent from " + s.getUserName() + " to " + sendTo);  ㊱
        memo.recycle();  ㊲
     db.recycle();
     s.recycle();
   } catch (NotesException n) {
   n.printStackTrace();
   gettxtStatus().setText("Error sending message.");  ㊳
   } finally {
   NotesThread.stermThread(); }  }  ㊴
```

Explanation

❶ Declare buttons to use in the applet.

❷ Declare labels to use on the applet.

❸ Declare the textarea object to use for the body field on the applet.

❹ Declare the text fields to use for the status, sendTo, and subject fields on the applet.

❺ The `actionPerformed` method handles all clicks of the mouse on defined objects. In our applet this includes the Send and Clear buttons.

❻ Determine if the Clear button was selected and act accordingly. The code handles the Clear button four times, once for each text field to be cleared. The calls could be combined into one if statement.

❼ Determine if the Send button was selected and act accordingly. The `sendIt` method is not called directly, but the code for the connection between the button and the code is called. A programmer would probably call the code directly from the event handler, but the VisualAge environment generates the code according to its rules.

⑧ Handle the Send button event; the `sendIt` method is called to compose and send the email message.

⑨ Handle the Clear send button event.

⑩ Set up the Send button on the applet's user interface.

⑪ Set up the `body` field on the applet.

⑫ Set up the `status` field on the applet.

⑬ Set up the `sendTo` field on the applet.

⑭ Method to handle uncaught exceptions.

⑮ The initialization method of a Domino applet. This replaces the `init` method in a normal applet.

⑯ Call the initialization method of the base class of the applet.

⑰ Set the name of the applet.

⑱ Set the background color of the applet window.

⑲ Set the size of the applet window.

⑳ Add the field label objects to the applet window.

㉑ Add the text field objects to the applet window.

㉒ Add the buttons to the applet window.

㉓ Call the initConnections method. This adds the listeners for events related to the objects that use connections (buttons).

㉔ The `sendIt` method handles the creation and sending of the email message.

㉕ Create a `String` object and populate it with the contents of the `sendTo` field.

㉖ Create a `String` object and populate it with the contents of the `subject` field.

㉗ Create a `String` object and populate it with the contents of the `body` field.

㉘ Initialize a `NotesThread` object.

㉙ Create a new Domino `Session` object. A session is created for the person's workstation on which the applet is run, since the `createSession` method with no parameters is used. A username and password could be specified.

㉚ Create a new Domino `Database` object. We use the Domino directory because we only need to use a `Database` object to create a Domino `Document` object for the mail memo.

㉛ Create a new Domino `Document` object for the mail memo.

㉜ Populate the `subject` field of the mail memo with the contents of the applet's subject field.

㉝ Populate the body field of the mail memo with the contents of the applet's `body` field.

㉞ Set the form property of the mail memo.

㉟ Send the mail memo, passing the recipient's name to the send method.

㊱ Populate the status field that states the memo was processed.

㊲ Recycle the Domino objects `Document`, `Database`, and `Session`.

㊳ Display error messages in the status field of the applet.

㊴ Dispose of the `NotesThread` object.

The graphical interface was designed via the Visual Composition Editor in VisualAge. The buttons, text fields, and other elements are laid out and items are connected together by dragging and dropping a connection between them. A connection can fire off any event or code. Figure 23.4 shows the layout of our applet.

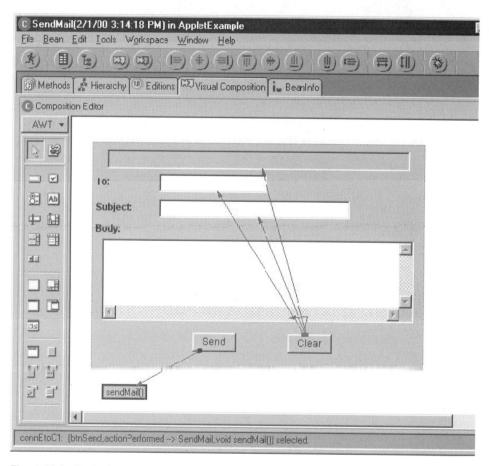

Figure 23.4 Designing an applet in VisualAge

Notice the connections between the Clear button and all fields, so the button can erase the contents of each. The Send button is connected to code (`sendit` function).

Once you have your applet designed and debugged, you can add it to a Domino form or page for use in Web browsers as well as the Notes client. Insert Applets into the design of pages or forms via the Create | Java Applet drop-down box (see figure 23.5).

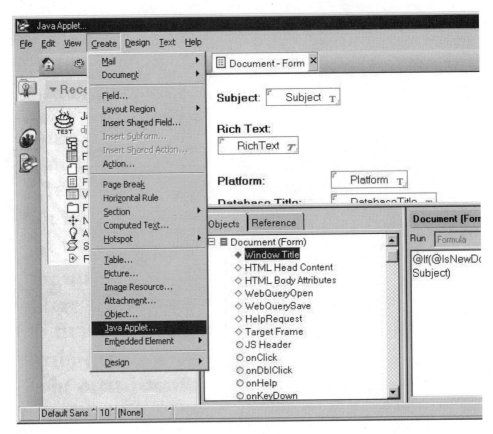

Figure 23.5   Inserting an applet into a Domino page

The next window, shown in figure 23.6, allows you to select the actual Java applet files (class and any resource files like images) to insert or import onto the Domino page or form. You select the files from a local directory and enter the base class name for the applet. You may link to an applet stored on a Web server (via its URL) as well.

Also, you can take advantage of the new Resources option in R5. It allows you to store Java applets, images, and more separately from the other design elements in a database. You can reference them in other design elements. This allows you to maintain an applet, image, and so forth in one location. It reduces the headaches of worrying where you used an item that has changed. Figure 23.7 shows a Java applet resource created for our applet.

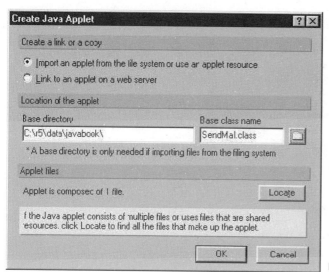

Figure 23.6   Inserting a Java applet

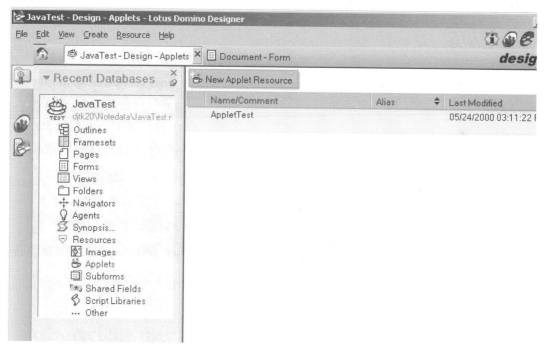

Figure 23.7   Java applet resource

You must tell Domino if an applet will access Domino objects from a browser client. You can accomplish this in the Java applet properties (right-click on the applet and select Properties) window. You must check the option entitled "Applet uses Notes

CORBA classes." This is not necessary for Lotus Notes clients. Figure 23.8 shows the Java applet properties.

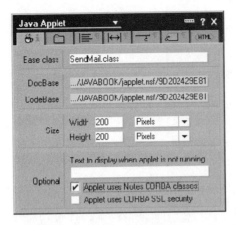

Figure 23.8
Java applet properties

If you are not using VisualAge for Java, you can use the JDK from SUN or any other IDE. VisualAge generates its own code for the connections and other aspects of the application. The following is the same code using the JDK. This code uses the Java 1.0 event model, whereas Example 23.3 took advantage of Java 1.1 event handlers.

Example 23.4   (Applet)

```
import lotus.domino.*;
import java.applet.*;
import java.awt.*;
public class Example_23_4 extends AppletBase {
  Document memo;
  Database db;
  TextField txtStatus = new TextField("",60);
  TextField txtSendTo = new TextField("",30);
  TextField txtSubject = new TextField("",30);
  TextArea txtBody = new TextArea("",1,30);
  Button btnSend = new Button("Send");
  Button btnClear = new Button("Clear");
  Label lblSendTo = new Label("Send To:");
  Label lblSubject = new Label("Subject:");
  Label lblBody = new Label("Body:");
  public void notesAppletInit() {
    super.notesAppletInit();
    setLayout(new FlowLayout());
    setSize(300,300);
    add(txtStatus);
    add(lblSendTo);
    add(txtSendTo);
    add(lblSubject);
    add(txtSubject);
    add(lblBody);
```

```
      add(txtBody);
      add(btnSend);
      add(btnClear);
      try {
       Session s = this.getSession();
       db = s.getDatabase("","names.nsf");
      } catch (NotesException n) {
       System.out.println("Error#" + n.id + " (" + n.text + ")");
      } catch (Exception e) {
       e.printStackTrace(); } }
   public boolean action(Event evt, Object arg) {
     if (evt.target.equals(btnSend)) {
      try {
       memo = db.createDocument();
       memo.replaceItemValue("Form","Memo");
       String sendTo = new String(txtSendTo.getText());
       String subject = new String(txtSubject.getText());
       String body = new String(txtBody.getText());
       memo.replaceItemValue("Subject",subject);
       memo.replaceItemValue("Body",body);
       memo.send(sendTo);
       txtStatus.setText("Message sent.");
      } catch (NotesException n) {
       System.out.println("Error#" + n.id + " (" + n.text + ")"); }
     } else if (evt.target.equals(btnClear)) {
      txtStatus.setText("");
      txtSubject.setText("");
      txtSendTo.setText("");
      txtBody.setText(""); }
    return(true); } }
```

23.8 STANDARD DOMINO APPLETS

Four design elements of a Domino application can be presented as Java applets when viewed in a browser. These elements include outlines, views, the rich-text field editor, and action bars. The Java applets provide the same functionality found in the Notes client. Figure 23.9 shows the outline Java applet.

Each Domino applet has its own Java archive file located in the domino\java directory of the Notes data directory. My installation directory is c:\r5, so the applets would be found in c:\r5\data\domino\java. Here is a list of the applet files:

- outline: outline.jar
- editor: editor.jar
- view: nvapplet.jar
- action bar: actionbar.jar

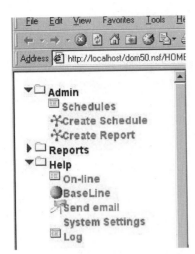

Figure 23.9
Outline applet

The size of the applets is rather large, so the download time associated with each can be a problem. For this reason, use them sparingly. The Properties window for each respective design element signals whether or not the applet is used. Each contains a "For Web Access" option. Figure 23.10 shows the selection for a view.

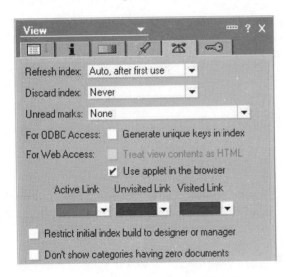

Figure 23.10
View "For Web Access" option

23.9 INSTALLING APPLETS LOCALLY

Applet download time determines whether an applet is successfully received in the user community. One way to avoid excessive download times is through the installation of the applet's class files on the client machine. This is not feasible with Internet applications that are accessed in all corners of the world, but it is another story within a controlled corporate environment.

Browsers search for Java class files in the following order:

1. Locally via directories specified in the system CLASSPATH variable
2. Locally in browser-specific directories
3. From the server via the applet tags ARCHIVE and CABBASE
4. Class files from the server

Installing the standard Domino applets (outline, view, action bar, and editor) on client machines involves extracting the class files from their respective Java archive (Jar) file and copying it to the appropriate directory on the client machine. The installation directory depends upon the browser used. Table 23.1 lists the directories for the Netscape and Microsoft (version 4 or higher) browsers.

Table 23.1 Java class location for major browsers

Browser	Directory
Netscape 3.x+ (Windows 95/98/NT)	\<netscape directory>\program\java\classes
Netscape 3.x+ (Macintosh)	\<netscape folder>\java\netscape-classes
Netscape 3.x+ (Unix)	Class files must be installed in the CLASSPATH.
Internet Explorer 4.x (Windows 95/98)	c:\windows\java\classes
Internet Explorer 4.x (Windows NT)	c:\winnt\java\classes

23.10 CHAPTER REVIEW

A Java applet is a special type of Java program that runs within a browser or the Lotus Notes client. A standard Java applet has certain predefined methods: `init`, `start`, `stop`, `destroy`, and `paint`. In addition, it extends the `Applet` class. A Domino applet extends the special `AppletBase` class and uses its own methods:

- `notesAppletInit`
- `notesAppletStart`
- `notesAppletStop`

  and

- `notesAppletDestroy`

These override the basic applet methods. You can use VisualAge for Java or another IDE to layout your applet. VisualAge has an excellent drag-and-drop utility for constructing applet user interfaces. You can import or link Java applets into a Domino form or page.

CHAPTER 24

Standalone applications

24.1 Overview   324
24.2 Main   325
24.3 Threads   325
24.4 Accessing a Domino server   326
24.5 Chapter review   328

24.1   OVERVIEW

A standalone Java application runs outside of the Domino environment. It is not an agent, servlet, or applet. It does not run in a Web browser. Rather, it runs by itself. It does require the JVM (Java Virtual Machine) to be installed on your system. The JVM interprets and executes the code.

Because it lives on a user's local drive, you must install a standalone Java application. It cannot take advantage of Domino replication like an agent or of a Web server like applets, but it can have read/write access to the local file system. Distribution of Java applications is the major drawback to a standalone application. On the design side, they are no different than any other code segments in this book. The only difference lies in the entry point for the Java code.

24.2 MAIN

The main method is defined as a class method (static). It is accessible to all other objects via its public declaration, and it returns no values (void). It has one parameter that is an array of strings containing command-line parameters, if there are any. Here is the format for the main method:

```
public static void main ( String[] args) {   method code }
```

Java applications require the main method.

24.3 THREADS

A Java application that takes advantage of the Domino Java classes must use threads through the NotesThread class. The NotesThread class extends the standard Java Thread class. There are three ways to implement it in your code. Which one of the three formats listed in table 24.1 you use determines the entry point for your application.

Table 24.1   Java application entry points

Entry point	Usage
main()	When using the sinitThread and stermThread methods of the NotesThread class
run()	Implementing the Runnable interface
runNotes()	Extending the NotesThread class

24.3.1 Extending the NotesThread class and using the runNotes method

The runNotes method is the entry point for code that extends the NotesThread class. That is, the application will begin execution in the runNotes method. To put this to use, you create a new object of your class and call the start method to instantiate the thread. Once the start method is called, the runNotes method of your class is called.

```
public class DominoThread extends NotesThread {
  public static void main(String[] args) {
   try {
     DominoThread testThread = new DominoThread();
     testThread.start();
   } catch (Exception e) {
     e.printStackTrace(); } }
  public void runNotes() {
//further code can go here } }
```

24.3.2 Implementing the Runnable interface

If your application implements the Runnable interface, the run method is the entry point of your code. To put it to use, a new object instance of your class is created and the start method is called. At this point, the run method of your class is called.

```
public class DominoThread implements Runnable {
 public static void main(String[] args) {
   try {
     DominoThread testThread = new DominoThread();
     NotesThread t = new NotesThread((Runnable) testThread);
     t.start();
   } catch (Exception e) {
     e.printStackTrace(); } }
 public void run() {
//further code can go here } }
```

24.3.3 Using the sinitThread and stermThread methods of the NotesThread class

You can use the sinitThread and stermThread methods of the NotesThread class to explicitly start and stop a thread.

```
public class DominoThread {
 public static void main(String[] args) {
   try {
     NotesThread.sinitThread();
   } catch (NotesException n) {
     System.out.println("Notes error (" + n.id + ") - " + n.text);
   } catch (Exception e) {
     e.printStackTrace();
   } finally {
     NotesThread.stermThread(); } }
```

24.4 ACCESSING A DOMINO SERVER

Once you decide the approach to use for creating a thread, you must access the Domino server. You can achieve this through the Session class. A Java application uses the NotesFactory class.

```
Session s = NotesFactory.createSession();
```

or

```
Session s = NotesFactory.createSession("server","username","password");
```

or

```
Session s = NotesFactory.createSession("server");
```

Once you create a Session object, all the Domino Java objects can be accessed in the same manner as in other code up to this point.

Let's take a look at accessing all documents in a database in example 24.1.

Example 24.1 (Standalone Application)

```
import lotus.domino.*;
public class Example_24_1 implements Runnable {
 public static void main(java.lang.String[] args) {  ❶
```

```
    try {
      Example_24_1 ex241 = new Example_24_1();   ❷
      NotesThread t = new NotesThread((Runnable)ex241);   ❸
      t.start();   ❹
    } catch (Exception e) {
      e.printStackTrace(); }   }
  public void run() {   ❺
    try {
      Session s = NotesFactory.createSession("");   ❻
      if (s != null) {   ❼
        Database db = s.getDatabase("","names.nsf");
        if (db != null) {
          DocumentCollection dc = db.getAllDocuments();
          Document doc = null;
          for (int x=1; x < dc.getCount(); x++) {
            doc = dc.getNthDocument(x);
            System.out.println(doc.getUniversalID());
            doc.recycle();}   ❽
          doc.recycle();   ❾
          dc.recycle();   ❿
          db.recycle(); }   ⓫
        else {
          System.out.println("Error accessing database."); }
          s.recycle(); }   ⓬
      else {
        System.out.print("Error - session could not ");
        System.out.println(" be established."); }
    } catch (NotesException n) {
      n.printStackTrace(); } } }
```

Explanation

❶ The Java code begins execution here.

❷ Create a new object instance of our class.

❸ Create a new `NotesThread` object for our object instance.

❹ Start the thread; execution of our application begins at the run method.

❺ Declare the method.

❻ Create a new `Session` object using settings in the local notes.ini file.

❼ Continue only if the `Session` object was properly created.

❽ Recycle the `Document` object each time through the loop. Resources are available for garbage collection.

❾ Recycle the `Document` object when finished accessing all documents.

❿ Recycle the `DocumentCollection` object.

⓫ Recycle the `Database` object.

⓬ Recycle the `Session` object.

Here is the same code extending the `NotesThread` class. The entry point for the application code in the example 24.2 is the `runNotes` method..

Example 24.2 (Applet)

```
import lotus.domino.*;
public class Example_24_2 extends NotesThread {
 public static void main(java.lang.String[] args) {
   try {
     Example_24_2 ex241 = new Example_24_2();
     ex241.start();
   } catch (Exception e) {
     e.printStackTrace(); }  }
 public void runNotes() {
   try {
     Session s = NotesFactory.createSession("");
     if (s != null) {
       Database db = s.getDatabase("","names.nsf");
       if (db != null) {
         DocumentCollection dc = db.getAllDocuments();
         Document doc = null;
         for (int x=1; x < dc.getCount(); x++) {
           doc = dc.getNthDocument(x);
           System.out.println(doc.getUniversalID());
           doc.recycle();}
         doc.recycle();
         dc.recycle();
         db.recycle(); }
       else {
         System.out.println("Error accessing database."); }
       s.recycle(); }
     else {
       System.out.print("Error - session could not ");
       System.out.println("be established."); }
   } catch (NotesException n) {
     n.printStackTrace(); } } }
```

24.5 CHAPTER REVIEW

A Java application is an application that runs outside of a browser and is not an applet. It takes advantage of the JVM (Java Virtual Machine) in order to run. The JVM is not a compiler, but it is an interpreter that processes the bytecode in the Java class file. A Java application that utilizes the Domino classes must use threads via the NotesThread class.

- A Java application runs by itself with no browser or server.
- A Java Virtual Machine (JVM) "runs" the application by interpreting the bytecode in a Java class file.
- A Java application must utilize threads via the NotesThread class. There are three approaches: implement the Runnable interface, extend the NotesThread class, and create the threads on your own via the sinitThread and stermThread methods.
- You can use the Session and NotesFactory classes to initialize a Domino session in a Java application.

C H A P T E R   2 5

Servlets

25.1 What is a servlet?   329

25.2 Java Servlet Development Kit (JSDK)   330

25.3 Structure of a servlet   330

25.4 Session tracking   335

25.5 Running servlets on Domino   337

25.6 The servlet life cycle   339

25.7 Accessing Domino objects via a servlet   340

25.8 Domino forms   343

25.9 Chapter review   344

25.1   WHAT IS A SERVLET?

A servlet is a Java program that runs on a server. It fills the same role as CGI (Common Gateway Interface) applications and Domino agents. The main advantage of a servlet is it is loaded into memory only once on the server. All calls to it after the initial load use the same instance. In contrast, CGI programs and Domino agents are loaded and run each and every time they are called. This is a great benefit with regard to system resources.

As stated earlier, servlets occupy the same space as a Domino agent. An agent resides in a Domino database, and the Domino server handles. The Web server manages a servlet. The servlet manager can be Domino (via the server document); you can load and utilize a third-party servlet manager. Not all Web servers support servlets, so be careful. An excellent example is the IBM WebSphere Application Server. It both supports servlets and can be integrated with Domino.

The major differences between a servlet and a Domino agent lie in two of Domino's most important features: replication and security. An agent lives and breathes in a Domino database. Therefore, it can take advantage of replication for distributing it to other locations and of Domino security for determining who can access the agent. Conversely, a servlet lives on the file system of the Web Application server. It runs with the security rights of the server, and you must copy or install it on other file systems as you desire.

Servlet:

- standard server-based Java program
- successor to Common Gateway Interface (CGI) programs
- offers better performance and security than CGI
- based on open standards
- Java Servlet Development Kit (JSDK) used for development

25.2   JAVA SERVLET DEVELOPMENT KIT (JSDK)

The classes you need in order to develop your own servlets are available in the Java Servlet Development Kit (JSDK). The JSDK is available for download from the Sun Java Web site (java.sun.com). There are different versions available, so be certain the version you choose is consistent with the servlet manager you will use. You install the JSDK 2.0 as a standard component of Domino R5, located in the root directory of your Domino installation. I have Domino installed in the r5 directory on my C drive, so here is the path to the JDSK:

```
C:\r5\jsdk.jar
```

If you use the Sun JSDK, you must add to your system CLASSPATH variable the path to the JSDK that you will use. Otherwise, follow the instructions of your development environment.

NOTE   Lotus will add support for servlet development to the Domino Designer Java IDE in a future release.

25.3   STRUCTURE OF A SERVLET

When you sit in front of your browser and enter a URL, a few things happen. Your browser sends a request to the specified Web server, the server processes the request, and a response is sent from the server to the browser. The browser can send two types of requests to the Web server, *get* and *post:*

- get: Retrieve information
- post: Send information (create a document, search, run an agent, and so on.)

You use the javax.servlet and javax.servlet.http packages from the JSDK when you develop a servlet for use on a Domino Web server (or any other HTTP server). You need to be concerned with three methods when you develop a servlet:

- `service`: This method is called each time the server requests a servlet. Usually, this method is not used for Web server (HTTP) servlets; it is more applicable to generic servlets.
- `doGet`: All get requests issued from the Web server to a servlet invoke this method. The format of this method is as follows:

```
public void doGet(HttpServletRequest req, HttpServletResponse res)
```

- `doPost`: All post requests issued from the Web server to the servlet invoke this method. The format of the method is as follows:

```
public void doPost(HttpServletRequest req, HttpServletResponse res)
```

> **NOTE** The `HttpServletRequest` object represents the request made to the Web server, and the `HttpServletResponse` object represents the response that will be sent to the requester.

Let's take a look at a basic servlet.

Example 25.1 (Servlet)

```
import java.io.*;
import javax.servlet.*;        ❶
import javax.servlet.http.*;

public class Example_25_1 extends HttpServlet {  ❷
  public void doGet(HttpServletRequest req, HttpServletResponse res)  ❸
    throws ServletException, IOException {
  res.setContentType("text/html");  ❹
  PrintWriter toBrowser = res.getWriter();  ❺
  toBrowser.println("<HTML>");  ❻
  toBrowser.println("<HEAD><TITLE>Example 25.1 - Servlet</TITLE></HEAD>");
  toBrowser.println("<BODY>");
  toBrowser.println("<H1>Example 25.1</H1>");
  toBrowser.println("<BR><HR><BR>");
  toBrowser.print("<H2>This was generated by the servlet");
  toBrowser.println("doGet method on a Domino server.</H2>");
  toBrowser.println("</BODY></HTML>"); }
  public void doPost(HttpServletRequest req, HttpServletResponse res)  ❼
    throws ServletException, IOException {
  res.setContentType("text/html");
  PrintWriter toBrowser = res.getWriter();
  toBrowser.println("<HTML>");
  toBrowser.print("<HEAD><TITLE>Example 25.1 - ");
  toBrowser.println("Servlet</TITLE></HEAD>");
  toBrowser.println("<BODY>");
  toBrowser.println("<H1>Example 25.1</H1>");
  toBrowser.println("<BR><HR><BR>");
  toBrowser.print("<H2>This was generated by the servlet");
  toBrowser.println("doPost method on a Domino server.</H2>");
  toBrowser.println("</BODY></HTML>"); } }
```

Explanation

❶ Import the required servlet package(s) for use in the code.

❷ Declare our new class; it must extend the `HttpServlet` class because we are working with a Web server.

❸ Declare the `doGet` method; it can throw two exceptions.

❹ Set the MIME type for the response (output) sent to the requester via the `setContentType` method of the `HttpServletResponse` class. The text/html type is used for browsers.

❺ Create a `PrintWriter` object to send output to the browser (requester).

❻ Send HTML to the browser.

❼ Declare the `doPost` method; it throws two exceptions.

You will notice that the `doGet` and `doPost` methods from example 25.1 take advantage of two servlet-specific objects: `HttpServletRequest` and `HttpServlet-Response`. I will refer to them as `request` and `response` objects for the sake of simplicity. Every servlet uses these objects, so they are very important. Basically, the `request` object gets data from the client, and the `response` object sends data to a client.

25.3.1   Servlet request object

The `HttpServletRequest` object encapsulates all information from a client or requester. Through the use of this object you gain access to the request headers, CGI variables, cookies, session tracking, and form data. Actually, it parses incoming form data and stores it as servlet parameters.

Here is a partial list of methods in the `HttpServletRequest` class:

- `getContentLength`: Returns request content length in bytes
- `getContentType`: Returns media type for the content, or null if unknown
- `getCookies`: Returns an array of cookie objects sent by the requester
- `getMethod`: Returns the `HTTP` method (post, get, and head are popular) used by the requester
- `getParameter(String name)`: Returns value of specified parameter. The servlet engine places all HTML form values into parameters. You should use this method for only single-value parameters.
- `getParameterNames`: Returns an Enumeration of `String` objects containing all parameters for a request
- `getParameterValue(String name)`: Returns all values for a parameter. Use this when a parameter has more than one possible value.
- `getPathInfo`: Returns extra path information associated with the request
- `getProtocol`: Returns the name and version of protocol used by the requester
- `getQueryString`: Returns a query string from the requester URL

- `getRemoteAddr`: Returns the IP address of the requester
- `getRemoteHost`: Returns the name of the requester/client
- `getRemoteUser`: Returns the name of the requester
- `getRequestURI`: Returns the Universal Resource Identifier (URI) of the request
- `getServerName`: Returns the name of the requester's server
- `getServerPort`: Returns the port on which the request was received
- `getServletPath`: Returns the URI of the servlet
- `getSession`: Returns the current session associated with the requester; creates one if necessary

> **NOTE** The `getSession` method has no relation to the Domino Java `getSession` method.

You will notice that a number of the methods for the `HttpServletRequest` object return CGI Environment Variable values. For instance, the `getRemoteAddr` method returns the REMOTE_ADDR CGI variable, and `getPathInfo` returns the CGI variable PATH_INFO.

25.3.2 Servlet response object

The `HttpServletResponse` class encapsulates all communication to a client or requester. This object grants access to all response headers, methods for setting cookies, HTTP status codes, and session tracking functions.

Here is a partial list of methods in the `HttpServletResponse` class:

- `addCookie(Cookie c)`: Adds a cookie to a response
- `getWriter`: Returns a `PrintWriter` object for the purpose of sending responses to the requester
- `sendRedirect(String url)`: Redirects the response to a specified location
- `setContentLength(int length)`: Sets the length of the content being sent to the requester. This sets the Content-Length HTTP header.
- `setContentType(String type)`: Sets the type of content being sent to the requester. It sets the Content-Type HTTP header.
- `setStatus(int code)`: Sets the HTTP Status Code

Example 25.2 demonstrates a number of the methods discussed so far, and figure 25.1 shows the output.

Example 25.2   (Servlet)

```
import java.io.*;
import java.util.*;
import javax.servlet.*;
import javax.servlet.http.*;
public class Example_25_2 extends HttpServlet {
```

```
public void doGet(HttpServletRequest req, HttpServletResponse res)
  throws ServletException, IOException {
res.setContentType("text/html");
PrintWriter out = res.getWriter();
out.println("<HTML><HEAD><TITLE>Example 25.2</TITLE></HEAD>");
out.println("<BODY>");
out.println("<BR><CENTER><H1>Example 25.2</H1></CENTER>");
out.println("<UL>");
out.println("<LI>CONTENT_LENGTH:   " + req.getContentLength()); ❶
out.println("<LI>CONTENT_TYPE:     " + req.getContentType());    ❷
out.println("<LI>REQUEST_METHOD:   " + req.getMethod());
out.println("<LI>PATH_INFO:        " + req.getPathInfo());
out.println("<LI>SERVER_PROTOCOL:  " + req.getProtocol());
out.println("<LI>QUERY_STRING:     " + req.getQueryString());
out.println("<LI>REMOTE_ADDR:      " + req.getRemoteAddr());
out.println("<LI>REMOTE_HOST:      " + req.getRemoteHost());
out.println("<LI>REMOTE_USER:      " + req.getRemoteUser());
out.println("<LI>SERVER_NAME:      " + req.getServerName());
out.println("<LI>SERVER_PORT:      " + req.getServerPort());
out.println("<LI>Servlet path:     " + req.getServletPath());
out.println("<LI>Request URI:      " + req.getRequestURI());
out.println("</UL>");
out.println("</BODY></HTML>");     } }
```

Explanation

❶ Send the contents of the CGI Environment variable to the requester (browser).

❷ Display the type of content sent via the response.

Output

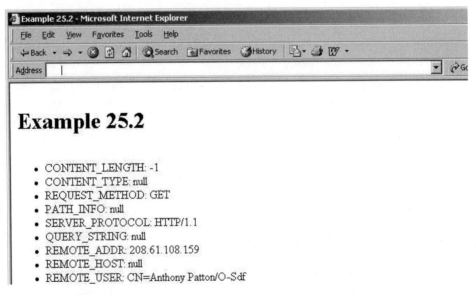

Figure 25.1   Example 25.2 output

25.4 SESSION TRACKING

The standard protocol used to serve Web pages, HTTP, is stateless. That is, it provides no way to recognize a user/client over more than one request. There are a variety of Web applications in which this presents a problem. The most common example used is a shopping cart Web site. A user wants to collect items (like going through your local grocery store with an actual cart) while shopping and pay for everything at once when he/she is ready.

Session tracking is a feature of servlets that allows a user to be identified (tracked) across more than one page request to a Web site. It was added to version 2.0 of the Servlet API (JSDK 2.0). It can store and track persistent data per each user session. You can use this in place of other techniques, such as hidden fields on a form or adding data to the end of a URL.

25.4.1 HttpSession object

A servlet assigns a session object to every visitor to a site. The object is of the `HttpSession` type. Servlets use this object to store and retrieve information pertaining to a visitor. The `HttpSession` class contains two methods, `putValue` and `getValue`, for storing and retrieving information pertaining to a session. Again, please do not confuse a servlet session with a Domino session.

Here is a partial list of `HttpSession` methods:

- `getCreationTime`: Returns the time a session object was created
- `getLastAccessTime`: Returns the last time a client sent a request for this session
- `getValue(String name)`: Returns the value for a specified key value; returns null for no matching key
- `getValueNames`: Returns a String array containing all key values for the session
- `invalidate`: Destroys a session object
- `putValue(String name, Object value)`: Stores an object with the associated key value
- `removeValue(String name)`: Removes the specified key and its value(s)

The `getSession` method of the `HttpServletRequest` class gets a handle on a client session. The `getSession` method accepts one `boolean` parameter that signals whether a new session should be created if it does not currently exist.

A client session does not last forever. A Web server destroys a session after a certain amount of inactivity; the default for most Web servers is 30 minutes. In addition, you can use the `invalidate` method of the `HttpSession` class to force the end of a client session. The point is that you should not store important data in session objects; you should use a database or cookies as a storage mechanism for crucial data.

Let's take a look at a simple example that puts everything together. Example 25.3 tracks the number of times a user accesses the servlet, and it could be called from different pages within the site to track site hits. Figure 25.2 shows the output.

Example 25.3   (Servlet)

```
import java.io.*;
import java.util.*;
import javax.servlet.*;           ❶
import javax.servlet.http.*;      ❷
public class Example_25_2 extends HttpServlet {
  public void doGet(HttpServletRequest req, HttpServletResponse res)
    throws ServletException, IOException {
    res.setContentType("text/html");        ❸
    PrintWriter out = res.getWriter();      ❹
    HttpSession s = req.getSession(true);   ❺
    Integer hits = (Integer)s.getValue("hits");   ❻
    if (hits == null) {
      hits = new Integer(1); }              ❼
    else {
      hits = new Integer(hits.intValue() + 1); }   ❽
    s.putValue("hits",hits);                ❾
    out.println("<HTML><HEAD><TITLE>Example 25.3</TITLE></HEAD>");
    out.println("<BODY>");
    out.println("<BR><CENTER><H1>Example 25.3</H1></CENTER>");
    out.print("<BR>You've accessed this servlet ");   ❿
    out.println(hits + " times.");
    out.println("</BODY></HTML>");     } }
```

Explanation

❶ Import the Java servlet classes.

❷ Import the Java Web server servlet classes.

❸ Set the content type of the response to html for the browser.

❹ Create a `PrintWriter` object for working with output to the browser.

❺ Create an `HttpSession` object for session-tracking purposes.

❻ Retrieve the value of the variable *hits* stored for the session.

❼ If the session variable did not exist, initialize our hits variable to one.

❽ If the session variable did exist, increment it by one.

❾ Store the updated hits variable for the session.

❿ Display the number of times the user *hit* the servlet. This number is incremented each time the page is reloaded.

Output

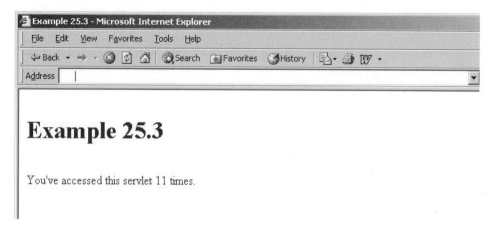

Figure 25.2   Example 25.3 output

NOTE   For more detailed information on servlets, check out *Java Servlets by Example* by Alan R. Williamson from Manning Publications.

25.5   RUNNING SERVLETS ON DOMINO

The Domino server document contains a section for servlet settings (see figure 25.3). It is located within the Internet Protocols section of the server document, in the Domino Web Engine section. The Java servlet support field has three options: None, Domino Servlet Manager, or Third-Party Servlet Support. These allow you to enable and disable servlet support. Currently (version 5.02b), the only third-party scrvlct engine supported is the IBM WebSphere Web Application server (www.ibm.com/websphere). Also, the Domino Servlet Manager allows you to specify the path to servlets. The path is the directory that will contain servlet files. The default setting is servlet, and it uses the Domino directory off of the Domino data directory as its starting point. For instance, I have my Domino server set up with a root directory of Domino5 on my D drive. I use the default servlet directory (Servlet URL path):

```
D:\Domino5\data\domino\servlet
```

In addition, you can specify the Java class path and servlet file extensions as well. You should keep separate entries in the servlet file extension field separated by commas. You can enable and disable session state tracking as well.

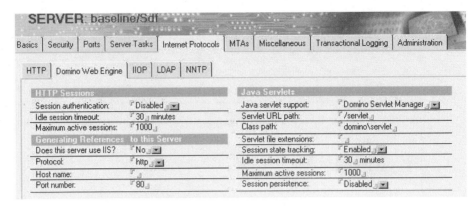

Figure 25.3   Domino servlet manager configuration

25.5.1   Domino servlet configuration file

The Domino Servlet engine includes support for a configuration file that specifies initialization parameters when it loads. The configuration file is a text file named Servlets.Properties. It must be located in your Domino data directory. I have my Domino server installed in the Domino5 directory on my D drive, so the path to my servlet configuration file is as follows:

```
D:\Domino5\data\Servlets.Properties
```

The servlet configuration file lets you specify a different name for your servlet than the file name. The next line in the configuration file registers a servlet named MyServlet using the code from example 25.3:

```
servlet.MyServlet.code = Example_25_3
```

Here is a breakdown of the line:

- `servlet`: Tells the system that the item specified is a servlet
- `MyServlet`: The unique name assigned to the servlet
- `code`: Tells the system that this is the code for the servlet
- `Example_25_3`: The actual servlet Java class file (located in the Domino servlet directory)

You can specify initial parameters in the configuration file as well. The next line specifies initialization arguments for the servlet:

```
servlet.MyServlet.initArgs = Tony Patton, two, three
```

Once you have specified servlet code and parameters, the startup directive tells the system which servlets to load when the servlet manager is started or restarted:

```
servlets.startup = MyServlet
```

Also, you can place comments in the configuration file with the numeric symbol (#). It should be the first character on the line. Here is the complete listing of our servlet configuration file with comments:

```
#Specify servlet code
servlet.Chapter251.code = Example_25_1
servlet.Chapter252.code = Example_25_2
#Specify the servlets to be loaded at startup
servlets.startup = Chapter251 Chapter252
```

Loading the servlets at startup will bypass the need to load the servlet the first time it is requested from a client, thus speeding up the load time.

25.6   THE SERVLET LIFE CYCLE

A servlet is loaded into memory only once. Every time it is loaded, the init and service methods execute—they execute once and only once when a servlet is loaded. When a client calls the servlet, the servlet's service() method is called and the doGet or doPost methods are executed, depending on the request.

Servlets are loaded into memory via one of two methods. The ServletManager loads servlets specified in the servlet configuration file (Servlets.Properties). The JVM (Java Virtual Machine) ClassLoader loads servlets loaded upon a client request. The client/requester sees no difference between the methods used to load a servlet. They realize the difference when a servlet is reloaded.

Servlets loaded by the ServletManager (configuration file) are reloaded every time the Web server is started. Servlets loaded by the JVM ClassLoader are loaded once and only once; they can only be reloaded by rebooting the Domino server. This scenario is true Domino 5, so it may change in the future. Keep an eye on the release notes for future Domino versions.

Use the ServletManager as much as possible, especially when you develop, test, and/or debug a servlet. If you combine the Domino **restart** command and the ServletManager, you can easily and quickly reload your servlet into server memory. Here is the command to restart the Domino Web server task:

```
tell http restart
```

You will notice when your Domino server loads that the ServletManager starts and loads any servlets specified in the servlet configuration file. Figure 25.4 demonstrates the initialization of the servlet engine and the loading of a servlet. The actual file name of the servlet is listed, but the name assigned in the servlet configuration file is used when a client or browser calls the servlet.

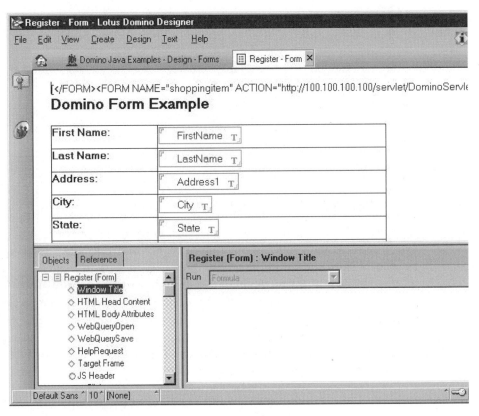

Figure 25.4 Starting the Domino server and ServletManager

25.7 ACCESSING DOMINO OBJECTS VIA A SERVLET

A servlet resembles a standalone Java application when it accesses Domino objects. The NotesFactory class instantiates a Domino Session object. Once the Session object is created, you can access Domino objects as usual. Remember that a Domino session and a servlet session are not the same. The servlet runs with server access rights if the NotesFactory class' createSession method is used without any parameters. Otherwise, a servlet's rights are determined by the user name/password pair specified in the createSession method. One note: You should never specify the server name in the createSession method when you work with servlets. Example 25.4 demonstrates how to access the Domino Directory (address book) from a servlet.

You must use a NotesThread object when you access Domino objects from a servlet. This entails the use of the sinitThread and stermThread methods of the NotesThread class. The sinitThread method creates a new NotesThread object, and the stermThread method destroys the NotesThread object. You should create the thread just before you access Domino objects, and destroy when you are finished.

```
NotesThread.sinitThread();
// code to access Domino objects
NotesThread.stermThread();
```

The best way to utilize the `NotesThread` class is by using a `try/catch/finally` block. You should terminate the thread in the finally block to ensure that it is always called.

```
try {
  NotesThread.sinitThread();
  // access Domino
} catch (NotesException n) {
  // handle the exception/error
} finally {
  NotesThread.stermThread(); }
```

Example 25.4   (Servlet)

```
import java.io.*;
import javax.servlet.*;          ❶
import javax.servlet.http.*;     ❷
import lotus.domino.*;           ❸

public class Example_25_4 extends HttpServlet {
  public void doGet(HttpServletRequest req, HttpServletResponse res)
     throws ServletException, IOException{
    res.setContentType("text/html");    ❹
    PrintWriter toBrowser = res.getWriter();   ❺
    toBrowser.println("<HTML>");
    toBrowser.println("<HEAD><TITLE>Example 25.4</TITLE></HEAD>");
    toBrowser.println("<BODY>");
    toBrowser.println("<H1>Example 25.4</H1>");
    try {
     NotesThread.sinitThread();      ❻
     Session s = NotesFactory.createSession();    ❼
     Database db = s.getDatabase("","names.nsf");   ❽
     DocumentCollection dc = db.getAllDocuments();   ❾
      toBrowser.print("Number of documents in ");    ❿
      toBrowser.println(db.getTitle() + " is  " + dc.getCount());
     dc recycle();
     db recycle();
     s recycle();
    }
     catch (NotesException n) {   ⓫
     System.out.println("Exception ID:  " + n.id);
     System.out.prinln("Exception description:  " + n.text);
    } finally {
     NotesThread.stermThread(); }    ⓬
    toBrowser.println("</BODY></HTML>"); } }
```

Explanation

❶ Import the Java servlet classes.

❷ Import the classes for using Web server servlets.

❸ Import the Domino Java classes.

❹ Call the `setContentType` method of the `HttpServletResponse` class to signal what type of content will be sent to the client/browser.

❺ Instantiate the `PrintWriter` object for sending content to the requester.

❻ Initialize a `NotesThread` object for accessing Domino objects.

❼ Instantiate a Domino `Session` object via the `NotesFactory` class. This servlet will run with the security access of the server.

❽ Get a handle to the Domino server's Domino Directory.

❾ Assemble a `DocumentCollection` object containing all documents from the Domino Directory.

❿ Display the title of the database and the number of documents.

⓫ Handle any Domino errors that are raised.

⓬ Destroy the `NotesThread` object used.

Example 25.5 specifies a user name and password for accessing the Domino server. For this reason, the servlet will run with the specified user's access level.

Example 25.5   (Servlet)

```
import java.io.*;
import javax.servlet.*;
import javax.servlet.http.*;
import lotus.domino.*;

public class Example_25_5 extends HttpServlet {
  public void doGet(HttpServletRequest req, HttpServletResponse res)
     throws ServletException, IOException{
   res.setContentType("text/html");
   PrintWriter toBrowser = res.getWriter();
   toBrowser.println("<HTML>");
   toBrowser.print("<HEAD><TITLE>Example 25.5 - );
   toBrowser.println("Servlet</TITLE></HEAD>");
   toBrowser.println("<BODY>");
   toBrowser.println("<H1>Example 25.5</H1>");
   try {
    NotesThread.sinitThread();
    Session s = NotesFactory.createSession("","Anthony
       Patton","password"); ❶
    Database db = s.getDatabase("","names.nsf");
    DocumentCollection dc = db.getAllDocuments();
    toBrowser.print("# of documents in Domino Directory:  ");
```

```
      toBrowser.println(dc.getCount());
      Agent agt = db.getAgent("Test");  ❷
      agt.run();  ❸
      agt recycle();
      dc recycle();
      db recycle();
      s recycle();
   } catch (NotesException n) {
     toBrowser.println("Error caught.");
   } finally {
     NotesThread.stermThread(); }
    toBrowser.println("<BR><HR><BR>");
    toBrowser.println("</BODY></HTML>"); } }
```

Explanation

❶ Create a new Domino `Session` object with the specified user name and password.

❷ Instantiate a Domino `Agent` object with the specified agent in the Domino database.

❸ Execute the agent.

Example 25.5 demonstrates how to execute an agent from a servlet, but you can call an agent from a URL as well. The latter technique is much simpler than using a servlet, but a servlet does let you specify a certain user run with server security. The URL technique relies upon the requester's access level:

http://domain.com/database.nsf/agentname?OpenAgent

25.8 DOMINO FORMS

Let's discuss one last item before we leave, using servlets on Domino forms. By default, Domino generates HTML form tags for its forms and documents. These tags direct the forms and documents to be handled by the Domino server, so you have to redirect them when you utilize a servlet. The trick is placing an ending HTML form tag at the beginning of your Domino form. Follow this by declaring a new form with a method that specifies the servlet. Figure 25.5 illustrates this.

The format of the HTML placed on the form is as follows:

```
[</FORM><FORM NAME="shoppingitem" ACTION="http://100.100.100.100/
    servlet/DominoServlet">]
```

The name parameter is optional, but the action parameter is required. The action parameter specifies the URL to use when processing the form.

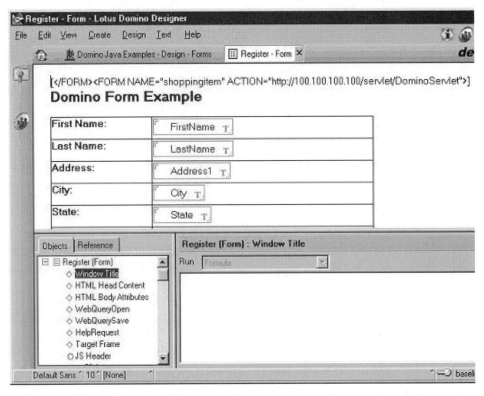

Figure 25.5   Using servlets with Domino-generated forms

25.9   CHAPTER REVIEW

Servlets:

- are triggered via a URL (Web address)
- can be included in Web pages via the <servlet> and </servlet> tags
- may be called directly by a Web server or a Java Server Page
- stay resident in memory once loaded
- can be set up to load on server startup
- can access HTTP parameters, cookies, and session state

A Java servlet is a Java application designed to be run on a Web server. The Domino Web server comes with a servlet engine that is set up in the Domino Server document in the Domino Directory. You can disable and replace this servlet engine with a third-party servlet engine. A browser sends data to a Web server via the post method and receives data via the get method. You need two methods of a servlet when you work with a Web server: doGet and doPost.

- A Java Servlet is a standard technology developed by Sun Microsystems for developing server-based Java applications.
- You can develop Java Servlets with the Java Servlet Development Kit (JSDK) available for downloading from the Sun Web site.
- A browser sends data to a Web server via the `post` method and receives data via the `get` method.
- The Domino Server contains a servlet engine, but you can replace it with a third-party product.
- Two Java packages from the JSDK are applicable to Domino servlet development: import javax.servlet and import javax.servlet.http.
- A Java servlet that utilizes a Web server takes advantage of two methods: `doGet` and `doPost`. These two methods handle browser requests and return data to the requesting client.

C H A P T E R   2 6

JDBC

26.1 What is JDBC?   346
26.2 SQL   346
26.3 Getting the Domino JDBC driver   348
26.4 JDBC URLs   348
26.5 Connecting to Domino   349
26.6 Statements   349

26.7   Executing   349
26.8   Results   349
26.9   Handling errors   352
26.10 Metadata   352
26.11 Servlets   353
26.12 Chapter review   356

26.1 WHAT IS JDBC?

Every enterprise has at least one database system in use. The majority has one or more disparate systems, and the data in every system is valuable to the business. The Java JDBC API provides applications access to these disparate systems. The standard language used in the JDBC is Structured Query Language (SQL). JDBC was introduced as a standard part of the Java JDK with version 1.1.

Each database system provides a JDBC driver for its system, so you must install the driver before you utilize JDBC to access its contents.

26.2 SQL

In order to implement JDBC with Domino properly, you must become familiar with general database concepts and the Structured Query Language (SQL). SQL is the industry standard language used to access relational database systems. Database vendors may add their own special functions for use with their products, but this is not a

346

concern when you work with JDBC. The best thing about SQL is that it is easy to learn. The intention of this chapter is not to teach SQL, but it does describe three commonly used SQL statements. When you work with relational database systems, you use SQL to retrieve values from a table. When you work with Domino, you use views as the source for SQL.

26.2.1 SELECT

SELECT is the most heavily used statement in SQL. It returns the chosen contents of one or more Domino views as a result table. You can use it to select all columns from a view or views, or specify only certain columns. An asterisk (*) signals that all columns are returned.

26.2.2 FROM

FROM must immediately follow a SELECT statement. It lists the one or more tables from which the result table is formulated.

Example 26.1

```
SELECT * FROM myView
```

Explanation

Returns every row and column of data from the view specified: myView.

Example 26.2

```
SELECT col2, col3 FROM myDominoView
```

Explanation

Returns every row but only the columns labeled col2 and col3 from the specified Domino view. The column title is used as the column identifier.

26.2.3 WHERE

The WHERE keyword allows you to filter the results from the SELECT statement. It can be very simple or very complex, but we will only cover simple cases. When you work with data from a Domino database, you can use WHERE to tell the system to return only those records in which a column value from a Domino view contains a specific value.

Example 26.3

```
SELECT * FROM myDominoView WHERE Name = "Tony Patton"
```

Explanation

Returns from the specified view (myDominoView) only those documents that contain the name.

Let's take a closer look at the Domino JDBC Driver before we apply our SQL knowledge.

26.3 GETTING THE DOMINO JDBC DRIVER

You can download the Domino JDBC driver for free from the Lotus Web site (www.lotus.com). The site contains instructions for downloading and installation. A Java Archive (Jar) file exists with the Domino JDBC driver in it. You can utilize it in your applications by specifying the Jar file in an import statement.

In addition to the Jar file, you can specify a Microsoft CAB file and system files (DLLs). The files installed for use with Window 95/98/NT follow:

```
JdbcDomino.jar
JdbcDomino.dll
JdbcDriver.dll
JdbcRNIDomino.dll
JdbcDomino.cab
```

NOTE   The Domino JDBC Driver is compatible beginning with the browsers Netscape Communicator 4.05 and Microsoft Internet Explorer 4.01 with service pack 1. It will not function properly with earlier versions.

26.3.1 Setting the CLASSPATH variable

Once you have the JDBC driver installed on your system, you must set up your system CLASSPATH variable accordingly. You only need to do this if you are using the Sun JDK command-line environment. The setup will differ in third-party IDEs like VisualAge for Java or JBuilder.

For the Sun JDK, I have the JDBC driver installed in the R5 directory on my C drive. Your installation will probably be different.

```
set CLASSPATH=c:\r5\jdbcsql\lib\JdbcDomino.jar
```

26.3.2 Importing the proper package

In order to use JDBC in your Java code, you must import the SQL package. You accomplish this with this line:

```
import java.sql.*;
```

26.4 JDBC URLS

Once you install JDBC, you can utilize a URL with it. The format of the Domino JDBC URL is as follows:

```
jdbc:domino:/database.nsf/directory/server
```

Here is a sample URL for accessing the Name and Address book on the server with the JDBC loaded:

```
jdbc:domino:/names.nsf
```

26.5 CONNECTING TO DOMINO

The `Connection` class in the JDBC package creates a connection to a Domino database for use with the Domino JDBC driver. Here is the format for creating a new `Connection` object:

```
Connection = DriverManager.getConnection("Domino JDBC URL","","");
```

> **NOTE** The last two parameters are user name and password; they are not used with Domino.

Here is an example of how to create a `Connection` object to connect to our Name and Address Book:

```
Connection con = DriverManager.getConnection("jdbc:domino:/names.nsf","","");
```

> **NOTE** When you connect to a Domino database, remember that a view is synonymous to a table in SQL.

26.6 STATEMENTS

Once you have created a SQL statement to return the desired results, you can apply it to a `Connection`. The `createStatement` method of the `Connection` object associates a statement with a connection.

```
Connection con = DriverManager.getConnection("jdbc:domino:/names.nsf","","");
Statement stmt = con.createConnection();
```

26.7 EXECUTING

Once you have formulated a SQL statement, you can apply it toward a database. You achieve this via the `execute` and `executeQuery` methods of the `Statement` class.

```
Connection con = DriverManager("jdbc:domino:/names.nsf","","");
Statement stmt = con.createConnection();
ResultSet res = stmt.executeQuery("sql statement");
```

or

```
ResultSet res = stmt.execute("sql statement");
```

26.8 RESULTS

As you can see in the previous section, a `ResultSet` object is returned once a SQL statement has been run against a database view. The `ResultSet` object contains all matching rows (and their columns) from the SQL statement. You can easily navigate the `ResultSet` to access individual elements in the `ResultSet` object.

The ResultSet object contains methods for accessing individual elements (columns) in individual rows that have been returned. In Domino, the column name in the view is used as the name of the item value to retrieve. The following statement uses the getString method to return the String value (if there is any) from the specified column in the ResultSet object:

```
rs.getString("column name");
```

There are numerous *get*-related statements for accessing values. Here is a short list:

- getString
- getBigDecimal
- getBoolean
- getByte
- getShort
- getInt
- getLong
- getFloat
- getDouble
- getBytes
- getDate
- getTime
- getTimeStamp

In addition to methods that retrieve specific data elements, there are a number of methods available for navigating a ResultSet object:

- isFirst: A boolean method that signals whether the current row is the first in the results
- isLast: A boolean method that signals whether the current row is the last in the results
- next: Retrieves the next row from the set; returns boolean signaling if there are no more rows
- previous: Retrieves the previous row from the set; returns boolean signaling if there are no previous rows
- last: Retrieves the last row from the set
- close: Closes the object

The following code uses the next, close, and getString methods:

```
Connection con = DriverManager("jdbc:domino:/names.nsf","","");
Statement stmt = con.createConnection();
ResultSet res = stmt.execute("sql statement");
while (res.next()) {
   System.out.println("First name:  " + res.getString("FirstName"));
   System.out.println("Last name:   " + res.getString("LastName")); }
res.close();
stmt.close();
con.close();
```

Example 26.4   (Standalone Application)

```
import java.sql.*;  ❶
import lotus.jdbc.domino.*;  ❷
public class Example_26_4 {  ❸
  public static void main(String[] args) {
    try {
      Class.forName("lotus.jdbc.domino.DominoDriver");  ❹
      String connStr = "jdbc:domino:/names.nsf";  ❺
      Connection con = DriverManager.getConnection(connStr, "",""); ❻
      String sql = "SELECT * FROM \"People\"";  ❼
      Statement stmt = con.createStatement();  ❽
      ResultSet rs = stmt.executeQuery(sql);  ❾
      ResultSetMetaData rsmd = rs.getMetaData();  ❿
      int numcols = rsmd.getColumnCount();  ⓫
      while (rs.next()) {  ⓬
        for (int i=1;i<=numcols;i++) {  ⓭
          Object obj=rs.getObject(i);  ⓮
          if (obj!=null) {  ⓯
            System.out.println(obj.toString()); } } }  ⓰
      rs.close();  ⓱
      stmt.close();  ⓲
      con.close();  ⓳
    } catch(ClassNotFoundException e) {  ⓴
      System.out.println("Could not load Domino driver.");
    } catch(SQLException e) {  ㉑
      System.out.println("SQLException caught:  " + e.getMessage());
    } catch(Exception e) {
      e.printStackTrace();} } }
```

Explanation

❶ Import the Java package for using SQL statements.

❷ Import the Domino JDBC driver.

❸ Declare the class.

❹ Retrieve the Domino JDBC driver to make sure it has been properly installed. A `ClassNotFoundException` is thrown if it is not found.

❺ Set up the Domino JDBC URL to use.

❻ Create a `Connection` object to the specified database using the Domino JDBC URL syntax.

❼ Set up SQL to apply to the database.

❽ Create a new `Statement` object.

❾ Create a new `ResultSet` object by executing the SQL statement on the database.

❿ Create a new `ResultSetMetaData` object; this returns the design of the database view.

⓫ Use the `getColumnCount` method of the `ResultSetMetaData` class to get the number of columns in the Domino view.

⑫ Loop through all rows returned in the ResultSet object.

⑬ A for loop is used with the number of columns to loop through all columns in a row.

⑭ Retrieve the current column as an Object.

⑮ Display its contents only if it exists.

⑯ Use the toString method of the Object to display its contents.

⑰ Close the ResultSet object.

⑱ Close the Statement object.

⑲ Close the Connection object.

⑳ Catch ClassNotFoundException errors; this will signal that the JDBC driver could not be loaded as a result of Item #4.

㉑ Catch any SQL errors.

26.9 HANDLING ERRORS

Example 26.4 gave a good look at the process of handling errors when you work with JDBC drivers. You want to make sure the JDBC driver exists, watch for SQL errors, and handle any generic errors.

You should place JDBC-related code in a try/catch block to properly handle any errors that may occur while you try to access a database via JDBC. The SQLException exception should be caught. It contains three methods—getMessage, getSQLState, and getErrorCode—that display information regarding the exception.

```
try {
  Connection con = DriverManager("jdbc:domino:/names.nsf","","");
  Statement stmt = con.createConnection();
  ResultSet res = stmt.execute("sql statement"");
} catch {SQLException e) {
    System.out.println("SQL error (" + e.getErrorCode() + ") - " + e.getErrorMessage());
} catch (Exception e) {
    e.printStackTrace(); }
```

26.10 METADATA

Metadata is a term used with most relational database management systems (RDBMS). It represents the configuration information for a database. When applied to Domino, metadata can be described as the layout of views. There are numerous methods for working with metadata, but this chapter will not cover all of them. Please refer to the JDBC documentation for more details.

JDBC provides two methods for working with metadata: DatabaseMetaData and ResultSetMetaData. These classes allow you to access metadata information regarding the database and a result set.

Let's take a brief look at the JDBC process before we cover integration with servlets. The steps involved in using JDBC are as follows:

1. Load the JDBC driver: Class.forName("lotus.jdbc.domino.DominoDriver");
2. Set the database: URL connection string ("jdbc:domino:/names.nsf");
3. Establish a connection: Connection con = DriverManager.getConnection(connStr, "","");
4. Create a SQL query: Statement stmt = con.createStatement();
5. Execute the query: ResultSet rs = stmt.executeQuery(sql);
6. Work with the results: rs.next();

26.11 SERVLETS

You can combine the power of JDBC with servlet technology to create servlets that interact with database stores, whether the database is Domino or Oracle, or any other database that has a JDBC driver.

Example 26.5 (Servlet)

```
import java.io.*;
import javax.servlet.*;
import javax.servlet.http.*;
import java.sql.*;
import lotus.jdbc.domino.*;

public class Example_26_5 extends HttpServlet {
  public void doGet(HttpServletRequest req, HttpServletResponse res) ❶
     throws ServletException, IOException{
   res.setContentType("text/html"); ❷
   PrintWriter toBrowser = res.getWriter();
   toBrowser.println("<HTML>");
   toBrowser.println("<HEAD><TITLE>Example 26.5 - Servlet</TITLE></HEAD>");
   toBrowser.println("<BODY>");
   toBrowser.println("<H1>Example 26.5</H1>");
   try {
    Class.forName("lotus.jdbc.domino.DominoDriver");
    String connStr = "jdbc:domino:/names.nsf";
    Connection con = DriverManager.getConnection(connStr, "","");
    String sql = "SELECT * FROM \"People\"";
    Statement stmt = con.createStatement();
    ResultSet rs = stmt.executeQuery(sql);
    ResultSetMetaData rsmd = rs.getMetaData();
    int numcols = rsmd.getColumnCount();
    toBrowser.println("<TABLE>");
    while (rs.next()) {
     toBrowser.println("<TR>"); ❸
     for (int i=1;i<=numcols;i++) {
      Object obj=rs.getObject(i);
      if (obj!=null) {
```

```
         toBrowser.println("<TD>" + obj.toString() + "</TD>"); } } ❹
     toBrowser.println("</TR>");}
   toBrowser.println("</TABLE>");
   rs.close();
   stmt.close();
   con.close();   }
 catch(ClassNotFoundException e)   {
   toBrowser.println("Could not load Domino driver.");   }
 catch(SQLException e)   {
   toBrowser.println("SQLException caught:   " + e.getMessage());   }
 catch(Exception e)   {
     e.printStackTrace();   }
toBrowser.println("<BR><HR><BR>");
toBrowser.println("</BODY></HTML>"); }   }
```

Explanation

❶ The doGet method of the servlet; it will handle the browser request.

❷ Set the type of content to be sent to the browser as html.

❸ Send the beginning of an HTML table row element.

❹ Display each item from the table in a single cell in the HTML table.

You could combine the power of a servlet with JDBC to exchange data between Domino and another data source. You can use a JDBC driver to access the non-Domino data source, and use the Domino Java classes to enter the data into a Domino database. Example 26.6 illustrates this scenario by copying records from a DB2 table into a Domino database.

Example 26.6   (Servlet)

```
import java.io.*;
import javax.servlet.*;
import javax.servlet.http.*;
import lotus.domino.*;
public class Example_26_6 extends HttpServlet {
 public void doGet(HttpServletRequest req, HttpServletResponse res)
    throws ServletException, IOException{
   res.setContentType("text/html");
   PrintWriter toBrowser = res.getWriter();
   toBrowser.println("<HTML>");
   toBrowser.print("<HEAD><TITLE>Example 26.6 - ");
   toBrowser.println("Servlet</TITLE></HEAD>");
   toBrowser.println("<BODY>");

   try {
     NotesThread.sinitThread();   ❶
     Session s = NotesFactoryCreateSession();   ❷
     Database db = s.getDatabase("","people.nsf");   ❸
     Document doc = null;   ❹
```

```
Class.forName(com.ibm.db2.jdbc.app.DB2Driver");  ❺
String connStr = "jdbc:db2:sample";
conn = DriverManager.getConnection(connStr, "user","password");  ❻
Statement stmt = conn.createStatement();  ❼
ResultSet rs = stmt.executeQuery("Select first, last, addr, city, st,  ❽
zip, phone from PersonTable");
while (rs.next()) {  ❾
  doc = db.createDocument();  ❿
  doc.replaceItemValue("Form","Person");  ⓫
  doc.replaceItemValue("FirstName",rs.getString(1));  ⓬
  doc.replaceItemValue("LastName", rs.getString(2));
  doc.replaceItemValue("Address", rs.getString(3));
  doc.replaceItemValue("City", rs.getString(4));
  doc.replaceItemValue("State", rs.getString(5));
  doc.replaceItemValue("ZipCode", rs.getString(6));
  doc.replaceItemValue("Telephone", rs.getString(7));
  doc.save();  ⓭
  doc.recycle();  ⓮
  toBrowser.println(rs.getString(2) + ", " + rs.getString(1));
  toBrowser.println(" copied to Domino.");
}
  db.recycle();  ⓯
  s.recycle();  ⓰
  stmt.close();  ⓱
 conn.close();
 toBrowser.println("<BR>Copy complete.</BODY></HTML>");
} catch(NotesException n) {
 n.printStackTrace();
} catch(ClassNotFoundException e)  {
 toBrowser.println("Could not load DB2 JDBC driver.");
} catch(SQLException e)   {
 toBrowser.println("SQLException caught:  " + e.getMessage());
} catch (Exception e) {
 e.printStackTrace();
} finally {
  NotesThread.stermThread(); } } }  ⓲
```

Explanation

❶ Create a new NotesThread object.

❷ Create a new Domino Session object using the Web server's access rights.

❸ Create a new Domino Database object.

❹ Create a Domino Document object for later use.

❺ Retrieve the DB2 JDBC driver to make sure it has been properly installed. A Class-NotFoundException is thrown if it is not found.

❻ Set up DB2 JDBC URL for use.

❼ Create a new Statement object.

❽ Create a new `ResultSet` object by executing the SQL statement on the database.

❾ Loop through all rows in the results of the SQL statement.

❿ Create a new Domino Document in the database.

⓫ Set the form value for the `Document` object.

⓬ Populate fields on the Document with values from the result set.

⓭ Save the newly created Document.

⓮ Recycle the `Document` object.

⓯ Recycle the `Database` object.

⓰ Recycle the `Session` object.

⓱ Close the `Statement` object.

⓲ Terminate the `NotesThread` object.

26.12 CHAPTER REVIEW

JDBC resembles the ODBC technology. The difference lies in the fact that the JDBC driver is more easily transported. The JDBC driver allows Java applets, servlets, or standalone applications to access database systems via Java. The JDBC driver for Domino facilitates Domino database access from Java. The JDBC driver is installed on the Domino Server, and Java code can utilize it. JDBC drivers are accessed via a specific JDBC URL syntax. Structured Query Language (SQL) is the standard language used to access relational database systems from JDBC. The SQL syntax is very straightforward, but you need a firm understanding of it and other database concepts before you can work with JDBC.

- JDBC is an acronym for Java DataBase Connectivity.
- SQL (Structured Query Language) is the standard syntax used to access databases via JDBC.

- You need a good understanding of SQL and basic database concepts to properly utilize JDBC in your application(s).

- Metadata is the design information for a database.

- A `Connection` object connects to a database.

- A SQL statement is applied to a database via JDBC, and the results are returned in the format of rows and columns.

- You can access the rows and columns of the results via the `ResultSet` object.

C H A P T E R   2 7

WebSphere

27.1 Overview 357
27.2 Versions 358
27.3 Getting the product 358
27.4 Installation with Domino 358
27.5 Administrative console 359

27.6 Java Server Pages (JSP) 359
27.7 JSP syntax 360
27.8 Support 360
27.9 Chapter review 361

27.1 OVERVIEW

The IBM WebSphere family of products facilitates the design, development, management, and deployment of Web sites. The products are comprised of the application server, studio development environment, performance pack, and site analysis. This chapter focuses on the application server.

The WebSphere Application Server is available in three flavors: Standard, Advanced, and Enterprise. Every edition allows the use of servlets, Java Server Pages, HTML, and XML to build advanced Web sites. IBM describes the advanced edition as a high-performance enterprise JavaBean server. You can use the enterprise edition to build high-transaction, high-volume applications that take advantage of enterprise JavaBeans (EJB) and CORBA components.

WebSphere is a Java application server designed for advanced applications that take advantage of JavaBeans, Java Server Pages, XML, and servlets. You can use it to serve straight HTML as well. It takes advantage of the Java environment installed on the host (server) machine, so a JDK must be properly installed and configured on the server.

357

WebSphere:

- Java Application environment
- cross-platform
- cross-web server
- built for Web applications
- runs on Microsoft Internet Information Server (IIS), Netscape Web servers, Apache, and Domino
- bundled with Domino beginning with version 5

27.2 VERSIONS

Version 3 is the current version at the time of writing this chapter. Version 3 includes full support for Java Server Pages (versions 0.91 and 1.0), Java Servlets 2.1, XML, and integration with VisualAge for Java. In addition, it is bundled with Domino on its own CD.

27.3 GETTING THE PRODUCT

You can download trial versions of the Advanced and Standard Editions from the IBM WebSphere Web site (www.ibm.com/websphere). You can order them as well.

27.4 INSTALLATION WITH DOMINO

You can use the WebSphere Application Server with a number of HTTP Servers. These include the IBM HTTP Server, Apache, Microsoft IIS, Netscape, and Domino 5. You must install and configure the Domino Server before you install WebSphere. Domino is one of the HTTP Server options when you install WebSphere. After you install it, you can designate WebSphere as the servlet engine to be used for all servlet requests issued to the Web server. Figure 27.1 shows the area of the Domino Server document where a non-Domino Servlet engine is designated.

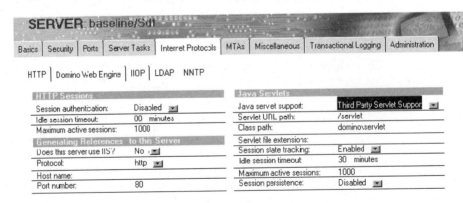

Figure 27.1   Domino non-Domino servlet engine designation (highlighted)

WebSphere:

- runs on a Domino HTTP server
- replaces a Domino servlet engine

Once you set up WebSphere as the servlet engine, servlets are stored in the servlets directory under the WebSphere installation directory. You can call any compiled Servlet classes stored in this directory from the servlet directory of your server.

```
server_ip_address/servlet/servlet_name
```

27.5   ADMINISTRATIVE CONSOLE

The administrative console is the management piece of WebSphere. It allows you to start and stop WebSphere services. This includes loading and unloading JDBC drivers and servlets.

> **NOTE**   One of the tricky aspects of using WebSphere as the servlet manager for your Domino server is that you must start the WebSphere servlet engine before you can use servlets.

> **NOTE**   The WebSphere Application Server requires an enormous amount of memory. I could not get the Administrative Console to load with anything less than 256 MB of memory.

27.6   JAVA SERVER PAGES (JSP)

Java Server Pages (JSP) is a technology developed by Sun Microsystems. It is similar to the Microsoft Active Server Pages (ASP) technology. It allows you to embed Java code, JavaBeans, and the results of a Java servlet in an HTML page. It also allows you to separate the data from the HTML; the HTML is separate from the business logic. WebSphere comes with full JSP documentation, and you can access more information via the Sun Web site (java.sun.com).

Java Server Pages:

- a server-side scripting framework for Web applications
- offers in-line HTML and logic on the same Java Server Page
- similar to Microsoft's Active Server Pages
- pluggable language architecture
- just-in-time compilation for fast performance
- targeted toward nonprogrammers because there is no compiling

> **NOTE**   For more Java Server Pages details, see *Web Development with JavaServer Pages* by Duane K. Fields and Mark A. Kolb. It is available from Manning Publications.

27.7 JSP SYNTAX

Java Server Page files are stored with the JSP extension. A JSP file can contain a combination of the following:

- HTML tags: JSP supports all valid HTML tags.
- NCSA tags: The WebSphere Application Server supports the following NCSA tags through JSP:
  - `config`
  - `echo var=variable`
  - `exec`
  - `filesize`
  - `include`
  - `lastmodified`
- `<SERVLET>` tags: These tags are used to call a servlet from the JSP. The structure of the servlet tags resembles that used for inserting regular Java applets into an HTML file:

```
<SERVLET NAME="name_of_servlet"
  CODE="servlet_class_filename"
  CODEBASE="URL_for_remote_learning"
  initparam1="initial_parameter_value">
<PARAM NAME="parameter_name" VALUE="parameter_value">
</SERVLET>
```

- JSP syntax:
  - `JSP Directives: <%@ and %>`
  - `Declarations: <%! and %>`
  - `Scriptlet tags: <% and %>`
  - `JSP expressions: <%= and %>`
  - `JavaBeans: <jsp:usebean>`

NOTE The JSP syntax for Java Beans has undergone major changes in the various versions of the JSP standard. The current syntax is shown above.

You can use Java Server Pages with Domino only with WebSphere (or another compatible Web server) installed.

27.8 SUPPORT

WebSphere can be a major pain to install and configure. There are a number of Internet newsgroups available from the IBM newsgroup server (news.software.ibm.com) for finding help. Here are a few:

- ibm.software.websphere.application-server
- ibm.software.websphere.commerce-suite
- ibm.software.websphere.perfpack

You can find additional help at the IBM WebSphere Web site.

27.9 CHAPTER REVIEW

The IBM WebSphere family of Web servers is a perfect complement to the Domino R5 Server. WebSphere extends the power of Domino by providing full support for Java Server Pages and more advanced Java servlet support. In addition, WebSphere can manage multiple JDBC drivers. The WebSphere administration console provides a nice graphical interface for managing the many facets of the environment.

- IBM WebSphere is a family of products for developing, deploying, and managing powerful Web-based applications.
- WebSphere is the perfect compliment to the Domino Server.
- WebSphere includes full support for Java Server Pages.
- Java Server Pages resemble the Microsoft Active Server Pages technology.
- Java Server Pages use the .jsp file extension and can include standard HTML, inline Java code, JavaBeans, and references to Java servlets.

CHAPTER 28

Lotus connectors

28.1 Java classes   363
28.2 JavaBeans   368
28.3 Chapter review   368

The majority of data in the corporate world is stored in enterprise systems such as Oracle, DB2, or Sybase. Lotus Connectors allow Domino to access enterprise data. Connectors operate at a layer between the enterprise data and services like Domino Enterprise Connectivity Services (DECS) and Lotus Enterprise Integration (LEI). Both services allow the Domino server to connect enterprise data through a simple user interface; the user points and clicks to make connections between data sources. In addition, Lotus has published a set of Java classes that you can use to take advantage of LEI/DECS services in your code. You can download the Java classes from the Lotus Web site (www.lotus.com/enterpriseintegration).

The Java classes are referred to the Lotus Connector Java classes. The classes give the same programming access as DECS. You should use the connectors if you need to access many different data types. Domino comes packaged with a few connectors, such as DB2 and ODBC, but connectors for ERP systems and other relational databases like Oracle must be purchased.

The great aspect of the Lotus Connector classes is that one object model is used for all connectors. That is, you learn the code once and that is it. The syntax of the code is the same no matter what connector you use. You can develop code for Oracle and easily transport it to DB2 or SAP. The only part of the code that will change is the connection.

28.1 JAVA CLASSES

You can download the Lotus Connector Java classes from the Lotus Web site (go to the developer's section). You will download a compressed file that contains a dll and Java Jar file (lcjava.dll and lcjava.jar). Place the files in your Domino installation directory and add the Jar file to your system CLASSPATH or equivalent setting for your IDE.

```
set CLASSPATH = c:\r5\lcjava.jar;
```

You must make the class files available to your code before you can use them. The following import statement handles this:

```
import lotus.lcjava.*;
```

The basic Java classes are LCSession, LCConnection, LCFieldList, and LCField.

28.1.1 LCSession

Each session has global state information that is managed by LEI. This state manages Lotus Connector libraries and connections, allocated objects, error and event information, count logs, and communications with the LEI Server.

A LCSession object is initialized with one and only one parameter, and that parameter is always set to zero (0).

```
LCSession lcs = new LCSession(0);
```

Methods. The LCSession class has a number of methods, but this chapter only covers a subset. Please refer to the Lotus documentation for more details. The LCSession class methods discussed here are the following:

- clearStatus: Clears the LCSession object's current status
- disablePooling: Disables connection pooling for the session
- enablePooling:Enables connection pooling for the session
- flushPool:The connection pool is destroyed, so all connections are destroyed as well.

28.1.2 LCConnection

The LCConnection class represents an instance of a Lotus connector. It manages individual connections within a session. You should use one connection for each individual data connection through a Connector in a session.

When you create a LCConnection object, you can use two properties: the name of the Connector and a Connector Token. The first parameter should match the name assigned to the connector in the Notes client, and the token should always be set to zero (0).

If you have a connection named "Test" in your LEI database, you would make a connection as follows:

```
LCConnection lccon = new LCConnection("Test", 0);
```

Methods.   Here are a few of the methods in the `LCConnection` class:

- `update`: Used to update data
- `select`: Used to query data
- `fetch`: Used to retrieve data and place it into local memory

Let's take a close look at the `setProperty` and `getProperty` methods.

setProperty(property, value).   The `setProperty` method sets a property of an `LCConnection` object to a specified value. The property parameter accepts a predefined constant to signal a property. Here is a partial list of constants:

- LCToken.DATABASE: Database string
- LCToken.FIELDLIST: List of fields in the connection
- LCToken.CONNECTOR: Connector object
- LCToken.INDEX: Index string
- LCToken.IS_CONNECTED: The connection made
- LCToken.IS_POOLED: The connection pooled
- LCToken.LIBRARY: Library name
- LCToken.METADATA: Metadata string
- LCToken.NAME: Object name
- LCToken.OPTION: Connector option
- LCToken.ORDERNAMES: Order field list
- LCToken.OWNER: Stored procedure string
- LCToken.PASSWORD: password string
- LCToken.POSITION: Stored procedure string
- LCToken.RECORD_LIMIT: Maximum number of records
- LCToken.SERVER: Server string
- LCToken.USERID: user id string

> **NOTE**   A complete list of `LCConnection` class properties is available in the Lotus Connector documentation.

getProperty.   The `getProperty` method of the `LCConnection` class retrieves values stored in the specified property.

28.1.3   LCFieldList

A fieldlist represents metadata for a record and may contain data for one or more record values. A fieldlist is a list of fields and field names with supporting functions. You can add, modify, retrieve, or list fields within a fieldlist in multiple ways. The handle type `LCFieldlist` represents a fieldlist.

Methods. Here is a partial list of `LCFieldList` class methods:

- `append (LCStream fieldname, int lcDataType)`: Appends a new field to the end of the list
- `free`: Frees up the list
- `getCount`: Returns the number of fields in the list
- `getField(int index, int lcStreamFormat, LCField field, LCStream fieldname)`: Retrieves a field from the list
- `getRecordCount`: Returns the number of records in the list of fields
- `insert(int index, LCStream newfield, int datatype)`: Inserts a new field into the list
- `remove(int index)`: Removes a field using its index value
- `replace(int index, LCStream oldField, int datatype)`: Replaces one field with another
- `setName(int index, LCStream newField)`: Assigns a new name to a field

28.1.4   LCField

A field is a data object that contains one or more data values of a designated data type. The handle type `LCField` represents a field.

Methods. Here is a partial list of `LCField` class methods:

- `getCurrency(int index, LCCurrency cur)`:
  Returns a value from the field index position and stores it in the LCCurrency object
- `getDateTime(int index, LCDateTime dt)`:
  Returns a value from the field index position and stores it in the dt LCDateTime object
- `getFloat(int index, java.lang.Float value)`:
  Returns a value from the field index position and stores it in the Float object
- `getInt(int index, java.lang.Integer value)`:
  Returns a value from the field index position and stores it in the Integer object
- `getNumeric(int index, LCNumeric value)`: Returns a value from the field index position and stores it in the LCNumeric object
- `getType`: Returns the type of data stored in the field
- `getTypeSize`: Returns the size of data stored in the field
- `getValueCount`: Returns the number of values stored in the field
- `isNull`: Signals whether or not a field's value is null

- `setCurrency(int index, LCCurrency)`:
  Assigns the `LCCurrency` object to the field index position
- `setDateTime(int index, LCDateTime)`:
  Assigns the `LCDateTime` object to the field index position
- `setFloat(int index, java.lang.Float)`:
  Assigns the `Float` object to the field index position
- `setInt(int index, java.lang.Integer)`:
  Assigns the `Integer` object to the field index position
- `setJavaString(int index, java.lang.String)`:
  Assigns the `String` object to the field index position
- `setNull(int index, Boolean)`:
  Assigns a boolean value to the field index position
- `setNumeric(int index, LCNumeric)`:
  Assigns the `LCNumeric` object to the field index position
- `toJavaInt`: Retrieves a value from the field as a Java int value
- `toJavaString`: Retrieves a value from the field as a Java `String` object

28.1.5 LCException

The `LCException` class handles all Lotus Connector exceptions just like any other Java exception, with a `try/catch/finally` block. Exceptions *must* be handled gracefully.

The `LCException` class has two methods:

- `getLCErrorCode`: Returns the error code
- `toString`: Returns a `String` object containing the error class name

We have seen the major classes in the Lotus Connector Java classes, so let's take a look at an example. Example 28.1 demonstrates the use of the Lotus Connector Java classes to transfer data from a Domino database to an external data source.

Example 28.1   (Domino Agent)

```
import java.io.PrintWriter;
import lotus.domino.*;
import lotus.lcjava.*;    ❶

public class Example_28_1 extends AgentBase {
  public void NotesMain() {    ❷
    try {
      Session s = getSession();
      AgentContext ac = s.getAgentContext();
      Document doc = ac.getDocumentContext();
      LCSession lcsess = new LCSession(0);    ❸
      LCConnection lccon = new LCConnection("OracleTest",0);    ❹
      lccon.setPropertyJavaString(LCTOKEN.DATABASE, "OracleTest");    ❺
      lccon.setPropertyJavaString(LCTOKEN.METADATA, "PeopleView");    ❻
      lccon.setPropertyJavaString(LCTOKEN.USERID, "TonyPatton");    ❼
```

```
lccon.setPropertyJavaString(LCTOKEN.PASSWORD, "password");  ⑧
lccon.connection();  ⑨
LCFieldlist keyFields = new LCFieldlist(1, LCFIELDF.TRUNC_PREC);  ⑩
LCFieldlist fields = new LCFieldlist(1, LCFIELDF.TRUNC_PREC);  ⑪
LCField empno = new LCField(LCTYPE.TEXT, 1);  ⑫
LCField firstname = new LCField(LCTYPE.TEXT, 1)  ⑬;
LCField midinit = new LCField(LCTYPE.TEXT, 1);
LCField lastname = new LCField(LCTYPE.TEXT, 1);
LCField streetaddr = new LCField(LCTYPE.TEXT, 1);
LCField city = new LCField(LCTYPE.TEXT, 1);
LCField state = new LCField(LCTYPE.TEXT, 1);
LCField zipcode = new LCField(LCTYPE.TEXT, 1);
Integer count = new Integer(0);
Document doc = ac.getDocumentContext();
keyFields.append ("EMPNO", LCTYPE.TEXT, field);
empno.setFlags( LCFIELDF.KEY);
empno.fromJavaString(doc.getItemValueString("EMPLOYEEID"));  ⑭
connection.select(keyFields,1, fields, count);  ⑮
int indx = 1;
Integer idx = new Integer(1);
int rcnt = 1;
int status = 0;
connection.fetch(fields, indx, rcnt, count);
fields.lookup("FIRSTNAME", field, idx);  ⑯
firstname.setJavaString(indx, doc.getItemValueString("FirstName"));  ⑰
fields.lookup("MIDINIT", field1, idx);
midinit.setJavaString(indx, doc.getItemValueString("Initial"));
fields.lookup("LASTNAME", field2, idx);
lastname.setJavaString(indx, doc.getItemValueString("LastName"));
fields.lookup("STREETADDR", field3, idx);
streetaddr.setJavaString(indx, doc.getItemValueString("StreetAddress"));
fields.lookup("CITY", field4, idx);
city.setJavaString(indx, doc.getItemValueString("City"));
fields.lookup("STATE", field5, idx);
state.setJavaString(indx, doc.getItemValueString("State"));
fields.lookup("ZIPCODE", field6, idx);
zipcode.setJavaString(indx, doc.getItemValueString("ZipCode"));
connection.setPropertyJavaBoolean(LCTOKEN.MAP_NAME, true);
connection.update(fields, indx, rcnt, count);  ⑱
connection.disconnect();  ⑲
doc recycle();
ac recycle();
s recycle();
} catch (Exception e) {
e.printStackTrace(); } }
```

Explanation

❶ Make the Lotus Connector Java classes accessible to the code.

❷ This is a Domino agent.

❸ Create a new Connector LCSession object.

❹ Create a Lotus Connection object using the specified entry.

❺ Set the Database property of the LCConnection object.

❻ Set the `MetaData` property of the `LCConnection` object. This is the table or view.

❼ Set the `Userid` property of the `LCConnection` object.

❽ Set the `password` property of the `LCConnection` object.

❾ Make the connection.

❿ Create a new `LCFieldList` object for key fields.

⓫ Create a new `LCFieldList` object for the other fields.

⓬ Create new `LCField` objects for the fields of data to be transferred from the Domino document. This object will hold the employee number value; this is the database key value.

⓭ Create a new `LCField` object for the `FirstName` field.

⓮ Store a value from Domino document in the corresponding `LCField` object.

⓯ Fetch the corresponding document from the external data source via the key field.

⓰ Get a pointer to the `FirstName` field.

⓱ Set the contents of the `FirstName` field to the value from the Domino document.

⓲ Commit the update to the external database.

⓳ Destroy the `LCConnection` object.

28.2   JAVABEANS

Lotus announced in early 2000 plans to develop JavaBeans to access Lotus Domino Connectors. JavaBeans will consist of four beans:

- LCBConnector
- LCBText
- LCBTextArea
- LCBLabel

The beans will be available for use in JavaBean development environments like VisualAge for Java. In VisualAge you can visually arrange or "wire" together beans by dragging and dropping beans and bean connections.

28.3   CHAPTER REVIEW

Lotus Connectors allow you to easily access non-Domino data from Domino. The Lotus Connectors Java classes take advantage of the Lotus Enterprise Integration (LEI) features of Domino. They allow you to take advantage of Lotus connectors in your code. The great aspect of the connector code is that it is transparent with respect to the back-end data source. That is, code designed to access Oracle will work with SAP, Sybase, or any other connector-supported data source. The only items in the code that you must change are specifics for the connection, not code changes. This makes it easy for the developer, since there is only one object model to learn.

CHAPTER 29

Third-party tools and code

29.1 ArNoNa CADViewer 369
29.2 JClass 372
29.3 Chapter review 374

Utilizing Java in your Domino application(s) opens up a whole new world. There are a variety of Java applets, code, and so forth available in today's marketplace. This chapter will explore utilizing a few third-party applets in a Domino application. Although this is only a small sampling of the market, it does give you a peek at the possibilities.

29.1 ArNoNa CADViewer

The CADViewer applet from ArNoNa Internet Software, Inc., www.cadviewer.com, is a Java-based viewer for viewing AutoCAD Drawing Web Format (DWF) and SVF files. SVF and DWF are standard formats for CAD files. You can use CADViewer in a standard HTML page, standalone, or embedded in a Domino application. (You can use it with any Web server.) Figure 29.1 shows a CAD drawing opened in a browser.

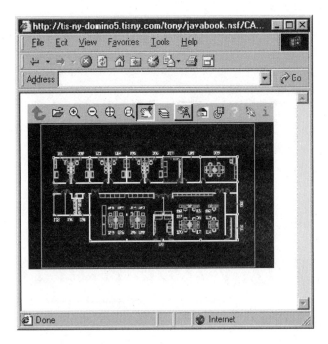

Figure 29.1 CADViewer applet

The applet allows the user to zoom in and out, move the drawing, change the background color, and perform many more actions. It allows you to view CAD drawings on any platform with a Web browser.

The CADViewer applet has its associated Java files, and you must specify the drawing to open. Also, it accepts a variety of applet parameters. I wanted to combine the power of the CADViewer applet with the Domino server. The Domino object store could be used to manage CAD drawing files; the applet is embedded on a Domino form or page. The Domino application consisted of the following items:

1 a Domino form used to store CAD drawing files

2 a Domino view for accessing CAD drawing files

3 a Domino form with the embedded applet

Figure 29.2 shows the basic form for storing CAD files.

Figure 29.3 shows the Domino form with the embedded Java applet.

Notice in Figure 29.3 that the parameters are visible in the bottom of the screen shot. There is the standard height parameter, but there are also two special CAD-Viewer parameters. The type parameter signals how the applet is presented to the user, and name specifies the drawing to be opened. We specify one of the CAD files composed in the separate form via the name parameter. Its value is "/tony/javabook.nsf/CADFILES/test/demo.dwl".

Figure 29.2 CAD file form

The setup works fine, but we need to store numerous CAD drawing files in our Domino database and view them via a browser. You can pass fields on a Domino form as parameters to an applet, so we add a field to the document with the applet. The field stores the path to the file. It will be referenced in the applet's parameter. Finally, the field is hidden from Web users.

Figure 29.4 shows the form in Domino Designer.

Notice that the field is specified as the value for the name parameter of the applet. Figure 29.5 shows one of the documents loaded in a browser.

Combining the power of the CADViewer applet and Domino provides a powerful solution. The many facets of Domino, like security, replication, and the object store, facilitate the easy management and distribution of the CADViewer files in an organization.

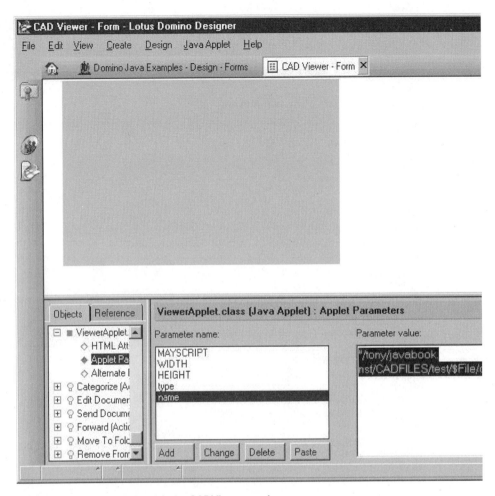

Figure 29.3   Domino form with the CADViewer applet

29.2   JCLASS

Visual representation of data adds excitement to an application, plus it is more intuitive. Domino developers want and need to graph data. Many turn to Microsoft Excel or Lotus 1-2-3. Domino R5 extends the possibilities by adding support for Java applets. There are a variety of charting tools available from third-party vendors. We will take a look at one in this section, the JClass Chart.

JClass is available from KL Group (www.klgroup.com). The Chart applet is just one of the numerous products they offer. JClass Chart allows you to present data in a variety of formats, including bar charts, stacked bars, and scattered plot graphs. Figure 29.6 shows a sample graph.

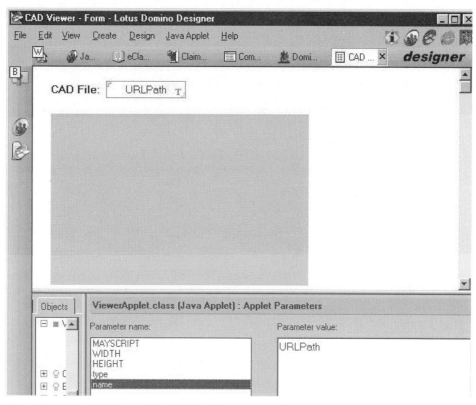

Figure 29.4   Domino form with a field used as a parameter

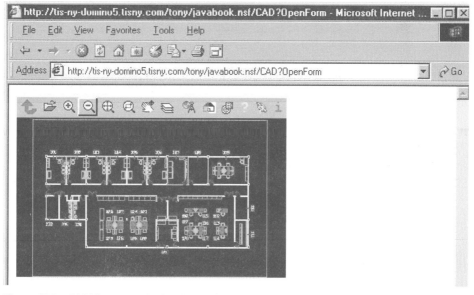

Figure 29.5   CADViewer applet in a browser

JClass Chart gives you the power to create sophisticated graphs and charts quickly and easily. Loaded with popular business and scientific charts, as well as a rich text format for customizing labels or mixing images and URLs with text, JClass Chart is fast and flexible. Packed with interactive features and integrated with all popular Java visual development environments, it's the choice of professionals!

You can utilize the JClass Chart applet in your Domino application using the same process as in section 29.1 for the CAD applet. Import the Java class files and set the appropriate parameters.

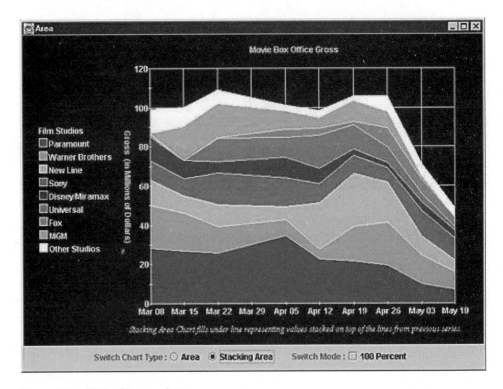

Figure 29.6   JClass Chart applet

29.3   CHAPTER REVIEW

The latest incarnation of Domino allows you to integrate Java applets in your applications. There are a variety of applets available. These include applets for charting data, viewing various types of files, and so on.

The future

30.1 OverViews   376
30.2 XML   376
30.3 Chapter review   380

The rapid advancement and acceptance of the Java programming language boggles the mind. It is unprecedented. The speedy rise has helped coin the term "Internet time." It describes the expeditious development of technologies such as the Internet, Java, and many others.

This rapid development has been introduced into the Lotus Notes/Domino realm. The product has been morphed into a powerful open-standards Web-application development platform. This confounds those who worked with Lotus Notes v3. The Lotus and IBM marriage continues to push the envelope with Domino. The future sees Domino wrapping its arms around XML and all its related technologies, integrated servlet support, portable digital assistant (PDAs) support, and more. It is indeed an exciting time to be involved.

This chapter covers a couple of topics that have been announced by Lotus, but no formal arrangements have been made. The first, OverViews, provides an easy way to present Domino data in a graphical format. Graphs are always easier to grasp than a page of black and white text. The other technology, XML, is the next big Internet-related phenomenon. It promises to change the face of data interchange.

30.1 OverViews

OverViews provide new, unique visualizations for navigating Domino database documents in a Notes client (or a Web browser). A standard Notes view lists selected fields from a subset of a database's documents in a user-specified ordering, sometimes with a hierarchical structure. In contrast, OverViews allow for the use of different user interfaces—such as a graph, map, or timeline—to present a view's list of documents. OverViews are interactive; they allow the user to navigate to specific documents and to control dynamically the visualizations (for example, by zooming in on the visualization or by controlling which fields are used to display the document set). Over-Views exploit Notes' ability to embed Java applets on a form as well as the Domino Objects interface for accessing Domino data from within a Java program.

OverViews are now in the research phase. You can obtain more information from the Lotus Research home page (www.lotus.com/research) by clicking on the Projects link.

OverViews use Java applets embedded within a Notes Form. The applets use the Domino Java Objects to access the document information. Although Java has been used to write agents in Domino, the research work has stressed combining the back-end classes with a graphical user interface that can be manipulated and used for document navigation. When a user requests that a document be opened, the necessary showDocument request is issued to the applet's appletContext. (This requires a "notes:" form of URL and not an "http:" form of URL to open the document within the Notes client.)

OverViews provide a general capability with some interesting properties. First, since an OverView is associated with a document, you can save it. When you set hidden document fields with the OverView state (e.g., level of zoom), the document becomes a record of the last settings for an information exploration. When you reopen the document, you return to the settings last used rather than begin anew. These saved OverViews can have their own view with the Notes client. Perhaps more interesting is the fact that after many OverViews have been saved, one might also want some form of OverView of OverViews.

The research Web site (www.lotus.com/research) has more up-to-date information, including interesting examples.

30.2 XML

Lotus has transformed the Lotus Notes product from a proprietary groupware package to a powerful Web Application Server (Domino) that has embraced Internet standards.

30.2.1 Current support

The current version of the Domino Web Application Server includes a couple of approaches for working with Domino data as XML. A Domino view is the standard way to present documents in a Domino database. Lotus has included a special directive that is placed at the end of a Domino view URL (Internet address). You can add the suffix ?ReadViewEntries to render the contents of a view as XML. Figure 30.1 shows the XML generated by using the suffix when accessing the list of people in the Domino Directory. The URL for the XML document in figure 30.1 is:

http://domino.server.address.com/names.nsf/People?ReadViewEntries

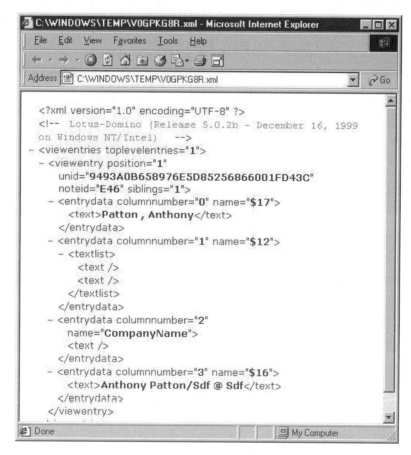

Figure 30.1 Domino-generated XML

> **NOTE** Figure 30.1 takes advantage of the XML parser included in Microsoft Internet Explorer 5. It displays XML documents in their tree format.

In addition, the back-end object model for accessing Domino objects via a development language such as Visual Basic, LotusScript, or Java allows you to generate

XML for specific documents in a Domino database. These two procedures are only the tip of the iceberg in terms of the future plans for XML-integration in Domino.

30.2.2 Future support

As you read this, Lotus is hard at work arranging XML support in Domino. In fact, they have developed their own language for working with Domino data. It is called DXL. DXL is the XML Schema for Domino data; it is the XML API to Domino data.

> **NOTE** The World Wide Web (W3C) has not yet finalized its *Recommendation on XML Schemas*. The document issued by W3C on April 7, 2000 is in "working draft" status. The rules within which DXL and other proprietary schemas must be constructed, therefore, are subject to change. Current information on the progress of XML schemata, and other XML technologies, is available at http://www.w3c.org/.

At first, it may sound like Lotus has rewritten XML to work with Domino, an approach you would expect from Redmond. Actually, this is how XML is designed. The markup language for Web pages, HTML, has a set of standard tags, but XML has no standard tags. XML is extensible, while HTML is not.

XML allows and encourages you to create your own tags to represent your data. This is where the true power of XML is realized. On the flip side, chaos can result if each and every organization and corporation develops its own XML tags. How would one know about the other's tags? Consistency and cooperation are the keys to the success of the XML standard.

For this reason, many industries like finance and organizations such as the Distributed Management Task Force (DMTF) have been quick to formalize a specific XML schema and Document Type Definition (DTD) for their niche. This simplifies the task of working with data for these organizations, and Lotus is no different when it comes to Domino.

Domino DXL has a DTD that defines all standard tags for working with Domino data. A DTD defines the structure, syntax, and vocabulary as it relates to the element and attribute set for a document. Lotus controls DXL like the finance industry controls its standard. In short, DXL contains all data concerning a Domino application. This includes design elements.

DXL:

- cannot and will never be interpreted by any Internet browser
- is not stored in a Domino database
- is not a good storage mechanism. Thus it does not replace the Domino database, but acts as a transfer medium for interacting with non-Domino systems.
- will not replace the Domino Web Server engine

Microsoft has lauded the next iteration of its Office Suite due to the fact that it stores everything as XML. It is fantastic that they have embraced open standards, but

XML is not a good storage format for data. In addition, the XML standard continues to evolve, so the underlying structure of Office documents is affected with each iteration of the XML standard. I keep expecting a new version of XML called MSXML to be announced.

Lotus has taken another approach with DXL. It lives and breathes within the Domino environment. It means nothing outside of Domino, so a conversion to standard XML is necessary in order for DXL to work outside the environment. Conversely, XML data must be converted to DXL before Domino can interpret it. This is where an XML parser or XLS Processor steps into the picture.

A parser is a mechanism for transforming and formatting XML data. It is the bridge between DXL and XML. A parser relies on the XML standard, so it is kept up-to-date with the evolving standard. For this reason, DXL is not concerned with the happenings of the World Wide Web Consortium (www.w3c.org) and the XML standard. Lotus will maintain DXL and let the processors handle the job of keeping up with XML.

Figure 30.2 presents the process of exporting data from Domino via DXL, and figure 30.3 shows the reverse process of importing XML into Domino.

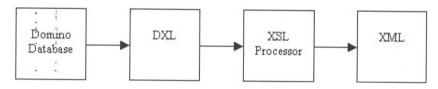

Figure 30.2   Exporting data from Domino via DXL

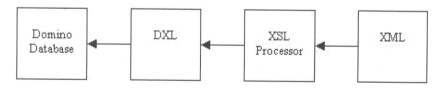

Figure 30.3   Importing data into Domino via DXL

30.2.3   LotusXLS

Lotus and IBM are making available an experimental implementation of an XSL processor. The World Wide Web Consortium (W3C) is developing the XSL specification. XSL provides powerful facilities for formatting and transforming XML documents. The LotusXLS processor is written in Java and conforms to the construction rules features of the draft XSL specification released by the W3C. LotusXLS is packaged as a JavaBean for use in client or server applications, as an applet for use in a Java-enabled Web browser, and as a command-line Java program.

30.3 CHAPTER REVIEW

Lotus and its parent IBM maintain and fund memberships in the W3C. Each has its own representatives in the associated standards committees, and each invests directly in technologies such as XSL. LotusXLS is a result of Lotus' work on XSL.

The annual pilgrimage of Lotus zealots to Orlando, Florida, USA (Lotusphere) offers more proof that XML is indeed a major part of Domino's future. If the truth was told, the hoopla associated with XML would be too much to ignore. It offers and promises solutions to standard IT problems. One of the most publicized is the sharing of data between disparate systems. XML will serve as a standard communication medium for all data-centric applications. It will replace the comma-delimited text file as the standard, and Lotus will support both in Domino.

Lotus and IBM continue to show vision when they adapt newer technologies. They know that Internet standards are ever-evolving. For this reason, they distanced themselves from XML by creating their own Domino standard (DXL). They can continue to develop DXL, and the Internet community can continue to work on XML. Other products that fully integrate the XML standard will run into the same problems as those experienced with other advancing technologies such as Java, HTML, and JavaScript.

CHAPTER 31

Example: shopping cart

31.1 Registration   382

31.2 Email agent   385

31.3 Individual store items   388

31.4 Checking out   393

31.5 Putting it all together   404

31.6 Notes   404

31.7 Chapter review   405

This chapter ties many topics from the book together into a Domino application. We need to develop an on-line storefront using Domino. Users will be able to browse store items, add items to their baskets, and check out as they desire. Also, users will have to register with the site to shop. The last requirement is the ability to send email messages to the customer service department for the store.

This chapter covers the following aspects of the Domino solution:

- A servlet and Domino form will handle the registration process. Users will be added to the default Domino Directory (names.nsf).

- The Domino agent is utilized to allow users to send customer service emails.

- The Domino database will house the individual items in the store.

- The Domino database will house orders submitted.

- A servlet will handle the "shopping cart" process. It will track items in a user's proverbial cart until checkout.

- A Domino servlet, form, and agent will handle the checkout process.

- Another Domino database will house the home page and various other aspects of the application.

31.1 REGISTRATION

Let's take a look at the registration servlet and form. In example 31.1, the servlet accepts field values from a Domino form, and adds the user to the Domino Directory and a group for accessing the site. Error messages are displayed accordingly.

Example 31.1 (Servlet)

```
import javax.servlet.*;
import javax.servlet.http.*;
import lotus.domino.*;
import java.io.*;
import java.util.*;
public class Example_31_1 extends HttpServlet {
 public void doGet(HttpServletRequest req, HttpServletResponse res)
    throws ServletException, IOException {
  res.setContentType("text/html");
  PrintWriter toBrowser = res.getWriter();
  toBrowser.println("<HTML>");
  toBrowser.println("<HEAD><TITLE>Example 31.1</TITLE></HEAD>");
  toBrowser.println("<BODY>");
  toBrowser.println("<H1>Example 31.1</H1>");
  String fname = req.getParameter("FirstName");     ❶
  String lname = req.getParameter("LastName");      ❷
  String addr1 = req.getParameter("Address1");
  String city = req.getParameter("City");
  String state = req.getParameter("State");
  String zip = req.getParameter("ZipCode");
  String phone = req.getParameter("Phone");
  String fax = req.getParameter("Fax");
  String company = req.getParameter("Company");
  String username = req.getParameter("Username");
  String password = req.getParameter("Password");
  String email = req.getParameter("EmailAddress");
  try {
   NotesThread.sinitThread();                       ❸
   Session s = NotesFactory.createSession();         ❹
   Database nab = s.getDatabase("","names.nsf");      ❺
   if (nab != null) {
    View vw = nab.getView("(username)");             ❻
    if (vw != null) {
     Document lookupDoc = vw.getDocumentByKey(username);    ❼
     if (lookupDoc != null) {
      toBrowser.println("Username already exists."); }      ❽
     else {
      Document personDoc = nab.createDocument();             ❾
      personDoc.replaceItemValue("Form","Person");           ❿
      personDoc.replaceItemValue("FirstName",fname);         ⓫
      personDoc.replaceItemValue("LastName",lname);
      personDoc.replaceItemValue("FullName",username);
      personDoc.replaceItemValue("ShortName",username);
      personDoc.replaceItemValue("HTTPPassword",password);
      personDoc.replaceItemValue("MailAddress",email);
      personDoc.replaceItemValue("CompanyName",company);
      personDoc.replaceItemValue("OfficeStreetAddress", addr1);
      personDoc.replaceItemValue("OfficeCity",city);
```

```
            personDoc.replaceItemValue("OfficeState",state);
            personDoc.replaceItemValue("OfficeZIP",zip);
            personDoc.replaceItemValue("OfficePhoneNumber",phone);
            personDoc.replaceItemValue("OfficeFAXPhoneNumber",fax);
            personDoc.replaceItemValue("Type","Person");
            personDoc.computeWithForm(false, false);    ⑫
            personDoc.save(true);    ⑬
            personDoc.recycle();
            View groupView = nab.getView("Groups");    ⑭
            Document groupDoc = null;
            if (groupView != null) {
               groupDoc = groupView.getDocumentByKey("WebUsers");    ⑮
              if (groupDoc != null) {
                 Item members = groupDoc.getFirstItem("Members");    ⑯
                 Vector values = members.getValues();    ⑰
                 if (!(values.contains(username)))    {    ⑱
                   members.appendToTextList(username);    ⑲
                   groupDoc.computeWithForm(false, false);    ⑳
                   groupDoc.save(true);    }    ㉑
                members.recycle();}
              groupDoc.recycle();
              groupView.recycle();    }
              else {
                 toBrowser.println("Error accessing group document.");    }    ㉒
              personDoc.recycle();
              lookupDoc.recycle();    }  }
          else{
             toBrowser.print("Error, username view could not";    ㉓
             toBrowser.println(" be found.");}
           vw.recycle();}
         else{
            toBrowser.println("Error, NAB not found.");}    ㉔
         nab.recycle();
         s.recycle();
      } catch (NotesException n) {
         toBrowser.println("Exception ID:    " + n.id);    ㉕
         toBrowser.println("Exception description:    " + n.text);    ㉖
        n.printStackTrace();
      } catch (Exception e) {
        e.printStackTrace();
      } finally {
         NotesThread.stermThread();    }
      toBrowser.print("Thank you, " + username);
      toBrowser.println(", you have been registered.");
      toBrowser.println("</BODY></HTML>");
   }}
```

Explanation

❶ Retrieve the `FirstName` field value from the form submitted to the servlet.

❷ Retrieve the `LastName` field value from the form submitted.

❸ Instantiate the `NotesThread` object for accessing Domino objects.

❹ Create a new Domino `Session` object for accessing the Domino server.

❺ Access the Domino Directory on the Domino server.

❻ Create a `View` object for accessing a specific view in the Domino Directory.

❼ Determine if the user already exists.

❽ Display a message if the user already exists in the Domino Directory.

❾ If the user does not exist, create a new person document in the Domino Directory.

❿ Set the form attribute for the new person document.

⓫ Populate fields on the new person document with values from the submitted form.

⓬ Compute fields on the new person document.

⓭ Save the Person document.

⓮ Retrieve a list of groups in the Domino Directory.

⓯ Locate a group document in the Domino Directory.

⓰ Create an `Item` object for the members field on the group document.

⓱ Create a `Vector` object containing all values from the members field.

⓲ Determine if the user is in the members field.

⓳ Add the user to the group.

⓴ Compute fields on the group document.

㉑ Save the changes made to the group document.

㉒ Display an error message in the browser if the group document cannot be found.

㉓ Display an error message in the browser if the user view is not found.

㉔ Display an error message in the browser if the Domino Directory does not exist.

㉕ Display an error id number for the exception caught.

㉖ Display error text for the exception caught.

The servlet is called from a Domino form. The Domino form must be tricked into calling the servlet. An ending HTML form tag is added to the top of the form to close the Domino-generated form tags. Another form tag is added with an action targeting the servlet. Here is the HTML pass-through for the top of the Domino form:

```
[</FORM><FORM ACTION=http://100.100.100.100/servlet/Ex311>]
```

NOTE The servlet was registered in the Servlets.Properties file as Ex311.

This directs the form to the servlet when you submit it. The Submit button has the following JavaScript code:

```
document.forms[1].submit();
```

Figure 31.1 displays the registration form (in design mode).

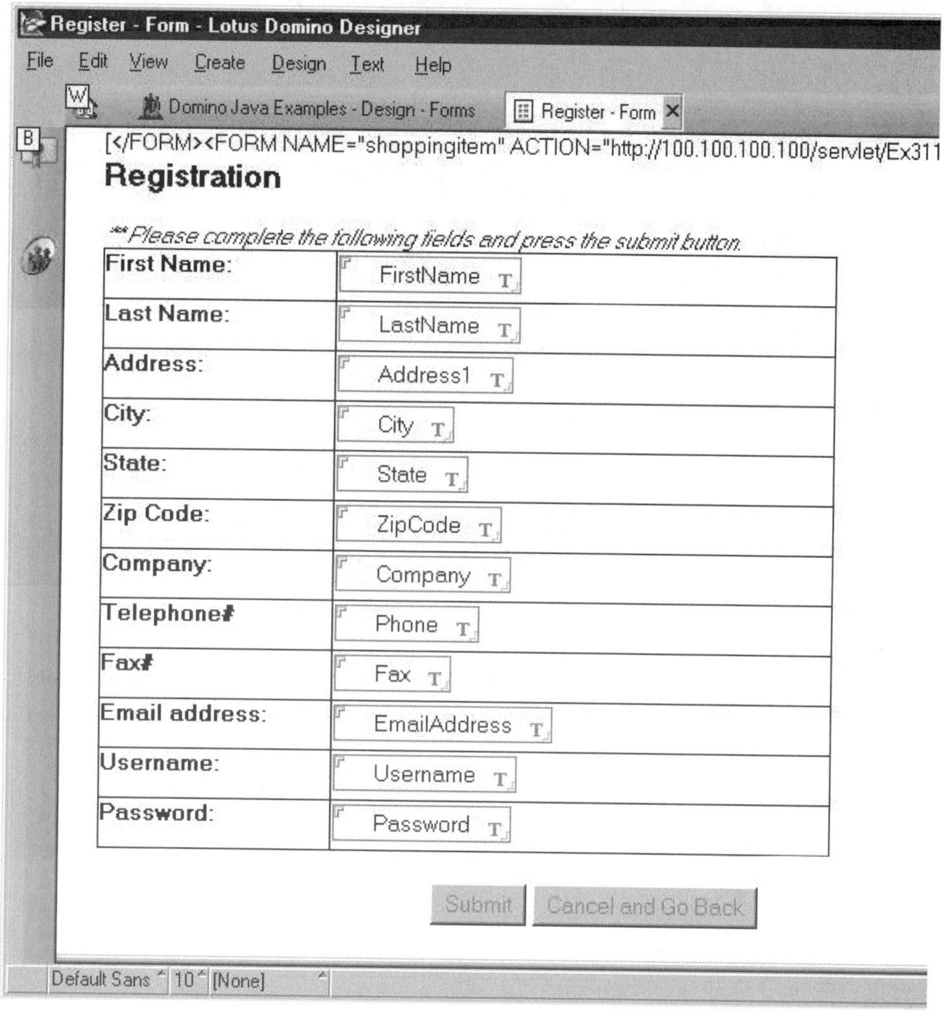

Figure 31.1   Registration form

31.2   EMAIL AGENT

Customer feedback is collected via a Domino form (see figure 31.2), and a Domino Java agent handles the sending of the feedback.

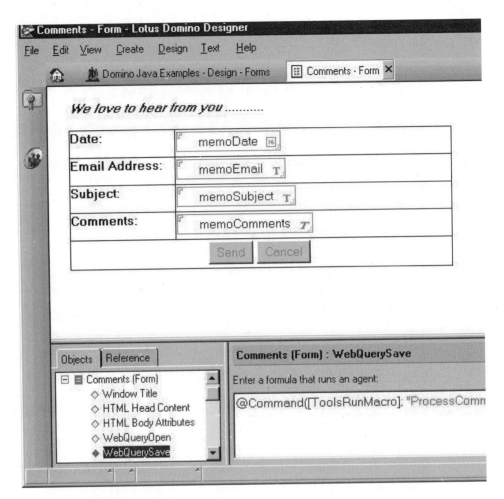

Figure 31.2 Comments form

The agent is specified in the WebQuerySave field. Let's take a look at the code in example 31.2:

Example 31.2 (Domino Agent)

```
import lotus.domino.*;
import java.io.PrintWriter;
public class Example_31_2 extends AgentBase {
 public void NotesMain() {
  try {
    Session s = getSession();
    AgentContext ac = s.getAgentContext();
    PrintWriter pw = this.getAgentOutput();
    Database db = ac.getCurrentDatabase();
    Document comments = ac.getDocumentContext();    ❶
    Document memo = db.createDocument();            ❷
    memo.replaceItemValue("Form","Memo");
```

```
String memoEmail = comments.getItemValue("memoEmail");
memo.replaceItemValue("From",memoEmail);     ❸

String memoSubject = comments.getItemValue("memoSubject");
memo.replaceItemValue("Subject",memoSubject);
String memoComments = comments.getItemValue("memoComments");
memo.replaceItemValue("Body",memoComments);
memo.computeWithForm(false, false);
memo.send("tpatton@tisny.com");     ❹
pw.println("<HTML><HEAD><TITLE>Comments</TITLE></HEAD><BODY>");
pw.print("<CENTER><H1>Thank you, your comments");     ❺
pw.println(" have been sent.</H1>");
pw.println("</CENTER></BODY></HTML>");
memo.recycle();     ❻
comments.recycle();
db.recycle();
ac.recycle();
s.recycle();
} catch(Exception e) {
e.printStackTrace(); } } }
```

Explanation

❶ Retrieve the document submitted by user.

❷ Create a new document for the memo.

❸ Copy values from the submitted document to the mail memo.

❹ Send the memo.

❺ Display a message to the user in the browser.

❻ Recycle object(s) used in our agent.

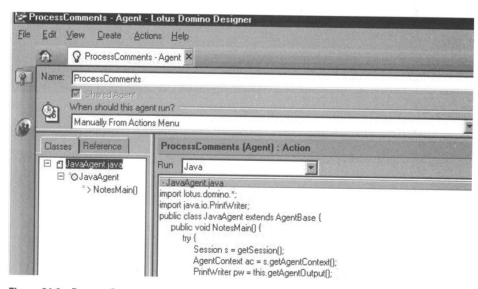

Figure 31.3   ProcessComments agent

Figure 31.4 shows the user comments document opened in a browser.

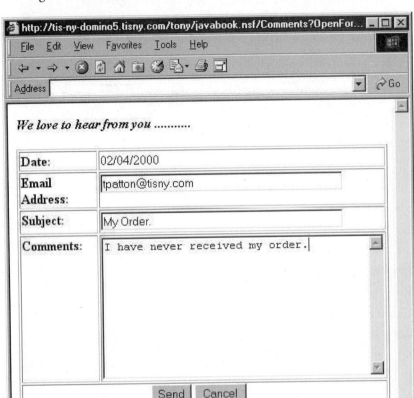

Figure 31.4 Comments form opened in a browser

Okay, we've looked at registration and sending comments. Let's turn our attention to the individual items that you can purchase. Items are maintained in their own Domino database.

31.3   INDIVIDUAL STORE ITEMS

Each item has the following information: id number, title, description, and price. This information is maintained via the Lotus Notes client. Figure 31.5 shows the form opened in the Domino Designer. There are two copies of each field. The first value is only displayed in the Notes client, and the other (with the Display suffix) is displayed in the browser. The fields with the Display suffix are computed and hidden from the Notes client, and the others are hidden from the Web client. Web users use the quantity field to enter the number of items they wish to order.

The form has the HTML form attribute included to point the form to the servlet once you submit it. We do not want the form submitted with nothing in the

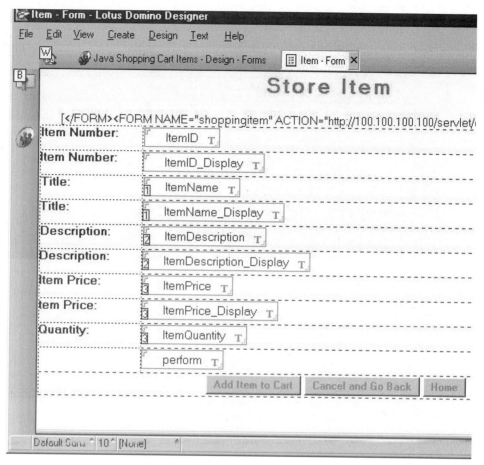

Figure 31.5 Store item form

`ItemQuantity` field, so we enter the following JavaScript code for the Add Item to Cart button:

```
if (document.forms[1].ItemQuantity.value == null)
{
  alert("Please enter a quantity.");
}
else
{
  document.forms[1].submit();
}
```

The code submits the form only if the `ItemQuantity` field contains some value. We could go further by checking for an appropriate numeric value. Figure 31.6 displays the form opened in a browser.

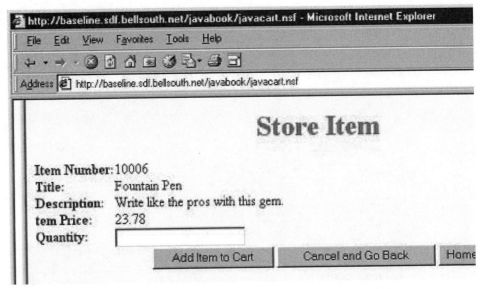

Figure 31.6 Store item form in a browser

Let's take a look at the servlet code that is called when the form is submitted. Session tracking records the items selected by a user. Only the item number and quantity are stored; the item number is used to look up related information from the Domino database.

Example 31.3   (Servlet)

```
import java.io.*;
import java.util.*;
import javax.servlet.*;
import javax.servlet.http.*;
import lotus.domino.*;
public class Example_31_3 extends HttpServlet {
  public void doGet(HttpServletRequest request, HttpServletResponse response)
     throws ServletException, IOException {
    HttpSession websession = request.getSession(true);  ❶
    response.setContentType("text/html");
    PrintWriter out = response.getWriter();
    Hashtable cartItems;  ❷
    Enumeration cartKeys;  ❸
    out.println("<HTML><HEAD>");
    out.println("<TITLE>Java Shopping Cart</TITLE></HEAD>");
    out.println("<BODY TEXT=\"#000000\" BGCOLOR=\"#FFFFFF\">");
    out.println("<CENTER>");
    try {
      String perform = request.getParameter("perform");  ❹
      String itemid = request.getParameter("ItemID");  ❺
      String quantity = request.getParameter("ItemQuantity");  ❻
      if (websession.isNew()) {  ❼
        websession.putValue("cart",new Hashtable()); }
```

```
  cartItems = (Hashtable)websession.getValue("cart");  ❽
  if (perform.equalsIgnoreCase("add")) {  ❾
   String findit = (String)cartItems.get(itemid);  ❿
   if (findit == null) {
    cartItems.put(itemid, quantity);  ⓫
   } else {
    int oldValue = new Integer(findit).intValue();
    int currentValue = new Integer(quantity).intValue();
     oldValue += currentValue;  ⓬
    Integer newValueI = new Integer(oldValue);
    String newValue = new String(newValueI.toString());
     cartItems.put(itemid, newValue);  } }  ⓭
   else if (perform.equalsIgnoreCase("remove")) {  ⓮
  cartItems.remove(itemid);  }
  NotesThread.sinitThread();  ⓯
  Session s = NotesFactory.createSession();  ⓰
  Database db = s.getDatabase("","javabook//javacart.nsf");  ⓱
  if (db != null) {
   View vw = db.getView("(ItemsByID)");  ⓲
   if (vw != null) {
    out.println("<TABLE CELLPADDING=\"5\" CELLSPACING=\"5\">");  ⓳
    out.print("<TR><TH COLSPAN=\"4\">Your Shopping");
    out.println("Cart</TH></TR>");
    out.print("<TR><TH>Item#</TH><TH>Item</TH>");
    out.println("<TH>Price</TH><TH>Quantity</TH></TR>");
    cartKeys = cartItems.keys();  ⓴
    int total = 0;  ㉑
    double totalDollars=0.0;
    while (cartKeys.hasMoreElements()) {  ㉒
     String key = (String)cartKeys.nextElement();  ㉓
     String value = (String)cartItems.get(key);  ㉔
     int q = new Integer(value).intValue();  ㉕
     total += q;  ㉖
     Document doc = vw.getDocumentByKey(key);  ㉗
     if (doc != null) {
      out.println("<TR><TD>");
      out.println(doc.getItemValueString("ItemID"));  ㉘
      out.println("</TD><TD>");
      out.println(doc.getItemValueString("ItemName"));  ㉙
      out.println("</TD><TD ALIGN=\"RIGHT\">");
      out.println(doc.getItemValueString("ItemPrice"));
      Double dTemp = new Double(doc.getItemValueString("ItemPrice"));
      totalDollars += (dTemp.doubleValue() * q);  ㉚
      out.println("</TD><TD>");
      out.println(value);
      out.println("</TD></TR>");
      doc.recycle();  ㉛
     } else {
      out.println("Document not found.");  } }
    vw.recycle();
    out.print("<TR><TH COLSPAN=\"2\" ALIGN");
    out.println("=\"RIGHT\">Total</TH>");
```

```
      out.print("<TH ALIGN=\"RIGHT\"><FONT COLOR=\"RED\">");
      out.print(totalDollars); ㉜
      out.print("</FONT></TH><TH><FONT COLOR=\"RED\">");
      out.print(total); ㉝
      out.println("</FONT></TH></TR>");
      out.println("</TABLE>");
    } else {
      out.println("View not found.");   }
    vw.recycle();
  } else {
    out.println("Database not found."); }
  db.recycle();
  s.recycle();
  NotesThread.stermThread(); ㉞
  out.print("<BR><BR><INPUT TYPE=\"SUBMIT\"");  ㉟
  out.print(" VALUE=\"Continue Shopping\" onClick = ");
  out.print("\'location.replace(\"/javabook/javacart.nsf/");
  out.println("StoreItems?OpenPage\");\'>");
  out.print("<INPUT TYPE=\"SUBMIT\"");
  out.print(" VALUE=\"Checkout\" onClick ");
  out.println("=\'location.replace(\"/servlet/checkout\");\'>");
  out.println("</BODY></HTML>");
}catch (NotesException n) {
  n.printStackTrace();
} catch (Exception e) {
  out.println(e.getMessage());
  out.println("Error caught"); } } }
```

Explanation

❶ Instantiate an HTTP `Session` object for session tracking.

❷ Create a `Hashtable` object to use to hold shopping cart items.

❸ Create an `Enumeration` object to access key values from the `Hashtable` object.

❹ Retrieve form values submitted; the perform value signals what type of action is to be taken with the item. A value of "add" means add the item to the user's shopping cart.

❺ Retrieve the ItemID submitted for the item.

❻ Retrieve the quantity submitted.

❼ If this is a new session for the user, create the shopping cart object.

❽ Retrieve the user's shopping cart from the HTTP `Session` object.

❾ Determine if the perform variable is "add".

❿ Retrieve the item submitted by the user from the user's shopping cart. This determines if the item is already in the cart.

⓫ Add the item to the user's cart if it isn't found.

⓬ If the item is found in the cart, increment the quantity in the cart with the new quantity submitted.

⓭ Add the item's new quantity to the cart. The `put` method of the `Hashtable` object will overwrite an existing entry (if it exists).

⓮ Determine if the perform variable contains "remove". The example does not utilize this, but you can use it to remove items from the shopping cart.

⓯ Instantiate the `NotesThread` object for working with Domino objects.

⓰ Create a new Domino `Session` object for the current server with the rights of the server.

⓱ Instantiate the `Database` object to the appropriate database.

⓲ Instantiate the `View` object to our lookup view for finding items by id.

⓳ Send HTML code to the browser. The code defines an HTML table to hold the contents of the user's shopping cart.

⓴ Populate the `Enumeration` object with the key values of the `Hashtable` object.

㉑ Initialize counter variables. These will track the total dollars and the total number of items ordered.

㉒ Loop through all elements in the `Hashtable` (shopping cart) object.

㉓ Get the key value for the current element. The key value is the item id. This will retrieve item information from the Domino database.

㉔ Get the quantity value from the `Hashtable` object.

㉕ Convert the quantity value into an integer.

㉖ Increment the quantity counter with the item's quantity value.

㉗ Retrieve the `Document` object from the View using the item's id number.

㉘ Print the item id in the HTML table.

㉙ Print the item's name in the HTML table.

㉚ Increment the total dollars counter with the dollar amount spent on the item.

㉛ Recycle the Domino `Document` object.

㉜ Display the total dollars spent by the user in the HTML table.

㉝ Display the total number of items selected by the user.

㉞ Terminate the `NotesThread` object.

㉟ Display the HTML button object that enables the user to continue shopping, thus returning him/her to the item listing.

Output

Figure 31.7 shows a sample output screen from the servlet. As you can see, the user has selected quite a few items.

31.4 CHECKING OUT

The checkout process combines the contents of the shopping cart with user information to form an order. The order is stored in a separate (secure) Domino database. A servlet is used to view the shopping cart and create the order document. Selecting the

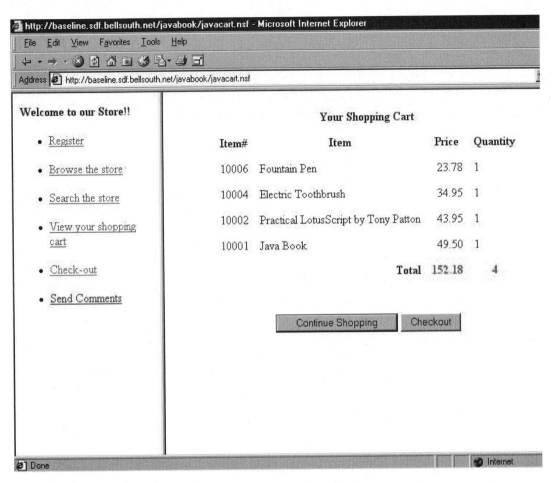

Figure 31.7 Example 31.3 output

Checkout link or button presents the user with the contents of the shopping cart and prompts him/her to enter a username and password. Let's take a look at the servlet code first.

In example 31.4, the servlet presents the user's shopping cart and the fields used to enter the user name and password. Most of the code is the same as in example 31.3.

Example 31.4   (Servlet)

```
import java.io.*;
import java.util.*;
import javax.servlet.*;
import javax.servlet.http.*;
import lotus.domino.*;
public class Example_31_4 extends HttpServlet  {
  public void doGet(HttpServletRequest request, HttpServletResponse response)
     throws ServletException, IOException  {
```

CHAPTER 31   EXAMPLE: SHOPPING CART

```
HttpSession websession = request.getSession(true);
response.setContentType("text/html");
PrintWriter out = response.getWriter();
Hashtable cartItems;
Enumeration cartKeys;
out.println("<HTML><HEAD>");
out.println("<TITLE>Checking Out</TITLE></HEAD>");
out.println("<BODY TEXT=\"#000000\" BGCOLOR=\"#FFFFFF\">");
out.println("<CENTER>");
try {
 cartItems = (Hashtable)websession.getValue("cart");
 NotesThread.sinitThread();
 Session s = NotesFactory.createSession();
 Database dbitems = s.getDatabase("","javabook//javacart.nsf");
 double totalDollars=0.0;
 if (dbitems != null) {
  View vw = dbitems.getView("(ItemsByID)");
  Document doc = null;
  if (vw != null) {
  out.println("<TABLE CELLPADDING=\"5\" CELLSPACING=\"5\">");
  out.println("<TR><TH COLSPAN=\"4\">Your Shopping Cart</TH></TR>");
  out.print("<TR><TH>Item#</TH><TH>Item</TH>");
  out.println("<TH>Price</TH><TH>Quantity</TH></TR>");
  cartKeys = cartItems.keys();
  int total = 0;
  while (cartKeys.hasMoreElements())  {
   String key = (String)cartKeys.nextElement();
   String value = (String)cartItems.get(key);
   int q = new Integer(value).intValue();
   total += q;
   doc = vw.getDocumentByKey(key);
   if (doc != null) {
    out.println("<TR><TD>");
    out.println(doc.getItemValueString("ItemID"));
    out.println("</TD><TD>");
    out.println(doc.getItemValueString("ItemName"));
    out.println("</TD><TD ALIGN=\"RIGHT\">");
    out.println(doc.getItemValueString("ItemPrice"));
    Double dTemp = new Double(doc.getItemValueString("ItemPrice"));
    totalDollars += (dTemp.doubleValue() * q);
    out.println("</TD><TD>");
    out.println(value);
    out.println("</TD></TR>");
    doc.recycle(); } }
  vw.recycle();
  out.print("<TR><TH COLSPAN=\"2\" ALIGN=\"RIGHT\">Total</TH>");
  out.print("<TH ALIGN=\"RIGHT\"><FONT COLOR=\"RED\">");
  out.print(totalDollars);
  out.print("</FONT></TH><TH><FONT COLOR=\"RED\">");
  out.print(total);
  out.println("</FONT></TH></TR>");
  out.println("</TABLE>");
  dbitems.recycle(); }
 vw.recycle();
```

```
    } else {
      out.println("Database not found.");    }
    s.recycle();
    NotesThread.stermThread();
    out.println("<FORM ACTION=\"http://baseline.sdf.bellsouth.net/servlet/create\">");  ❶
    out.print("<CENTER><TABLE><TR><TH COLSPAN=\"2\">");  ❷
    out.println("Please enter your username and password.</TH></TR>");
    out.print("<TR><TH>Username:</TH><TD><INPUT TYPE");
    out.println("=\"TEXT\" NAME=\"username\"></TD></TR>");
    out.print("<TR><TH>Password:</TH><TD><INPUT TYPE");  ❸
    out.println("=\"PASSWORD\" NAME=\"password\"></TD></TR></TABLE>");
    out.print("<BR><BR><INPUT TYPE=\"SUBMIT\" VALUE=");  ❹
    out.print("\"Process Order\" ");
    out.println("onClick=\'document.forms[0].submit();\'>");
    out.print("<INPUT TYPE=\"SUBMIT\" VALUE=\"Cancel\" ");
    out.println("onClick=\'history.go(-1);\'>");
    out.println("</FORM></BODY></HTML>");
  } catch (NotesException n) {
    n.printStackTrace();
  } catch (Exception e) {
    out.println(e.getMessage());
    out.println("Error caught");  } } }
```

Explanation

❶ Print HTML for the form to accept the user name and password submission. The contents of the form (user name and password) are passed to the servlet specified.

❷ Display the user name and password fields in a table.

❸ Display the password field.

❹ The HTML code for the Submit button that appears on the form.

The last servlet calls example 31.5. It is registered as create in the Servlets.Properties file.

Example 31.5   (Servlet)

```
import java.io.*;
import java.util.*;
import javax.servlet.*;
import javax.servlet.http.*;
import lotus.domino.*;
public class Example_31_5 extends HttpServlet  {
  public void doGet(HttpServletRequest request, HttpServletResponse response)
      throws ServletException, IOException  {
    HttpSession websession = request.getSession(true);
    response.setContentType("text/html");
    PrintWriter out = response.getWriter();
    Hashtable cartItems;
    Enumeration cartKeys;
    out.println("<HTML><HEAD>");
    out.println("<TITLE>Checking Out</TITLE></HEAD>");
```

```
out.println("<BODY TEXT=\"#000000\" BGCOLOR=\"#FFFFFF\">");
out.println("<CENTER>");
try {
 cartItems = (Hashtable)websession.getValue("cart");
 NotesThread.sinitThread();
 Session s = NotesFactory.createSession();
 Database dbitems = s.getDatabase("","javabook//javacart.nsf"); ❶
 Database nab = s.getDatabase("","names.nsf"); ❷
 double totalDollars=0.0;
 if ((dbitems != null) & (nab != null))  {
  View vw = dbitems.getView("(ItemsByID)");
  Document doc = null;
  websession.putValue("itemList",new Vector()); ❸
  websession.putValue("quantityList", new Vector()); ❹
  websession.putValue("priceList", new Vector()); ❺
  websession.putValue("nameList", new Vector()); ❻
  Vector itemList = (Vector)websession.getValue("itemList"); ❼
   Vector quantityList = (Vector)websession.getValue("quantityList");
   Vector priceList = (Vector)websession.getValue("priceList");
   Vector nameList = (Vector)websession.getValue("nameList");
  if (vw != null) {
   out.println("<TABLE CELLPADDING=\"5\" CELLSPACING=\"5\">");
   out.println("<TR><TH COLSPAN=\"4\">Your Shopping Cart</TH></TR>");
   out.print("<TR><TH>Item#</TH><TH>Item</TH>");
   out.print("<TH>Price</TH><TH>Quantity</TH></TR>");
   cartKeys = cartItems.keys();
   int total = 0;
   while (cartKeys.hasMoreElements())  {
    String key = (String)cartKeys.nextElement();
    String value = (String)cartItems.get(key);
    int q = new Integer(value).intValue();
    total += q;
    doc = vw.getDocumentByKey(key);
    if (doc != null) {
     out.println("<TR><TD>");
     out.println(doc.getItemValueString("ItemID"));
     itemList.addElement(doc.getItemValueString("ItemID")); ❽
     out.println("</TD><TD>");
     out.println(doc.getItemValueString("ItemName"));
     nameList.addElement(doc.getItemValueString("ItemName")); ❾
     out.println("</TD><TD ALIGN=\"RIGHT\">");
     out.println(doc.getItemValueString("ItemPrice"));
     priceList.addElement(doc.getItemValueString("ItemPrice")); ❿
     Double dTemp = new Double(doc.getItemValueString("ItemPrice"));
     totalDollars += (dTemp.doubleValue() * q);
     out.println("</TD><TD>");
     out.println(value);
     quantityList.addElement(value); ⓫
     out.println("</TD></TR>");
     doc.recycle();  }
    vw.recycle();
    out.print("<TR><TH COLSPAN=\"2\" ALIGN=\"RIGHT\">");
```

```
        out.print("Total</TH><TH ALIGN=\"RIGHT\"><FONT COLOR=\"RED\">");
        out.print(totalDollars);
        out.print("</FONT></TH><TH><FONT COLOR=\"RED\">");
        out.print(total);
        out.println("</FONT></TH></TR>");
        out.println("</TABLE>");
        dbitems.recycle();  }
vw.recycle();
String username = request.getParameter("username");  ⑫
vw = nab.getView("(username)");  ⑬
if (vw != null) {
 doc = vw.getDocumentByKey(username);  ⑭
 if (doc != null)  {
   out.println("<BR><BR><TABLE>");
   String fname = doc.getItemValueString("FirstName");  ⑮
   String lname = doc.getItemValueString("LastName");  ⑯
   String addr = doc.getItemValueString("OfficeStreetAddress");
   String city = doc.getItemValueString("OfficeCity");
   String state = doc.getItemValueString("OfficeState");
   String zip = doc.getItemValueString("OfficeZip");
   String tele = doc.getItemValueString("OfficePhoneNumber");
   out.println("<TR><TD>Name:</TD><TD>");
   out.println(fname + " " + lname);
   out.println("</TD></TR><TR><TD>Address</TD><TD>");
   out.println(addr);
   out.println("</TD></TR><TR><TD>City</TD><TD>");
   out.println(city);
   out.println("</TD></TR><TR><TD>State</TD><TD>");
   out.println(state);
   out.println("</TD></TR><TR><TD>Zip</TD><TD>");
   out.println(zip);
   out.println("</TD></TR><TR><TD>Telephone</TD><TD>");
   out.println(tele);
   out.println("</TD></TR></TABLE>");
   out.println("<FORM ACTION=\"http://baseline.sdf.bellsouth.net/
       servlet/process\">");  ⑰
   out.print("<INPUT TYPE=\"HIDDEN\" TYPE=\"TEXT\"");  ⑱
   out.print(" NAME=\"orderTotal\" VALUE=\"");
   out.println(totalDollars +"\">");
   out.print("<INPUT TYPE=\"HIDDEN\" TYPE=\"TEXT\"");
   out.println(" NAME=\"UserName\" VALUE=\"" + username +"\">");
   out.print("<INPUT TYPE=\"HIDDEN\" TYPE=\"TEXT\"");  ⑲
   out.println(" NAME=\"LastName\" VALUE=\"" + lname +"\">");
   out.print("<INPUT TYPE=\"HIDDEN\" TYPE=\"TEXT\"");  ⑳
   out.println( NAME=\"FirstName\" VALUE=\"" + fname +"\">");
   out.print("<INPUT TYPE=\"HIDDEN\" TYPE=\"TEXT\"");
   out.println(" NAME=\"Address\" VALUE=\"" + addr +"\">");
   out.print("<INPUT TYPE=\"HIDDEN\" TYPE=\"TEXT\"");
   out.println(" NAME=\"City\" VALUE=\"" + city +"\">");
   out.print("<INPUT TYPE=\"HIDDEN\" TYPE=\"TEXT\"");
   out.println(" NAME=\"State\" VALUE=\"" + state +"\">");
   out.print("<INPUT TYPE=\"HIDDEN\" TYPE=\"TEXT\"");
```

```
            out.println(" NAME=\"ZipCode\" VALUE=\"" + zip +"\">");
            out.print("<INPUT TYPE=\"HIDDEN\" TYPE=\"TEXT\"");
            out.println(" NAME=\"Telephone\" VALUE=\"" + tele +"\">");
            vw.recycle();
            nab.recycle();
          } else {
            out.println("User information could not be retrieved."); } }
        } else {
          out.println("Database(s) not found."); }
        s.recycle();
        NotesThread.stermThread();
        out.print("<BR><BR><INPUT TYPE=\"SUBMIT\" VALUE=");
        out.print("\"Process Order\" ");
        out.println("onClick=\'document.forms[0].submit();\'>");
        out.print("<INPUT TYPE=\"SUBMIT\" VALUE=\"Cancel\"");
        out.println(" onClick=\'history.go(-1);\'>");
        out.println("</FORM></BODY></HTML>");
      } catch (NotesException n) {
        n.printStackTrace();
      } catch (Exception e) {
        out.println(e.getMessage());
        out.println("Error caught");   } } }
```

◼

Explanation

❶ Set the `Database` object to the orders database.

❷ Set the `Database` object to the Domino Directory.

❸ Create a session `Vector` object to hold item id numbers.

❹ Create a session `Vector` object to hold item quantities.

❺ Create a session `Vector` object to hold item prices.

❻ Create a session `Vector` object to hold item names.

❼ Retrieve `Vector` object(s) from the `Session` object.

❽ Add an item id number to the `Vector` object, thus adding it to the `Session` object.

❾ Add an item name to the `Vector` object, thus adding it to the `Session` object.

❿ Add an item price to the `Vector` object, thus adding it to the `Session` object.

⓫ Add an item quantity to the `Vector` object, thus adding it to the `Session` object.

⓬ Retrieve the user's name from the servlet parameter from the previous form. This is used to retrieve user information from the Domino Directory.

⓭ Retrieve the lookup view from the Domino Directory.

⓮ Set the `Document` object to the user's Domino Directory entry.

⓯ Get the user's first name from the `Document` object.

⑯ Get the user's last name from the `Document` object.

⑰ Send HTML to the browser. A form is set up for the final step in creating an order. The user will be presented with shopping cart items, the total, and user information. If everything is correct, the user should click the Process Order button to create an order in the orders database.

⑱ Display fields to be passed to the next servlet as hidden HTML fields. This line displays the total amount of the order.

⑲ Display the user's first name as a hidden HTML field.

⑳ Display the user's last name as a hidden HTML field.

The final piece of the order creation process is the actual creation of the order in the orders database. The servlet in example 31.6 is called from the previous servlet; it takes values passed as hidden HTML fields and `Session` objects to create the actual order document. A thank-you message is displayed in the browser.

Example 31.6 (Servlet)

```
import java.io.*;
import java.util.*;
import javax.servlet.*;
import javax.servlet.http.*;
import lotus.domino.*;
public class Example_31_6 extends HttpServlet  {
  public void doGet(HttpServletRequest request, HttpServletResponse response)
     throws ServletException, IOException  {
   HttpSession websession = request.getSession(true);
   response.setContentType("text/html");
   PrintWriter out = response.getWriter();
   out.println("<HTML><HEAD>");
   out.println("<TITLE>Processing Order</TITLE></HEAD>");
   out.println("<BODY TEXT=\"#000000\" BGCOLOR=\"#FFFFFF\">");
   out.println("<CENTER>");
   try {
    Vector itemIDs = (Vector)websession.getValue("itemList");        ❶
    Vector itemQuantity = (Vector)websession.getValue("quantityList");   ❷
    String Username = request.getParameter("UserName");      ❸
    String orderTotal = request.getParameter("orderTotal");    ❹
    Vector itemPrices = (Vector)websession.getValue("priceList");   ❺
    Vector itemNames = (Vector)websession.getValue("nameList");   ❻
    NotesThread.sinitThread();      ❼
    Session s = NotesFactory.createSession();
    Database ordersDB = s.getDatabase("","javabook//jvorders.nsf");   ❽
    if (ordersDB != null) {
      Document doc = ordersDB.createDocument();    ❾
      doc.replaceItemValue("Form","Order");
      doc.replaceItemValue("orderCustomerID",Username);    ❿
      doc.replaceItemValue("orderStatus","Open");
      doc.replaceItemValue("orderItemNumber",itemIDs);    ⓫
```

```
        doc.replaceItemValue("orderItemDesc",itemNames);
        doc.replaceItemValue("orderItemQuantity",itemQuantity);
        doc.replaceItemValue("orderItemPrice",itemPrices);
        doc.replaceItemValue("orderTotal",orderTotal);
        doc.save(); ⓬
        doc.recycle();
        ordersDB.recycle();
      } else {
        out.println("Database not found."); }
      s.recycle();
      NotesThread.stermThread(); ⓭
      out.println("<BR><BR>");
      out.println("<H1>Thank you for your order.</H1>");
      out.println("</CENTER></BODY></HTML>");
    } catch (NotesException n) {
      n.printStackTrace(); }
    catch (Exception e) {
      out.println(e.getMessage());
      out.println("Error caught"); } } }
```

Explanation

❶ Retrieve the Vector object of item numbers ordered from the servlet's Session object.

❷ Retrieve the Vector object containing item quantities ordered from the servlet's Session object.

❸ Retrieve the user name from the servlet's parameters (passed as an HTML form field).

❹ Retrieve the order total from the servlet's parameters.

❺ Retrieve the Vector object of item prices.

❻ Retrieve the Vector object of item names.

❼ Instantiate a NotesThread object.

❽ Create a Database object to access the orders database.

❾ Create a new order document in the orders database.

❿ Populate fields on the order with values retrieved from the servlet Session object.

⓫ Populate the multi-valued field on the order with a Vector object.

⓬ Save the new order.

⓭ Dispose of the NotesThread object.

All of the servlets are registered and started in the Servlets.Properties file. This allows them to be called by names other than the actual class file names. Here is the Servlets.Properties file for our application:

```
servlet.order.code = Example_31_3
servlet.checkout.code = Example_31_4
servlet.Ex311.code = Example_31_1
servlet.create.code = Example_31_5
servlet.process.code = Example_31_6
servlets.startup = order checkout Ex311 create process
```

Let's take a look at the checkout process via screen shots. The three screens displayed in figures 31.8 through 31.10 show the user selecting the checkout link, hitting the process order button to retrieve user information, and selecting the process order button a final time to create the order.

Figure 31.8   Selecting the checkout link

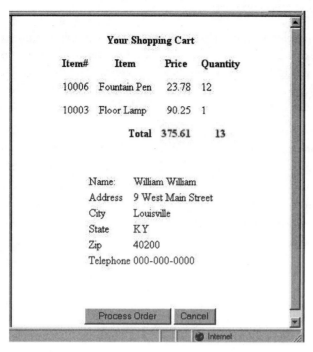

Figure 31.9   Pressing the First Process Order button

Figure 31.10   Creating the order

31.5 PUTTING IT ALL TOGETHER

The application assembled in this chapter is very basic—a simple frameset consisting of Domino pages is used to present the site. The user can choose to browse store items, view the shopping cart, check out, log in, or register. Figure 31.11 shows the opening page for the site.

31.6 NOTES

The application code presented in this chapter is not intended for production use. This chapter has used servlets extensively for the purpose of demonstration, but other techniques may be more appropriate. Server load and other tests must be performed to determine the most appropriate solution. In addition, security has not been considered in any aspect of the application.

Figure 31.11 Store home page

31.7 CHAPTER REVIEW

The introduction of Java into the Domino environment has opened up new technologies and possibilities. In this chapter we have explored the extensive use of servlets and Domino Java code to develop the framework for a Domino-based store. The store allows users to browse and select items, and asks them for user information upon checkout.

C H A P T E R   3 2

More examples

32.1 Extracting attachments   407

32.2 Removing a user from ACL   408

32.3 Exporting   409

32.4 XML exporting   410

32.5 Creating a newsletter   411

This chapter includes numerous sample Java agents that you may find useful.

32.1 EXTRACTING ATTACHMENTS

The agent in example 32.1 detaches attachments from all documents in a view, saving them to a local drive.

Example 32.1   (Domino Agent)

```
import lotus.domino.*;
import java.util.Vector;
import java.util.Enumeration;
import java.io.PrintWriter;
public class Example_32_1 extends AgentBase {
  public void NotesMain() {
    try {
      Session s = this.getSession();
      AgentContext ac = s.getAgentContext();
      Database db = ac.getCurrentDatabase();
      PrintWriter pw = this.getAgentOutput();
      View vw = db.getView("Attach");
      if (vw != null) {
        Document doc = null;
        RichTextItem rtf = null;
        EmbeddedObject eo = null;
        doc = vw.getFirstDocument();
        while (doc != null) {
          rtf = (RichTextItem)doc.getFirstItem("Attach");
          if (rtf != null) {
            Vector v = rtf.getEmbeddedObjects();
            Enumeration e = v.elements();
            while (e.hasMoreElements()) {
              eo = (EmbeddedObject)e.nextElement();
              if (eo.getType() == EmbeddedObject.EMBED_ATTACHMENT) {
                eo.extractFile("C:\\" + eo.getSource());
                pw.println(eo.getSource() + " detached."); } } }
          doc = vw.getNextDocument(doc); }
        eo.recycle();
        rtf.recycle();
        vw.recycle(); }
      db.recycle();
      ac.recycle();
      s.recycle();
    } catch(Exception e) {
      e.printStackTrace(); } } }
```

32.2 REMOVING A USER FROM ACL

The agent in example 32.2 removes the designated user from every database ACL.

Example 32.2 (Domino Agent)

```java
import lotus.domino.*;
import java.util.Vector;
import java.util.Enumeration;
import java.io.PrintWriter;
public class Example_32_2 extends AgentBase {
  public void NotesMain() {
    try {
      String nameToDelete = "Charles Barkley";
      Session s = this.getSession();
      AgentContext ac = s.getAgentContext();
      PrintWriter pw = this.getAgentOutput();
      DbDirectory dbdir = s.getDbDirectory(null);
      Database db = dbdir.getFirstDatabase(DbDirectory.DATABASE);
      ACL dbacl = null;
      ACLEntry entry = null;
      Log log = s.createLog("Name Cleanup Agent");
      Vector logRecipients = new Vector();
      logRecipients.addElement(s.getUserName());
      log.openMailLog(logRecipients, "Name Cleanup Agent results");
      while (db != null) {
        dbacl = db.getACL();
        if (dbacl != null) {
          entry = dbacl.getEntry(nameToDelete);
          if (entry != null) {
            entry.remove();
            dbacl.save();
            dbacl.recycle();
            entry.recycle();
            log.logAction(nameToDelete + " removed from " + db.getTitle()); } }
        db = dbdir.getNextDatabase(); }
      log.close();
      log.recycle();
      dbdir.recycle();
      ac.recycle();
      s.recycle();
    } catch(Exception e) {
      e.printStackTrace(); } } }
```

32.3 EXPORTING

The agent in example 32.3 exports all person documents to a comma-delimited file. Only select fields are used from the Person document.

Example 32.3 (Domino Agent)

```java
import lotus.domino.*;
import java.io.*;
import java.io.PrintWriter;
public class Example_32_3 extends AgentBase {
 public void NotesMain() {
   try {
     Session s = this.getSession();
     AgentContext ac = s.getAgentContext();
     Database db = s.getDatabase("","names.nsf");
     PrintWriter pw = this.getAgentOutput();
     View vw = db.getView("People");
     if (vw != null) {
     DataOutputStream outFile = new DataOutputStream(new
         BufferedOutputStream(new FileOutputStream("c:\\people.txt")));
      Document doc = vw.getFirstDocument();
      while (doc != null) {
        String firstName = doc.getItemValueString("FirstName");
        String lastName = doc.getItemValueString("LastName");
        String address = doc.getItemValueString("OfficeStreetAddress");
        String city = doc.getItemValueString("OfficeCity");
        String state = doc.getItemValueString("OfficeState");
        String zip = doc.getItemValueString("OfficeZIP");
        outFile.writeBytes("\"" + lastName + "\",\" " + firstName);
        outFile.writeBytes("\",\" " + address + "\",\" " + city);
        outFile.writeBytes("\",\" " + state + "\",\" " + zip + "\"\n");
        doc = vw.getNextDocument(doc); }
      vw.recycle();
      outFile.close();}
     db.recycle();
     s.recycle();
   } catch(IOException e) {
     System.out.println("IO Exception");
   } catch(Exception e) {
     e.printStackTrace(); } } }
```

32.4 XML EXPORTING

The code in example 32.4 extends example 32.3 by exporting to an XML formatted file.

Example 32.4 (Domino Agent)

```java
import lotus.domino.*;
import java.io.*;
import java.io.PrintWriter;
public class Example_32_4 extends AgentBase {
 public void NotesMain() {
   try {
     Session s = this.getSession();
     AgentContext ac = s.getAgentContext();
     Database db = s.getDatabase("","names.nsf");
     PrintWriter pw = this.getAgentOutput();
     View vw = db.getView("People");
     if (vw != null) {
      DataOutputStream outFile =
        new DataOutputStream(
          new BufferedOutputStream(
            new FileOutputStream("c:\\peoplexml.txt")));
      outFile.writeBytes("<?xml version=\"1.0\"");
      outFile.writeBytes("encoding=\"UTF-8\"?>\n");
      outFile.writeBytes("<people>\n");
      Document doc = null;
      doc = vw.getFirstDocument();
      while (doc != null) {
       String firstName = doc.getItemValueString("FirstName");
       String lastName = doc.getItemValueString("LastName");
       String address = doc.getItemValueString("OfficeStreetAddress");
       String city = doc.getItemValueString("OfficeCity");
       String state = doc.getItemValueString("OfficeState");
       String zip = doc.getItemValueString("OfficeZIP");
       outFile.writeBytes("<person>\n");
       outFile.writeBytes("<firstname>")
       outFile.writeBytes(firstName);
       outFile.writeBytes("</firstname>\n");
       outFile.writeBytes("<lastname>");
       outFile.writeBytes(lastName);
       outFile.writeBytes("</lastname>\n");
       outFile.writeBytes("<address>");
       outFile.writeBytes(address);
       outFile.writeBytes("</address>\n");
       outFile.writeBytes("<city>");
       outFile.writeBytes(city);
       outFile.writeBytes("</city>\n");
       outFile.writeBytes("<state>");
       outFile.writeBytes(state);
       outFile.writeBytes("</state>\n");
       outFile.writeBytes("<zipcode>");
       outFile.writeBytes(zip);
       outFile.writeBytes("</zipcode>\n");
       outFile.writeBytes("</person>\n");
```

```
       doc = vw.getNextDocument(doc); }
      vw.recycle();
      outFile.writeBytes("</people>\n");
      outFile.close();}
     db.recycle();
     s.recycle();
    } catch(IOException e) {
     System.out.println("IO Exception");
    } catch(Exception e) {
     e.printStackTrace(); } } }
```

32.5   CREATING A NEWSLETTER

The agent in example 32.5 creates a newsletter containing documents that match the search criteria and mails it to a group of users defined in a profile document in the database.

Example 32.5   (Domino Agent)

```
import lotus.domino.*;
import java.util.Vector;
import java.io.PrintWriter;
public class Example_32_5 extends AgentBase {
 public void NotesMain() {
  try {
    Session s = this.getSession();
    AgentContext ac = s.getAgentContext();
    Database db = ac.getCurrentDatabase();
    PrintWriter pw = this.getAgentOutput();
    Document profileDoc = db.getProfileDocument("Newsletter","Newsletter");
    if (profileDoc != null) {
     String search=profileDoc.getItemValueString("SearchPhrase");
     Vector recipients = profileDoc.getItemValue("Recipients");
     DocumentCollection dc = db.FTSearch(search);
     if (dc.getCount() > 0) {
      Newsletter news = s.createNewsletter(dc);
      news.setSubjectItemName("Subject");
      news.setDoSubject(true);
      Document memo = news.formatMsgWithDoclinks(db);
      memo.appendItemValue("Form","memo");
      memo.appendItemValue("Subject","Profile Matches");
      memo.send(false, recipients);
      memo.recycle();
      news.recycle();}
     dc.recycle();
     profileDoc.recycle();}
    db.recycle();
    ac.recycle();
    s.recycle();
   } catch(Exception e) {
    e.printStackTrace(); } } }
```

Domino Java class reference

A.1 ACL CLASS

Methods

```
addRole
createACLEntry
deleteRole
getEntry
getFirstEntry
getNextEntry
renameRole
removeACLEntry
save
```

Properties

InternetLevel (read/write)
isUniformAccess (read/write)
Parent (read-only)
Roles (read-only)

A.2 ACLENTRY CLASS

Methods

```
disableRole
enableRole
isRoleEnabled
remove
```

Properties

IsAdminReaderAuthor (read/write)
IsAdminServer (read/write)
IsCanCreateDocuments (read/write)
IsCanCreateLSOrJavaAgent (read/write)
IsCanCreatePersonalAgent (read/write)
IsCanCreatePersonalFolder (read/write)
IsCanCreateSharedFolder (read/write)
IsCanDeleteDocuments (read/write)
IsGroup (read/write)
IsPerson (read/write)
IsServer (read/write)
IsPublicReader (read/write)
IsPublicWriter (read/write)
Level (read/write)
Name (read/write)
NameObject (read-only)

```
Parent (read-only)
Roles (read-only)
UserType (read/write)
```

A.3   AGENT CLASS

Methods

```
remove
run
runOnServer
save
```

Properties

```
Comment (read-only)
CommonOwner (read-only)
IsEnabled (read/write)
IsNotesAgent (read-only)
IsPublic (read-only)
IsWebAgent (read-only)
LastRun (read-only)
Name (read-only)
Owner (read-only)
Parent (read-only)
Query (read-only)
ServerName (read/write)
Target (read-only)
Trigger (read-only)
```

A.4   AGENTCONTEXT CLASS

Methods

```
unprocessedFTSearch
unprocessedSearch
updateProcessedDoc
```

Properties

```
CurrentAgent (read-only)
CurrentDatabase (read-only)
DocumentContext (read-only)
EffectiveUserName (read-only)
LastExitStatus (read-only)
LastRun (read-only)
SavedData (read-only)
UnprocessedDocuments (read-only)
```

A.5 DATABASE CLASS

Methods

compact
createCopy
createDocument
createFromTemplate
createOutline
createReplica
createFolder
FTDomainSearch
FTSearch
getAgent
getDocumentByID
getDocumentByUNID
getDocumentByURL
getForm
getOutline
getProfileDocCollection
getProfileDocument
getURLHeaderInfo
getView
grantAccess
open
queryAccess
remove
replicate
revokeAccess
search
updateFTIndex

Properties

ACL (read-only)
Agents (read-only)
AllDocuments (read-only)
Categories (read/write)
Created (read-only)
CurrentAccessLevel (read-only)
DesignTemplateName (read-only)
FileName (read-only)
FilePath (read-only)
FolderReferencesEnabled (read/write)
Forms (read-only)
IsDelayUpdates (read/write)

IsFTIndexed (read-only)
IsMultiDBSearch (read-only)
IsOpen (read-only)
IsPrivateAddressBook (read-only)
IsPublicAddressBook (read-only)
LastFTIndexed (read-only)
LastModified (read-only)
Managers (read-only)
MaxSize (read-only)
Parent (read-only)
PercentUsed (read-only)
ReplicaID (read-only)
ReplicationInfo (read-only)
Server (read-only)
Size (read-only)
SizeQuota (read/write)
TemplateName (read-only)
Title (read-only)
Views (read-only)

A.6   DATERANGE CLASS

Methods
None

Properties
EndDateTime (read/write)
Parent (read-only)
StartDateTime (read/write)
Text (read/write)

A.7   DATETIME CLASS

Methods
adjustDay
adjustHour
adjustMinute
adjustMonth
adjustSecond
adjustYear
convertToZone
setAnyDate
setAnyTime

```
setNow
timeDifference
toJavaDate
```

Properties

```
DateOnly (read-only)
GMTTime (read-only)
IsDST (read-only)
LocalTime (read/write)
Parent (read-only)
TimeOnly (read-only)
TimeZone (read-only)
ZoneTime (read-only)
```

A.8 DBDIRECTORY CLASS

Methods

```
createDatabase
getFirstDatabase
getNextDatabase
openDatabase
openDatabaseByReplicaID
openDatabaseIfModified
openMailDatabase
```

Properties

```
Name (read-only)
Parent (read-only)
```

A.9 DOCUMENT CLASS

Methods

```
appendItemValue
computeWithForm
copyAllItems
copyItem
copyToDatabase
createReplyMessage
createRichTextItem
encrypt
generateXML
getAttachment
getFirstItem
getItemValue
getItemValueDouble
```

```
getItemValueInteger
getItemValueString
hasItem
makeResponse
putInFolder
remove
removeFromFolder
removeItem
renderToRTItem
replaceItemValue
save
send
sign
```

Properties

```
Authors (read-only)
ColumnValues (read-only)
Created (read-only)
EmbeddedObjects (read-only)
EncryptionKeys (read/write)
FolderReferences (read-only)
FTSearchScore (read-only)
HasEmbedded (read-only)
IsDeleted (read-only)
IsEcryptOnSend (read/write)
IsNewNote (read-only)
IsProfile (read-only)
IsResponse (read-only)
IsSaveMessageOnSend (read/write)
IsSentByAgent (read-only)
IsSigned (read-only)
IsSignOnSend (read/write)
IsValid (read-only)
Items (read-only)
Key (read-only)
LastAccessed (read-only)
LastModified (read-only)
NameOfProfile (read-only)
NoteID (read-only)
ParentDatabase (read-only)
ParentDocumentUNID (read-only)
ParentView (read-only)
Responses (read-only)
```

```
Signer (read-only)
Size (read-only)
UniversalID (read-only)
Verifier (read-only)
```

A.10 DOCUMENTCOLLECTION CLASS

Methods

```
addDocument
deleteDocument
FTSearch
getDocument
getFirstDocument
getLastDocument
getNextDocument
getNthDocument
getPrevDocument
putAllInFolder
removeAll
removeAllFromFolder
stampAll
updateAll
```

Properties

```
Count (read-only)
IsSorted (read-only)
Parent (read-only)
Query (read-only)
```

A.11 EMBEDDEDOBJECT CLASS

Methods

```
activate
doVerb
extractFile
remove
```

Properties

```
ClassName (read-only)
FileSize (read-only)
Name (read-only)
Object (read-only)
Parent (read-only)
Source (read-only)
```

Type (read-only)
Verbs (read-only)

A.12 *FORM CLASS*

Methods

remove

Properties

Aliases (read-only)
Fields (read-only)
FormUsers (read/write)
IsProtectReaders (read/write)
IsProtectUsers (read/write)
IsSubForm (read-only)
Name (read-only)
Parent (read-only)
Readers (read/write)

A.13 *INTERNATIONAL CLASS*

Methods

None

Properties

AMString (read-only)
CurrencyDigits (read-only)
CurrencySymbol (read-only)
DateSep (read-only)
DecimalSep (read-only)
IsCurrencySpace (read-only)
IsCurrencySuffix (read-only)
IsCurrencyZero (read-only)
IsDateDMY (read-only)
IsDateMDY (read-only)
IsDateYMD (read-only)
IsDST (read-only)
IsTime24Hour (read-only)
Parent (read-only)
PMString (read-only)
ThousandsSep (read-only)
TimeSep (read-only)
TimeZone (read-only)

```
Today (read-only)
Tomorrow (read-only)
Yesterday (read-only)
```

A.14 ITEM CLASS

Methods
```
abstractText
appendToTextList
containsValue
copyItemToDocument
remove
```

Properties
```
DateTimeValue (read/write)
IsAuthors (read/write)
IsEncrypted (read/write)
IsNames (read/write)
IsProtected (read/write)
IsReaders (read/write)
IsSaveToDisk (read/write)
IsSigned (read/write)
IsSummary (read/write)
LastModifed (read-only)
Name (read-only)
Parent (read-only)
Text (read-only)
Type (read-only)
ValueDouble (read/write)
ValueInteger (read/write)
ValueLength (read-only)
Values (read/write)
ValueString (read/write)
```

A.15 LOG CLASS

Methods
```
close
logAction
logError
logEvent
openAgentLog
openFileLog
```

```
openMailLog
openNotesLog
```

Properties

```
IsLogActions (read/write)
IsLogErrors (read/write)
IsOverwriteFiles (read/write)
NumActions (read-only)
NumErrors (read-only)
Parent (read-only)
ProgramName (read/write)
```

A.16 NAME CLASS

Methods

None

Properties

```
Abbreviated (read-only)
Addr821 (read-only)
Addr822Comment1 (read-only)
Addr822Comment2 (read-only)
Addr822Comment3 (read-only)
Addr822LocalPart (read-only)
Addr822Phrase (read-only)
ADMD (read-only)
Canonical (read-only)
Common (read-only)
Country (read-only)
Generation (read-only)
Given (read-only)
Initials (read-only)
IsHierarchical (read-only)
Keyword (read-only)
Language (read-only)
Organization (read-only)
OrgUnit1 (read-only)
OrgUnit2 (read-only)
OrgUnit3 (read-only)
OrgUnit4 (read-only)
PRMD (read-only)
Parent (read-only)
Surname (read-only)
```

A.17 NEWSLETTER CLASS

Methods
```
formatDocument
formatMsgWithDoclinks
```

Properties
IsDoScore (read/write)
IsDoSubject (read/write)
Parent (read-only)
SubjectItemName (read/write)

A.18 OUTLINE CLASS

Methods
```
addEntry
createEntry
getFirst
getLast
getNext
getNextSibling
getParent
getPrev
getPrevSibling
moveEntry
removeEntry
save
```

Properties
Alias (read-only)
Comment (read-only)
Name (read-only)

A.19 OUTLINEENTRY CLASS

Methods
```
setAction
setNamedElement
setNoteLink
setURL
```

Properties
Alias (read/write)
Database (read-only)

Document (read-only)
EntryClass (read-only)
Formula (read-only)
FrameText (read/write)
HasChildren (read-only)
ImagesText (read/write)
IsHidden (read/write)
IsInThisDb (read-only)
IsPrivate (read-only)
Label (read/write)
Level (read-only)
NamedElement (read-only)
Type (read-only)
URL (read-only)
View (read-only)

A.20 REGISTRATION CLASS

Methods

addCertifierToAddressBook
addServerToAddressBook
addUserProfile
addUserToAddressBook
crossCertify
deleteIDOnServer
getIDFromServer
getUserInfo
recertify
registerNewCertifier
registerNewServer
registerNewUser
switchToID

Properties

CertifierIDFile (read/write)
CreateMailDb (read/write)
Expiration (read/write)
IDType (read/write)
IsNorthAmerican (read/write)
MinPasswordLength (read/write)
OrgUnit (read/write)
RegistrationLog (read/write)
RegistrationServer (read/write)

StoreIDInAddressBook (read/write)
UpdateAddressBook (read/write)

A.21 REPLICATION CLASS

Methods
clearHistory
reset
save

Properties
CutoffDate (read-only)
CutoffInterval (read/write)
IsAbstract (read/write)
IsCutoffDelete (read/write)
IsDisabled (read/write)
IsDoNotBrowse (read/write)
IsDoNotCatalog (read/write)
IsHideDesign (read/write)
IsIgnoreDeletes (read/write)
IsIgnoreDestDeletes(read/write)
IsMultiDbIndex (read/write)
IsNeverReplicate (read/write)
IsNoChronos (read/write)
Priority (read/write)

A.22 RICHTEXTITEM CLASS

Methods
addNewLine
addPageBreak
addTab
appendDocLink
appendParagraphStyle
appendRTItem
appendStyle
appendText
embedObject
getEmbeddedObject
getFormattedText

Properties
EmbeddedObjects (read-only)

A.23 RichTextParagraphStyle class

Methods

```
clearAllTabs
setTab
setTabs
```

Properties

```
Alignment (read/write)
FirstLineLeftMargin (read/write)
InterLineSpacing (read/write)
LeftMargin (read/write)
Pagination (read/write)
RightMargin (read/write)
SpacingAbove (read/write)
SpacingBelow (read/write)
Tabs (read-only)
```

A.24 RichTextStyle class

Methods

None

Properties

```
Bold (read/write)
Color (read/write)
Effects (read/write)
Font (read/write)
FontSize (read/write)
Italic (read/write)
Parent (read-only)
PassThruHTML (read/write)
StrikeThrough (read/write)
Underline (read/write)
```

A.25 Session class

Methods

```
createDateRange
createDateTime
createLog
createName
createNewsLetter
createRegistration
```

```
createRichTextParagraphStyle
createRichTextStyle
evaluate
freeTimeSearch
getDatabase
getDbDirectory
getEnvironmentString
getEnvironmentValue
getURLDatabase
resolve
setEnvironmentVar
```

Properties

```
AddressBooks (read-only)
AgentContext (read-only)
CommonUserName (read-only)
International (read-only)
IsOnServer (read-only)
NotesVersion (read-only)
Platform (read-only)
ServerName (read-only)
UserName (read-only)
UserNameList (read-only)
UserNameObject (read-only)
```

A.26 VIEW CLASS

Methods

```
clear
createViewNav
createViewNavFrom
createViewNavFromCategory
createViewNavFromChildren
createViewNavFromDescendants
createViewNavMaxLevel
FTSearch
getAllDocumentsByKey
getAllEntriesByKey
getChild
getColumn
getDocumentByKey
getEntryByKey
getFirstDocument
getLastDocument
```

```
getNextDocument
getNextSibling
getNthDocument
getParentDocument
getPrevDocument
getPrevSibling
refresh
remove
```

Properties

Aliases (read-only)
AllEntries (read-only)
BackgroundColor (read-only)
ColumnCount (read-only)
ColumnNames (read-only)
Columns (read-only)
Created (read-only)
HeaderLines (read-only)
IsAutoUpdate (read/write)
IsCalendar (read-only)
IsCategorized (read-only)
IsConflict (read-only)
IsDefaultView (read-only)
IsFolder (read-only)
IsHierarchical (read-only)
IsModified (read-only)
IsPrivate (read-only)
IsProtectReaders (read/write)
LastModifed (read-only)
Name (read-only)
Parent (read-only)
Readers (read/write)
RowLines (read-only)
Spacing (read-only)
TopLevelEntryCount (read-only)
UniversalID (read-only)

A.27 VIEWCOLUMN CLASS

Methods

None

Properties

Alignment (read-only)
DateFmt (read-only)
FontColor (read-only)
FontFace (read-only)
FontPointSize (read-only)
FontStyle (read-only)
Formula (read-only)
HeaderAlignment (read-only)
IsAccentSensitiveSort (read-only)
IsCaseSensitiveSort (read-only)
IsCategory (read-only)
IsField (read-only)
IsFormula (read-only)
IsHidden (read-only)
IsHideDetail (read-only)
IsIcon (read-only)
IsResize (read-only)
IsResortAscending (read-only)
IsResortDescending (read-only)
IsResortToView (read-only)
IsResponse (read-only)
IsSecondaryResort (read-only)
IsSecondaryResortDescending (read-only)
IsShowTwistie (read-only)
IsSortDescending (read-only)
IsSorted (read-only)
ItemName (read-only)
ListSep (read-only)
NumberAttrib (read-only)
NumberDigits (read-only)
NumberFormat (read-only)
Parent (read-only)
Position (read-only)
TimeDateFmt (read-only)
TimeFormat (read-only)
TimeZoneFmt (read-only)
Title (read-only)
Width (read-only)

A.28 *ViewEntry CLASS*

Methods

getPosition

Properties

ChildCount (read-only)
ColumnIndentLevel (read-only)
ColumnValues (read-only)
DescendantCount (read-only)
Document (read-only)
FTSearchScore (read-only)
IndentLevel (read-only)
IsCategory (read-only)
IsConflict (read-only)
IsDocument (read-only)
IsTotal (read-only)
IsValid (read-only)
NoteID (read-only)
Parent (read-only)
SiblingCount (read-only)
UniversalID (read-only)

A.29 *ViewEntryCollection CLASS*

Methods

addEntry
deleteEntry
FTSearch
getEntry
getFirstEntry
getLastEntry
getNextEntry
getNthEntry
getPrevEntry
putAllInFolder
removeAll
removeAllFromFolder
stampAll
updateAll

Properties

Count (read-only)
Parent (read-only)
Query (read-only)

A.30 VIEWNAVIGATOR CLASS

Methods
getChild
getCurrent
getFirst
getFirstDocument
getLast
getLastDocument
getNext
getNextCategory
getNextDocument
getNextSibling
getNth
getParent
getPos
getPrev
getPrevCategory
getPrevDocument
getPrevSibling
gotoChild
gotoEntry
gotoFirst
gotoFirstDocument
gotoLast
gotoLastDocument
gotoNext
gotoNextCategory
gotoNextDocument
gotoNextSibling
gotoParent
gotoPos
gotoPrev
gotoPrevCategory
gotoPrevDocument
gotoPrevSibling

Properties
CacheSize (read/write)
MaxLevel (read/write)
ParentView (read-only)

Error codes

Error No.	Error Code
4000	NOTES_ERR_ERROR
4001	NOTES_ERR_SYS_OUT_OF_MEMORY
4002	NOTES_ERR_SYS_LOAD_OUT_OF_MEM
4003	NOTES_ERR_SYS_FILE_NOT_FOUND
4004	NOTES_ERR_SYS_DICT_NOT_ON_PATH
4005	NOTES_ERR_ERROR2
4008	NOTES_ERR_SYS_RESOURCE_NOT_FOUND
4009	NOTES_ERR_SYS_LOADING_RESOURCE
4010	NOTES_ERR_SYS_LOCKING_RESOURCE
4011	NOTES_ERR_SYS_FREEING_RESOURCE
4012	NOTES_ERR_SYS_NOSUCH_RESOURCE
4016	NOTES_ERR_SYS_WARNING_TITLE
4026	NOTES_ERR_MAIL_COPEN_FAILED
4027	NOTES_ERR_MAIL_PAOPEN_FAILED
4028	NOTES_ERR_MAIL_LAOPEN_FAILED
4029	NOTES_ERR_MAIL_VIM_MESSAGE
4030	NOTES_ERR_MAIL_CANT_CREATE
4031	NOTES_ERR_MAIL_UNKNOWN_PROP
4032	NOTES_ERR_MAIL_INVALID_MSG
4033	NOTES_ERR_MAIL_NOPUBLIC_GRP
4034	NOTES_ERR_MAIL_NOPRIVATE_GRP
4035	NOTES_ERR_MAIL_GRPCREATE_FAILED
4036	NOTES_ERR_MAIL_GROUP_DELETED
4037	NOTES_ERR_MAIL_NAME_REQUIRED
4038	NOTES_ERR_FAILURE
4039	NOTES_ERR_NOSUCH_VIEW
4040	NOTES_ERR_NOFTINDEX
4041	NOTES_ERR_DBCREATE_FAILED
4042	NOTES_ERR_DBDELETE_FAILED
4043	NOTES_ERR_DBOPEN_FAILED
4044	NOTES_ERR_INVALID_FORMULA
4045	NOTES_ERR_INVALID_DATE
4046	NOTES_ERR_COPY_FAILED
4047	NOTES_ERR_VIEWOPEN_FAILED
4048	NOTES_ERR_NOTEDEL_FAILED
4049	NOTES_ERR_NEXTITEM_FAILED
4050	NOTES_ERR_FINDITEM_FAILED
4051	NOTES_ERR_MODLOAD_FAILED
4052	NOTES_ERR_PROCFIND_FAILED
4053	NOTES_ERR_RTWRITE_FAILED
4054	NOTES_ERR_RTCONVERT_FAILED
4055	NOTES_ERR_FTSRCH_FAILED

Error No.	Error Code
4056	NOTES_ERR_QUERY_FAILED
4057	NOTES_ERR_DOCSEARCH_FAILED
4058	NOTES_ERR_ITEMCOPY_FAILED
4059	NOTES_ERR_CREATENOTE_FAILED
4060	NOTES_ERR_DBNOACCESS
4061	NOTES_ERR_UNAME_LOOKUP
4062	NOTES_ERR_SESOPEN_FAILED
4063	NOTES_ERR_DATABASE_NOTOPEN
4064	NOTES_ERR_SESSION_DATECONV
4065	NOTES_ERR_SESSION_VALNOTSUPP
4066	NOTES_ERR_CANT_GETNTH
4067	NOTES_ERR_ATTACH_FAILED
4068	NOTES_ERR_DETACH_FAILED
4069	NOTES_ERR_EXTRACT_FAILED
4070	NOTES_ERR_DIRSEARCH_FAILED
4071	NOTES_ERR_BAD_INDEX
4072	NOTES_ERR_NOSUCH_DIRECTORY
4073	NOTES_ERR_CDTEXTCREATE_FAILED
4074	NOTES_ERR_CDASSIM_FAILED
4075	NOTES_ERR_NOT_RT_ITEM
4076	NOTES_ERR_FORMCOMP_FAILED
4077	NOTES_ERR_FORMEVAL_FAILED
4078	NOTES_ERR_ITEMCREATE_FAILED
4079	NOTES_ERR_DECRYPT_FAILED
4080	NOTES_ERR_NOTLOCAL_IDX
4081	NOTES_ERR_FTIDX_FAILED
4082	NOTES_ERR_NOTEOPEN_FAILED
4083	NOTES_ERR_RENDER_FAILED
4084	NOTES_ERR_FILENOTFOUND
4085	NOTES_ERR_UNKNOWN_TYPE
4086	NOTES_ERR_FILEOPEN_FAILED
4087	NOTES_ERR_FILEWRITE_FAILED
4088	NOTES_ERR_DATE_NOTSET
4089	NOTES_ERR_NODBNAME
4090	NOTES_ERR_TEMPLCOPY_FAILED
4091	NOTES_ERR_BAD_UNID
4092	NOTES_ERR_UNAME_REQ
4093	NOTES_ERR_GETACL_FAILED
4094	NOTES_ERR_ACLENTRY_FAILED
4095	NOTES_ERR_ACL_INVALID
4096	NOTES_ERR_QUERYACL_FAILED
4097	NOTES_ERR_REFRESH_FAILED
4098	NOTES_ERR_OLEPKG_FAILED
4099	NOTES_ERR_TMPFILE_FAILED

Error No.	Error Code
4100	NOTES_ERR_RTRENDER_FAILED
4101	NOTES_ERR_WRONG_CLASS
4102	NOTES_ERR_INVALID_ID
4103	NOTES_ERR_INVALID_AGENT
4104	NOTES_ERR_VIEWCLONE_FAILED
4105	NOTES_ERR_NOVIEWNAME
4106	NOTES_ERR_NEWSGROUPDB_FAILED
4107	NOTES_ERR_NONEWSGROUPNAME
4108	NOTES_ERR_READFILE_FAILED
4135	NOTES_ERR_LOG_DBOPEN_FAILED
4136	NOTES_ERR_LOG_FOPEN_FAILED
4137	NOTES_ERR_LOG_CDCREATE_FAILED
4138	NOTES_ERR_LOG_MAILLOG_FAILED
4139	NOTES_ERR_MEM_HVPOOLFULL
4150	NOTES_ERR_COPYACL_FAILED
4151	NOTES_ERR_DOC_NOTINVIEW
4152	NOTES_ERR_NOFTQUERY
4153	NOTES_ERR_NOITEMNAME
4154	NOTES_ERR_NOTEUPDATE_FAILED
4155	NOTES_ERR_NOTELOCATE_FAILED
4156	NOTES_ERR_VIEWDEL_FAILED
4157	NOTES_ERR_LOG_CONSTRUCT_FAILED
4158	NOTES_ERR_SEM_ALLOC_FAILED
4159	NOTES_ERR_LOOKUP_FAILED
4160	NOTES_ERR_SEND_FAILED
4161	NOTES_ERR_NCREATE_FAILED
4162	NOTES_ERR_MACRO_IDTBL_FAILED
4163	NOTES_ERR_MACRO_RUN_FAILED
4164	NOTES_ERR_DBOPEN_NOTLOCAL
4165	NOTES_ERR_SIGN_NOPERM
4166	NOTES_ERR_ENCRYPT_NOPERM
4167	NOTES_ERR_ENCRYPT_FAILED
4168	NOTES_ERR_NOSENDTO
4169	NOTES_ERR_LOG_EVENTPUT_FAILED
4170	NOTES_ERR_LOG_INVALID_EVTYPE
4171	NOTES_ERR_LOG_INVALID_SEVERITY
4172	NOTES_ERR_NO_NEWSLETTERDOCS
4173	NOTES_ERR_MAILDBOPEN_FAILED
4174	NOTES_ERR_NEWSLETTER_FAILED
4175	NOTES_ERR_DFLT_VID_FAILED
4176	NOTES_ERR_KEYFIND_FAILED
4177	NOTES_ERR_RTTEXT_FAILED
4178	NOTES_ERR_RTDOCLINK_FAILED

Error No.	Error Code
4179	NOTES_ERR_NOPERM_DISKIO
4180	NOTES_ERR_NOPERM_SIGN
4181	NOTES_ERR_NOPERM_ENCRYPT
4182	NOTES_ERR_NOPERM_ENVIRON
4183	NOTES_ERR_NOPERM_ANY
4184	NOTES_ERR_NOSERV_DB
4185	NOTES_ERR_INVALID_DB
4186	NOTES_ERR_INVALID_CREDEL
4187	NOTES_ERR_INVALID_DOC
4188	NOTES_ERR_DBS_MUST_MATCH
4189	NOTES_ERR_RESPONSE_FAILED
4190	NOTES_ERR_NOLISTS
4191	NOTES_ERR_CONTAINS_FAILED
4192	NOTES_ERR_MUSTBE_STRING
4193	NOTES_ERR_DESVIEW_FAILED
4194	NOTES_ERR_ITEMARR_FAILED
4195	NOTES_ERR_SRVSEARCH_FAILED
4196	NOTES_ERR_UNKNOWN_SRCHTYPE
4197	NOTES_ERR_MUSTCALL_FIRSTDB
4198	NOTES_ERR_ALLDOCS_FAILED
4199	NOTES_ERR_ITYPENOT_TEXT
4200	NOTES_ERR_INVALID_ITYPE
4201	NOTES_ERR_NOSUCH_FOLDER
4202	NOTES_ERR_ADDRBOOK_FAILED
4203	NOTES_ERR_NOTCONTEXT_DB
4204	NOTES_ERR_LTDACCESS_FAILED
4205	NOTES_ERR_LTDUPDATE_FAILED
4206	NOTES_ERR_BADVIEW_VERSION
4207	NOTES_ERR_NEED_ADT
4208	NOTES_ERR_ACLWRITE_FAILED
4209	NOTES_ERR_RENAME_FAILED
4210	NOTES_ERR_NOSUCH_ROLENAME
4211	NOTES_ERR_PRIVNAME_FAILED
4212	NOTES_ERR_READPRIV_FAILED
4213	NOTES_ERR_DELPRIV_FAILED
4214	NOTES_ERR_DELENTRY_FAILED
4215	NOTES_ERR_NOSERV_EVENTS
4216	NOTES_ERR_INVALID_ACLENTRYNAME
4217	NOTES_ERR_ENTRYNAME_FAILED
4218	NOTES_ERR_NOTLOCAL_REPL
4219	NOTES_ERR_REPL_FAILED
4220	NOTES_ERR_NOTLOCAL_COMPACT
4221	NOTES_ERR_COMPACT_FAILED
4222	NOTES_ERR_TIMEADJUST_FAILED

Error No.	Error Code
4223	NOTES_ERR_NOSUCH_EMBED
4224	NOTES_ERR_NOSUCH_EOFILE
4225	NOTES_ERR_NOSUCH_PATH
4226	NOTES_ERR_EMBEDARR_FAILED
4227	NOTES_ERR_NOADDRS_FOUND
4228	NOTES_ERR_DUP_ROLENAME
4229	NOTES_ERR_CANTCREATE_FOLDER
4230	NOTES_ERR_NOTERENDER_FAILED
4231	NOTES_ERR_NOFROMFIELD
4232	NOTES_ERR_TEXTLIST_FAILED
4233	NOTES_ERR_NOTA_DOCUMENT
4234	NOTES_ERR_VALIDATE_FAILED
4235	NOTES_ERR_ABSTRACT_BUFFER
4236	NOTES_ERR_ABSTRACTING_TEXT
4237	NOTES_ERR_DESAGENT_FAILED
4238	NOTES_ERR_MIXED_ARRAY
4239	NOTES_ERR_INVALID_DOCLINK
4240	NOTES_ERR_TEXTLIST_BAD_INPUT
4241	NOTES_ERR_CANTREMOVE
4242	NOTES_ERR_CANTENCRYPT
4243	NOTES_ERR_CANTCLOSEDB
4244	NOTES_ERR_CANTRUN_OLEOBJ
4345	NOTES_ERR_CANTSHOW_OLEOBJ
4246	NOTES_ERR_NOEMBEDDED_OBJ
4247	NOTES_ERR_NOSUCH_EMBEDCLASS
4248	NOTES_ERR_CANTGET_DBSUMMARY
4249	NOTES_ERR_CANTCOPY_ITEMTYPE
4250	NOTES_ERR_NEED_DB
4251	NOTES_ERR_NEED_NOTE
4252	NOTES_ERR_CANT_LINK_OLE1
4253	NOTES_ERR_ROLENAME_TOOBIG
4254	NOTES_ERR_EOARRAY_FAILED
4255	NOTES_ERR_ATTACHINFO_FAILED
4256	NOTES_ERR_QUOTAINFO_FAILED
4257	NOTES_ERR_DOCNOTSAVED
4258	NOTES_ERR_ACLNEXT_INVALID
4259	NOTES_ERR_NOTAFILE
4260	NOTES_ERR_CANTFIND_ATTACHMENT
4261	NOTES_ERR_NOSUCH_VERB
4262	NOTES_ERR_DOVERB_FAILED
4263	NOTES_ERR_INVALID_ADTTYPE
4264	NOTES_ERR_FTQUERY_FAILED
4265	NOTES_ERR_NOSUCH_DBID
4266	NOTES_ERR_OPENBYRID_FAILED

Error No.	Error Code
4267	NOTES_ERR_BAD_UNPROCFT
4268	NOTES_ERR_AGENT_NO_RECURSION
4269	NOTES_ERR_CANTGET_MAILSERVER
4270	NOTES_ERR_BAD_NOTEID
4271	NOTES_ERR_DBSECURITY
4272	NOTES_ERR_DELETE_AGENT
4273	NOTES_ERR_RUN_AGENT
4274	NOTES_ERR_NOSUCH_DOCINDEX
4275	NOTES_ERR_BAD_SOURCE_CLASS
4276	NOTES_ERR_CANT_CHANGE_DEFACL
4277	NOTES_ERR_LINKNOCLASS
4278	NOTES_ERR_CANTDO_ARRAYOFARRAY
4279	NOTES_ERR_SESSION_CLOSED
4280	NOTES_ERR_CANTOPEN_URLDB
4281	NOTES_ERR_NEED_URL
4282	NOTES_ERR_INVALID_URL
4283	NOTES_ERR_INVALID_URLHEADER
4284	NOTES_ERR_NOSUCH_URLHEADER
4285	NOTES_ERR_NOUNPROC_DOCS
4286	NOTES_ERR_EMBED_FAILED
4287	NOTES_ERR_NODEL_CURRENTDB
4288	NOTES_ERR_INVALID_TIMEEXPR
4289	NOTES_ERR_RECURSIVE_RENDER
4290	NOTES_ERR_INVALID_ITEM
4291	NOTES_ERR_NOMOVETO_PRIV1STUSE
4292	NOTES_ERR_SAMESRV_REPLICA
4293	NOTES_ERR_CANT_SIGN
4294	NOTES_ERR_NO_MATCH
4295	NOTES_ERR_AMBIGUOUS_MATCH
4296	NOTES_ERR_DBALREADY_OPEN
4297	NOTES_ERR_OLE_NOTAVAIL
4298	NOTES_ERR_ARRAY_NOGOOD
4299	NOTES_ERR_REGARG_NOTGIVEN
4300	NOTES_ERR_MISSING_CERTID
4301	NOTES_ERR_NOCERT_CTX
4301	NOTES_ERR_REGFAILED
4303	NOTES_ERR_SRVREGFAILED
4304	NOTES_ERR_CERTREGFAILED
4305	NOTES_ERR_XCERTFAILED
4306	NOTES_ERR_RECERTFAILED
4307	NOTES_ERR_NOSUCH_BOOL
4308	NOTES_ERR_CANTSWITCH_ID
4309	NOTES_ERR_NOSUCH_MAILPATH
4310	NOTES_ERR_BAD_IDFILE

Error No.	Error Code
4311	NOTES_ERR_CANTADD_USER
4312	NOTES_ERR_CANTADD_SERV
4313	NOTES_ERR_CANTADD_CERT
4314	NOTES_ERR_NOCURRENT_AGENT
4315	NOTES_ERR_AGENTLOG_FAILED
4316	NOTES_ERR_NOSUCH_CERTIDTYPE
4317	NOTES_ERR_NOCURRENT_FTRESULT
4318	NOTES_ERR_IDTBL_FAILED
4319	NOTES_ERR_PROF_ARG_MISSING
4320	NOTES_ERR_NOSUCH_PROFILE
4321	NOTES_ERR_PROFUPDATE_FAILED
4322	NOTES_ERR_PROFDELETE_FAILED
4323	NOTES_ERR_NOSUCH_ARG
4324	NOTES_ERR_WRONG_UNID_LEN
4325	NOTES_ERR_DESFORM_FAILED
4326	NOTES_ERR_FORMDEL_FAILED
4327	NOTES_ERR_NOCLOSE_CURRDB
4328	NOTES_ERR_FREETIME_FAILED
4329	NOTES_ERR_UNIFORM_FAILED
4330	NOTES_ERR_GETOPTION_FAILED
4331	NOTES_ERR_MARKREAD_FAILED
4332	NOTES_ERR_MARKUNREAD_FAILED
4333	NOTES_ERR_MULTIDB_FAILED
4334	NOTES_ERR_ADDPROF_FAILED
4335	NOTES_ERR_ULOOKUP_FAILED
4336	NOTES_ERR_INVALID_OBJECT
4337	NOTES_ERR_STAMP_FAILED
4338	NOTES_ERR_BAD_ORGUNIT
4339	NOTES_ERR_BAD_FTSORT
4340	NOTES_ERR_NOTCONTEXT_COLLEC
4341	NOTES_ERR_ECLACCESS_FAILED
4342	NOTES_ERR_W32DOM_FAILED
4343	NOTES_ERR_W32DOM_NOFIRSTUSER
4344	NOTES_ERR_W32DOM_BADPLATFORM
4345	NOTES_ERR_W32DOM_BADNETAPI32
4346	NOTES_ERR_W32DOM_DOMAIN_CONTROLLER
4347	NOTES_ERR_TOOMANY_SORT_KEYS
4348	NOTES_ERR_BAD_KEYTYPE
4349	NOTES_ERR_CANT_SELF_ASSIMILATE
4350	NOTES_ERR_CANT_SELF_COPY
4351	NOTES_ERR_POP3_FAILED
4352	NOTES_ERR_ARRCREATE_FAILED
4353	NOTES_ERR_AGSAVE_FAILED
4354	NOTES_ERR_CANTREMOVE_AGC

Error No.	Error Code
4355	NOTES_ERR_CANTENCRYPT_AGC
4356	NOTES_ERR_RTSTYLE_CREATEFAILED
4357	NOTES_ERR_RTSTYLE_APPENDFAILED
4358	NOTES_ERR_RTSTYLE_BADFONT
4359	NOTES_ERR_NO_CONTEXTDB
4360	NOTES_ERR_NULL_APPENDLIST
4361	NOTES_ERR_NOSUCH_JAVA_TYPE
4362	NOTES_ERR_INVALID_JARRAY
4363	NOTES_ERR_RTSTYLE_BADBOOL
4364	NOTES_ERR_RTSTYLE_BADFONTSIZE
4365	NOTES_ERR_RTSTYLE_BADCOLOR
4366	NOTES_ERR_RTSTYLE_BADEFFECT
4367	NOTES_ERR_NOTREMOTE_DB
4368	NOTES_ERR_RTITEM_EXISTS
4369	NOTES_ERR_NOFORM
4370	NOTES_ERR_NOTA_VECTOR
4371	NOTES_ERR_SERVER_SWITCH
4372	NOTES_ERR_DBDIR_THREAD
4373	NOTES_ERR_NO_COLLECTION
4374	NOTES_ERR_NOT_IN_SESSION
4375	NOTES_ERR_INVALID_NAME
4376	NOTES_ERR_DELETED
4377	NOTES_ERR_NOT_LOCAL
4378	NOTES_ERR_INVALID_RANGE
4379	NOTES_ERR_OBJECT_NOT_FOUND
4383	NOTES_ERR_INVALID_TIMEZONE
4386	NOTES_ERR_FOLDERREFS_NOT_SUPPORTED_BY_DB
4387	NOTES_ERR_DBFOLDERREFS_NOT_ENABLED
4391	NOTES_ERR_VIEWNAV_BAD_ENTRY
4392	NOTES_ERR_VIEWNAV_BAD_MAX
4393	NOTES_ERR_VIEWNAV_BAD_POS
4394	NOTES_ERR_VIEWNAV_BAD_PARENT
4395	NOTES_ERR_NOT_IMPLEMENTED
4396	NOTES_ERR_VIEW_INVALID_COLUMN
4397	NOTES_ERR_RTPSTYLE_APPENDFAILED
4398	NOTES_ERR_RTPSTYLE_TOOMANYTABS
4399	NOTES_ERR_RTPSTYLE_OUTOFRANGE
4400	NOTES_ERR_RTPSTYLE_BADALIGN
4401	NOTES_ERR_RTPSTYLE_BADSPACING
4402	NOTES_ERR_RTPSTYLE_BADPAGINATE
4403	NOTES_ERR_ACL_MISSING
4404	NOTES_ERR_SESSION_MISSING
4405	NOTES_ERR_DATABASE_MISSING

Error No.	Error Code
4406	NOTES_ERR_DOCUMENT_MISSING
4407	NOTES_ERR_VIEW_MISSING
4408	NOTES_ERR_PARENT_MISSING
4409	NOTES_ERR_NOT_RICHTEXT
4410	NOTES_ERR_PSTYLE_MISSING
4411	NOTES_ERR_REMOVEALL_FAILED
4412	NOTES_ERR_ENTRY_NOT_FROM_COLLECTION
4413	NOTES_ERR_NOTE_NOT_FROM_COLLECTION
4414	NOTES_ERR_ADDENTRY_DUP
4415	NOTES_ERR_ADDENTRY_FAILED
4416	NOTES_ERR_MACRO_SNM_ENABLE_FAILED
4417	NOTES_ERR_SYNCH_RUN_AGENT
4418	NOTES_ERR_SYNCH_NOOLE
4419	NOTES_ERR_RTPSTYLE_BADTABTYPE
4420	NOTES_ERR_GETALLENTRIES_FAILED
4421	NOTES_ERR_EXECUTESETUP_FAILED
4422	NOTES_ERR_MAXDBSIZE_EXCEEDED
4423	NOTES_ERR_INVALID_NAV
4424	NOTES_ERR_VNLEVEL
4425	NOTES_ERR_SVRACCESS_FAILED
4426	NOTES_ERR_NOT_IN_VIEW
4427	NOTES_ERR_NOT_IN_DB
4428	NOTES_ERR_PROP_NOT_AVAIL
4429	NOTES_ERR_NOT_IN_ACL
4430	NOTES_ERR_NO_LOGS_OPEN
4431	NOTES_ERR_CACHE_SZ_INVALID
4432	NOTES_ERR_VIEW_ENTRY_REMOVED
4433	NOTES_ERR_VIEW_ENTRY_DELETED
4434	NOTES_ERR_DOCUMENT_DELETED
4435	NOTES_ERR_ERR_NOTES_SYNCH_INVALIDOP
4436	NOTES_ERR_CREATEOUTLINE_FAILED
4437	NOTES_ERR_HTML_GENFAILED
4438	NOTES_ERR_CREATE_DOCCOLL_FAILED
4439	NOTES_ERR_EXECUTESETUP_FAILED2
4440	NOTES_ERR_CANTUPDATE_FOLDER
4441	NOTES_ERR_RTITEM_MISSING
4442	NOTES_ERR_NO_AUTHORIZATION
4443	NOTES_ERR_NAME_MISSING
4444	NOTES_ERR_ITEM_MISSING
4445	NOTES_ERR_DATERANGE_MISSING
4446	NOTES_ERR_VIEWENTRY_MISSING
4447	NOTES_ERR_VIEWENTRY_OR_DOC_MISSING
4448	NOTES_ERR_OUTLINE_MISSING
4449	NOTES_ERR_DATETIME_MISSING

Error No.	Error Code
4450	NOTES_ERR_VNAV_CAT_PARENT
4451	NOTES_ERR_VNAV_CAT_GOTO
4452	NOTES_ERR_INVALID_SIZE
4453	NOTES_ERR_REGSERVER_NOTSET
4454	NOTES_ERR_NOT_ATTACHMENT
4455	NOTES_ERR_NOT_RESOLVED
4456	NOTES_ERR_INVALID_IOR
4457	NOTES_ERR_GETIOR_FAILED
4458	NOTES_ERR_INVALID_DATESPEC
4459	NOTES_ERR_INVALID_TIMESPEC
4460	NOTES_ERR_CANTSAVE_CURRENTAGENT
4461	NOTES_ERR_CANTDISABLE_MANUALAGENT
4462	NOTES_ERR_BAD_ENTRYDOC
4463	NOTES_ERR_UNINITIALIZED_THREAD
4464	NOTES_ERR_INVALIDATED_OBJECT
4465	NOTES_ERR_ACL_ROLE_INVALID
4466	NOTES_ERR_ARG_DELETED
4467	NOTES_ERR_ACLENTRY_MISSING
4469	NOTES_ERR_ADDDOC_DUP

index

Symbols

// 29

A

abstractText 105
access levels 154
accessing embedded objects 123
ACL 50, 154, 156, 165, 410
ACL class 156–158
ACL object 156
ACL window 156
ACLEntry class 156, 159, 163, 167
ACLEntry objects 166
actionbar.jar 322
activate 124
addDocument 137
addEntry 225
addNewLine 110
addPageBreak 110
addRole 166
addTab 110
adjustDay 201
adjustHour 201
adjustMinute 201
adjustMonth 201
adjustSecond 201
adjustYear 201
Agent class 170, 172, 180
Agent Log
    template file 152
    window 146

agent log 147, 149
Agent object 170
AgentBase class 19, 291
AgentContext
    class 132, 140, 170, 182,
        185, 187, 191, 194, 275
    object 46
    Session property 43
AgentRunner 303
AgentRunner class 291–293, 303
    setup 293
AgentRunner database 304
AllDocuments 51
AND 264
appendDocLink 110
appendItemValue 80, 95
appendParagraphStyle 116
appendRTItem 111
appendStyle 112
appendText 111
appendToTextList 106
Applet class 308, 310
AppletBase class 307, 310
applets 307
appletviewer 295, 297
arrays 29
attachments 125, 127, 409
Authors property 86, 98

B

backslash 25
boolean 26
browser pane 11
browsers 274
byte 26

C

CADViewer applet 370
Calendar class 217
Canonical property 193
carriage returns 110, 112, 272
case 28
casting 32
CGI 330, 333
char 25
ClassLoader 340
CLASSPATH 291, 295, 349, 364
classpath 293
clearAllTabs 119
clearHistory 52
collection 131, 133, 137
column 61, 65
columns 60, 65
ColumnValues 86
comma-delimited file 411
comments 29
Common Name (CN) 189
Common property 193
CommonOwner 172

CommonUserName 43
compact 50
computeWithForm 83
Concatenation 26
Connection class 350
Connection object 350
connectors 363
constructor method 31
constructors 235–236
containsValue 106
continue 29
convertToZone 202
convertZone 202
copyAllItems 83
copying document 83
copyItem 84
copyItemToDocument 106
copyToDatabase 84
CORBA 290, 295, 297, 307, 321
create a new document 84
createCopy 50
createDatabase 54
createDateRange 43, 207
createDateTime 43, 198
createDocument 79
createEntry 226
createFromTemplate 50
createLog 43, 145
createName 43
createNewsletter 43, 257
createOutline 221
createRegistration 43
createReplica 50
createReplyMessage 84
createRichTextItem 85, 108
createRichTextParagraphStyle 43, 116
createRichTextStyle 43, 112
createSession 34, 341
createStatement 350
createViewNav 70
createViewNavFrom 71
createViewNavFromCategory 71
createViewNavFromChildren 71
createViewNavFromDescendents 71

createViewNavMaxLevel 71
creating a class 233
creating a link object 127
creating a new rich text item 108
creating embedded objects 123
curly braces 25
CutoffDate 52
CutoffInterval 52

D

Database class 45, 50–51, 58, 79, 132, 141, 156, 170, 221, 238
Database object 55, 84, 157, 183
DatabaseMetaData 354
Date class 217
Date object 217
DateOnly 199
DateRange class 206
DateSep 210
DateTime class 201, 205, 212
date-time fields 214
DateTime object 55, 197–198, 202–203, 211, 213–214, 268
Date-time values 197
DateTimeValue 100
DbDirectory class 46, 54–55
DbDirectory object 46
DebugAgentBase class 291, 293, 303
decrement 27
DECS 363
deleteDocument 137
deleteRole 167
deleting objects 128
destroy 308
difference between two Date/ Time objects 205
disableRole 167
do 28
document 84
Document class 78, 80, 96–97, 123, 132
Document object 78, 86, 88, 107, 133, 136

Document parameter 133
Document property 68, 100
DocumentCollection class 131, 140, 184
DocumentCollection object 87, 136–137, 139, 141, 159, 183, 222, 257, 264, 267
DocumentContext 187, 275
DocumentContext class 284
doGet 332
Domino Designer 6, 237
  browser pane 11
  Compile 14
  documentation 20
  Edit Project 14
  Export 14
  object browser 13
  reference browser 12
Domino Designer IDE 290
Domino JDBC driver 349–350
Domino log 146
Domino Servlet engine 339
Domino Servlet Manager 338
doPost 332
double 25
doVerb 124
DXL 379

E

editor.jar 322
EffectiveUserName 191
else 28
else if 28
EmbeddedObject class 123, 128
EmbeddedObjects property 86
embedObject 123, 125
enableRole 167
encrypt method 85
Encrypted property 98
EncryptionKeys 86
EndDateTime 206
Enumeration object 131, 394
environment variables 91, 274, 334–335
error handling 36

escape character 25, 125
evaluate 43
exception 36, 137
execute 350
executeQuery 350
Exporting 411
extends 31
extractFile 124

F

file logging 146
final 31
finalize 37
float 25
FolderReferences 86
folders 77, 85, 139
for 27, 135
Form events
  WebQueryOpen 21
  WebQuerySave 21
formatDocument 258
formatMsgWithDoclinks 258
Free-time search 208
freeTimeSearch 44, 208
FROM 348
FTSearch 136–137, 238, 264,
  266, 268
FTSearchScore 86
full-text indexes 155, 263, 269
full-text search 75, 86, 136

G

garbage collection 37
ger 340
getACL 156
getAgent 51
getAllDocumentsByKey 266
getAttachment 85
getColumn 60
getColumns 61
getCount 132, 135
getCurrent 72, 75
getCurrentAgent 183
getCurrentDatabase 183
getDatabase 44

getDBDirectory 44
getDocument 133, 137
getDocumentByID 51
getDocumentByKey 266–267
getDocumentByUNID 51
getDocumentByURL 51
getDocumentContext 275
getFirst 72, 222
getFirstDatabase 55
getFirstDocument 72, 133
getFirstEntry 159
getFirstItem 82, 96, 107
getForm 51
getFormattedText 111
getInternational 210
getInternetLevel 158
getItems 96
getItemValue 80
getItemValueDouble 80
getItemValueInteger 80
getItemValueString 80
getLast 72
getLastDocument 72, 133
getNext 72, 223
getNextCategory 72
getNextDatabase 55
getNextDocument 72, 133
getNextEntry 159
getNextSibling 72, 223
getNth 72
getNthDocument 135
getOutline 51, 221
getParameterDocID 180
getParent 72, 158, 223
getPos 72
getPrev 72, 223
getPrevCategory 72
getPrevDocument 72, 136
getPrevSibling 72, 223
getProfileDocCollection 51, 141
getProfileDocument 51
getRoles 158
getSession 336
getToday 212
getTomorrow 212
getURLHeaderInfo 51

getUserNameList 190
getUserNameObject 190
getView 51, 58
getViews 58–59
getWriter 334
getYesterday 212
gotoChild 73
gotoEntry 73
gotoFirst 73
gotoFirstDocument 73
gotoLast 73
gotoLastDocument 73
gotoNext 73
gotoNextCategory 73
gotoNextDocument 73
gotoNextSibling 74
gotoParent 74
gotoPos 74
gotoPrev 74
gotoPrevCategory 74
gotoPrevDocument 74
gotoPrevSibling 74
GregorianCalendar class 217

H

hasEmbedded 86
Hashtable object 394
hasItem 82, 96
hierarchical name 193–194
HTML 308, 344, 386, 390,
  398, 402
HTTP 285
HTTP environment
  variables 274
HTTP Session object 394
HttpServletRequest class 336
HttpServletRequest object 333
HttpServletResponse class 334,
  343
HttpSession class 336

I

IDE 289
if 28
IIOP 60, 137, 307

implements 30
import 7, 30
increment 27
init 308
int 25
International 43
International class 209
International object 210–211, 213
InternetLevel 158
IsAbstract 52
IsCutoffDelete 52
isDeleted 86
IsDisabled 52
IsDocSubject 258
IsDoScore 258
isEncryptOnSend 86
isFolder 77
isFTIndexed 263–264
IsIgnoreDeletes 52
IsIgnoreDestDeletes 52
isNewNote 87
isProfile 87
isResponse 87
isRoleEnabled 167
isSaveMessageOnSend 87
isSentByAgent 87
isSigned 87
isSignOnSend 87
isUniformAccess 158
isValid 87
Item 98
    constants 103
    type property 103
item
    accessing 96
    creating 95
    removing 97
Item class 95, 100
Item object 96
Items property 87

J

jar 295
Java 7, 11, 295
    console 19

Data types 25
    import 7
Java class path 338
Java Console Window 187
Java Server Pages 271, 297, 358, 360
Java Virtual Machine (JVM) 2
java.util package 217
java.util.Date object 197, 203
JavaBeans 369
javac 295
JavaScript 387
javax.servlet 331
javax.servlet.http 331
JClass 373
jdb 295
JDBC 297, 347, 349–350, 352, 354, 357
JDBC URLs 349
JDK 291, 295, 321, 347, 349, 358
JSDK 331, 336
JVM 325, 340

K

Key 87

L

LastAccessed 87
LastModified 87, 100
LCConnection 364
LCConnection object 365
LCException 367
LCException class 367
LCField 364, 366
LCFieldList 364–365
LCSession 364
LEI 363–364
LocalTime 199
Log 145
log activity 152
Log object 146
logAction 146–147
logError 146–147

logging
    of activity 145
    to a Domino database 152
    to a file 149
Logging via Email 149
Logical AND 26
Logical OR 26
long 25
Lotus Domino Toolkit for Java 292
LotusScript 2–3
LotusXLS 380

M

mail logging 146
makeResponse 85
Memory management/ recycle 37
metadata 353
moveEntry 226

N

Name class 189, 192
Name object 190–191
Name property 100
NameOfProfile 87
Names property 98
ncso.jar 290
ncsoc.jar 290
newsletter 413
Newsletter class 257–258
Newsletter object 257
NOT 264–265
NoteID 87, 180
notes.jar 290, 293
notesAppletDestroy 311
notesAppletInit 310
notesAppletStart 310
notesAppletStop 311
NotesError 37
NotesException 36–37
NotesFactory class 34, 327, 341
NotesThread class 36, 326, 341
nvapplet.jar 322

O

object browser 13
ODBC 357
OLE 86, 107, 123–124
openAgentLog 145, 147
openDatabase 55
openDatabaseByReplicaID 55
openDatabaseIfModified 55
openFileLog 145
openMailDatabase 55
openMailLog 145
openNotesLog 145
OR 264
Outline class 221–222
Outline object 221, 225
outline.jar 322
OutlineEntry class 221
OutlineEntry object 223, 225
outlines 220
overloading 32
OverViews 377

P

package 30
paint 308
Parent property 100, 133, 206
ParentDatabase 87
ParentDocumentUNID 87
ParentView 87
PrintWriter class 40, 187, 272
PrintWriter object 279, 284, 334, 343
Priority 52
private 30, 234
profile Document 87, 91
profile document 87, 92, 141, 280, 283, 413
Protected 30, 98
public 30, 234
putAllInFolder 139
putInFolder 85

Q

queryAccess 50

R

Readers 98
ReadViewEntries 378
recycle 37
reference browser 12
remove 85, 97, 124, 128, 163, 179
removeAllFromFolder 139
removeEntry 226
removeFromFolder 85
removeItem 86, 97
renameRole 167
renderToRTItem 86
replaceItemValue 80–81, 95
replicate 50
Replication class 51–52, 55
replication history 52
reports 249
reset 52
response document 87
Responses property 87
restart command 340
ResultSet object 351
ResultSetMetaData 354
rich text field 86
RichTextItem 112, 116
RichTextItem class 107, 112, 123
RichTextItem object 107, 110, 125
RichTextParagraphStyle class 116
RichTextParagraphStyle object 119–121
RichTextStyle class 112
RichTextTab class 121
RichTextTab objects 119
roles 158, 165
run 179
runnable interface 326
runNotes 326
runOnServer 179

S

save 52, 226
SaveToDisk 98
script libraries 240, 243
searches 106
searching 75, 262, 266
SELECT 348
service 332
servlet 330–331, 333–334, 336–338, 340, 344–345, 354, 358, 383, 392, 395, 402
servlet settings 338
ServletManager 340
ServletManger 340
Servlets.Properties 339–340, 404
Session class 39, 112, 116, 190, 194, 197, 207–208, 210
Session object 45, 402
session tracking 336
setAnyDate 202
setAnyHour 202
setContentType 343
setInternetLevel 158
setLocalDate 202
setLocalTime 203
setNow 203
setTab 119, 121
setTabs 120–121
setUniformAccess 158
Shared Java Libraries 243
shopping cart 336, 382, 396
short 25
sign 86
Signed property 98
Signer property 87
sinitThread 327, 341
Size property 87
soft deletes 86
Special keys 21
SQL 347, 349–350, 354
stampAll 140, 184
standalone applications 325
start 308, 326
StartDateTime 206
Statement class 350

static 31
stermThread 327, 341
stop 308
SubjectItemName 258
Summary property 98
Sun JDK 294–295
switch 28
switch/case 28, 175
SYSEDIT 295

T

Tabs vector 119
text file logging 147
Text property 100, 206
third-party tools 370
this 233
threads 326
timeDifference 203, 205
Today property 211, 213
toJavaDate 203
Tomorrow property 211, 213
try/catch/finally 342, 367
type property 100, 103

U

UniversalID 88
unProcessedFTSearch 183
unProcessedSearch 183

updateAll 140, 184
updateFTIndex 269
updateProcessedDoc 140
URL 220, 279, 344
user name 39, 192
UserName 43

V

validation 83
ValueDouble 100
ValueInteger 100
ValueLength 100
Values property 100
ValueString 100
Vector class 29
Vector element 238
Vector object 131, 190, 266
Verifier 88
view
 deleting 76
 refreshing 76
 searching 75
 working with 58
View class 58, 65, 69–70, 76, 132, 267
view columns 60
view entries 65
View object 222

ViewColumn class 61
ViewColumn object 60, 64
ViewEntry class 65, 68–69
ViewEntry object 72
ViewEntryCollection 65
ViewEntryCollection class 69
ViewNavigator class 65, 70, 75
ViewNavigator object 72
VisualAge 312
VisualAge for Java 297, 303, 321, 369

W

WebQueryOpen 21, 170, 246, 278, 280
WebQuerySave 21, 170, 246, 278–280, 388
WebSphere 297, 330, 338, 358
WHERE 348
while 28

X

XML 358, 376–379, 412

Y

Yesterday property 211, 213